A Cormac McCarthy Companion

A Cormac McCarthy Companion

The Border Trilogy

Edited by
Edwin T. Arnold and
Dianne C. Luce

University Press of Mississippi
Jackson

www.upress.state.ms.us

Copyright © 2001 by University Press of Mississippi
The following articles were first published in *The Southern Quarterly* and are used by permission: "Autotextuality, or Dialogic Imagination in Cormac McCarthy's Border Trilogy" by Christine Chollier; " 'Go to sleep': Dreams and Visions in the Border Trilogy" by Edwin T. Arnold; " 'Wars and rumors of wars' in Cormac McCarthy's Border Trilogy" by John Wegner; " 'As of some site where life had not succeeded': Sorrow, Allegory, and Pastoralism in Cormac McCarthy's Border Trilogy" by George Guillemin; "The World on Fire: Ethics and Evolution in Cormac McCarthy's Border Trilogy" by Jacqueline Scoones; "The Vanishing World of Cormac McCarthy's Border Trilogy" by Dianne C. Luce; "Cowboy Codes in Cormac McCarthy's Border Trilogy" by Phillip A. Snyder; "Boys Will Be Boys and Girls Will Be Gone: The Circuit of Male Desire in Cormac McCarthy's Border Trilogy" by Nell Sullivan; all copyright © 2000 by *The Southern Quarterly*.

All rights reserved
Manufactured in the United States of America

Library of Congress Cataloging-in-Publication Data

A Cormac McCarthy companion : the Border trilogy / edited by Edwin T. Arnold and Dianne C. Luce.
p. cm.
Includes bibliographical references and index.
ISBN 1-57806-400-7 (cloth : alk. paper)—
ISBN 1-57806-401-5 (pbk. : alk. paper)
1. McCarthy, Cormac, 1933– Border trilogy. 2. Mexican-American Border Region—In literature. 3. Western stories—History and criticism. I. Arnold, Edwin T. II. Luce, Dianne C.

PS3563.C337 B6733 2001
813'.54—dc21   2001026170

British Library Cataloging-in-Publication Data available

Contents

Introduction   vii

**Autotextuality, or Dialogic Imagination
in Cormac McCarthy's Border Trilogy**   3
Christine Chollier

**"Go to sleep":
Dreams and Visions in the Border Trilogy**   37
Edwin T. Arnold

**"Wars and rumors of wars" in
Cormac McCarthy's Border Trilogy**   73
John Wegner

**"As of some site where life had not succeeded":
Sorrow, Allegory, and Pastoralism in
Cormac McCarthy's Border Trilogy**   92
George Guillemin

**The World on Fire:
Ethics and Evolution in Cormac McCarthy's Border Trilogy**   131
Jacqueline Scoones

**The Vanishing World of
Cormac McCarthy's Border Trilogy** 161
Dianne C. Luce

Cowboy Codes in Cormac McCarthy's Border Trilogy 198
Phillip A. Snyder

Boys Will Be Boys and Girls Will Be Gone:
The Circuit of Male Desire in Cormac McCarthy's Border Trilogy 228
Nell Sullivan

**Crossing from the Wasteland into the Exotic
in McCarthy's Border Trilogy** 256
J. Douglas Canfield

Notes on Contributors 271
Index 273

INTRODUCTION

This volume is intended as a companion to our earlier collection of essays, *Perspectives on Cormac McCarthy* (1993, rev. ed. 1999). In that book, we brought together studies of all of McCarthy's major writings, with the exception of his play *The Stonemason*. Now we have chosen to concentrate on a specific, unified body of work—*All the Pretty Horses* (1992), *The Crossing* (1994), and *Cities of the Plain* (1998)—the three novels that comprise McCarthy's Border Trilogy. McCarthy spent some fifteen years writing this story. If one also included his first western, *Blood Meridian* (1984), which might rightfully be seen as prologue to the trilogy, then almost half of his writing career has been devoted to these western novels. Many would consider them his best work, although that issue will no doubt continue to be debated.

As we now know, the Border Trilogy had its genesis in a screenplay entitled "Cities of the Plain" that McCarthy wrote in the early 1980s (see Arnold's "The Last of the Trilogy: First Thoughts on *Cities of the Plain*" in *Perspectives* 221–47). In that version, the characters of John Grady and Billy (with no last names) anticipate their later manifestations in the novels, although the Billy we find in the screenplay is a secondary figure and the emphasis is on John Grady's story. After unsuccessful attempts to place the screenplay, McCarthy recast the material in novel form, although it is unclear just when he decided to use the material in fiction. It may always have been his intention, or the decision may have evolved later, as it became clear that a film of "Cities" would not be made.

According to Gary Fisketjon, McCarthy's editor at Knopf, McCarthy at first planned to write only two books, both on John Grady, one elaborating his background and the second covering the events in the screenplay. At some point these two books turned into three, as Billy began to emerge as a more significant figure. Thus, reserving the narrative in the screenplay for his final volume, McCarthy wrote *All the Pretty Horses*, devoted to John Grady Cole, and then turned to Billy Parham in *The Crossing*, before bringing them both together in *Cities of the Plain*. The ending of the trilogy, then, was always waiting for the other two books to arrive. John Grady's death and Billy's grief make up the inevitable conclusion towards which all events in the preceding novels converge.

The idea of "trilogy" is an intriguing one, and in recent years some notable American writers have explored the possibilities of the form. Toni Morrison, for example, has identified *Beloved* (1987), *Jazz* (1993), and *Paradise* (1999) as three interrelated books: although they are connected neither by recurring characters nor specific events, they hold together in their historical examination of the African-American experience from slavery to contemporary times and in their exploration of varieties of destructive love. On the other hand, Peter Matthiessen's "Everglades Trilogy," composed of *Killing Mister Watson* (1990), *Lost Man's River* (1997), and *Bone by Bone* (2000), recounts the events, both actual and imagined, leading to the murder of Edgar J. Watson from three different approaches, including Watson's own first person narrative. Madison Smartt Bell is presently completing his own trilogy detailing the 18th century slave revolt in Haiti led by Toussaint Louverture; the first two volumes, *All Souls' Rising* (1996) and *Master of the Crossroads* (2000) have already appeared. Expanding the form, over the last two decades, Louise Erdrich has created a growing, interconnected clan chronicle in such books as *Love Medicine* (1984), *Tracks* (1988), and *The Bingo Palace* (1994), while other writers like John Updike and Phillip Roth have returned again and again to fictional representatives such as Harry Angstrom and Nathan Zuckerman in multiple works. Although we have not tried to compare McCarthy's trilogy with these roughly contemporaneous novel sequences, or with earlier notable American trilogies such as John

Dos Passos's *U.S.A.* or William Faulkner's Snopes Trilogy, it is clear that he is working within a revitalized tradition.

At the time of its original publication, *Perspectives on Cormac McCarthy*, a revised version of our 1992 special McCarthy issue of *The Southern Quarterly*, was the first collection devoted to McCarthy's writings, preceded only by Vereen Bell's groundbreaking work, *The Achievement of Cormac McCarthy* (1988). By the time our revised edition of *Perspectives*, which included new essays on *The Crossing* and *Cities of the Plain*, came out in the spring of 1999, other studies and anthologies had remarkably expanded the scholarly examination of McCarthy. *Sacred Violence: A Reader's Companion to Cormac McCarthy*, edited by Wade Hall and Rick Wallach, appeared in 1995; Robert L. Jarrett's Twayne monograph *Cormac McCarthy* followed in 1997. Later, in Fall 1999, the journal *Southwestern American Literature* published an issue focused primarily on McCarthy's western writings, guest-edited by Wallach.

The beginning of the new century has so far witnessed further examples of McCarthy scholarship. In the Spring of 2000 *The Southern Quarterly* published our second special McCarthy issue, which forms the foundation of this collection. Next, Barcley Owens's study *Cormac McCarthy's Western Novels* was published by University of Arizona Press (2000), and Wallach recently brought out a comprehensive collection of essays, both original and previously published, on all of McCarthy's work under the title *Myth, Legend, Dust: Critical Responses to Cormac McCarthy* (Manchester University Press, 2000).

As should be clear, McCarthy scholarship has so far been dominated by articles and essays, many of them quite brief in scope (the majority of the articles in the Wallach anthologies were selected from presentations given at the annual meetings of the Cormac McCarthy Society, from its genesis in 1992 to the near present). Meanwhile, dissertations on McCarthy continue to be written both in the United States and abroad, and we should expect to see more of them turned into books and monographs, such as Owens's. But at this point the need for in-depth studies of McCarthy's writing, both southern and western, remains great. The lengthy and complex essays in this collection point the way for the kind of work we feel McCarthy's novels deserve, a mid-point, perhaps, between conference proceedings and the kind of full-length explorations we anticipate in the future.

In this collection we have brought together diverse readings of the trilogy, using both traditional and newer critical approaches. We have challenged our authors to undertake extended treatments of the Border Trilogy, to consider the complex ways in which each book relates to the others: the matrix of linkages among them. In editing the volume, we discovered that the articles themselves formed a web of interrelated interpretations—always complementary if not always in agreement with one another.

Christine Chollier's treatment of dialogics in the trilogy offers a close examination of its narrative voice(s) and style. George Guillemin places the trilogy within the American pastoral tradition, emphasizing the concept of loss, while Phillip Snyder approaches it through the more contemporary cowboy codes of the American Western. Snyder's discussion of masculine Western images is balanced against Nell Sullivan's feminist approach to the trilogy's cowboys, which explores their enacting of the feminine within the context of this tradition.

Dianne Luce's study of the history and literary representation of the wolf hunt addresses masculine roles from that more restricted perspective and, like John Wegner's exploration of the war history underpinning the trilogy, provides evidence of the historical grounding of the works. Jacqueline Scoones's treatment of place, technology, and environmental ethics joins the articles by Luce and Guillemin to form a cluster of varied eco-critical approaches to the trilogy. Moreover, Scoones's discussion of war and technology complements Wegner's exploration of the several wars in the background (or foreground) of the novels' actions.

Edwin Arnold's examination of the dreams and visions so prominent in the characters' experience demonstrates how the trilogy maintains significant technical and thematic links to all of McCarthy's earlier works. Arnold's essay and, to a lesser extent, Luce's point to the presence of a spiritual or mystical sensibility in McCarthy's work—a seriousness of moral vision that has not always been recognized. Finally, Douglas Canfield's theological existentialist reading of the trilogy, which considers the spiritual vision of its "vatic" passages from the perspective of Heidegger and Kant and further explores McCarthy's depiction of Mexico and the question of his cultural imperialism, offers commentary on and a possible synthesis of various approaches critics have taken to the trilogy.

In 1999, Everyman Library published the trilogy in a single volume, further emphasizing its status as one extended tale. We feel that the three novels of the Border Trilogy, taken as a whole, represent McCarthy's working in the full maturity of his talent and in a scope surpassing anything he has done before. Stylistically breathtaking, structurally and philosophically complex, subtly nuanced, this is a tale that will continue to reward and challenge readers to come.

Edwin T. Arnold
Dianne C. Luce
December 2000

Note:

Because of their wider availability, we have chosen to cite the Vintage paperback issues of McCarthy's works rather than first editions (the publications are textually identical). In quoting from McCarthy's texts, we have silently followed his consistent practice of omitting diacritical marks in Spanish. We are grateful to Francisco Pérez, of the Humanities Department of Midlands Technical College, for his advice concerning translations of McCarthy's Spanish throughout this volume.

We have used the following abbreviations for McCarthy's works:

APH	*All the Pretty Horses*	S	*Suttree*
BM	*Blood Meridian*	St	*The Stonemason*
C	*The Crossing*	OD	*Outer Dark*
COG	*Child of God*	OK	*The Orchard Keeper*
COP	*Cities of the Plain*	"WAM"	"Whales and Men"

A Cormac McCarthy Companion

AUTOTEXTUALITY, OR DIALOGIC IMAGINATION IN CORMAC MCCARTHY'S BORDER TRILOGY

Christine Chollier

By writing three southern novels—*The Orchard Keeper*, *Outer Dark*, and *Child of God*—which were followed by the atypical semi-autobiographical *Suttree*, then shifting to the revisionist southwestern novel of collective bloodshed—*Blood Meridian*—which was followed by a series of three southwestern works conspicuously called a trilogy, Cormac McCarthy has obviously foregrounded the oscillation of his creative work between continuity and discontinuity. The sample of his prose which can be found in the Border Trilogy may nevertheless be scrutinized for its own sake, especially with a view to unearthing traces of what Mikhail Bakhtin called dialogism, that is to say the presence of another's voice inside a given voice.[1] It might seem paradoxical to emphasize dialogic relations in a trilogy whose narrator so easily transgresses the tenets of modernism by inhabiting "every aspect of a story except the consciousness of its characters" so that we are "rarely if ever permitted into their thoughts or emotions" (Wallach 60). And indeed, McCarthy's narrator apparently fits Wayne Booth's definition of the (implied) author who "sees more deeply and judges more profoundly than his presented characters" (Booth 74) much better than Bakhtin's, in which the freedom of the character has superseded the lack of freedom of the objectivized hero, and not the author's superior consciousness but the hero's self-consciousness is the dominant of representation: "The hero's discourse in its response to discourses of the other characters *and* the discourse of the author is, for Bakhtin, the novel's principal object of representation" (Bialostosky 212). However, as Bakhtin argued in the essay "Discourse in the Novel," "even in those places where the author's voice seems at first glance to be unitary and consistent, direct and unmediatedly intentional, beneath that smooth single-languaged surface we can nevertheless uncover prose's three-dimensionality,[2] its profound speech diversity, which enters the project of style and is its determining factor" (*The Dialogic Imagination* 315). A monologue—or a single-voiced, monologic novel—is thus often more dialogic—more double-voiced—than it first appeared to be, because, although it seeks to objectify reality, it cannot totally deny or silence another voice, which continues to compete to make itself heard. If Bakhtin's definition of dialogism as an exchange of words and ideas occurring between two different speakers in what is not true dialogue, what is not directly quoted discourse, can be adopted here,[3] then intertextuality, intratextuality and autotextuality emerge as three different forms of dialogism. Intertextuality, as Michael Riffaterre also said, consists in eliminating one meaning of the previous text to produce another; it is a form of literary dialogics which has already interested some critics of McCarthy studies.[4] Intratextuality seeks connections among the works of a given writer to trace their progression; it is also a form of dialogism which has been examined by critics.[5] Autotextuality tracks several forms of vocal exchange within a given novel.[6]

Bakhtin's theory of dialogics relies on the notion that the word is always inherited, already inhabited by another's voice and meant for another: "The internally dialogized word is both multifaceted and multidirected, existing at the confluence of two planes. Articulated in the present, it is oriented toward both past and future as its principal temporal considerations. With regard to the spatial, it refers to the object (itself permeated by past and future intentions), to previous users of the word (in some necessarily differing set of contexts), and to those who have yet to employ it (in some as yet undefined context)" (Danow 92). Danow also explains that Bakhtin's usage of the Russian term *slovo* may be translated as "word" or "discourse," like the Greek *logos*, "since a single word may in a given situation represent an entire discourse bearing its own ideology, intent, or special meaning" (Danow 80). Thus, in this study, "word" will mean "discourse," "speech," "word," or "language," unless otherwise stated. In a work of literature, dialogism occurs whenever the word "is directed both toward the object of speech, like an ordinary word, and toward *another word*, toward *another person's speech*" (Bakhtin, *Dostoevsky* 153). Also called *heteroglossia*, it defines the presence of another's speech in one's language, serving to express authorial intentions in a refracted way; consequently, it contains two voices and two meanings.[7] The double-voiced word is dialogic in that the writer[8] makes use of another's word—itself already imbued with an original intent, unless Adamic language ever existed—by blending his own intentions within it. The writer thus injects his own (opposing, supportive, ironic, or travestied) meaning into that of the original speaker. This original speaker can be another writer—in which case the relation with this other work is intertextual, another voice from another book by the same author—in which case the relation is intratextual, or another voice from the same work—in which case the relation is autotextual. Thus, the study of autotextual connections in the Border Trilogy will concentrate on dialogic relationships between the narrator's and the characters' voices, or between one character's voice and another's, within a given novel. As dialogics excludes the study of dialogue—direct discourse as dialogue—for reasons which have already been mentioned,[9] it is legitimate to wonder whether one can scrutinize the writer's intentions within a character's word, however refracted they may be, in novels which appear extroverted narratives carried largely through direct discourse and character interactions and mediated by an omniscient narrator who, in addition, hardly ever allows one into the characters' inner lives. In fact, the narrator's refusal to give us access to the character's motivations may be his own way of acknowledging the freedom of the character, the autonomy of the dreamer-traveler which is put forward in the epilogue of *Cities of the Plain*. The Epilogue serves several functions, among which is that of metafictional commentary on the whole trilogy. The man Billy meets is a dreamer/creator whose traveler/creature "has no substance and therefore no history but . . . whatever he may be or of whatever made he cannot exist without a history" (274). Billy's companion has said just before that he can not "rob the traveler of his own autonomy lest he vanish altogether" (274). So McCarthy's characterless enterprise has its limits, as suggested by the creator himself: if he totally robbed the characters of their autonomy, they would disappear from the fiction altogether. The notion of character would then disappear, just as the notion of self, which is what Dana Phillips has suggested about *Blood Meridian*.[10] In fact, very fruitful for the purpose of this study are those rare but rewarding instances where the vision and voice of the narrator intersect with those of the character. But for them to intersect, they have to be distinct from the first.

From a theoretical point of view the question of focalization should always be kept separate from that of voice: "who sees?" is a different question from "who speaks?" because perception can be focused on a character while the narrating voice remains that of the extra- or hetero-diegetic narrator.[11] "Thus, speaking and seeing, narration and focalization, may, but need not, be attributed to the same agent" (Rimmon-Kenan 72). However, internal focalization can extend a character's sphere of influence, or zone of influence, in the text. When John Grady and Rawlins arrive at *La Púrisima*, one of the first marvels they encounter is Alejandra riding her horse:

a young girl came riding down the road and passed them and they ceased talking. She wore english riding boots and jodhpurs and a blue twill hacking jacket . . . and her black hair was loose under [her hat] and fell halfway to her waist and as she rode past she turned and smiled and touched the brim of the hat with her crop and the vaqueros touched their hatbrims one by one down to the last of those who'd pretended not even to see her as she passed. (APH 94)

"[T]hey ceased talking" refers to the group of vaqueros including John Grady and Rawlins. Rawlins' question afterward ("Did you see that little darlin?") and John Grady's fascinated gaze ("He was still looking down the road where she'd gone") make it clear that they are the focal characters and that John Grady is the more important focalizer, as the emphasis on Alejandra's beautiful long black hair shows[12] and his love-at-first-sight syndrome also points out ("There was nothing there to see but he was looking anyway"). The narrating voice here is of course that of the narrator, but the focalizer is John Grady, for the benefit of having the implied reader see the girl through the boy's loving eyes. Such a device is utilized at crucial moments in the narratives.

In *The Crossing*, Billy does not meet the wolf in the mountains; he is met by her. She is reported to be the agent of the encounter: "the wolf stood up to meet him" (52). But the meeting has been prepared by Billy's attempt to see through the eyes of the animal, "to see the world the wolf saw" (51). Before their eyes converge, the boy's observation is modelled on his father's. The heifer he finds dead at the edge of trees is described in a paragraph which sounds like a report addressed to his father: "It was lying on its side in the shadow of the woods with its eyes glazed over and its tongue out and she had begun to feed on it between its rear legs and eaten the liver and dragged the intestines over the snow and eaten several pounds of meat from the inside of the thighs. The heifer was not quite stiff, not quite cold" (32). Billy's intimacy with the wolf teaches him to see the world the wolf sees, as the beautiful farewell scene shows. After closing the wolf's eyes, he

closed his own eyes that he could see her running in the mountains, running in the starlight where the grass was wet and the sun's coming as yet had not undone the rich matrix of creatures passed in the night before her. Deer and hare and dove and groundvole all richly empaneled on the air for her delight, all nations of the possible world ordained by God of which she was one among and not separate from. Where she ran the cries of the coyotes clapped shut as if a door had closed upon them and all was fear and marvel" (C 127).

Billy's attempt to focus his perception on the animal's and to model his voice on hers testifies to his dialogic relationship with the wolf. Between these two episodes the wolf is taken away from Billy to the fair where the boy finds her under a tent:

She was lying in the floor of the cart in a bed of straw. They'd taken the rope from her collar and fitted the collar with a chain and run the chain through the floorboards of the cart so that it was all that she could do to rise and stand. Beside her in the straw was a clay bowl that perhaps had held water. (C 105)

Internal focalization allows the narrator to have Billy discover the conditions of the wolf's imprisonment. The reasoning embedded in the description and suggested by the logical link "so that" and the adverb "perhaps" further takes us into Billy's consciousness. The adverb raises doubts as to the men's concern for the animal: it contains Billy's doubts as well as the narrator's. Later on, Billy "made his way along the edge of the crowd":

> They were a strange egality of witnesses there gathered and among the merchants from adjacent towns and the neighboring hacendados and the petty hidalgos de gotera come from as far as Agua Prieta and Casas Grandes in their tightly fitted suits there were tradesmen and hunters and gerentes and mayordomos from the haciendas and from the ejidos and there were caporals and vaqueros and a few favored peons. There were no women. (C 113)

Through Billy's eyes we see men from all walks of life join in the carnivalesque familiarization of violence—here, the wolf's fight with dogs. However, one voice underscores the absence of women to say that the would-be democratic blurring of hierarchical borderlines does not go so far as to break down the barriers between men and women. This voice must be that of the narrator because at this stage in the story the boy is not yet alive to male and female relationships.[13] His innocent gaze round the place merely registers the absence of women. The narrator's knowledge of the progress of women's rights—and his awareness of female readers' possible objections—then impinges on Billy's observation. In *Cities of the Plain*, when Billy visits the White Lake to try to buy Magdalena on John Grady's behalf, he is first met by the smiling, Lucifer-like Tiburcio who leads him down corridors, through doors, until he has reached the point where he must wait to talk to Eduardo:

> An old woman with one eye came down the corridor and tapped at one of the doors. When she saw him there she blessed herself with the sign of the cross. The door opened and she disappeared inside and the door closed and the corridor stood empty once again in the soft blue light.
> When the silver door opened the alcahuete motioned him inside with a cupping motion of his thin ringed fingers. (COP 130)[14]

The one-eyed old woman is already well-known to the reader but she is new to the focal character, which explains the narrator's use of the indefinite article.

Such examples as the ones quoted above show that the language of the narrator is sometimes permeated with the vision of a character. But that character is not necessarily the protagonist: Billy, John Grady and Rawlins are perceived as *güeros* by the Mexicans, whose vision contaminates the narrator's word when the scene is seen through their eyes:

> That the wolf was loose save for his grip on her collar did not escape the notice of the men who had entered the ring. They looked at one another. Some began to back away. The wolf stood against the güero's thigh with her teeth bared and her flanks sucking in and out and she made no move. (C 117)[15]

The focalizers are those men who look upon Billy as a stranger, just as the *carretero* who "looked back at the animal and looked at the deputy. His eyes moved over the waiting pilgrims now reassembled until he met the eyes of the young extranjero from whom the wolf had been appropriated" (C 101).[16]

After the wolf's death Billy's world becomes disenchanted. The narrator's psycho-narration conveys the character's consciousness:

> He could feel the horse's hooves muted on the cobbled rocks of the river floor and hear the water sucking at the horse's legs. The water came up under the animal's belly and he could feel the cold of it where it leaked into his boots. A last lone rocket rose over the town and revealed them midriver and revealed all the country about them, the shoreland trees strangely enshadowed, the pale rocks. A solitary dog from the town that had caught the scent of the wolf on the wind and followed him out stood frozen on the beach on three legs standing in that false light and then all faded again into the darkness out of which it had been summoned. (C 125)

The concentration of such words as "enshadowed," "darkness" (which has already appeared in the previous paragraph), "pale," "faded," "cold," "frozen," "lone," "solitary," effectively renders Billy's feelings of alienation which are then projected onto the landscape by his consciousness.[17] Thus, although internal focalization should not be mistaken for an instance of the double-voiced word, it nevertheless gives us access to the characters' inner lives, which remain mediated and dominated by the narrator's voice. Internal focalization does not lead us directly to dialogism but it certainly extends the character's sphere of influence because it appears at the confluence of two planes; it interweaves the narrator's voice and the character's consciousness.

According to Bakhtin's theory of the word, the character's consciousness and voice are likely to be inhabited by other voices. In *All the Pretty Horses*, Blevins and Rawlins may well be enemies or rivals; they are nevertheless connected by the same attempt to borrow the words (and voice) of popular wisdom when it suits them, even while denying it: "You never know when you'll be in need of them you've despised," says Blevins to John Grady, aiming at Rawlins' negative attitude toward him (72); "A goodlookin horse is like a goodlookin woman, [Rawlins] said. They're always more trouble[18] than what they're worth. What a man needs is just one that will get the job done" (89). Each borrowed speech is saturated with other people's uses of the word in other contexts to the point that it is almost emptied of meaning: it has become a *cliché*. Blevins borrows a biblical maxim from the language of the other Jimmy Blevins, the radio preacher, drawing attention to the possibility that he may also have borrowed his identity. Rawlins uses a simile which is all the more irrelevant as he is neither married nor attached and as the previous conversation has been centered upon Blevins' inability to prove the horse belongs to him. This is ironically underlined by John Grady's similar replies in both cases:

Where the hell'd you hear that at? (72)
Where'd you hear that at? (89)

The dishonesty of the two pretenders is emphasized by the similarity between both Blevins' and Rawlins' answers ("I dont know").[19] McCarthy's narrator thus points to dialogic relations between the characters while injecting his own comment into John Grady's, using his double-voiced word to highlight the duplicity in Rawlins' and Blevins' own words.

A special case of borrowing appears in the long words of such talkative characters as Don Héctor, Alfonsa and Eduardo. When John Grady is invited to play pool by the *hacendado*, the game is meant to be a kind of agonistic challenge which will allow Alejandra's father to put the young man to the test at several levels. Of course, it repeats the agonistic chess game with Alfonsa which has taken place before. The "hacendado beat him easily," we are told (144), and Don Héctor seizes the opportunity of this man-to-man situation to warn the boy in veiled terms against coveting Alejandra. First, he tells him about the chapel whose sanctity he would not let anyone—even a priest—dissolve; his word contains and fights another, which metaphorically refers to the sanctuary of his daughter's person. Second, like the other members of his family—Alfonsa (227–39) and Alejandra (141)—he does not separate the history of his kin from that of his country and thus never separates his own language from the language of his kin. This twofold history and language allow him to tell John Grady that his marriage with Alejandra will never be permitted by recalling Alfonsa's possible but doomed engagement to Francisco Madero's brother, Gustavo: "Alfonsita may have been engaged to be married to Francisco's brother. I'm not sure. In any case my grandfather would never have permitted the marriage" (144).[20] Another example of *double-entendre* can be found in Alfonsa's chess-game, which is also highly agonistic:

It occurred to him that she might be curious to know if he would throw the game and he realized that he had in fact already considered it and he knew she'd thought of it before he had. (133)

Chess stategy consists in controlling one's impulsive moves while anticipating the adversary's moves to checkmate him, *i.e.*, to render him powerless. John Grady wins two games and she wins the third one. The chess game is then replaced by a conversation in which John Grady is a mere listener but in which chess tactics have been transferred to what is at stake: Alejandra's future. Actually Alfonsa tries to make her monologue more dialogic than it is by connecting John Grady's (first, minor) scar with her own finger accident and by struggling with her own past when dealing with her grandniece (135). Nevertheless, Alfonsa is the kind of person who can very well anticipate the adversary's reply, and in this she is opposed to Don Héctor: "Héctor said that you would not come here. I assured him he was wrong" (227). That is why she is so good at strategy.

In *Cities of the Plain*, Eduardo's offended reaction to Billy's well-chosen question about Magdalena's freedom is a provocative, stratified retort: "You think I am a whiteslaver" (134). It contains at least two meanings and two voices. First, Eduardo redirects the accusation of coming from a country of slaveholders—of being one of them—at Billy, the *güero* from North America. It may not be completely irrelevant to suggest also that "(to) slaver" can be read in the written word—if not in the spoken word—and interpreted as "(to) show great desire for, lust after," which echoes the mention that Eduardo is in love with Magdalena. Such a pun—if there be a pun—comes from the sphere of the narrator or that of the implied author. However, there is yet another layer of meaning, which Eduardo had certainly not expected and which must have been implanted by the narrator or the implied author. It could read as follows: yes, a northerner has a right to suspect a southern pimp of slave-holding because prostitution is a form of slavery in that the pimp's properties have alienated their right to stop working for their employer, just as slaves cannot end their contract simply by giving notice. Eduardo's word thus contains two hostilely juxtaposed meanings which make one language—the narrator's—impinge on another—the character's. The procurer utilizes language in a provocative way and the narrator utilizes the same language to achieve a totally different effect that debunks the former's. The internally dialogized word appears as a two-sided act which can engage in polemic when it contains two diametrically opposed views.

Siding or not siding with a character's determination, belief, perception is part and parcel of McCarthy's narrator's game of creating undifferentiation and differentiation, continuity and discontinuity. He can take us into the wolf's subjectivity ("She ate till her belly dragged and she did not go back. She would not return to a kill. She would not cross a road or a rail line in daylight. She would not cross under a wire fence twice in the same place. These were the new protocols. Strictures that had not existed before. Now they did" [C 25]), just as he can distance himself from the character's supposed knowledge:

Once he rode her up out of a bed in a windbreak thicket on the south slope where she'd slept in the sun. Or thought he rode her up. (C 32)
He already knew that she was smarter than any dog but he didnt know how much smarter. (C 82)

We have seen that the character's perception can haunt the narration, and that the narrator's voice can inhabit the character's voice. Conversely, the character's consciousness can encroach upon the narrator's language.[21] Just before Billy and Boyd come across Keno, they ride through the town of Morelos, with Boyd sleeping against his elder brother's back on the same horse, and "they took the road south where he had followed the pilgrims to the fair in the spring of that same year so long ago" (C 180). "[I]n the spring of that same year" is an objective time-marker which originates from the narrator's point of view whereas "so long ago" is a subjective time-marker which is imbued with Billy's consciousness.[22] The boy's and the narrator's voices are closely intertwined within a sentence. These two different voices particularly interact upon each other in (free) indirect discourse which brings into play a plurality of speakers and attitudes.

Free indirect discourse (or thought), as Dorrit Cohn explains, aims at the presentation of a character's discourse (or thoughts) in the third person and the tense of the narration; it resorts to a technique whereby the narrative voice relays the character's discourse (or thoughts) indirectly, while retaining syntactical features of the character's voiced or mental discourse.[23] When Billy meets Boyd's girlfriend in Namiquipa, as Boyd has asked him to, the two riders are left together and they share an intimacy which is new to both. The girl tells Billy about the life of her grandmother, which, as usual in McCarthy's Mexico, is blended with that of the country—more particularly that of the Revolution:

> She said that her grandmother was skeptical of many things in this world and of none more than men. . . . Her grandmother spoke to her often of men and she spoke with great earnestness and she said that rash men were a great temptation to women. . . . She said that to be a woman was to live a life of difficulty and heartbreak. . . . And she said that since this was so nor could it be altered one was better to follow one's heart in joy and in misery than simply to seek comfort for there was none. To seek it was only to welcome in the misery and to know little else. She said that these were things all women knew yet seldom spoke of. (322)

What is striking here is the polyphonic use of the third-person pronoun "she": the first occurrence of the pronoun refers to the girl while the second one pertains to the grandmother; but the following ones can be interpreted either as the grandmother's word reported by the girl ("[My grandmother] said that . . .") or as the girl's word reported by the narrator. Actually the second hypothesis is supported by the conjunction "Lastly she said" and the beginning of the next paragraph ("She had finished eating"). However, the borderline between the two women's voices is blurred by the similarities between the two destinies during a bird's-eye view sort of reading: the language, which is inherited from the grandmother—and was probably already a legacy—is taken up by the girl and addressed to Billy as a sample of female knowledge. The two destinies, past, present and future, seem to merge. And the grandmother's discourse is reinforced by the support it is given by the girl. It is even quoted by the narrator in the sole instance of free indirect discourse to be found in this paragraph: "To seek it was only to welcome in the misery and to know little else." Nothing here distinguishes the narrator's voice from the women's, except the past tense. The effect which is achieved is not polemics but trust, agreement, reinforcement through fusion.

Free indirect thought—or narrated monologue, as Dorrit Cohn terms it—allows the narrator to blend narration and quotation and to merge his voice with the character's mental discourse. When Billy sees the gypsies' play, he watches "with interest" but can "make little of it" (219), which is dramatized by the rest of the paragraph:

The company was perhaps describing some adventure of their own in their travels and they sang into each other's faces and wept and in the end the man in buffoon's motley slew the woman and slew another man perhaps his rival with a dagger and young boys ran forward with the curtain hems to draw them shut and the mules standing in their traces raised their heads up out of their sleep and began to shift and step. (219)

Billy is designated as the focal character of the scene ("He watched the play") and the rest of the paragraph as his thoughts ("The company was perhaps describing . . ."). Narrated monologue enables the narrator to trace the boy's efforts to understand something which does not cohere. The numerous conjunctions "and" add the events to each other without providing them with logic, order or differentiation: the mules and the young boys drawing the curtains shut are placed on the same level as the actors playing roles; the actors are all fused in the collective "they" at the beginning, which gives the impression that they all do the same thing and that it is confusing; when differentiated, the actors are simply men or women, etc. Two attempts at interpretation can be traced in the adverb "perhaps." The confusion is either the consequence of the stage director's bad job or Billy's closed mind, which recalls John Grady's inability to make sense of his mother's play (*APH* 21). The blurring of enunciative borderlines makes it impossible to identify the narration as omniscient. Free indirect discourse and narrated monologue create internal dialogism where direct discourse pretends to quote the character's words without narratorial intervention and indirect discourse makes the narrator's voice predominant. They merge the narrator's presentation of the events with the character's; they produce the dual voice studied by Roy Pascal in *The Dual Voice: Free Indirect Speech and Its Functioning in the Nineteenth-Century European Novel*. The text thus appears as a hybrid in which the narrating voice and a character's can either express themselves in chorus or compete for supremacy. McCarthy does not seem to use free indirect discourse and narrated monologue for the sake of polemics. But, as Bakhtin shows, the two voices can be converging or diverging. McCarthy's travestied words—multi-layered words—bear evidence of both directions.

Dialogue—direct discourse—is often used as a subdued battleground between opposed characters: John Grady and his mother, John Grady and his father, Rawlins and Blevins, the boys and the authorities, the boys and Pérez, John Grady and Alfonsa, John Grady and Alejandra in *All the Pretty Horses*; Billy and the wolf haters, Billy and Boyd, the boys and the (Mexican or American military) authorities, the boys and the villains in *The Crossing*; Billy and John Grady about the latter's quixotic attitude, the boys and the pimps, etc. in *Cities of the Plain*. When McCarthy injects another's word into a character's word, the two voices generally converge, unlike what happens between two voices in direct discourse.

In *All the Pretty Horses*, Alfonsa's speech is polyphonic and heteroglossic. It is inhabited, among others, by feminist ideas ("I grew up in a world of men" [135]; "The societies to which I have been exposed seemed to me largely machines for the suppression of women" [230]), ideas she has found in books ("By the time I was sixteen I had read many books and I had become a freethinker. In all cases I refused to believe in a God who could permit such injustice as I saw in a world of his own making" [232]), her interpretation of poverty, which intersects with that of the Madero brothers ("I began to see how the world must become if I were to live in it. . . . Francisco began to set up schools for the poor children of the district. He dispensed medicines. Later he would feed hundreds of people from his own kitchen" [233]), the family paternalist tradition she also inherits from her father ("My father was outspoken in his views concerning the responsibilities of the landed class" [236]), a kind of anti-Hegelian conception of history ("It is supposed to be true that those who do not know history are condemned to repeat it. I dont believe knowing can save us" [239]). Some of these discourses may appear to clash, but they co-exist in Alfonsa's language, and she even manages to reconcile them with each other in her *Weltanschauung*: "[Gustavo] was never meant to be a soldier. I think they did not understand Mexico. Like my father he hated bloodshed and violence. But perhaps he did not hate it enough. Francisco was the most deluded of all. He was never suited to be president of Mexico" (238). Alfonsa "suffers" from the symptom McCarthy mentioned to artistic director Douglas Wager: "even people who are buried alive go over their life stories to stay sane. Verification of one's story to someone else is essential to living . . . ; our reality comes out of the narrative we create, not out of the experiences themselves" (Arnold, *Stonemason* 121). The narrative of her life is a multi-layered discourse nurtured by several traditions—the old world's and the new world's, among others, articulated in the present and oriented toward the future ("My grandniece is the only future I contemplate" [239]): the repudiation of John Grady as a suitor and the purchase of his release in return for Alejandra's renunciation are replies anticipating further response. She combines the data in her life as she moves pawns on a chessboard. Alfonsa finds herself at the intersection of past, present and future. Comprehension of the past usages of words and response to their yet unutilized potential dialectically merge and interact in her thoughts.

In *The Crossing*, after the wolf's death and retrieval by Billy, the boy's feelings of alienation reach a climax, as has been said above:

As he rode he sang old songs his father once had sung in the used to be and a soft *corrido* in spanish from his grandmother that told of the death of a brave *soldadera* who took up her fallen soldierman's gun and faced the enemy in some old waste of death. (125–6)

He sings songs he has heard two dear relatives sing before, and through these songs he reaches across time and space toward his kin. The voices of the relatives, the narrator and the protagonist converge to weave together past, present and future. Indeed, the *corrido* he sings connects his own story with Boyd's future story: Billy, like the *soldadera*, has taken up his rifle and faced the enemy, but the victim is the she-wolf; according to the legend, Boyd takes up his gun and shoots the *gerente* but "the güerito and his novia die in each other's arms for they have no more ammunition" (381). In the songs Billy's past, present (and future) intersect, which has a soothing effect, as the rhythm of the following sentences suggests:

The night was clear and as he rode the moon dropped under the rim of the mountain and stars began to come up in the east where it was darkest. They rode up the dry course of a creekbed in a night suddenly colder, as if the moon had had warmth to it. Up through the low hills where he would ride all night singing softly as he rode. (126)

Billy learns it is difficult to run counter to the legends surrounding the wolf and those dealing with his brother. Boyd's legend is inspired by previous stories. His girlfriend asserts that "all the world knew that the güerito had killed the gerente from Las Varitas. The man who had betrayed Socorro Rivera and sold out his own people to the Guardia Blanca of La Babícora" (322). Because the truth "aint what come out of somebody's mouth" (as John Grady maintains in *All the Pretty Horses* [168]), Billy tries to make the history right: "the manco had fallen from his horse and broken his back and ... he himself had seen it happen" (322). But it is of no avail. Similarly, the legend of his wolf draws on other stories: "they'd put up a sign at the front that gave her history and the number of people she was known to have eaten" (104) because

An old woman said that the wolf had been brought from the sierras where it had eaten many schoolchildren. Another woman said that it had been captured in the company of a young boy who had run away naked into the woods. A third said that the hunters who had brought the wolf down out of the sierras had been followed by other wolves who howled at night from the darkness beyond their fire and some of the hunters had said that these wolves were no right wolves. (102)

The double-voiced word can also contain the narrator's axiologic judgment about the society which is represented in his story. I have argued elsewhere that McCarthy is sensitive to individual rebellion against market economies which involve the commodification of animals and human beings.[24] In *All the Pretty Horses*, the three runaway boys have to buy *sotol* from caravans because they do not have enough change to buy water (66). Then they come across a Mexican who offers to trade wax for Blevins (76). After being released from the Saltillo prison as a result of a transaction he has refused for himself ("Some people dont have a price" [193]), John Grady has grown into a young man who is well aware of the distortions trade entails. At the end of the novel, his wry sense of humor is directed at those distorted human relationships, and more particularly at the men who are chasing him and the captain he has abducted: "You must owe them sons of bitches money" (270). The character's ironical voice, which aims at specific circumstances, and the narrator's parodic voice, whose target is the global commodification of human beings, converge toward criticism in that humorous sally.

What has been implied previously is that the double-voiced word is mainly the locus of passive dialogism, that is to say that it consists in using another's word to express one's own orientations. It can also be active, diverging, that is to say, engage in polemics. When John Grady prepares to see Alejandra for the last time and maybe induce her to change her mind as to their break-up, he buys her "a very plain silver necklace" (APH 248), thus putting into practice "what his father had once told him, that scared money cant win and a worried man cant love" (247). He buys the present and "paid the woman what she asked" (248). Such an inconspicuous clause would go unnoticed if it did not contain two competing meanings which are deliberately introduced by the narrator: either the sentence is equivalent to "he paid for it"—but then why does the narrator add "what she asked"?—or it includes an axiological judgment about the price asked for the necklace, which equates it with extortion, and John Grady nevertheless pays for it because he is in no mood to argue or to bargain. This may pass for a detail but it reveals the way the narrator's voice may work.

In *Cities of the Plain*, when John Grady looks for Magdalena in whorehouses, the narrator tells us about his investigation: "He walked up Tlaxcala and up Mariscal and entered another such place and sat at the bar" (37). "[A]nother such place" is a euphemism that the narrator pretends to borrow from self-righteous people's language. The lack of quotation marks does not prevent the reader from detecting a stranger's phrase in the narrator's speech. The clash between the ironical use of the euphemistic phrase and its serious use bears witness to the narrator's unintimidated readiness to introduce places like whorehouses or subjects like prostitution into fiction.

The double-voiced word which is the focus of this study can emerge as the locus of a character's oscillation between two phases of his ego. These two phases are not successive in time but they co-exist at a given moment. In *All the Pretty Horses*, Rawlins obliquely voices his doubts as to his and John Grady's plans to run away:

Just seems too damn easy in a way. (31)
Wonder what all they're doin back home? (36)

Well suppose you were ill at ease and didnt know why. (37)
You think there'll be a day when the sun wont rise? (60)
I wish it was mornin. (87)

Each subject is raised to mean something else and to convey fear: Rawlins' "I said I wouldnt [quit you]" (91) suggests that were it not for his given word, he would give up. Rawlins' voiced doubts betray an inner conflict between the self he models on John Grady's own dreamed self and his former Texan self: both phases compete, and their conflict has not yet been settled by history. McCarthy nevertheless cautiously avoids suggesting nostalgia. Billy, for example, cannot turn the clock backward: "He thought to become again the child he never was" (C 129).

In *The Crossing*, Billy must carry out a mission he has been given by his father: "If by any chance at all she should be in a trap you come and get me. Unless her leg is broke. If her leg is broke shoot her. Otherwise she'll twist out" (30). When he finds the wolf caught by the right forefoot, he "tried to remember what his father had said. If her leg were broke or she were caught by the paw" (53). The sentence, which starts as narrated monologue, takes up part of his father's speech but leaves it unfinished. The missing part concerns what the boy will not do: shoot her. The father's discourse is thus truncated and cannibalized, and his voice is silenced and repressed.

Later, like Rawlins, Billy voices his doubts:

If anybody was to see this, he told [the wolf], they'd come and carry me off to the loonybin in a rig just like it. (80)
All right, he said. Dont get stupid on me now. He wasnt talking to the wolf. She gets hold of you, he said, they wont even find a beltbuckle. (81)

The narrator's comment on this dialogue ("He wasnt talking to the wolf") supports the reader's impression that there is an internally dialogized word embedded within a speech which is apparently addressed to the animal. This internally dialogized word is the battleground of a conflict between two phases of the ego: the ego that transgresses parental interdiction and the ego which is determined to return the wolf to the mountains.

The narrative voice often underlines the character's hesitation between two courses of action and his oscillation between two moral stands. When Billy, at the beginning of his quest, comes across an old rancher, "He knew the old man wanted to hear that he was trapping coyotes and he wouldnt lie, or wouldnt exactly lie" (37). The two final segments take us into the boy's subjective assessment of what is best for the old man, for himself, and for the sake of moral values. The narrative voice conveys that competition through psycho-narration. Later, toward the end of the story, when Billy is told to sign his mother's name on the parental consent form to be taken in the army, he signs Louisa May Parham: "His mother's name was Carolyn" (338). The narrator's laconic information is more than just that: it suggests that Billy is reluctant to sign the name of his dead mother, and thus to commit forgery.

The characters are not the only ones to be inhabited by several voices, including the voice of their social and moral norm. The narrator's own voice may be inhabited by another, more critical, counterpart. At the beginning of *The Crossing*, Billy's father is described: "Like a man bent on fixing himself someway in the world. Bent on trying by arc or chord the space between his being and the world that was. If there be such space" (22). The speaker's difficulty at describing the indescribable is expressed first by the simile and then by the restriction which follows. In fact the reliability of language in reflecting reality, visible or not, is discussed through the circumlocutions which are scattered throughout the text:

> Such road as it was soon ceased to be road at all. (187)
> They ate in what passed for a cafe in that rawlooking country. (239)
> An hour later and they came to a crossroads. Or they came to a place where a gullied rut ran down out of the mountains from the north.... (251)

Each periphrasis testifies to the presence of a critical authority who questions the notion of the transparency of language and its aim at representation. The two voices—the voice which says and the voice which questions—coexist and balance each other.

Proleptic statements need to be examined because they can originate from a diverging voice. They can prefigure serious and tragic events such as Niño's wound (after Boyd, other *niños* are wounded, as Dianne Luce has observed ["Road" 202]) or the separation of the two brothers, as the diva seems to foresee (C 230). As do all proleptic phrases, they encourage the reader to read the story backward. But they can also be contained within the word of a character who announces his own future unknowingly and at his own expense: they draw on dramatic irony which sustains a duplicity of meaning which is perceived by the writer and the reader but is unknown to the character. In *All the Pretty Horses*, Rawlins is that kind of character who says something that anticipates the actual outcome, but not at all in the way he means it:

You aint ridin with us, said Rawlins. You'll get us thowed in the jailhouse. (41)
You're just a deadhead. (44)
Suppose, he said, that we wanted to trade that horse off for one less likely to get us shot. (47)
Get shot dead for horsestealin it dont mean a damn thing to him. He expects it. (80)
I always wanted to be a bad man. (121)
What I see is you fixin to get us fired and run off the place. (138)
There aint much happenin out there [in the Mexican countryside], is there? (88)²⁵

In *All the Pretty Horses*, John Grady jokes with the little Mexican girls, but his words are also unfortunate when he introduces himself as a thief and a bandit: "Sí. Ladrones muy famosos. Bandoleros" (156; Yes. Very famous robbers. Bandits). In each case, the character acts in a way grossly inappropriate to the actual circumstances, or expects the opposite of what fate holds in store. What is meant as a joke to exorcise the uncertain future provides a frame to the narrator's diverging announcement of the characters' tragic destinies.

Apart from the use of "and" and that of participles, what characterizes McCarthy's prose is his conspicuous utilization of analogy which reinforces characterization, or acts as a purely textual link, independent of story-causality, or emphasizes similarity or contrast. Unlike metaphors, the comparing link "as if" or "like" maintains the presence of the agent who makes the comparison. That is why that link foregrounds the arbitrary quality of the comparison. It is also the locus of another voice which tugs in the opposite direction, that of artificial resemblance, almost that of difference:

He tried to see into her eyes but the light played off the glass of her spectacles and one of the panes was half opaque with dirt as if perhaps she had no vision in that eye and saw no need to clean it. (C 297)

The drovers when they saw him raised their hands in greeting and cried out. Almost as if they'd been expecting to come upon him soon or late. (C 401)

Here, the twofold role of McCarthy's comparison is underlined by a modifying adverb, such as "perhaps" or "almost," which further invalidates the similarity which has been established previously and yet is not completely erased by the opposite movement. Like "as if," the link "like" is a double-voiced word, because it introduces resemblance—more often than not with a *cliché*—and initiates departure from *cliché*. In "they had the look of storybook riders" (C 213), resemblance is undermined by the comparison with fictional characters, which defuses referential illusion. The comparison is no longer part of what Barthes termed "effects of reality" because identification through likeness is not guaranteed by the narrator. But, just as *cliché* is avoided for the sake of discontinuity, avoidance of *cliché* is also undermined in an ironical reversal: "They looked like what they were, outcasts in an alien land" (C 296). The clash between what is expected—hiatus between being and appearances—and what is given—identity between being and appearances—ironically underscores the perversion involved in reading and writing habits which transform avoidance of *cliché* into *cliché*. "And it is precisely at the juncture of cliché and departure from cliché that the book works its most wondrous charms," Rick Wallach argues about *Cities of the Plain* (57). When the reader expects a stereotypical saloon fight at the end of *The Crossing*, no brawl ensues:

He looked at the man who'd warned him not to turn but that was all the warning that man had. (363)

When Billy, who has fallen into an ambuscade, is expected to be robbed or wounded or killed, the boy remains safe but there is a victim nevertheless: the Niño horse (394–97). The reader is thus made to hear two voices which tug in opposite directions, one toward stereotype and one toward what is not stereotype. It is indeed the task of the narrator—as the priest at Huisiachepic tells Billy in one long tale within the tale—to produce many stories of one: "Always the teller must be at pains to devise against his listener's claim—perhaps spoken, perhaps not—that he has heard the tale before" (155), we are told in a self-reflexive loop.

What sounds like metafictional comments within the story contains the implied reader's voice lodged within the narrator's tale. That device is not merely used but performed at the end of *All the Pretty Horses* when John

Grady comes back to talk to the judge, who tells him, "I dont believe anybody could make up the story you just now got done tellin us" (288). It is thus the fictional character of the judge of human affairs who tells the boy that his story cannot be a figment of anyone's imagination, in a kind of dialectical reversal. John Grady's story is not directly guaranteed by the implied author's voice but by a fictional character's voice, which is paradoxical and controversial. The judge takes over from the narrator—the voice which actually tells the story made up by the implied author and to whom the reader has become accustomed—who is about to be erased: "those stories which speak to us with the greatest resonance have a way of turning upon the teller and erasing him and his motives from all memory" (COP 277). Just before vanishing, the narrative voice wants to rectify possible mistakes: "It just bothered me that you might think I was somethin special. I aint," John Grady says to the judge (APH 293). The protagonist should not be taken for a hero, we are told. The closing of *The Crossing*, with the gypsy's insistence on representation and illusion, is also a valediction to both character and reader. At the end of each book—including *Cities of the Plain*—the implied author writes a farewell scene to his character whose fate is going to escape him: "The proprietary claims of the dreamer upon the dreamt have their limits. I cannot rob the traveler of his own autonomy lest he vanish altogether" (COP 274).

Although John Grady and Billy can speak Spanish perfectly, Mexico appears as a Tower of Babel where *double-entendre*, even within a given language, reinforces the duplicity of meaning. All in all, the protagonist's quest is a quest for meaning which he cannot discover in Texas or New Mexico; John Grady has had "the notion that there would be something in the story itself to tell him about the way the world was or was becoming but there was not. There was nothing in it at all" (APH 21); Billy is told that "no man knew what the wolf knew" (C 45). Their adventures into the Mexican microcosm are therefore emblematic of the quest and condition of Everyman.[26]

McCarthy uses Spanish words to achieve effects of reality—to create referential illusion—for example for toponyms (*tienda, bodega, ejido, alameda, paseo, hacienda,* etc.) or socio-economic roles (*hacendado, dueña, alguacil, jefe, criada, alcahuete, cucinera, sepulturero,* etc.). But language is also represented as the locus of power or the instrument of power. Indeed, the character who imposes one language rather than another on his interlocutor turns out to be the socially superior one or the one who eventually gets the upper hand. *All the Pretty Horses* effectively illustrates that agonistic function of language. When Don Héctor imposes the English language ("We can speak english") on a John Grady who is ready and willing to speak Spanish ("Como le convenga": However it suits you [113]), it is because he wants to test the boy's honesty rather than the boy's linguistic abilities. However, just as the misunderstanding about Blevins cannot be avoided due to John Grady's tactical error, linguistic misunderstanding also seems to be inevitable:

[The stallion] is enroute.
He's where?
Enroute. From Mexico. (114)

The difficulty is reinforced by the presence of a strange word borrowed from French. However, John Grady is signed as the loser of the contest with the *hacendado*, at least from a linguistic point of view.[27] What is at stake is already the question of the stolen horse, as Alfonsa will explain later on: "The affair of the stolen horse was known here even before you arrived. The thieves were known to be Americans. When he questioned you about this you denied everything" (*APH* 228). On the other hand, when neither the conflicting subject of Alejandra's future nor that of the stolen horse is at stake, the *hacendado* and the boy can share their interest in horses. Then their good relationship is dramatized by a linguistic exchange in which they shift back and forth between both languages:

I'd like to ride him. Con su permiso. [If I may.]
The hacendado nodded. Yes, he said. Of course.
[. . .]
Le gusta? [Do you like him?] said the hacendado.
John Grady nodded. That's a hell of a horse, he said. (126)[28]

Just before John Grady and Rawlins are taken to the Saltillo prison, they are questioned by the Mexican captain who has had them arrested. They are told to speak English ("Speak english please. You come to buy cattle?" [164]), even though the captain is far from mastering the language as well as Don Héctor and needs Rawlins' explanations:

To shoot game.
Ghem?
Game. To hunt. Cazador [Hunter]. (165)

His difficulties can even create linguistic *quid pro quo*: "You must co-po-rate" (163).

McCarthy's narrator is obviously sensitive to the hiatus created by, on the one hand, the need of linguistic expression and, on the other, the inadequacy of language. John Grady, for example, leaves home to find "country," which he believes is missing or disappearing on the northern side of the border. While the narrator repeatedly insists on "the new country," the boy continues to believe in "country": "Well, he said. There's a lot of country out there" (89). At the end of the novel, when he is told "This is still good country," he answers: "Yeah. I know it is. But it aint my country" (299). Although he seems to have understood the difference between the two, he has found neither. Language has previously played the same trick on him in a conversation with Alejandra's great-aunt. When he replies that the emphasis put on women's honor does not seem right to him, she answers that it is "not a matter of right" (137). The shift from adjective to noun is not his, but it is nevertheless made at his expense. Thus language can also be subjected to a duplication which affects meaning.

The introduction of foreign words into the narrative is a way for the narrator to suggest the characters' alienation even more forcefully and to create powerful effects of meaning. At the end of Part One in *The Crossing*, Billy follows the crowd, including the *alguacil*, to the *hacienda* where the wolf is going to be exhibited:

the alguacil and his party were passing along the alameda four and six abreast, calling out to one another, many of them garbed in the gaudy attire of the norteño and of the charro all spangled and trimmed with silver braid, the seams of their trousers done with silver shells. (106)

When the cart carrying the wolf is attacked by dogs, "The alguacil and his minions stood in their stirrups and shouted after them, laughing and whooping" (109). The term "minions" certainly means obsequious followers, servile agents who carry out the *alguacil*'s orders. But it also ironically refers to the carnivalesque "gaudy attire" imported from the North, which unexpectedly transforms these dependants into effeminate favorites in what is supposed to be the "world of men" Alfonsa deplores in *All the Pretty Horses*. The narrator's use of foreign etymology introduces a subversive voice into the frame of the story.

The dialogic exchange among several languages produces carnivalesque distortion. The singular "money" becomes the plural "monies" when the Spanish speaker believes or wants his addressee to believe that a lot of money is at stake (COP 58, C 409). According to the concepts of onomastics, Wolfenbarger has a predatory temperament, which John Grady perfectly suspects (COP 115). The expression "Todo el mundo" (all the world; everyone) tells a German-speaking reader that death (*Tod*) is everywhere in the world. But it is the Spanish language which is given pride of place on the carnivalesque stage. John Grady does not know yet how desperate he will be when he tells Rawlins he looks like a *desperado* (APH 36, 55). Considering that the Spanish-sounding word is the alteration of the past participle of the verb *despedir*, which means "to discharge," "to emit," "to throw off," "to give off," "to take leave," the word's strata are not limited to "reckless criminal" but go further to include alienation and even John Grady's repudiation as a suitor. The town of Encantada that John Grady and Rawlins ride into and out of several times (APH 77, 154, 228) is a typically dialogized name in which McCarthy superimposes the mystery and fear created by Melville's Enchanted Islands ("The Encantadas")[29] and the terror and fear he creates in his own story. After "John Grady Cole's Expulsion from Paradise" (Morrison), Mexico has become a disenchanted place, if not an inferno recalling Dante's.

In *The Crossing*, Billy's first attempt to recuperate the wolf comes up against the crowd and the hostility of the *hacendado*'s son. In order not to lose face in front of his people, the young *hacendado* questions Billy. The investigation starts in English but switches to Spanish when Billy tries to drive home the point that he just wanted to pass through Mexico: "Pasar o traspasar?" the young master of language retorts (119). Because it can mean "to trespass" and "to inflict agony or suffering," *traspasar* links the theme of transgression with that of suffering and cruelty, which Billy incarnates. His transgression—of parental order and of boundaries—results in the wolf's cruel suffering, and in his own. More generally speaking, the theme of transgression has been internally dialogized by the text. When Billy visits Don Arnulfo in quest of Echols's secrets, which he could not find in the old trapper's cabin, he is told, "The wolf is like the copo de nieve [snowflake]. ... If you catch it you lose it" (46). What is said would not be so interesting if it were not what the text performs—or refuses to perform. In this case, the subsequent events perform exactly that: Billy loses the wolf just after catching her. Old Don Arnulfo's words have come true. What is also inspiring is that all transgressions are recycled in a dream of Billy's, which connects them. In this dream, Billy reaches out his arms to a company of wolves who see him and touch his face with their muzzles but vanish into the snow and the dark night. Here the wolves will not let themselves be caught: they remain free and inaccessible even though contact has been made possible. The second part of the dream takes place inside the house, with Boyd thinking his elder brother has run away from home and saying that their parents will not wake (295–6). Thus the dream reconfigures not only Billy's special relationship with wolves (except that the one who chooses between freedom and captivity is the wolf), but also his transgression of parental order (Billy's parents will not wake because they are dead due in part to his misjudgment), and his failure to live up to his brother's expectations (Boyd pleads that Billy will not desert him). This dream and the others help Billy express his guilt, but they do not relieve him totally of self-reproach. Boyd has been interred in San Buenaventura, Billy is eventually told, which means that he has not been as lucky in his adventures as the name of the place might suggest. His bones are carried by Billy across the frontier and buried in the town of Animas, where his soul will rest among many others: *animas* meaning "souls."

It is in *Cities of the Plain* that McCarthy deploys his linguistic forces most effectively. John Grady meets a young bootblack whom he calls *bolero*, which means "shoeshine boy" and "liar," both meanings being adapted in that the young bootblack is also someone who reconfigures the world through speech: "If there's somethin I want to be a different way from what it is then that's how I say it is. What's wrong with that?" (97). The second sense may be attributed to John Grady or to the narrator: it defines the very young boy as both a bootblack and a teller of tales. When Billy visits Eduardo and brings John Grady's money to buy Magdalena from her pimp, Tiburcio calls him "the trujamán" (129). The *alcahuete* may well play on the two meanings of "counselor," "advisor" and also "interpreter" or "translator," as Billy is acting as a go-between. However, the implied author has probably also grafted another sense onto the first two: that of "broker," "trader," which introduces the analogy between prostitution—sex trade—and slavery. Thus either the procurer's deputy acknowledges the commodification of the prostitutes, while highlighting John Grady's and Billy's own ambiguous part in the trade, or the reference to trade originates solely from the implied author. The latter's polyphonic use of the Spanish word within a dialogic situation weaves together several readings of Tiburcio's utterance.

At the end of Part One, John Grady walks back through the streets of Juárez, hearing nightvendors who "trundled their carts or drove their small burros before them. They called out leeen-ya. They called out quero-seeen-a" (82). What they sell is *leña* (firewood) and *kerosén*, or *kerosina*, or *queroseno*. McCarthy's choice of *kerosina* allows him to transform the word into a lament: *quero* sounds like *quiero* (I want, I need) and *seen-a*, like a girl's name—just as *leeen-ya* conjures up [Magda]lena. The narrator thus projects lovesick John Grady's distorted perception of the outside world onto that world: "Plying the darkened streets and calling out like old suitors in search themselves of maids long lost to them" (82). While being the implied author's prefiguration of John Grady's tragic loss, the vendors' word is reinterpreted by another consciousness which is inhabited by both character and narrator. Although the narrator explicitly gives us the key to the dialogic relationship between the two meanings—thus depriving the reader of the pleasure of finding the pun—the implied author has made the most of the polyphonic potential of the Spanish word *kerosina*. The implied author's usage of a foreign language like Spanish may well be motivated by the phonetic, morphologic or semantic system of that language. Spanish being stereotypically considered as the vehicle of romantic lament, he has firmly implanted John Grady's new dream into stereotype the better to depart from it afterward.

Bakhtin posited the freedom of the character and the independence of his mind to distinguish the narrator's sphere of influence from the character's and to examine the exchanges between the two. McCarthy's characters often "dialogize" their language, i.e., use another's word to instill their own meaning into the first one, particularly if the exchange takes place between two different languages for the sake of stylization or parody, or for the sake of irony and polemic.

In *All the Pretty Horses*, Alejandra meets John Grady in Zacatecas for the last time. The town of Zacatecas may not have been chosen only for geographical or historical reasons. Indeed, *zacatecas* is another name for *sepultureros* (gravediggers), which marks the town as an appropriate place to inter one's love: Alejandra has agreed to come to Zacatecas to bury their relationship. She has traded the death of their love for the life of the lover.[30] She insists on showing him a small plaza where her grandfather died for the Revolution in 1914. In addition to her attempt not to romanticize his death, her translation of the street names points to her resignation: "As for the Street of Desire [la Calle del Deseo] it is like the Calle de Noche Triste [Sorrowful Street].[31] They are but names for Mexico" (253). Alejandra has made the name of the streets into the projection of her state of mind—an objective correlative of her feelings which she extends to the country of Mexico.[32]

After she has gone, John Grady leaves the hotel, gets drunk, gets in a fight and wakes in a strange room: "He remembered a man in silhouette at the end of a street who stood much as Rawlins had stood when last he saw him, half turned in farewell, a coat slung loosely over one shoulder. Who'd come to ruin no man's house. No man's daughter" (255). In John Grady's angry monologue "ruin" ironically recycles all the words he has heard before: Don Héctor's speech about the desecration of the chapel (144) and the "ruined" Madero family (145), Alfonsa's concern with the notions of "tainted blood" (229), "family curse" (229), "devastation" (234), "honor" (137), and "gossip" (136). John Grady thus mockingly interprets the world and judges others in terms of "ruin," derisively using Alejandra's family's criteria to repudiate them all the more forcefully. His monologue can be read as self-repudiation, expressing his guilt feelings when he compares himself with Rawlins, or a speech addressed to Alejandra's family, simultaneously conveying his repudiation of them and his self-exoneration. Interestingly the term "ruin" overlaps *The Crossing* to follow John Grady into *Cities of the Plain*, where he renovates the little house which is in ruins (145) but will eventually die because, as Alfonsa has declared, "Those whom life does not cure death will" (APH 238).

In *Cities of the Plain*, Billy has become a more talkative and bawdy character.[33] But Billy is no match for Eduardo, who is also endowed with the gift of language, as the knife-fight shows.[34] When faced with Billy for the second time, after Magdalena's death, Eduardo tells him that "everything that has come to pass has been the result of your friend's coveting of another man's property and his willful determination to convert that property to his own use without regard for the consequences" (240). Here Eduardo uses "to convert" in the sense of "to appropriate another's property without right to one's own use," dismissing the meaning of "to exchange for something of equal value," which corresponds to John Grady's offer.

The epilogue of *Cities of the Plain* is a highly carnivalesque and dialogized section, not only because it superimposes a dream inside the dream within the tale and self-reflexive comments on the art of narrating stories, but also because of the strange dialogue the two characters share. Billy is cast in the role of the listener who may be naïve (a prey to referential illusion), tired of the narrator's convolutions, or unwilling to suspend disbelief. He constantly challenges the stranger's distinctions between the dreamer and the subject of the dream:

Because if you were the same then one would know what the other knew.
As in the world.
Yes.
But this is not the world. This is a dream. In the world the question could not occur. (272)
   I think you got a habit of makin things a bit more complicated than what they need to be. Why not just tell the story?
   ... I should point out to you that you are the one with the questions. (278)
I suppose you're fixin to tell me he survived havin his head lopped off. (283)

Despite the naïve quality of Billy's questions, the tale about the dream within the dream is a monologue which is dialogic. Billy's question "Did he dream?" (272) seems to orient the man's narrative and does open new vistas for the teller: "Let us say that the events which took place were a dream of this man whose own reality remains conjectural" (272). Moreover, the speaker's rhetorical questions testify to the coexistence of his own questions with another's, as though he anticipated those questions from the outside (272, 285). Lastly, the implied author's words form another layer of meaning consisting in self-reflexive statements. The superimposition of these strata makes for the complex and parodic quality of the Epilogue. It is part and parcel of the carnivalesque familiarization of the world which is foregrounded by McCarthy's prose fiction.

Such stratified words can also be found in the long tales within the narrative that McCarthy has interspersed in *The Crossing*. The long speeches of the priest in the church, of the blind man, and of the gypsy include others' speeches: not only other characters' thoughts or utterances, which they report through direct or indirect discourse, but other people's possible beliefs, objections, and replies. The gypsy's tale, for example, anticipates the widespread opinion that what men see is reality in order to make a slightly different point: "what men do not understand is that what the dead have quit is itself no world but is also only the picture of the world in men's hearts" (413). Although they are primarily addressed to Billy, these speeches imply many other utterances, possible and virtual. They themselves co-exist within the novel, build upon each other[35] and interact with Billy's story, as when the gypsy tells Billy that looking after the past is like looking after a dream (411).

In the town where Billy and Boyd find the horse Keno at a German doctor's house, a thin old man sketches in the dust "a portrait of the country they said they wished to visit," but "When he was gone the men on the bench began to laugh" (184). Then they launch themselves into a dialogue discussing the quality of the old man's map and then the relevance of any map. The first speaker observes that a map is based on mere landmarks and that it cannot represent the whole country; being that incomplete, it is but the picture of a trip. That point is dismissed by a second man who points out the original drawer's good will, saying that there are other dangers than losing one's way. The previous speaker insists that a bad map is worse than no map at all. Another man on the bench joins the conversation and supports this view, saying that anyway dogs would piss on that bad map, while the second speaker repudiates his argument. The discussion goes on until the boys leave the place and the *tertulia* disbands. The *tertulia* illustrates McCarthy's carnivalization of the Mexican world. It can be considered as the Hispanic reincarnation of the Socratic dialogue—itself one of the forerunners of the modern novel, according to Bakhtin ("Composition and Genre in Dostoevsky's Novels," *Dostoevsky*)—in that it also resorts to syncrisis and anacrisis. Syncrisis is a rhetorical device by which opposite views on a given subject are compared, as is the case with the relevance and accuracy of the thin old man's map. Anacrisis consists in the art of challenging the interlocutor to debate, which is second nature to these disputants. The *tertulia* is one of the comic and serious genres which Bakhtin viewed as the precursors of the novel. Its introduction into McCarthy's novel mirrors and reduplicates the writer's use of dialogism as a key principle.

McCarthy's southwestern texts are no monologic, organically unified wholes. Just as the trilogy distances the reader from the ideology of cowboy stories, exposing its contradictions and laying bare the artifice surrounding their production, it constructs a polyphony of equally valid voices, while suggesting that not all meanings are equally valid. After all, the ideas of the judge in *Blood Meridian* and those of Eduardo in *Cities of the Plain* lead to violence and death. "Instead of integrating heterogeneous genre elements into a stable system whose vision of truth enjoys the approval of institutionalized orthodoxies, Bakhtin foregrounds their dialogical, multi-voiced dispersion and their full polyphonic diversity and disparity," wrote critic Evelyn Cobley (333). The same could be said of McCarthy, who binds heterogeneous voices together to create the impression that reality is constructed out of signs. However, although "our reality comes out of the narrative we create" (quoted in Arnold, *"The Stonemason,"* 121), the Epilogue subversively suggests that it offers no escape from the interminable circularity of representations. The stories of discontinuity and continuity within McCarthy's narratives of discontinuity and contradictions owe much to the way late-twentieth century man interprets his own historical condition: "For the world [/word] to survive it must be replenished daily" (C 293).

Acknowledgments

I would like to express my gratitude to Pierre Schaeffer, my colleague and friend from Strasburg University, for sharing his knowledge and documents on Bakhtin.

Notes

1. A more elaborate definition can be given: dialogism, or the relations between the speaker's utterances with regard to both his own past and future statements and those (past and future) of another. Mikhail Mikhailovich Bakhtin's concept of the word was developed mainly in *Rabelais and His World*, *Problems of Dostoevsky's Poetics* and *The Dialogic Imagination; Four Essays by M. M. Bakhtin*.
2. For Bakhtin the three dimensions of any discourse, including discourse in prose fiction, are time and space (who speaks and under what conditions he speaks), the object of discourse (what he speaks about), and the addressee (for whom it is meant).
3. Within represented discourse Bakhtin distinguishes between monologic speech (direct discourse) and dialogic speech, which is internally dialogized discourse. The latter, which is also termed double-voiced speech, can be active (polemical) dialogism or passive dialogism, which makes use of another's word to express its own intentions and is divided into converging dialogism (stylization) and diverging dialogism (parody). To simplify matters, I shall replace "active dialogism" by "diverging bivocality" and "passive dialogism" by "converging bivocality."
4. See, among others, George Guillemin's comparative studies of Faulkner's *Light in August* and *Outer Dark* in " 'Books Made out of Books': Some Instances of Intertextuality with Southern Literature in *Outer Dark*," Holloway 28–34; John M. Grammer, "A Thing Against Which Time Will Not Prevail: Pastoral and History in Cormac McCarthy's South," Arnold and Luce 29–44; and Dianne C. Luce, "The Road and the Matrix: The World as Tale in *The Crossing*," Arnold and Luce 195–220.
5. See, among others, Edwin T. Arnold, "The Mosaic of McCarthy's Fiction," Hall and Wallach, 17–23, or by the same author, "The Last of the Trilogy: First Thoughts on *Cities of the Plain*," Arnold and Luce 221–47; and Jay Ellis, "Arcs Within the Arc," Holloway 35–9.
6. For specific definitions of autotextuality, see Lucien Dällenbach, "Intertexte et Autotexte," *Poétique* 27 (1976): 282–96.
7. Bakhtin posits the freedom of the character—a notion which now makes many critics' hair stand on end—in order to make the existence of both the character's and author's intentions plausible.
8. Bakhtin used the terms "writer" or "author" where we would say "narrator" or "implied author" today. For the sake of simplicity, I shall employ "writer" or "author" when quoting Bakhtin or explaining his theory.
9. It has often been noted that Bakhtin uses the term "polyphony" when complete internal and external dialogism occurs between a plurality of fully valid voices (*Dostoevsky*). Here we are concerned with internal dialogism.
10. Dana Phillips argues for McCarthy's character as language, not as self (440).
11. For example, the beginning of Section One, Chapter Two in *Manhattan Transfer* concentrates on Ed Thatcher's voice through "narrated monologue" and "reported monologue" (see Dorrit Cohn for the terminology); then it shifts to Ed's perception through the device of internal focalization. The two devices are used separately to achieve specific effects.
12. John Grady's senses focus on Alejandra's black hair (APH 139, 142) just as they will on Magdalena's (COP 6, 69, 70, 229).

13. Some of his first initiatory epiphanies will be the scene of the diva's bath (C 220) and Boyd's girlfriend's speech (C 321–9).
14. This quotation supports Dianne C. Luce's argument that space is narrow in *Cities of the Plain*, as opposed to the wide open spaces of the first two books in the trilogy. See Arnold, "The Last of the Trilogy," 235, and Luce, "The Road and the Matrix," 217, note 21. A place of small rooms which can be "latched only from without" (73) and is kept by someone who never parts with her set of keys is called a prison. The silver door opens onto a golden cage where all that glitters is not gold (66). The narrator goes so far as to connect the White Lake and the city of Juárez through the metaphor of the glass-tiara (67, 87). The city of queans who parade as queens is thus a huge brothel where girls had better steer clear of ice palaces and glass palaces.
15. See also APH 95; C 363.
16. The word "appropriated" may well contain the narrator's ironical comment on a verb which means "to make one's own" but which also insists that you make something your own by stealing it from someone else: to appropriate is to take for one's own use, especially illegally or without permission.
17. This is certainly an exception to McCarthy's attempt at unmediated description of Nature. Here, Billy is dejected; therefore, the weather is cold, beings are solitary, and the landscape is dark. Thus, the landscape entertains a relation of story-causality with the character.
18. The word "trouble" would deserve a whole analysis for itself. It is used as a euphemism by the Mexican officials who warn the boys against "trouble," which is ominous but weak, considering the real trouble the protagonists meet in all three novels. That word has even been internalized by Rawlins after he and John Grady have heard it so many times: "All my life I had the feelin that trouble was close at hand," he says to his partner after they have been released (APH 208).
19. In a study of intratextuality we might have noted that Boyd also borrows and recycles words: "Drygulch us? Yeah. Where'd you hear that at? I dont know" (C 251). Boyd is also connected with Blevins and Rawlins through that specific use of language.
20. Later Alfonsa will tell John Grady that she and Gustavo were never engaged (APH 236). We may also wonder if the Spanish diminutive is meant not only to express affection but also to convey the meaning "small" or "unimportant," in which case the belittling effect would be the narrator's ironical comment and echo to Alfonsa's own complaint: "The societies to which I have been exposed seemed to me largely machines for the suppression of women" (230); "I grew up in a world of men" (135).
21. That may explain why some critics have spoken of an amorphous narrator. See George Guillemin's "As of some site where life had not succeeded": Sorrow, Allegory, and Pastoralism in Cormac McCarthy's Border Trilogy" in this volume.
22. As Boyd is asleep, his consciousness is not taken into account but it is possible to attribute that weariness to both boys. This does not alter our conclusion. The same effect is struck in the following sentence: "where he had ridden another horse in another time long ago" (C 355).
23. In the following example: "There could be no thought of people being left behind. Who would permit such a thing?" (C 218), the question is that of the character, just as the wording is supposed to be, but the tenses are those of the narrating authority.
24. See my "'I aint come back rich, that's for sure' or The Questioning of Market Economies in Cormac McCarthy's Novels," *Southwestern American Literature* 25.1 (Fall 1999): 43–9.

25. Blevins is also a good one for unfortunate words: "I'm double bred for death by fire" (*APH* 68).

26. To a certain extent, McCarthy's trilogy echoes *Under The Volcano*, about which Malcolm Lowry wrote: "The scene is Mexico, the meeting place, according to some, of mankind itself. . . . Its geographical remoteness from us, as well as the closeness of its problems to our own, will assist the tragedy each in its own way. We can see it as the world itself, or the Garden of Eden, or both at once. Or we can see it as a kind of timeless symbol of the world on which we can place the Garden of Eden, the Tower of Babel and indeed anything else we please. It is paradisal: it is unquestionably infernal" (*Selected Letters* 67).

27. See also Nancy Kreml, "Stylistic Variation and Cognitive Constraint in *All the Pretty Horses*," Hall and Wallach 137–48. Another word, a Spanish word, which John Grady does not understand is *rechoncha* (chubby; *APH* 117).

28. Similarly, after he has been released from the prison and as he arrives at Don Héctor's ranch, John Grady is called "Juan" by the *vaqueros*, a token of his integration into the society of Spanish workers (*APH* 226).

29. Themselves dialogical sketches because Melville skillfully "plagiarized" from his reading (legends) and his own experience in the South Seas. Otherwise called The Galapagos, those islands dramatize the English name they were given by being prone to create mystery, fear and enchantment, and showing humanity reduced to the lower level of existence. McCarthy's interest in Melville's tales may surface in the last book in the trilogy which compares the cities to islands ("that precious insularity common to cities of the desert" *COP* 71), the "blue prairies" to the sea (*COP* 115), and a cab to a boat (*COP* 246).

30. "You should of left me there," John Grady tells Alfonsa. "You would have died," she replies (*APH* 229).

31. The *Calle de Noche Triste*, historically associated with the defeat of Cortez, recurs in *Cities of the Plain*.

32. "She did not sleep and when he woke in the dawn she was standing at the window wearing his shirt" (*APH* 252).

33. Edwin Arnold notes that the second Billy is but a parody of the first. See "The Last of the Trilogy," 232.

34. See Edwin Arnold's analysis of the fight in "The Last of the Trilogy," 231.

35. See Dianne Luce's in-depth study in "The Road and the Matrix."

Works Cited

Arnold, Edwin T. "Cormac McCarthy's *The Stonemason*: The Unmaking of a Play." *Southern Quarterly* 33.2–3 (1995): 117–29.

———. "The Last of the Trilogy: First Thoughts on *Cities of the Plain*." Arnold and Luce. 221–47.

Arnold, Edwin T., and Dianne C. Luce, eds. *Perspectives on Cormac McCarthy*. Rev. ed. Jackson: UP of Mississippi, 1998.

Bakhtin, Mikhail Mikhailovich. *Rabelais and His World*. Trans. Hélène Iswolsky. Cambridge: M.I.T. P, 1968.

———. *Problems of Dostoevsky's Poetics*. Trans. Caryl Emerson. 1973. Minneapolis: U of Minnesota P, 1984.

———. *The Dialogic Imagination; Four Essays by M. M. Bakhtin*. Ed. Michael Holquist. Trans. Caryl Emerson and Michael Holquist. Austin: U of Texas P, 1981.

Bialostosky, Don H. "Booth's Rhetoric, Bakhtin's Dialogics and the Future of Novel Criticism." *Novel, A Forum on Fiction* 18.3 (1985): 209–16.

Booth, Wayne. *The Rhetoric of Fiction*. 2nd ed. Chicago: U of Chicago P, 1983.

Cobley, Evelyn. "Mikhaïl Bakhtin's Place in Genre Theory." *Genre. A Quarterly Devoted to Generic Criticism* 21.3 (1988): 321–38.

Cohn, Dorrit. *Transparent Minds: Narrative Modes for Presenting Consciousness in Fiction*. Princeton: Princeton UP, 1978.

Danow, David K. "M. M. Bakhtin's Concept of the Word." *American Journal of Semiotics* 3.1 (1984): 79–97.

Hall, Wade, and Rick Wallach, eds. *Sacred Violence: A Reader's Companion to Cormac McCarthy*. El Paso: Texas Western P, 1995.

Holloway, David, ed. *Proceedings of the First European Conference on Cormac McCarthy*. Miami: Cormac McCarthy Society, 1999.

Lowry, Malcolm. *Selected Letters of Malcolm Lowry*. Ed. Harvey Breit and Margerie Bonner Lowry. Harmondsworth: Penguin, 1985.

Luce, Dianne C. "The Road and the Matrix: The World as Tale in *The Crossing*." Arnold and Luce 195–219.

McCarthy, Cormac. *All the Pretty Horses*. New York: Vintage, 1993.

———. *Blood Meridian or the Evening Redness in the West*. New York: Vintage, 1992.

———. *Cities of the Plain*. New York: Vintage, 1999.

———. *The Crossing*. New York: Vintage, 1995.

Morrison, Gail M. "John Grady Cole's Expulsion from Paradise." Arnold and Luce 175–94.

Pascal, Roy. *The Dual Voice: Free Indirect Speech and Its Functioning in the Nineteenth-Century European Novel*. Manchester: Manchester UP, 1977.

Phillips, Dana. "History and the Ugly Facts of Cormac McCarthy's *Blood Meridian*." *American Literature*. 68.2 (1996): 433–60.

Riffaterre, Michael. "Syllepsis." *Critical Inquiry* 6.4 (1980): 625–38.

Rimmon-Kenan, Shlomith. *Narrative Fiction: Contemporary Poetics*. London and New York: Methuen, 1983.

Wallach, Rick. "Three Dreams: [T]he Bizarre Epilogue of *Cities of the Plain*." Holloway 57–61.

"Go to sleep"

Dreams and Visions in the Border Trilogy

―――◆·▸◂·◆―――

Edwin T. Arnold

More and more language seemed to me to be an aberration by which we had come to lose the world. Everything that is named is set at one remove from itself. Nomenclature is the very soul of secondhandness. . . . When I began to think that way I began to see the true extent of our alienation. What if there existed a dialogue among the lifeforms of this earth from which we had excluded ourselves so totally that we no longer even believed it to exist? Could it be that dialogue which we still sense in dreams? Or in those rare moments of peace when the world seems in some sense to be revealed to us and to be proper and right? I knew that dreams were prelingual. . . . Language is a way of containing the world. A thing named becomes that named thing. It is under surveillance. We were put into a garden and we turned it into a detention center.

—McCarthy, "Whales and Men" 57–58

He said that the religious experience is always described through the symbols of a particular culture and thus is somewhat misrepresented by them. He indicated that even the religious person is often uncomfortable with such experiences and accounts of them, and that those who have not had a religious experience cannot comprehend it through second-hand accounts, even good ones like James's [The] Varieties of Religious Experience. He went on to say that he thinks the mystical experience is a direct apprehension of reality, unmediated by symbol, and he ended with the thought that our inability to see spiritual truth is the greater mystery.

—Garry Wallace, "Meeting McCarthy" 138

And in the last days it shall be, God declares that . . . your young men shall see visions, and your old men shall dream dreams.

—Acts 2. 17

Hushabye,/Don't you cry,/Go to sleepy, little baby.

—Traditional lullaby

And he no longer cared to tell which were things done and which dreamt.

—McCarthy, *The Orchard Keeper* 245

It may be that all of Cormac McCarthy's writings constitute a prolonged dream. Reading McCarthy's works—any one of them—is an experience not quite real. We are never in the present world, neither in time nor history. Even though the locales are most often identifiable, for the author is unusually precise about streets, towns, distances, dates (he maps the world with the nuanced eye of a master literary cartographer), there is nonetheless always the sense that this is some world never quite our own. Perhaps it is the warp of the dream that confounds us, or the brilliant clarity of the vision that momentarily repositions us through revelation.

McCarthy's works assume that there are multiple ways of experiencing the world, ranging from heedless, alienated ignorance to mystical, perhaps divine, insight. The dream, experienced while asleep, and the vision, which comes during periods of more immediate awareness, are narrative devices McCarthy employs to provide insight into both characters and experiential possibilities. Some would maintain that McCarthy's novels through *Blood Meridian* are largely brutish affairs, unrelieved by the possibilities of self-knowledge or transcendence of any sort. I quote Denis Donoghue as an example, who maintains, "The main characters in these [first] three novels [*The Orchard Keeper*, *Outer Dark*, and *Child of God*] are like recently arrived primates, each possessing a spinal column but little or no capacity of mind or consciousness. A few of the minor characters are ethically precocious; that is, they are kind by nature and instinct, like the doctor who helps Rinthy [Holme, in *Outer Dark*]. But most of them, and especially Culla [Rinthy's brother], live on a subsistence level of feeling and cognition" (260). The college-educated and obviously intellectual Cornelius Suttree provides a contrast to these early characters, but Donoghue finds that this novel in general "does not depend on Suttree's particular intelligence but on a comprehensive sense of life which is innate to McCarthy's narrative and dispersed throughout his pages" (263). The kid in *Blood Meridian*, again like the earlier characters, seems without much self-knowledge or desire thereof, at least until the final episodes of the novel. The Border Trilogy, however, gives us more sympathetic characters in John Grady Cole and Billy Parham, and some of us have read these last three books (especially *The Crossing*) as deeply moral works that comprise an extended spiritual quest. But to divide McCarthy's work in this fashion, to separate the trilogy from the stories and characters preceding it, misreads in both directions. If McCarthy's southern protagonists often appear unthinking or inhumanly obtuse to us, perhaps we are too dogmatically equating verbal expression with self-awareness, and silence with stupidity. That these characters do experience intense feelings and fears and conflicts seems inarguable to me, and nowhere are these emotions more clearly revealed than in their dreams and carefully depicted moments of perception and revelation.[1]

Why we dream has never been adequately explained: despite all manner of investigation and theories, dreaming remains one of the basic physiological and psychological mysteries.[2] However, the belief that dreams provide a different way of seeing and knowing ourselves and the world(s) around us dates back at least to the Assyrian "dream books" and Egyptian, Greek, and Roman concepts that dreams could be means of divine information passed from the gods to mankind. In the Bible, God speaks through dreams to certain selected men in the Old Testament like Jacob (Gen. 28.12–17), Joseph (Gen. 37.5–10; in verse 19 his brothers call him "this dreamer"), Solomon (1 Kings 3.4–14), and Nebuchadnezzar (chapter 2 of the Book of

Daniel).³ Some of these dreams require interpreters gifted by God, men such as Joseph and Daniel who must read the meaning inherent in the puzzling dream images. In Numbers, God distinguishes between dream and more direct forms of communication. God tells Moses, Aaron, and Miriam, "Hear my words: If there is a prophet among you, I the Lord make myself known to him in a vision, I speak with him in a dream. Not so with my servant Moses; he is entrusted with all my house. With him I speak mouth to mouth, clearly, and not in dark speech; and he beholds the form of the Lord" (12.6–8). Elihu tells Job that "when deep sleep falls upon men, while they slumber on their beds" God "opens the ears of men, and terrifies them with warnings, that he may turn man aside from his deed, and cut off pride from man; he keeps back his soul from the Pit" (Job 33.15–18). In the New Testament, Mary and Joseph receive clear warnings from an angel of God in dreams (the first two chapters of Matthew) and the apostle Paul experiences visions containing instructions or assurance (Acts 18.9–10). These messages direct the dreamers in their actions once awake, give them foreknowledge they could not otherwise have.

The modern interpretive concepts of dreams, linked most often to the schools of Sigmund Freud and Carl Jung, emphasized psychological as well as physical determinants for dreaming. Both men felt dreams gave access to the unconscious. Freud theorized that they revealed individual, unacknowledged wishes and desires hidden beneath the surface of everyday knowing; Jung expanded the idea of the psyche from the personal unconscious to the collective unconscious as well, which acted as a storage of primordial images common to all people and expressed by selected archetypes. Dreams, each believed, offered evidence from the sleeping world for interpretation in the wakeful state, but Freud disapproved of Jung's "mystical" bent. McCarthy's use of dreams seems closer to the Jungian concept than to the Freudian, for they are often "mystical" in their manner. Indeed, the stranger Billy meets in the epilogue to *Cities of the Plain* appears to speak to the idea of inherited collective knowledge: "The world of our fathers resides within us," he says. "Ten thousand generations and more. . . . At the core of our life is the history of which it is composed and in that core are no idioms but only the act of knowing and it is this we share in dreams and out. Before the first man spoke and after the last is silenced forever" (281). Still more recent theories have discussed dreams in terms of the physical structure of the brain as a functioning organ within the body complex, and through comparisons of the sleeping brain and the dream function to resting computers and programs that "clean up" unnecessary bits of junk knowledge so that the waking brain/computer can function more efficiently. And yet still others say that dreams have no meaning whatsoever, are random neuron firings to which we later give structure and narrative through our inherent need to order our existence.

Despite the Jungian connection, it is not my intent to argue that Cormac McCarthy uses the dream motif in his books to represent any particular concept, although, given the little we know about McCarthy's interests in science and philosophy, it seems likely that he has read and thought deeply on these matters. We must also acknowledge the probable literary influence of such dream writers as Borges, Castaneda, and Garcia Marquéz, whose forays into realms of magical realism are surely reflected in McCarthy, most obviously in the Border Trilogy. But what I am interested in is how McCarthy uses both the dream experience and the visionary moment in his fiction, and for what ultimate purpose.

McCarthy's southern works often employ the dream as an essential element of their narratives. His first published story, "Wake for Susan" (October 1959 in *The Phoenix*, the literary supplement to the University of Tennessee's student paper *Orange and White*), has a dream-like quality as the young boy Wes, his imagination sparked by a tombstone in an abandoned graveyard, envisions the life of the young woman buried there. "From a simple carved stone, the marble turned to a monument; from a gravestone, to the surviving integral tie to a once warm-blooded, live person. Wes pictured Susan" (4). He furthermore "pictures" himself into her story so deeply that when he "wakes" (the double meaning of the word is significant) from this visionary idyll, he is "drained and empty" (6).[4] Dianne C. Luce has suggested that *The Orchard Keeper*, in a similar fashion, "may be read as John Wesley Rattner's partly imagined reconstruction of his childhood as he contemplates the gravestone of his dead mother" ("Road" 204). Like Wes, John Wesley (the similarity in names hints at the similarity in character) is acutely at one with the natural world, as is one of his mentors, the old mountain man Arthur Ownby. David Paul Ragan notes, "Uncle Ather's values derive in part from his vital connection with the natural world. . . .

His mystical knowledge bridges the gap between the areas in which Uncle Ather grounds his understanding of life's purpose and meaning—the web of human life and the mountain wilderness—and provides the rationale for his most significant actions" (22–23). The old man is given to visions and dreams, and John Wesley reveals his own growing sympathetic awareness with some otherworld apart from that of the everyday, as evidenced by the transcendent value he places on the dead hawk, victim of civilization and commerce (and in this, he clearly anticipates Billy Parham and the she-wolf).

The incestuous and cowardly Culla Holme of *Outer Dark* and, even more appalling, *Child of God*'s peeping, creeping, necrophilic Lester Ballard prove harder cases, but Culla's opening nightmare (5–6) tells us all we need to know of his suppressed guilt—he is McCarthy's version of Hawthorne's Reverend Dimmesdale, with the leader of the dark triune filling in for Chillingworth—while Lester's dream, occasioned by the forgotten memory of his suicide father "on the road coming home whistling, a lonely piper" (170), is surprisingly gentle, mournful, and touching. "He dreamt that night that he rode through woods on a low ridge. . . . Each leaf that brushed his face deepened his sadness and dread. Each leaf he passed he'd never pass again. . . . He had resolved himself to ride on for he could not turn back and the world that day was as lovely as any day that ever was and he was riding to his death" (170–71). This unanticipated glimpse into Lester's distraught soul comes immediately after he sits high above the world "that he'd once inhabited" (169) and weeps as he watches the "diminutive progress of all things in the valley, the gray fields coming up black and corded under the plow, the slow green occlusion that the trees were spreading" (170). There is an awful need for love and belonging even in a creature such as Lester, his dream affirms, and in this manner McCarthy opens Ballard's heart to us in all its twisted yearning.

Suttree is a book filled with visions and dreams, and it is sometimes difficult to determine which world Suttree inhabits. States of drunkenness, of psychedelic perception, of hyper-awareness spiraling away from and beyond ratiocination, are those in which Suttree confronts his own inner guilt, self-disgust, alienation, and reaches for some form of rescue.[5] The hallucinatory reel of these episodes (reflecting similar scenes in Joyce's *Ulysses* and Burroughs's *Naked Lunch*, to name two likely influences) counterpoint equally brilliant examples of dispassionate expository description that mirror the physical everyday life of Knoxville and its environs. Still, this is not a life many of us know, and the narrator tells us in the prologue that we will be witnesses to the strange and bizarre: "*We are come to a world within the world. In these alien reaches, these maugre sinks and interstitial wastes that the righteous see from carriage and car another life dreams*" (4). For all practical purposes, Suttree exists in a state of purgatory in which he is beset by dreams and visions. Some are mixtures of memory and projection: "In a dream I walked with my grandfather by a dark lake and the old man's talk was filled with incertitude. I saw how all things false fall from the dead. We spoke easily and I was humbly honored to walk with him deep in that world where he was a man like all men" (14). Others seem more like spiritual warnings or prophecies of damnation, similar to Culla Holme's nightmare of the final eclipse in *Outer Dark*. Suttree speaks: "I'd like these shoes soled I dreamt I dreamt. An old bent cobbler looked up from his lasts and lapstone with eyes dim and windowed. Not these, my boy, they are far too far gone, these soles. . . . You must forget these and find others now" (79). One of his worst dreams is peopled by images and horrors taken from the first three books:

By the side of a dark dream road he'd seen a hawk nailed to a barn door. But what loomed was a flayed man with his brisket tacked open like a cooling beef and his skull peeled, blue and bulbous and palely luminescent, black grots his eyeholes and bloody mouth gaped tongueless. The traveler had seized his fingers in his jaws, but it was not alone this horror that he cried. Beyond the flayed man dimly adumbrate another figure paled, for his surgeons move about the world even as you and I. (86)

The most baroque of Suttree's dreams (or, better, visions, since he is not asleep) are caused by starvation (during his retreat to the mountains near Gatlinburg, Tennessee), drugs (the dwarf Mother She's sexual voodoo), and illness (his hallucinations induced by typhoid fever). The last of these brings about Suttree's primary revelations: "I know all souls are one and all souls lonely" (459); "[God] is not a thing. Nothing ever stops moving" (461); and "I learned that there is one Suttree and one Suttree only" (461). Each of these realizations about the interconnectedness of the universe, the sacred wholeness of all creation, anticipates the later truths of the Border Trilogy.

Suttree leaves Knoxville at the end of the book, heading west one would assume, as does John Wesley Rattner and as did McCarthy himself when he moved from Tennessee to El Paso in the late 1970s. Suttree is pursued as he leaves, tracked by "[a]n enormous lank hound . . . like a hound from the depths" (471). The narrative voice concludes the book:

> Somewhere in the gray wood by the river is the huntsman and in the brooming corn and in the castellated press of cities. His work lies all wheres and his hounds tire not. I have seen them in a dream, slaverous and wild and their eyes crazed with ravening for souls in this world. Fly them. (471)

The huntsman, a personification of death and judgment, reappears in the sweaty delirium that is *Blood Meridian*, in a description that echoes the words and phrasings of *Suttree*'s conclusion:

> The dust the party raised was quickly dispersed and lost in the immensity of that landscape and there was no dust other for the pale sutler who pursued them drives unseen and his lean horse and his lean cart leave no track upon such ground or any ground. By a thousand fires in the iron blue dusk he keeps his commissary and he's a wry and grinning tradesman good to follow every campaign or hound men from their holes in just those whited regions where they've gone to hide from God. (44)

In dream fashion, Death the huntsman with his hound becomes Death the sutler (a provisioner or "tradesman," an identity that also curiously links him to the tinker in *Outer Dark*), who "hound[s] men from their holes . . . where they've gone to hide from God." Suttree is translated into the kid who, a century earlier, also leaves Tennessee for the west. The lost souls of McAnally Flats—"*Illshapen or black or deranged, fugitive of all order, strangers in everyland*" (S 4) become the fugitive scalp hunters, "a pack of viciouslooking humans . . . bearded, barbarous, clad in the skins of animals stitched up with thews and armed with weapons of every description" (BM 78), whose company the kid joins.

Blood Meridian is a delirious book, an extended nightmare of history. To read it is to enter the darker places of the imagination, to witness the malignity of humankind at its worst. Perhaps we can do this only in the dream state. The novel also marks a change in McCarthy's use of dreams, for here they become more portentous, parabolic, the sort of mysterious biblical "dark speeches" that must be interpreted, puzzled out. One dream in particular challenges simple reading and seems to direct us to one of the book's underlying theses.

Donoghue rightly notes that "we have to apprehend the Kid's principles by default, he never speaks of them. The judge is all speech, endlessly voluble, the Kid is silence" (272). Furthermore, the kid, as far as we know, is not generally given to visions or dreams,[6] apparently to his psychological detriment since the horrors he performs and witnesses build internally until, following his year with the scalp hunters, he "began to speak with a strange urgency of things few men have seen in a lifetime and his jailers said that his mind had come uncottered by the acts of blood in which he had participated" (305). After Glanton and most of his gang have been slaughtered at Yuma Ferry, the kid, who has escaped, is arrested in San Diego. There he wakes one morning to find the demonic Judge Holden sitting outside his jail cell. Holden comes to confront the kid with his failure to commit himself totally to the group. "For it was required of no man to give more than he possessed nor was any man's share compared to another's. Only each was called upon to empty out his heart into the common and one did not. Can you tell me who that one was?" "It was you," the kid answers. "You were the one" (307). There is truth to both statements, for the kid has remained apart from his fellows and the fullness of their deeds, while the judge has used the gang throughout the book, directing and manipulating them for his own purposes. "Time to be going," Holden comically and yet ominously says before disappearing. "I have errands." "The kid closed his eyes. When he opened them the judge was gone" (308). The dream-like quality of the visitation, occurring as it does in an apparent false waking (the kid's repetitive opening and closing of his eyes suggests various stages of sleeping and dreaming, until he "wakes" to an empty room), further illustrates the kid's unexpressed guilt (the scene recalls Culla's dream in *Outer Dark*) and further suggests that the judge is of a supernatural kind, like some incubus or terrible force, "something that had better been left sleeping" (147), indeed.

What then follows is a series of hauntings by the judge. They first occur when the kid is anesthetized to remove the remnant of an arrow shaft from his leg. "In that sleep and in sleeps to follow the judge did visit. Who would come other?" (309). In these dreams the judge, uncharacteristically, does not speak—"A great shambling mutant, silent and serene" (309). At this point, the book's narrator steps from the background, stops the account after some 300 pages of story, to ponder the judge:

Whatever his antecedents he was something wholly other than their sum, nor was there system by which to divide him back into his origins for he would not go. Whoever would seek out his history through what unraveling of loins and ledgerbooks must stand at last darkened and dumb at the shore of a void without terminus or origin and whatever science he might bring to bear upon the dusty primal matter blowing down out of the millennia will discover no trace of any ultimate atavistic egg by which to reckon his commencing. (309–10)

Although the kid has long been intrigued and vexed by the judge, these are not likely his own thoughts, not, in any case, as expressed in this lofty vocabulary. As in *Child of God*, the teller of the tale apparently finds it necessary to address his audience directly in order to remind us of the greater mysteries represented by the individual characters, Lester Ballard or Judge Holden.[7] Whatever Judge Holden is, the narrator tells us, he cannot be adequately explained through science or logic. We might, in fact, read the passage as a refutation of scientific thinkers like Freud who believe there is always a discoverable point, an identifiable action that ultimately explains. This is what the judge maintains: "Your heart's desire is to be told some mystery," he tells members of the gang. "The mystery is that there is no mystery" (252). Yet, as Tobin responds to the kid, the inexplicable judge is by his very existence proof of the mystery in the world he intends to deny. And as McCarthy himself has said, that we do not ordinarily apprehend this mystery is the larger question (Wallace 138).

In the dream the kid next looks into the judge's "small and lashless pig's eyes" (310), but what is it he sees? On the one hand he appears to see his fate, his name written in the judge's ledger, suggesting that he has already been enslaved by the judge, fated to his doom.[8] But the kid also seems to perceive in these eyes the unfathomable nature of evil, perhaps to realize that evil is not an individual, separate thing but very much an essential part of the system of existence. This is a profoundly metaphysical moment for the kid, and he is eventually changed by it. One might compare it to Job's ultimate perception of God's awful grandeur that joins fortune and misfortune, good and bad, in one inexplicable whole; or to Jacob Boehme's vision of the "Byss and the Abyss" of which he wrote, "For I had a thorough view of the universe as in a chaos, wherein all things are couched and wrapt up, but it was impossible for me to explicate the same" (quoted in James 411).

Edwin T. Arnold 47

The kid's first reaction, however, is to search for a gun to protect himself, entirely in keeping with his character and place.

The dream then continues with one of McCarthy's more gnostic images, that of the "coldforger" who works in the judge's shadow, a "false moneyer" who "seeks favor with the judge" as he creates fraudulent coinage (310). This dream figure has been read in different ways and may derive from numerous sources.[9] Certainly there are biblical echoes to be considered, chief among them the sayings of Christ recounted in Matthew, Mark, and Luke concerning the question of proper authority and the difference between spiritual and worldly goods. When the Pharisees attempt to "entrap him in his talk," asking "Is it lawful to pay taxes to Caesar, or not?" Christ answers, "Bring me a coin, and let me look at it. . . . Whose likeness and inscription is this?" When they answer "Caesar's," he replies, "Render to Caesar the things that are Caesar's, and to God the things that are God's" (Mark 12.13–17, RSV; see also Matthew 22.17–32 and Luke 20.22–25). We should note that the account in Matthew (Chapter 22) also contains the verse concerning "the outer darkness; there men will weep and gnash their teeth" (22.13) from which McCarthy took the title of his second novel; and the coldforger is described in similar terms as "perhaps under some indictment and an exile from men's fires . . ." (310).

There are echoes of other figures in the image of the coiner, ranging from Pluto, god of the underworld, to Spenser's melancholy gnome-like Mammon, who lives in hell making money (*Fairie Queen*, 2, vii), to Blake's mythic Los, the smithy who works at the command of Urizen just as the coldforger works to please the judge. Although there are important differences between Urizen and Holden, both wish to control the world by denying or obliterating mystery through logic and science. "Here alone I in books formd of metals,/Have written the secrets of wisdom,/The secrets of dark contemplation," Urizen says, and in the "Book/Of eternal brass, written in my solitude" he sets down "One command, one joy, one desire,/One curse, one weight, one measure,/One King, one God, one Law" ("The [First] Book of Urizen," chapter 2, 24–26, 32–33, 38–40). Los (who has been torn from the side of Urizen) helps this powerful demon to forge the chains that will bind man through the limitations and assumptions of reason alone, which confines and organizes and thus diminishes the world. Similarly, the coldforger is "at contriving from cold slag brute in the crucible a face that will pass, an image that will render this residual specie current in the markets where men barter" (310). Thus he works in the material world of commerce and Caesar, not the transcendent one of God, and, as "false moneyer," he aids the judge in his on-going deception and corruption.

We might extend the dream meaning yet further. Jacques Derrida has compared words to coins in order to discuss the signified-signifier conundrum. Money, he notes, has representational rather than intrinsic value, just as words and language are sounds and systems that stand in for the things and ideas being communicated. In McCarthy's unpublished screenplay "Whales and Men," language is described by the character Peter Gregory as "a thing corrupted by its own success. What had begun as a system for identifying and organizing the phenomena of the world had become a system for replacing those phenomena. For replacing the world. . . . Everything that is named is set at one remove from itself. . . . Language is a way of containing the world. A thing named becomes that named thing. It is under surveillance" (57–58).[10] Add, then, to this representation a counterfeit image, a deceptive inscription, an intentionally duplicitous or false word, and understanding is yet more distorted, further misdirected. There is thus an implied connection in the kid's dream between coins and words, and between the art of the coldforger and language itself. The "coldforger" is, as the identification suggests, both a maker (one who forges, creates) and a deceiver (one who forges, imitates intending to defraud). Working under the judge he makes coins, "coins" words, and, as the glib judge himself acknowledges, there are in this world "coins and false coins" (246) aplenty.

Peter Gregory concludes his thoughts on words and representation by saying, "We were put into a garden and we turned it into a detention center" ("WAM" 58). He might well be paraphrasing Blake as well as describing Judge Holden, who would contain the world in his ledgers and who "detains" through language and protocol. "The freedom of birds is an insult to me," Holden proclaims. "I'd have them all in zoos" (BM 199), while Blake declares in "The Marriage of Heaven and Hell," "How do you know but ev'ry Bird that cuts the airy way,/Is an immense world of delight, clos'd by your senses five?" ("A Memorable Fancy" 35). "Words are things," the judge insists, approving of the very state Gregory abhors. "Their authority transcends [man's] ignorance of their meaning" (85).[11] Blake again anticipates the judge in another "Memorable Fancy" in which he "was in a Printing house in Hell & saw the method in which knowledge is transmitted from generation to generation." Truths are processed, "took the forms of books & were arranged in libraries" (39), thus robbing them of their original meaning and essence. In *Blood Meridian*, the "will to deceive" which may "post men to fraudulent destinies" (120) seems an inherent part of the dark world itself, the "state of dismal woe" Blake imagined. "Of this is the judge judge and the night does not end" (310).[12]

Certainly dreams, like words, may deceive. "So do not listen to your prophets, your diviners, your dreamers, your soothsayers, or your sorcerers. . . . For it is a lie which they are prophesying to you, with the result that you will be removed far from your land, and I will drive you out, and you will perish," the prophet Jeremiah warns (27.9–10). And there are characters who are led astray by their fantasies in McCarthy's work. But if "deep" dreams are prelingual, as Peter Gregory maintains, then they may also provide direct contact to the true and essential, unmediated by conscious formulation of symbolic substitution or undistorted by intentional misrepresentation. They may provide access to the "ordinate world" not generally perceived (although perhaps occasionally intuited)[13] in everyday human existence. McCarthy's reiterative use of dreams and visions suggests that this narrative device is more than a convenient literary trope; rather it strongly implies the author's conviction that some ultimate source, some godhead perhaps, exists beyond the range of our normal waking knowing.

All of the preceding forms a lengthy prelude to the point of this essay, the examination of dreams and visions in the Border Trilogy itself. If "They rode on" is the recurring chorus of *Blood Meridian*,[14] "Go to sleep" could be the primary incantation of the Border Trilogy. Indeed, one of the many possible manifestations of "borders" in the trilogy is that between this world and that of sleep, between our waking awareness and the mysterious knowing of the dream.

All the Pretty Horses begins with John Grady Cole viewing his grandfather's corpse. "That was not sleeping," he thinks. "That was not sleeping" (3). John Grady here, probably unconsciously, alludes to and contradicts both Jesus, who says of Jarius's daughter, "The child is not dead but sleeping" (Mark 5.39; see also Matt. 9.24 and Luke 9.52) and Prince Hamlet's meditation: "To die, to sleep;/To sleep: perchance to dream" (*Hamlet*, 3. 1.

64–65). If he has read Shakespeare, then perhaps he recognizes the similarity between Hamlet's situation and his own.[15] He is roused to action not by the ghost of his father, but by another spectral vision "like a dream of the past," that of the "lost nation . . . out of the north," the "nation and ghost of nation passing in a soft chorale" along the old Comanche road (5). This passage describes a thing both ancient and otherworldly, and yet McCarthy suggests that the vision is not imagined by the boy or present to him only. Indeed, even after John Grady "must turn the pony up onto the plain and homeward," the "warriors would ride on in that darkness they'd become, rattling past with their stone-age tools of war in default of all substance and singing softly in blood and longing south across the plains to Mexico" (6). The vision, then, exists independent of the boy—these ghostly figures out of the past are still a very real part of the world, whether seen or not, whether "alive" or not. At this moment the boy has the eyes and the spirit to witness them, but they do not depend on his witnessing for their existence. By the end of the book, he himself will become a similar vision, witnessed by the descendants of this "lost nation," who "stood and watched him pass and watched him vanish upon that landscape solely because he was passing. Solely because he would vanish" (301). Since John Grady is moving toward death (and also toward legend) throughout the trilogy, this is an apt and appropriate conclusion (with more than a few similarities to the ending of *Suttree* as well).

But the John Grady we meet at the beginning of *All the Pretty Horses* is still a sixteen-year-old boy with hopes and aspirations, motivated by romantic ideas. The first pages of the novel comprise an extended leavetaking of home, parents, girlfriend; then John Grady, reflected in the window of the San Angelo Federal Building, like Alice "stepped out of the glass forever" (29) and into another world. The episodes that make up this first chapter reveal John Grady and Rawlins's naïvete and good hearts, but they also plant the seeds for the tragedies that will follow. By the end of the chapter, the boys are deep in the Mexican state of Coahuila, hired to work as hands on the fabulous *Hacienda de Nuestra Señora de la Purísima Concepción*. They have seen Don Héctor Rocha y Villareal's daughter Alejandra, and John Grady has begun to fantasize of a life with her on this magnificent ranch, a miraculous replacement for the family and land he has lost back in Texas. The chapter ends with Rawlins talking to John Grady as they lie in their bunks. "This is some country, aint it?" Rawlins says. "Yeah. It is," John Grady answers. "Go to sleep." "This is how it was with the old waddies, aint it?" Lacey persists. "How long do you think you'd like to stay here?" "About a hundred years," John Grady replies. "Go to sleep" (96).

Chapter 2 might very easily be read as an extended dream experienced in that sleep. Obviously we are not meant to take this possibility literally—the events that follow are "real" in the world of the novel—but the boys' experiences at the *hacienda* do comprise the kind of adolescent fantasy found in youthful adventure tales. Some have criticized the book for exactly this quality, the unlikeliness of it all, but that may be the point of the tale. After all, the title of the book comes from a lullaby in which the baby is being sung to sleep with the promise that "When you wake,/You shall have/All the pretty little horses."[16] The boys have not yet been mastered by the world, wakened to its harshness, although John Grady has been warned by his dying father of this inevitability during their last conversation. "We're like the Comanches was two hundred years ago. We dont know what's goin to show up here come daylight. We dont even know what color they'll be" (25–26), he says, almost as if he, too, had once shared his son's vision of the ghostly tribe.[17]

Don Héctor's ranch is edenic—"In the lakes and in the streams were species of fish not known elsewhere on earth and birds and lizards and other forms of life as well all long relict here for the desert stretched away on every side" (97).[18] Here John Grady has moments of transcendence in which the earth itself becomes an animate being, like the horses he rides: "he lay looking up at the stars in their places and the hot belt of matter that ran the chord of the dark vault overhead and he put his hands on the ground at either side of him and pressed them against the earth and in that coldly burning canopy of black he slowly turned dead center to the world, all of it taut and trembling and moving enormous and alive under his hands" (119). His thoughts, however, are directed primarily on Alejandra, and it must be noted that the boy's dreams at this stage are focused on his own egotistical desires, his personal, physical passions. Nowhere is this clearer than in the grandly written description of John Grady's thoughts as he rides and commands the great stallion. The narrative voice captures the boy's surging emotions:

While inside the vaulting of the ribs between his knees the darkly meated heart pumped of who's will and the blood pulsed and the bowels shifted in their massive blue convolutions of who's will and the stout thighbones and knee and cannon and the tendons like flaxen hawsers that drew and flexed and drew and flexed at their articulations and of who's will all sheathed and muffled in the flesh and the hooves that stove wells in the morning groundmist and the head turning side to side and the great slavering keyboard of his teeth and the hot globes of his eyes where the world burned. (128)[19]

He watches the girl cross the countryside during a storm: "riding erect and stately until the rain caught her up and shrouded her figure away in that wild summer landscape: real horse, real rider, real land and sky and yet a dream withal" (132); and some nights later, while he is "asleep in his bunk in the barn" (139), she comes to him in the dark and he gives himself over to her. "Tell me what to do. . . . I'll do anything you say" (140). They ride at night to the lake where they swim naked. McCarthy's description of Alejandra anticipates that given of the wolves in *The Crossing*. "She was so pale in the lake she seemed to be burning. Like foxfire in a darkened wood. That burned cold. Like the moon that burned cold." She asks if he desires her. "God yes, he said" (141).

Before she returns to Mexico City, Alejandra comes to John Grady "for nine nights running . . . at God knew what hour and stepping out of her clothes and sliding cool and naked against him in the narrow bunk all softness and perfume and the lushness of her black hair falling over him and no caution to her at all. Saying I dont care I dont care. Drawing blood with her teeth where he held the heel of his hand against her mouth that she not cry out" (142). There are characteristics of the succubus, the demon of sleep who assumes female shape and comes to men in dreams, in this description. Certainly this is a harsh judgment and in many ways completely unfair to Alejandra, but at no other time in the book is John Grady's own judgment so faulty, his sense of loyalty and honor so compromised. He has lied and has betrayed the trust placed in him by Don Héctor, as well as by others like his partner Lacey Rawlins, who has warned him repeatedly to use common sense. As soon as Alejandra leaves, the dream, erotic and indulgent, ends when "at gray daybreak two men entered his cubicle with drawn pistols and put a flashlight in his eyes and ordered him to get up" (149). Later the Dueña Alfonsa will spell out the truth for the boy: "Those whom life does

Edwin T. Arnold 53

not cure death will. The world is quite ruthless in selecting between the dream and the reality, even where we will not. Between the wish and the thing the world lies waiting" (238).

John Grady has experienced a delusional dream in this chapter, an intoxicating fantasy that has led him into danger and from which he must now extricate himself if he can. After their arrest, Lacey asks John Grady if he has tried to wake Don Héctor in order to make sense of the situation. When John Grady admits that he has not, Lacey informs him, "They said he was awake. They said he'd been awake for a long time. Then they laughed" (155). That Don Héctor has known the truth about the boys, and has perhaps suspected John Grady's relationship with his daughter, is appropriately expressed in terms of such wakefulness, and we now realize that the father has, in earlier conversations, cautioned the boy against the very deeds John Grady subsequently commits.[20]

In jail he dreams of horses, of dream horses, variations of the "picturebook horses" in his grandfather's painting (16). This is also a dream of freedom, for he runs among them "in a field on a high plain" (161), and it is further a recognition of something more he finds in that "high world" and that is "a resonance that was like a music among them and they were none of them afraid horse nor colt nor mare and they ran in that resonance which is the world itself and which cannot be spoken but only praised" (161–62). Here we have an example of an experience beyond words—it "cannot be spoken but only praised." Here the dream offers the direct, unmediated moment, the physical, fundamental awareness of the world's "resonance." The term refers to the intensification or enrichment of a sound or feeling. In physics, it describes the effect one vibrating body has on another body: the movement of the first is translated to the second so that both bodies come to move together. In this sense, the transcendent wonder of the "high world" is transmitted through the medium of dream to the ordinary world in which the boy lives and provides him with momentary escape from the "detention center" in which he now finds himself. The resonance of the dream repeats a long-held McCarthy concept that all life is flux, that all being is energy, that, as we read in *Suttree*, "Nothing ever stops moving."[21]

Still later, in the Saltillo prison, John Grady knows that he must stay awake to survive. After he has been badly cut in the knife fight in which he kills his attacker, he finally does sleep and dreams of the dead, "standing about in their bones and the dark sockets of their eyes that were indeed without speculation bottomed in the void wherein lay a terrible intelligence common to all but of which none would speak" (205). Rawlins will later comment, "Dying aint in people's plans, is it?" (210); but from this point on John Grady comes to accept, and perhaps finally to desire, his death. Dreams as forms of visitation from the dead date at least to ancient Greek mythology and become a recurring trope in the Border Trilogy, in which the dead are never far from the living, whether historically—as in the constant social memories of the Mexican Revolution—or personally. When John Grady returns to *La Purísima* to retrieve both his belongings and, he fervently hopes, Alejandra herself, he "thought what sort of dream might bring him luck" and thinks to dream of the girl. Instead, before sleeping, he remembers a ghostly visitation while in the Saltillo prison by the murdered Jimmy Blevins, a time when "Blevins came to sit beside him and they talked of what it was like to be dead and Blevins said it was like nothing at all and he believed him." Blevins now replaces Alejandra in John Grady's dream, and, in fact, comes to negate her and any "luck" she might bring him: "He thought perhaps if he dreamt of him enough he'd go away forever and be dead among his kind and the grass scissored in the wind at his ear and he fell asleep and dreamt of nothing at all" (225).

It is noteworthy that Blevins's exact words go unrecorded in this account, for dream figures rarely speak directly in the trilogy, as if their thoughts were communicated by means other than speech. The stranger Billy meets in the epilogue to *Cities of the Plain* addresses this question while describing his own dream: "It is not the case that there are small men in your head holding a conversation. There is no sound," he says. "So what language is that? In any case this was a deep dream for the dreamer and in such dreams there is a language that is older than the spoken word at all. The idiom is another specie and with it there can be no lie or no dissemblance of the truth" (280–81). After his death, Boyd Parham will prove an equally mute visitor to his brother Billy in *The Crossing*. "When finally he did ask him what it was like to be dead Boyd only smiled and looked away and would not answer" (400). Again in *Cities of the Plain* Billy will dream first of his sister, "dead seventy years and buried near Fort Sumner. He saw her so clearly.... When she passed the house he knew that she would never enter there again nor would he see her ever again and in his sleep he called out to her but she did not turn or answer him but only passed on down that empty road in infinite sadness and infinite loss" (265–66). And still later he sees Boyd once more: "One night he dreamt that Boyd was in the room with him but he would not speak for all that he called out to him" (290). These figures give ghostly evidence of some otherworldly existence, but there can be no direct telling for such communication seems impossible between the dead and those who still draw breath on earth.

Billy will live to be an old man, but John Grady is fated to a short life. *All the Pretty Horses* alerts us to this fact, although we cannot know the specifics at the time without having read *Cities of the Plain*, in which the events are accomplished. Alejandra tells the boy, "I saw you in a dream. I saw you dead in a dream. . . . They carried you through the streets of a city I'd never seen. It was dawn. The children were praying. Lloraba tu madre. Con más razón tu puta" (252; Your mother was crying. More to the point, your whore). "Dont say that. You cant say that," John Grady replies, but it's not his death that he denies, it's that she dreams he dies for a whore. At this point, he thinks Alejandra is describing herself in the dream, since he *would* die for her if the situation demanded, and it is her reputation that he tries to uphold in his denial. He cannot yet anticipate any woman besides her, much less the prostitute Magdalena. Later, when Alejandra refuses to marry him, "He felt something cold and soulless enter him like another being and he imagined that it smiled malignly and he had no reason to believe that it would ever leave" (254). He drinks recklessly, starts a fight, and the next morning he remembers "things from the night of whose reality he was uncertain." Among his recollections is that of "a vacant field in a city in the rain and in the field a wooden crate and he saw a dog emerge from the crate into the slack and sallow lamplight like a carnival dog forlorn and pick its way brokenly across the rubble of the lot to vanish without fanfare among the darkened buildings" (255). The boy's dramatic, self-pitying, and destructive response to Alejandra's decision reveals how little he has actually learned from his experiences at this point—he is still a sixteen-year-old boy. The bleak image, moreover, specifically foretells the place of his dying, to which he will be brought by the same unchecked anger and despair. All the signs prove true; all the warnings fail to prevent this doom. In some ways, John Grady's plight is put into words by Ben Telfair in McCarthy's play *The Stonemason*, in which Telfair says, "I had a dream and this dream was a cautionary dream and a dream I did not heed." Ben dreams that "I had died or the world had ended and I stood waiting before the door of some ultimate justice which I knew would open for me" (112). Like John Grady, Ben Telfair wants to be "justified," but he finally learns, "Ultimately there is no one to tell you if you are justified in your own house" (105). "Because we cannot save ourselves unless we save all ourselves," he finally realizes. "I had this dream but did not heed it. And so I lost my way" (113), as will John Grady himself.

John Grady's last dream in the book is again one of horses, and it reveals, I think, a more mature acceptance of the tragic nature of the world. This time the horses do not run; rather they "moved gravely among the tilted stones like horses come upon an antique site where some ordering of the world had failed and if anything had been written on the stones the weathers had taken it away again. . . ." A deeper order, however, resides in the horses' hearts, "a place where no rain could erase it" (280). Once again McCarthy echoes lines from *The Stonemason*. Ben Telfair says of his grandfather, one of the last of the traditional masons:

What holds the stone trues the wall as well and I've seen him check his fourfoot wooden level with a plumb bob and then break the level over the wall and call for a new one. Not in anger, but only to safeguard the true. To safeguard it everywhere. . . . I see him standing there over his plumb bob which never lies and never lies and the plumb bob is pointing motionless to the unimaginable center of the earth four thousand miles beneath his feet. Pointing to a blackness unknown and unknowable both in truth and in principle where God and matter are locked in a collaboration that is silent nowhere in the universe and it is this that guides him as he places his stone one over two and two over one as did his fathers before him and his sons to follow and let the rain carve them if it can. (66–67)

Both descriptions accept a natural balance, a universal collaboration between material and spiritual, a "true" that endures in the center of rocks and in the hearts of horses and men. The priest in *The Crossing* expresses this presence in another manner. "Men do not turn from God so easily you see," he tells Billy Parham. "Not so easily. Deep in each man is the knowledge that something knows of his existence. Something knows, and cannot be fled nor hid from. To imagine otherwise is to imagine the unspeakable" (148).

Following this dream John Grady Cole becomes more aware of the mysterious workings of the world. "When he woke there were three men standing over him" (280). In dream-like fashion (there is little logic to the scene or explanation for it) he is rescued by these miraculous "Men of the country" (281), a benevolent version of the three nightmen who stalk the wastelands of *Outer Dark*. Then, returning to the United States, he shoots a doe for food and watches her die: "and she looked at him and her eyes were warm and wet and there was no fear in them and then she died. . . . The sky was dark and a cold wind ran through the bajada and in the dying light a cold blue cast had turned the doe's eyes to but one thing more of things she lay among in that darkening landscape. Grass and blood. Blood and stone. Stone and the dark medallions that the first flat drops of rain caused upon them." The interrelationship of all things, the "living" and the "inanimate," is here clarified for the boy:

He thought that in the beauty of the world were hid a secret. He thought the world's heart beat at some terrible cost and that the world's pain and its beauty moved in a relationship of diverging equity and that in this headlong deficit the blood of multitudes might ultimately be exacted for the vision of a single flower. (282)

John Grady's realization that the balance and beauty of the world exist beyond any rational, anthropocentric sense of "equity" is paralleled by Billy Parham's equally mystical moment in *The Crossing* after he has killed the she-wolf and prepares to bury it. "He took up her stiff head out of the leaves and held it or he reached to hold what cannot be held, what already ran among the mountains at once terrible and of a great beauty, like flowers that feed on flesh." The description captures many of the images we have already discovered:

What we may well believe has power to cut and shape and hollow out the dark form of the world surely if wind can, if rain can. But which cannot be held never be held and is no flower but is swift and a huntress and the wind itself is in terror of it and the world cannot lose it. (127)

The Crossing is a book predicated on dreams and visions. Its narrative structure is established on such recitations as essentially as on other premodern forms such as the parables that are interpolated throughout the text. Oddly enough, its protagonist, Billy Parham, is often skeptical of the ideas inherent in these communications. For example, he discounts Boyd's fearful dreams of "this big fire out on the dry lake" with the commonsense reply, "There aint nothin to burn on a dry lake." "These people were burnin. The lake was on fire and they was burnin up," Boyd continues. "People have dreams all the time. It dont mean nothin," Billy insists. "Then what do they have em for?" Boyd asks. It's a good question, one Billy can't answer, and he simply repeats himself: "You just had a bad dream is all. It dont mean somethin bad is goin to happen. . . . It dont mean nothin." "Go to sleep," he tells Boyd three times (35–36), as if sleep, the medium of dreams, might somehow provide an escape from them.

Boyd's disturbing dream of fire prefigures a doom, "somethin bad," to be sure, but it also hints at something mystical as well, a quality also found in the primal nature of the she-wolf. "When the flames came up her eyes burned out there like gatelamps to another world. A world burning on the shore of an unknowable void. A world construed out of blood and blood's alcahest and blood in its core and in its integument because it was that nothing save blood had power to resonate against that void which threatened hourly to devour it" (73–74). Moreso than in *All the Pretty Horses*, dreams in *The Crossing* often have this apocalyptic quality about them, and this book is in essential ways—structural, thematic—the dark center of the trilogy, the profound mystery that gives foundation to the more conventional stories that bracket it. "Apocalypse" in Christian literature means to reveal, usually through divine disclosure and often through dreams and visions or the mediation of angels or other such otherworldly messengers. Unlike prophecies, which anticipate specific future events, often in very individual, personal terms (like John Grady's death, spelled out in *All the Pretty Horses* but not accomplished until *Cities of the Plain*), apocalyptic writings describe eternal truths, secrets held by God that transcend both individual and human history, that in fact assume the culmination of history in the final days. This ultimate revelation looks beyond earthly events to the transcendently spiritual and is often coded in symbolism, as in the Book of Revelation. Thus we may read *The Crossing* (the title itself has multiple meanings, inherently spiritual), with its old wise men and women who give warnings or gifts, its unaccountable, vaguely angelic strangers who tell complex stories demanding exegesis or symbolic interpretation, its moments of sudden illumination leading to supra-rational states of awe or even majestic terror, as a book of revelation itself, a mystical text in the guise of a western adventure.

There are, as already noted, dreams in this novel that serve the traditional purposes of caution, warning, prediction. When Billy, for another example, takes the wolf into Mexico, he dreams one night that "a messenger had come in off the plains from the south with something writ upon a ledgerscrap but he could not read it. He looked at the messenger but that face was obscured in shadow and featureless and he knew that the messenger was messenger alone and could tell him nothing of the news he bore" (82–83). Later, after Billy has killed the wolf and has become an outrider from civilization, an "orphan" according to some, a foolish raggedy man (much like Lester Ballard in *Child of God*) to others, he is warned in a dream that (again like Lester) he might eventually find himself totally alienated from humanity. "He slept and in his sleep he dreamt of wild men who came to him with clubs and their teeth were filed to points and they gathered round him and warned him of their work before they even set about it" (135–36). The dream (similar to Suttree's nightmare described earlier) causes Billy to return to his own country, and on the way he encounters the priest, the unaccountable figure who attempts to instruct the boy through his lengthy tale of the heretic. This heretic, we learn, after despairing of God's justice in the world, became a "bearer of messages. He carried a satchel of leather and canvas secured with a lock. He had no way to know what the messages said nor had he any curiosity concerning them. . . . He was simply a messenger" (147).[22] Thus, Billy's earlier dreams are in a sense confirmed and continued by the priest's tale, which again warns Billy that he himself stands in danger of becoming a figure with no meaning, a Bartleby-like symbol with no connection to the rest of humankind.

The Crossing contains three major dream-like or visionary episodes that mark the development of its main character. In *All the Pretty Horses*, John Grady Cole grows toward a more mature understanding of the nature of loss and of justice, although, as we have seen, he will continue to force his personal issues to a violent and destructive conclusion. Billy Parham's journey is ultimately more devastating, spiritually, for he learns the greater truth of humanity's misplaced vanity and ultimate insignificance. Billy will experience the apocalyptic moment, will come to the place described by the old wolf trapper (and fellow outcast) Don Arnulfo as that where "acts of God

60 *Dreams and Visions in the Trilogy*

and those of man are of a piece. Where they cannot be distinguished. . . . He said that it was at such places that God sits and conspires in the destruction of that which he has been at such pains to create" (47).

Billy's initial visionary experience (the first described to us, at any rate) occurs on the first page of the novel. He wakes to hear the howl of wolves and dresses in the dark, careful not to disturb his brother or parents, for this is a personal and private moment. The portrait of the wolves reminds one of Sherwood Anderson's magical image of the wild dogs in "Death in the Woods":

> After a time all the dogs came back to the clearing. They were excited about something. Such nights, cold and clear, and with a moon, do things to dogs. It may be that some old instinct, come down from the time when they were wolves and ranged the woods in packs on winter nights, comes back into them. . . . They began to play, running in circles in the clearing. Round and round they ran, each dog's nose at the tail of the next dog. In the clearing, under the snow-laden trees and under the wintry moon they made a strange picture, running thus silently, in a circle their running had beaten into the soft snow. The dogs made no sound. They ran around and around in a circle. (127)

McCarthy describes the wolves as follows:

> They were running on the plain harrying the antelope and the antelope moved like phantoms in the snow and circled and wheeled and the dry powder blew about them in the cold moonlight and their breath smoked palely in the cold as if they burned with some inner fire and the wolves twisted and turned and leapt in a silence such that they seemed of another world entire. . . . Loping and twisting. Dancing. Tunneling their noses in the snow. Loping and running and rising by twos in a standing dance and running on again. (4)

When they return, the mystical seven of them, they sense Billy's presence, and for one moment boy and wolves acknowledge one another, in a manner similar to Isaac McCaslin's numinous meeting with Old Ben, the crippled bear in Faulkner's *Go Down, Moses*. "When he got back to the house Boyd was awake but he didnt tell him where he'd been nor what he'd seen. He never told anybody" (5). This apparition—and it is either a dream or an extraordinary night experience, its reality imbued with an intoxication beyond the events themselves—is precious to the boy. Although he doesn't tell, he surely also does not forget. Indeed, after Boyd is shot, Billy, frantically searching for his brother, revisits the moment. He dreams that he is making his way through deep snow "toward a darkened house and the wolves had followed him as far as the fence." Rather than dance, the wolves huddle together and whine, fretful, and then they gather about the boy:

He knelt in the snow and reached out his arms to them and they touched his face with their wild muzzles and drew away again and their breath was warm and it smelled of the earth and the heart of the earth. When the last of them had come forward they stood in a crescent before him and their eyes were like footlights to the ordinate world and then they turned and wheeled away and loped off through the snow and vanished smoking into the winter night. (295)

As the dream continues, Billy enters his house, and Boyd is there, himself waking from a fearful dream (dreams within dreams, foreshadowing Billy's later experience with the stranger in the epilogue of *Cities of the Plain*, who also dreams of a dreamer). In Billy's dream, Boyd tells him that, in his sleep, he had feared that Billy had run away. "You wont run off and leave me will you Billy?" he asks, and Billy promises that he will not. Twice he instructs his brother (in the dream) to "Go to sleep," adding, "Hush. You'll wake them." And then we are told, "But in the dream Boyd only said softly that they would not wake"(296). His whisper is a sad reminder of both the wolf's and his parents' fates, and a premonition of Boyd's forthcoming abandonment of his brother and of his own death. It also reflects Billy's later determination to recover Boyd's body and bring it home (such a simple transposition of letters—body/Boyd—marks Boyd's passage from life to death and memory).

The second experience is the one already mentioned, the spiritual metamorphosis that occurs when Billy prepares to bury the she-wolf. As he rides from town, the last of the fireworks explode behind him against the black sky. He passes a "burntout catherinewheel" (125), a flammable pinwheel whose design is derived from an instrument of torture, an appropriate symbol of Billy's own case. He crosses the river as a "last lone rocket" soars and illuminates him on his horse, the wolf's body draped across the bow of his saddle (just as he carried Boyd as a child, and will, in *Cities*, carry John Grady's pup). A "solitary dog" follows him, "frozen on the beach on three legs standing in that false light and then all faded again into the darkness out of which it had been summoned" (125). After he reaches the mountains earlier promised to the wolf, Billy "fell asleep with his hands palm up before him like some dozing penitent. When he woke it was still dark" (126). It is in this borderstate of consciousness that he merges spirits with the wolf, experiences with or through her the magnificence of her final freedom in the ordinate world: "Deer and hare and dove and groundvole all richly empaneled on the air for her delight, all nations of the possible world ordained by God of which she was one among and not separate from" (127). The scene parallels John Grady's prison dream of running with the wild horses, once again emphasizing that often unacknowledged "resonance" at the heart of the world. Afterwards, however, as is often the case after such a shattering revelation, Billy finds his common existence repugnant, cold, and all too hard.

Billy experiences other illuminations of varying intensity during his travels, hears other stories of similar moments, but the boy is unable to get beyond his essential sense of alienation. After years of wandering, he comes to that place foretold by Don Arnulfo, "where acts of God and those of man are of a piece" (47). This revelation is accomplished by the first atomic explosion at the White Sands test site, Trinity, New Mexico, at 5:29:45 a.m. on 16 July 1945, which Billy witnesses from afar. It clearly is an apocalyptic event, one of both terror and truth. Billy has earlier sought shelter from the rain, has chased an old dog from the ruined building each had chosen for comfort and protection. This dog, a three-legged monstrosity that encapsulates so many images of trinity in the novel—the lame she-wolf, the three-legged dog at the river, the floating church that "stands on three legs" in the town of Caborca (149), the three major parables told to Billy in his wanderings—serves as Billy's double, as emblem of all outcasts and aliens denied the common bond. Billy's act is unusually mean-spirited, quite at odds with the lessons of charity he should have learned in his journeying. It is after this selfish act that, in the early morning, he suddenly wakes "in the white light of the desert noon," a light that immediately begins to fade "[a]s if a cloud were passing over the sun" (425). In this "false light" he sees its source, a "dim neon bow," which itself pales so that the "noon in which he'd woke was now become an alien dusk and now an alien dark" and soon is again replaced by the black night. "After a while he sat in the road. He took off his hat and placed it on the tarmac before him and he bowed his head and held his face in his hands and wept," we are told, a recollection of his posture at the wolf's grave and a traditional one for penitents or pilgrims who seek enlightenment. "He sat there for a long time and after a while the east did gray and after a while the right and godmade sun did rise, once again, for all and without distinction" (425–26).

The Gospel of Mark foretells the last days of tribulation that precede the Second Coming of Christ. "False Christs and false prophets will arise and show signs and wonders to lead astray, if possible, the elect," Jesus warns. "But in those days, after that tribulation, the sun will be darkened, and the moon will not give its light, and the stars will be falling from heaven, and the powers in the heavens will be shaken. And then they will see the Son of man coming in clouds with great power and glory" (Mark 13.22, 24–25). I have elsewhere discussed McCarthy's paraphrase in the last section of Matthew 5.45, which reads in part, "for he makes his sun rise on the evil and on the good, and sends rain on the just and on the unjust," Christ's description of common grace in the Sermon on the Mount.[23] In one way, then, this final visionary moment reenacts Billy's earlier revelation while burying the she-wolf. In another, it emphasizes the spiritual essence of the book, leaving Billy crying, for the third time, and seeking somehow to make amends for his own failure of kindness. The love shown the proud wolf is replaced by thoughtless cruelty to the pathetic dog. If Billy cannot recognize the bond that exists among all living and god-made things, then how can he hope for himself any similar grace? As Ben Telfair has said, "Because we cannot save ourselves unless we save all ourselves" (St 113). The human arrogance of the moment, the explosion of the bomb that works by dismantling the structure of the universe, and the challenge it thus throws down to the divinely ordered world, so honored in *The Stonemason*, stand at odds with the central meaning of *The Crossing*. As the priest tells Billy,

So everything is necessary. Every least thing. This is the hard lesson. Nothing can be dispensed with. Nothing despised. Because the seams are hid from us, you see. The joinery. The way in which the world is made. We have no way to know what could be taken away. What omitted. (143)

This, I think, is the revelation Billy experiences in this instant of fear, confusion, and abasement. The naïve, magical joy of his first vision of the dancing wolves is forever replaced by a darker, more profound understanding of human vanity, an arrogance so great that it threatens the fundamental pattern established by the creative god, a destruction in which that god itself now seems willing to "conspire." The apocalyptic nature of the event, the allusions to Armageddon, and the deep abjection Billy feels, all capture a sense of biblical judgment at hand. Nevertheless, the awful majesty of this final scene concludes the book on a note both horrifying and strangely hopeful. We might look one last time at *The Stonemason*, published in the same year as *The Crossing* and so very close to it in theme and rhetoric. The play concludes with Ben Telfair's final vision of his dead grandfather, Papaw:

He came out of the darkness and at that moment everything seemed revealed to me and I could almost touch him. . . . He was just a man, naked and alone in the universe, and he was not afraid and I wept with a joy and a sadness I'd never known and I stood there with the tears pouring down my face and he smiled at me and he held out both his hands. Hands from which all those blessings had flowed. Hands I never tired to look at. Shaped in the image of God. To make the world. To make it again and again. To make it in the very maelstrom of its undoing. Then as he began to fade I knelt in the grass and I prayed for the first time in my life. I prayed as men must have prayed ten thousand years ago to their dead kin for guidance and I knew that he would guide me all my days and that he would not fail me, not fail me, not ever fail me. (132–33)[24]

Thus, in the midst of destruction is hope for regeneration, for mercy. Papaw's vision fades like the atomic explosion, "in the very maelstrom of its undoing," but it leaves Ben Telfair with a sense of strange peace. We cannot know what Billy feels, but the great melancholy that inflicts his soul never completely destroys it, and he never completely loses the ability to trust and to love.

In comparison to the profound, weighty narrative of *The Crossing* (and some would say the book is too self-important, too caught up in philosophical-theological rumblings and ramblings, although I am obviously not of that camp), *Cities of the Plain* may at first seem a retreat or, as the priest might say, a "colindancia" to the reader. But this is a deceptive novel. Simple in its plot, conventional, even at times clichéd, in its characters, the most overtly sentimental of McCarthy's works, *Cities* is nonetheless a magical book, a dream narrative, with Billy Parham as the primary dreamer. It moves of its own pace, is told through memory and apparition, sleep its recurring state. How many times do its characters bid one another good night? How often do they think on a world recalled only in dreams? A past life, a dead love, a tender knowledge of loss: these are the sad, lovely moments that stay with one after reading the book. It is a novel built on sighs. The story takes place largely at night, in the dark. Old Mr. Johnson wanders the early morning hours in some mid-world, unable to distinguish between then and now, but he is only the most obvious of the characters who yearn for what's gone. John Grady, Billy, Mac McGovern, Troy, JC: can we find someone other than the villainous Eduardo (who echoes both Judge Holden and the Dueña Alfonsa), who is not caught in this limbo? It is Eduardo who mocks the dream: "Men have in their minds a picture of how the world will be," he tells Billy. "The world may be many different ways for them but there is one world that will never be and that is the world they dream of. Do you believe that?" "Let me sleep on it," Billy answers sardonically (134–35).

The story is told in the vocabulary and at times the logic of sleep and dreams. Tiburcio is "A morbid voyeur, a mortician. An incubus of uncertain proclivity..." (183). John Grady dreams of "things he'd heard and that were so although she'd never spoke of them" (103), a nightmare in which his sexual fears and jealousies concerning Magdalena are expressed in the most garish, gothic manner imaginable, a scene almost demonic in its presentation. He wants to save her, and we are later told that "[a]ll his early dreams were the same. Something was afraid and he had come to comfort it" (204). But John Grady moves "from dream to dream" in this book, and his sleep is constantly disturbed by anticipation of his own death: He finds himself "alone in some bleak landscape where the wind blew without abatement and where the presence of those who had gone before still lingered on in the darkness about" (104), an echo of the opening of *All the Pretty Horses* (3). He sees himself dressed in a suit, preparing for both wedding and burial simultaneously: "He buttoned the coat and stood. His hands crossed at the wrist in front of him" (204). Magdalena lives in a world half-way between the real and the other: she is an epileptic whose seizures take her into another realm; the other prostitutes think her possessed or caught in some divine rapture and dip their handkerchiefs in her blood. She is murdered by Tiburcio early on the morning she hopes to escape to John Grady. "In the cold dawn all that halfsordid world was coming to light again," we are told, and she "said a silent goodbye to everything she knew and to each thing she would not see again" (224). She is almost overtaken by a seizure, but "[t]he cold pneuma passed. She should have called it back" (225), the narrator comments, for she wakes from this state to see the "smiling Tiburcio," her murderer, walking toward her.

But the chief dreamer is Billy, who has tried so often to deny the power or significance of dreams. The epilogue to *Cities* provides McCarthy's primary disquisition on the nature of dreams and dreaming, a summation of all that has gone before in his work.[25] The stranger Billy meets in the dream world of 2002—unreal to us today because of its futurity but equally unreal because Billy has now entered another consciousness altogether, despite his continued insistence on logic and fact—encourages Billy to take comfort in the knowledge provided by such a state of knowing. "Our waking life's desire to shape the world to our convenience invites all manner of paradox and difficulty," he tells Billy. "All in our custody seethes with an inner restlessness. But in dreams we stand in this great democracy of the possible and there we are right pilgrims indeed. There we go forth to meet what we shall meet" (283–84). The complication provided by the "dream-within-a-dream" structure of the stranger's tale is further complicated by the possibility that Billy may be dreaming the stranger himself and thus also the stranger's dream and the dream imbedded in that dream. Moreover, since we are reading a work of fiction, and McCarthy, as author, is himself "dreaming" Billy and the stranger and all that comes between them, we must always be aware that we can never in this world find that primary level of "reality" or "fact," which is, of course, the whole point of the epilogue. As Billy notes, "A dream inside a dream might not be a dream" (273); it might, in other words, be a deeper truth than we can otherwise know.[26]

"Two worlds touch here," the stranger tells Billy (285), and although Billy would like to insist even now, as he did years ago to Boyd, that a dream is "just a dream" (284) and not to be taken seriously—"I aint thought about em at all. I've just had em" (277), he tells the stranger—at heart Billy knows, or hopes to discover, that what the stranger says is so. The book strongly suggests that it is. "You'll see things on the desert at night that you cant understand," Mr. Johnson tells John Grady earlier in the book. "Your horse will see things.... I aint talkin about spooks. It's more like just the way things are. If you only knew it" (124). "Of such dreams and of the rituals of them there can also be no end," the stranger says. "The thing that is sought is altogether other. However it may be construed within men's dreams or by their acts it will never make a fit. These dreams and these acts are driven by a terrible hunger. They seek to meet a need which they can never satisfy, and for that we must be grateful" (287). Dreams, he suggests, continue to remind us of what we fail to apprehend in our daily existence, but they cannot and should not "satisfy" our yearning for that "other," else we would cease to strive for it.

"I got to get on," Billy says in farewell. "I hope your friends await you," the stranger answers. "And I," Billy concurs (288). Billy's friends, of course, are all dead, and his hope to meet them again reveals the old man's essential goodness and faith, despite all he has suffered and lost in his long life. He is now like the old dog to which he denied shelter at the end of *The Crossing*. We leave him in transition, in bed awakened from one dream—of his lost "bud" Boyd, but also of John Grady, with whom Boyd has merged in Billy's mind—and in movement toward another, final, place of consolation. "I'm not what you think I am. I aint nothin," Billy tells Betty, the mother of the family that has charitably taken him in.[27] "I know who you are," she simply replies. "You go to sleep now. I'll see you in the morning" (292). Here the story ends, with Billy's drifting off, leaving this world, blessed and perhaps finally justified by the touch of her hand and the kindness of her heart.[28] "That was not sleeping," John Grady thinks on the first page of *All the Pretty Horses*. "You go to sleep now," the last page of *Cities of the Plain* directs. The visionary experience that is the Border Trilogy comes between, and it offers us a different way of seeing the world(s), of finding our place therein.

Notes

1. Rick Wallach has also made this point in his essay "Three Dreams: [T]he Bizarre Epilogue of *Cities of the Plain*." *Proceedings of the First European Conference on Cormac McCarthy*. Ed. David Holloway. Miami: The Cormac McCarthy Society, 1999: 57–61.

2. There are far too many works, both popular and scientific, on dreams and dream theory to offer anything other than a minimal listing. Sigmund Freud's *The Interpretation of Dreams* (1900) and C. G. Jung's many writing on dreams found in *The Collected Works of C. G. Jung* (Bollingen Series), 20 vols. (1953–1979) form the basis for any consideration. Other works that have gained wide readerships or offer useful basic information include Erich Fromm, *The Forgotten Language* (1951), Ann Faraday, *Dream Power* (1972), Christopher Evans, *Landscapes of the Night: How and Why We Dream* (1983), Stephen La Berge, *Lucid Dreaming* (1985), Carlos

Castaneda, *The Art of Dreaming* (1993), and Ernest Hartman, *Dreams and Nightmares* (1998). Opinions vary widely as to the significance of some of these studies.

3. For further discussion, see "Dreams" in *The Oxford Companion to the Bible*. Ed. Bruce M. Metzger and Michael D. Coogan (New York and Oxford: Oxford UP, 1993) 171.

4. For further discussion of these early "dreams" in McCarthy's writings, see Dianne C. Luce's " 'They aint the thing': Artifact and Hallucinated Recollection in Cormac McCarthy's Early Frame-Works" (*Myth, Legend, Dust: Critical Responses to Cormac McCarthy*. Ed. Rick Wallach. Manchester and New York: Manchester UP, 2000) 21–36.

5. See William C. Spencer, "Altered States of Consciousness in *Suttree*." *Southern Quarterly* 35.2 (1997) 87–92, for further discussion of these ideas.

6. Even the most hallucinatory waking moments in *Blood Meridian*, such as the Indian attack across the lake bed during which inverted phantom images of the warriors are reflected in the sky above them (109), have rational explanations. Such explanations, however, do not necessarily mitigate the eeriness of the moment.

7. "He could not swim, but how would you drown him? . . . You could say that he's sustained by his fellow men, like you. Has peopled the shore with them, calling to him. A race that gives suck to the maimed and the crazed, that wants their wrong blood in its history and will have it. But they want this man's life" (COG 156).

8. Ledgerbooks in McCarthy's work serve as images of rationality, of logical knowing, or of justification, earthly versions of God's traditional Book of Judgment. Characters wish to point to "proofs" in these books in order to make their cases, to explain their actions. In addition to the judge's ledger, in which he intends to record and order and thus to control all existence, we might also consider Ben Telfair's "job book" in *The Stonemason*: he has listed his work, his "good deeds," in this book, but when he attempts to use it to argue his worth before God, he finds "that the pages were yellowed and crumbling and the ink faded and the accounts no longer clear and suddenly I thought to myself fool fool do you not see what will be asked of you?" (112). There is also a "ledgerscrap" in one of Billy Parham's dreams discussed later in this essay. One might further consider the ledgerbook in which Isaac McCaslin discovers his family's history in Faulkner's *Go Down, Moses*.

9. Leo Daugherty discusses this figure at length in his essay "Gravers False and True: *Blood Meridian* as Gnostic Tragedy" (Arnold and Luce, *Perspectives* 159–74. See esp. 166–68). One might also consult the archives of the "Forum" located at the Cormac McCarthy Home Pages website (http//www.cormacmccarthy.com) for a variety of opinions on this figure.

10. See Dianne C. Luce, "The Road and the Matrix" for further discussion of the importance of "Whales and Men" to McCarthy's novels, especially *The Crossing*.

11. Phillip A. Snyder observes, "In McCarthy's borderlands, language bears the same weight of reality as do physical performance and natural phenomena, his style aspiring to achieve a tangible substance to match the reality of his plot and setting." See Snyder, "Cowboy Codes in Cormac McCarthy's The Border Trilogy" in this collection, 223.

12. Like so many great writers, McCarthy confronts the inadequacies and dangers of words even as he practices his own wordcraft with growing mastery and authority. We might question to what extent the coldforger represents both the artist—he "seemed an artisan and a worker in metal"—and the con artist much like Melville's Confidence-Man. McCarthy explored the limitations of the artist in his play *The Stonemason*, in which the maker, a builder in stone, tries to follow the path of nature. "According to the gospel of the true mason God has laid the

stones in the earth for men to use and he has laid them in their bedding planes to show the mason how his own work must go" (10). This understanding is of God as Prime Mover who places within nature the designs man might copy to achieve his own form of order and art, even with the realization that his creation will be but a sad imitation of the original thing or path itself. McCarthy also addresses the human artist in the epilogue to his last novel, *Cities of the Plain*, and there he again seems to admit the inevitable failure of any human endeavor, artistic or otherwise (see Arnold, "The Last of the Trilogy," Arnold and Luce, *Perspectives* 221–47, esp. 242–43). But can there also be a false artist who intentionally misleads? Also, see Wallace, who quotes McCarthy as follows:

> He said that he felt sorry for me because I was unable to grasp this concept of spiritual experience. . . . He asked if I'd ever read William James's *The Varieties of Religious Experience*. I had not. His attitude seemed to indicate that in this book were the answers to many of the questions posed during our evening discussion. I was nonplussed.
> "Truth," McCarthy said about what writers must accomplish in their writing.
> "But what exactly is truth?" I asked.
> "Truth," he repeated, his implications tacit. (138)

13. An example of the intuited separation between these two "worlds" is reflected in Lacey Rawlins's comment to John Grady in *All the Pretty Horses*:

> You ever get ill at ease? said Rawlins.
> About what?
> I dont know. About anything. Just ill at ease.
> Sometimes. If you're someplace you aint supposed to be I guess you'd be ill at ease. Should be anyways.
> Well suppose you were ill at ease and didnt know why. Would that mean that you might be someplace you wasnt supposed to be and didnt know it?
> What the hell's wrong with you?
> I dont know. Nothin. I believe I'll sing. (37)

14. See Bernard Schopen, " 'They Rode On': *Blood Meridian* and the Art of Narrative." *Western American Literature* 30.2 (1995) 179–94.
15. Jennifer Fraser has drawn a number of other similarities between John Grady and Hamlet in her unpublished essay "The Border Trilogy: McCarthy's Marriage of *Figura*."
16. Dianne C. Luce makes the point that the "pretty horses of the title come to represent any fantasy, dream, wish, or object of desire to which one might aspire or feel entitled to . . ." (156). She also discusses John Grady's growth in terms of "waking" from a dream. (" 'When you wake' 155–67).
17. One might compare many of the previously-discussed passages to the view of the world described by William Faulkner in such works as *Go Down, Moses*, his meditation on man and nature, the world we know and the world sometimes revealed to us. In the section "The Old People," for example, Isaac McCaslin kills his first buck and "Sam Fathers marked his face with the hot blood which he had spilled and he ceased to be a child and became a hunter and a man" (132). Shortly thereafter Isaac sees what must be a phantom deer, the spirit of the woods. He tries to explain it to his cousin McCaslin Edmonds, and Cass responds. "Think of all that has happened here, on this earth. All the blood hot and strong for living, pleasuring, that has soaked back into it. . . . And all that must be somewhere; all that could not have been invented

and created just to be thrown away. And the earth is shallow; there is not a great deal of it before you come to the rock. And the earth dont want to just keep things, hoard them; it wants to use them again." "But I saw it!" Isaac insists, fearing that Cass misunderstands the literalness of the event. "I saw him!" "Steady," Cass replies. "I know you did. So did I. Sam took me in there once after I killed my first deer" (138–39).

18. The *hacienda* is located "along the edge of the Bolsón de Cuatro Ciénagas in the state of Coahuila" (97). Despite the paradisaical qualities, McCarthy's description of the basin is not exaggerated, for it is a unique geographical area and supports a variety of fish and other aquatic life forms not found elsewhere in the world. Much of the area is now under the management of the Nature Conservancy, which is attempting to protect the special quality of the region. I am grateful to Robert G. McCready, Northeast Mexico Program Manager of The Nature Conservancy of Texas (and a devoted reader of the Trilogy), for information concerning Cuatro Ciénagas.

19. McCarthy's use of "who's" rather than the more appropriate pronoun "whose" is intriguing. On the one hand it specifies a "who," a thing that exists and possesses, and in this sense emphasizes the existence of some higher force. However, in the typescript of "Whales and Men," we find this sentence: "The question whether [whales] are as smart as we are is not a real question. Smarter at what? From who's point of view?" (23), which appears to be a simple grammatical mistake.

20. See Christine Chollier's essay "Autotextuality, or Dialogic Imagination in Cormac McCarthy's Border Trilogy," in this collection for further discussion of Don Héctor's warnings.

21. A great deal is happening in this passage. As Dianne Luce pointed out to me, McCarthy here echoes in his vocabulary Dylan Thomas's "Fern Hill," in which the poet remembers being "green and carefree, famous among the barns/About the happy yard and singing as the farm was home" (ll. 10–11). The poem continues:

> And then to awake, and the farm, like a wanderer white
> With the dew, come back, the cock on his shoulder: it was all Shining, it was Adam and maiden,
> The sky gathered again
> And the sun grew round that very day.
> So it must have been after the birth of the simple light
> In the first, spinning place, the spellbound horses walking warm
> Out of the whinnying green stable
> On to the fields of praise. (ll.28–36)

"Fern Hill" is also alluded to in *Child of God*, in Lester's dream of his father and the heartbreaking beauty of the world (170–71). But the passage goes beyond Thomas's lyrical romanticism. In theoretical physics, the ongoing exploration into the structure of the world of subatomic particles posits a unified theory of the universe. This "theory of everything" now concentrates on "string theory," which holds that the smallest scales of material within the atom are "loops of vibrating string." As Brian Greene puts it in his book *The Elegant Universe*, "Far from being a collection of chaotic experimental facts, particle properties in string theory are the manifestation of one and the same physical feature: the resonant patterns of vibration—the music, so to speak—of fundamental loops of strings" (15–16).

22. Consider Ben Telfair's vision of his dead grandfather in *The Stonemason*: "I saw him here

twice in the evening just at dusk and I tried small tricks to make him appear again. . . . Or maybe it was a dream. I saw him with a great stone that he carried with much labor and I thought it was like a boundary stone and I looked for some mark or inscription on the stone but there was none. It was just a stone. Nothing is finally understood. Nothing is finally arrived at" (131).

23. See my essay "McCarthy and the Sacred: A Reading of *The Crossing*" forthcoming in James Lilley, ed. *Cormac McCarthy* (University of New Mexico Press, 2002).

24. "Hands" serve as a major trope in these later works, especially *The Crossing*, *The Stonemason*, and *Cities of the Plain*. In these they represent the shared humanity of all peoples and illustrate McCarthy's insistence on the idea that we are all one. In *The Crossing*, for example, the heretic takes the priest's hand "as of the hand of a comrade" and compares it to his own: "and he said see the likeness. This flesh is but a memento, yet it tells the true. Ultimately every man's path is every other's. There are no separate journeys for there are no separate men to make them. All men are one and there is no other tale to tell" (156–57). In "Whales and Men" McCarthy extends this human connection to other forms of creation in the scene where Kelly McAmon "places her hand alongside the skeleton hand [of a right-whale] in the illustration. Her hand is about the same size as the page illustration" (83).

25. See my "The Last of the Trilogy: First Thoughts on *Cities of the Plain*" for further discussion of the dream narrative in this epilogue, esp. 241–43.

26. The comic interlude concerning Oren's observations on the brains of a horse (149–52)—"A horse has got two brains. He dont see the same thing out of both eyes at once. He's got a eye for each side" (150)—merges strangely with the stranger's dream(s) at this point. Both episodes emphasize seeing in different ways and attempting to bring those two views together in some compatible and understandable fashion.

27. Billy's self-deprecation is very similar to John Grady's comment to the judge at the end of *All the Pretty Horses*: "I guess what I wanted to say first of all was that it kindly bothered me in the court what you said. It was like I was in the right about everthing and I dont feel that way. . . . I dont feel justified." The judge's response is "Son . . . you strike me as somebody that maybe tends to be a little hard on theirselves. . . . Maybe the best thing to do might be just to go on and put it behind you" (290–91).

28. A comparison might be made here to Rinthy Holme in *Outer Dark*, whose search for her child ends in the place of its death. "Shadows grew cold across the wood and night rang down upon these lonely figures and after a while little sister was sleeping" (237–38).

Works Cited

Anderson, Sherwood. "Death in the Woods." *Sherwood Anderson: Short Stories*. New York: Hill and Wang, 1962. 121–32.

Arnold, Edwin T. "The Last of the Trilogy: First Thoughts on *Cities of the Plain*." Arnold and Luce, *Perspectives* 221–47.

Arnold, Edwin T., and Dianne C. Luce, eds., *A Cormac McCarthy Companion: The Border Trilogy*. Jackson: UP of Mississippi, 2001.

Arnold, Edwin T., and Dianne C. Luce, eds. *Perspectives on Cormac McCarthy.* Rev. ed. Jackson: UP of Mississippi, 1999.

Blake, William. *The Poetry and Prose of William Blake.* Ed. David V. Erdman. Garden City, NY: Doubleday, 1970.

Chollier, Christine. "Autotextuality, or Dialogic Imagination in Cormac McCarthy's Border Trilogy," Arnold and Luce, *Companion* 3–36.

Daugherty, Leo. "Gravers False and True: *Blood Meridian* as Gnostic Tragedy." Arnold and Luce, *Perspectives* 159–74.

Donoghue, Denis. "Teaching *Blood Meridian.*" *The Practice of Reading.* New Haven: Yale UP, 1998. 259–77.

Faulkner, William. *Go Down, Moses.* New York: Library of America, 1994.

Greene, Brian. *The Elegant Universe.* New York: Norton, 1999.

Hall, Wade, and Rick Wallach, eds. *Sacred Violence: A Reader's Companion to Cormac McCarthy.* El Paso: Texas Western P, 1995.

James, William. *The Varieties of Religious Experience.* New York: Longmans, Green. 1925.

Luce, Dianne C. "The Road and the Matrix: The World as Tale in *The Crossing.*" Arnold and Luce, *Perspectives* 195–219.

———. " 'When you wake': John Grady Cole's Heroism in *All the Pretty Horses.*" Hall and Wallach 155–67.

McCarthy, C. J., Jr. [Cormac]. "Wake for Susan." *The Phoenix* [U of Tennessee]. Oct. 1959: 3–6.

McCarthy, Cormac. *All the Pretty Horses.* New York: Vintage, 1993.

———. *Blood Meridian or The Evening Redness in the West.* New York: Vintage, 1992.

———. *Child of God.* New York: Vintage, 1993.

———. *Cities of the Plain.* New York: Vintage, 1999.

———. *The Crossing.* New York: Vintage, 1995.

———. *The Orchard Keeper.* New York: Vintage, 1993.

———. *Outer Dark.* New York: Vintage, 1993.

———. *The Stonemason.* New York: Vintage, 1995.

———. *Suttree.* New York: Vintage, 1992.

———. "Whales and Men." Unpublished ts. Cormac McCarthy Papers. Southwestern Writers Collection. Albert B. Alkek Library. Southwest Texas State U, San Marcos.

Ragan, David Paul. "Values and Structure in *The Orchard Keeper.*" Arnold and Luce, *Perspectives* 17–27.

Shakespeare, William. "Hamlet, Prince of Denmark." *The Complete Works of William Shakespeare.* Ed. Hardin Craig. Glenview, IL: Scott, Foresman, 1961. 898–943.

Snyder, Phillip A. "Cowboy Codes in Cormac McCarthy's Border Trilogy." Arnold and Luce, *Companion* 198–227.

Thomas, Dylan. "Fern Hill." *The Collected Poems of Dylan Thomas.* New York: New Directions, 1953. 178–79.

Wallace, Garry. "Meeting McCarthy." *Southern Quarterly* 30.4 (1992): 134–39.

"WARS AND RUMORS OF WARS" IN CORMAC MCCARTHY'S BORDER TRILOGY

John Wegner

> Evenin Mr Johnson, he said.
> Evenin son.
> What's the news?
> The old man shook his head. He leaned across the table to the windowsill where the radio sat and turned it off. It aint news no more, he said. Wars and rumors of wars.
>
> —*Cities of the Plain* 61

> The Modern Era has nurtured a dream in which mankind, divided into its separate civilizations, would someday come together in unity and everlasting peace. Today, the history of the planet has finally become one indivisible whole, but it is war, ambulant and everlasting war, that embodies and guarantees this long-desired unity of mankind. Unity of mankind means: No escape for anyone anywhere.
>
> —Kundera, *The Art of the Novel* 10–11

War is the central thesis to McCarthy's southwestern works. *The Crossing* begins between World War I and World War II with America on the verge of the Depression, and *Cities of the Plain* essentially ends in 1952 as America's presence in Korea grows. John Grady Cole's father returns from a World War II p.o.w. camp sick and dying; *The Crossing* ends with Billy's witness of the "strange false sunrise . . . of the Trinity Test" (Hunt 31); and *Cities of the Plain* begins with John Grady's drinking with Troy, a war veteran. Even more pervasive are the accounts of the Mexican Revolution that become integral parts of the trilogy's narrative: Dueña Alfonsa's story to John Grady about Francisco I. Madero; Billy's encounters with the blind revolutionary and the patriot in the bar late in *The Crossing*; and Travis's story in *Cities of the Plain* of crossing the border after the fighting in Juárez. The two wars that form the backdrop of the trilogy represent opposite ends of the spectrum. The Mexican Revolution was fought on horseback and train track by peasants and ill-equipped soldiers. The war's most popular figure was a barbaric, illiterate guerilla warrior, Pancho Villa. World War II, on the other hand, was the first great technological war, fought from the air and ended with arguably the twentieth century's most significant and deadly discovery, the atomic bomb. In McCarthy's Border Trilogy, these two wars act as historical frames for the novels, defining and mapping the world in which these characters must live and survive.

The journey of *Blood Meridian*'s kid prefigures both the importance of war and the multiple international crossings of John Grady Cole and Billy Parham in the Border Trilogy.[1] His movement from Tennessee to Texas begins directly after the Mexican/American War (1846–1848), and he participates in various filibustering gangs whose goals are to rid the earth of the heathen tribes below the newly-formed border and make a little money while doing it. The kid flits in and out of the lives of the famous and infamous, known and unknown figures of the West and other fictional characters based closely upon historical persons. In essence, the kid actively participates in American expansion West and South.[2] Concomitantly, the epilogue to *Blood Meridian* seems to foreshadow *All the Pretty Horses*, *The Crossing*, and *Cities of the Plain*.[3] While there are many philosophical implications of the man "*progressing over the plain by means of holes*" (BM 337), he is quite literally digging fence posts, fence posts John Grady Cole and Lacey Rawlins wish did not exist and fence posts Billy and Boyd Parham will burn for firewood on their first trip to Mexico. John Grady and Billy's nostalgia for a time before the man digging post holes, the time of the kid's youth, is a product of naïveté, Hollywood, picture books, and youthful exuberance—a romanticizing of pre-World War I America.

McCarthy's *Blood Meridian*, however, is not necessarily part one of a border tetralogy. Ostensibly (and perhaps paradoxically), his first southwestern novel offers a counter-argument to the trilogy's almost wistful and romantic look at the pre-industrial Southwest. In a type of midrash on his own work, McCarthy offers a pre-revisionary comment on his own nostalgic western novels, revealing "the impossibility of separating ourselves from the events of our past that we now find to be morally objectionable" and that "American history [is] a series of violent cultural transformations, a history of slaughtered selves and strange, incongruous births" (Parrish and Spiller 463). John Grady, in particular, would have done well to read *Blood Meridian* before setting out across the border searching for his Big Rock Candy Mountain. McCarthy's novels are bound by their region, just as the Southwest remains bound to itself and its history. It is a region re-defined from the Mexican North to the American Southwest by war, and it is a region where some areas still have more in common with Mexico City than New York City.

The kid enters Texas and the Southwest shortly after the American defeat of Mexico and during the negotiations regarding the Treaty of Guadalupe Hidalgo. At this pivotal moment in history America creates the border that John Grady and Billy will later cross.[4] The kid's life of isolation and degradation spans both the American Civil War and Mexico's war with Spain. When he meets Elrod on the plains and the judge in the jakes, Porfirio Díaz has recently gained the Presidency in Mexico, superseding Benito Juárez, who successfully defended Mexico against Maximilian and Spain's attempts to reassert its colonial power in Mexico. During the war, Juárez' "capital city" was El Paso del Norte, a city vital for supplying weapons and American money. Juárez' victory was crucial to the United States' and Mexico's relations because his fierce Mexican pride created an anti-American sentiment that persists even today.[5] When Díaz wrested control from Juárez (an Indian peasant who rose to power), he opened Mexico's border to rich U.S. investors who appropriated the land and resources, oppressing the Mexican population with foreign economic interests. The northern Mexico and southwestern United States in which McCarthy sets his four southwestern novels exist in the aftermath of 110 years of revolution and war. Mexico's revolving door began with Miguel Hidalgo y Costillo's cry for Mexican independence from Spain (1810) and continued for the next 100 years: Agustin de Iturbide (1821); Santa Anna (1823–1855); Benito Juárez and Melchor Ocamp Ignacio Comonfort (1855–1872); Porfirio Díaz (1876–1910). A hundred years after the Hidalgo-led revolution, Mexico was still in turmoil with a revolution led by Francisco I. Madero (1910), who was joined (at first) by Emiliano Zapata and Pancho Villa. Madero gave way to Victoriano Huerta (1913), who quickly lost the presidency to Venustiano Carranza (1914). The next three years were marked by violent civil war and interim presidents. In 1917 under Carranza's leadership, Mexico crafted its Constitution (a constitution still in use today), but Carranza was assassinated in 1920 and Alvaro Obregón became President. Obregón's election effectively marked the end of the revolution. Despite sporadic revolutionary violence in Mexico, Obregón was a strong leader who served a four year presidency that helped stabilize the Mexican government after ten years of revolution.

In the midst of this bloodshed below the border, McCarthy's characters live both in the historical moment and in its aftermath. Glanton's gang lays the groundwork for men like William Randolph Hearst to enter into the Mexican economy and buy *La Babícora*, a purchase that occurred only six years after the kid meets the judge in the jakes. Unlike the kid, who rides with historical men, the boys from the Border Trilogy simply live in the historical aftermath of bloodshed in Mexico. The anti-American sentiment, Magdalena's difficult (and fatal) attempt to cross the border, and Eduardo's hatred for the leprous paradise north of the border in *Cities of the Plain* are all products of history, but they are not part of an archived historical moment in that history. They are, in other words, the stuff of fiction. From the exact dates and weather patterns of *Blood Meridian* to the vague location of the White Lake brothel, McCarthy's southwestern works grow less historically and geographically specific. It is this distinction that separates the completed Border Trilogy from *Blood Meridian*. History, an important, viable character in *Blood Meridian*, becomes an influence—a secondary, subtle motivator—in the trilogy, where it is the human responses to that historical influence that take center stage. John Grady Cole may believe "in individualism, free will, volition . . . [and that] every man born on this planet is an

Adam, free of memory and external constraint, able to shape his illimitable 'self' in any way he chooses" (Pilkington 320). However, the history lesson John Grady learns from Dueña Alfonsa contradicts that American ideal. Instead, he learns, as Quijada tells Billy, that the "soul of Mexico is very old" (C 385); the past influences and controls the present. The scalping, filibustering gangs like Captain White's and Glanton's prefigured the economic filibustering gangs led by Hearst. This continual and oppressive American presence fueled the 1910 Mexican Revolution that tightened the border restrictions the Treaty of Guadalupe Hidalgo had created. John Grady and Billy travel to a Mexico controlled by the PRI, the *Partido Revolucion Institucional*, a political party created in 1938. Creating a political party that institutionalizes the revolution, in effect, implies that the government represents the revolution and its ideas for reform. By the same token, the government eliminates the need for any new revolutions, implying that Mexico is in a constant state of controlled revolution and change. For Mexico, then, the revolution is continual and ongoing, hence the past is a significant part of the present.

Whether history or myth, McCarthy's trilogy seems to contend that "the past that was differs little from the past that was not" (BM 330). When Billy Parham talks to the traveler in the epilogue to *Cities of the Plain*, the narrator tells him that "This story like all stories has its beginnings in a question" (277). The traveler's story, a story within a story "in what we must imagine to be some unknown infinitude of alternate being and likeness," is a retold narrative explaining why the Mexican narrator drew a map of his life (275). His tale of a dreamer and a group of men engaging in a "blood ceremony that was then and is now an affront to God" blurs boundaries between dreams and reality and contends that there is a common history among all men, hence a common history among cities, among nations (280). The narrator's discussion of "common histories" and his story about his dreamt dreamer's dream, with all of its inherent philosophical complexities, seem to de-construct boundaries that separate men and generations: "Two worlds touch here" within the traveler's story (276; 285). That point of contact mirrors the lives of John Grady Cole and Billy Parham. Ostensibly, the question that begins the story of the two protagonists of the trilogy asks whether "His history is the same as yours or mine" (COP 285). This duality reflects the opening of the trilogy just as the "candleflame and the image of the candleflame caught in the pierglass" introduce us to John Grady (APH 3). If we treat these as one, then it is necessarily true that history is a shared experience and boundaries themselves do little to separate the effects of events where two worlds touch. The image and the reality (the myth and the history) are not two distinct objects; both become "twisted and righted" when the wind blows (APH 3).

Much of what is twisted and righted historically is war. McCarthy's southwestern fiction consistently provides historical reminders of the "[w]ars and rumors of wars" (COP 61) that Mr. Johnson hears on the radio, and these rumors constantly remind us that history and all the events of history revolve around war and revolution. The constant of McCarthy's southwestern fiction is the effect of war on men and women. The dominant historical event of the Southwest has been the revolutions in Mexico that created a new border between the wealthy United States and the poverty-stricken Mexican people. The battles south of the border influenced America's readiness for World War I, and the United States returned to the Southwest to perfect its ability to end world wars by building and testing the atomic bomb. Yet, even that capability does not stop the military intrusion on the land and its people as the government plans to buy Mac McGovern's ranch to extend the White Sands Missile Range.[6] McCarthy's southwestern fiction rejects the judge's admonition that "If war is not holy man is nothing but antic clay" (BM 307). Rather, these novels cry out against the meaninglessness of war and the repetitive historical patterns that create war, arguing that war will simply bury man in the clay that much faster. The Border Trilogy rejects the clichéd hope that to know history is to avoid repeating it. It argues that "The war changed everthing" (COP 78), but McCarthy does not specify which war because they are all the same, caused by the same types of events. The change is constantly revolving, violently and inevitably, and "[w]ars and rumors of war" dominate the discourse of the twentieth century.

The two wars that dominate the trilogy are the Mexican Revolution and World War II, and America's involvements in both of these conflicts are defining moments in American history. Both Don Héctor and Dueña Alfonsa speak "of the revolution and of the history of Mexico . . . and of Francisco Madero" (APH 144).[7] Madero's revolution was intended to recreate Mexico and end the dictatorships that oppressed the worker and peasant.

While it is true that the revolutionary party claimed victory after 1917, the poverty in Mexico that John Grady and Billy see subverts the rhetoric of change. The revolution offered hope to the masses that free elections could create equality. Even though Don Héctor correctly dismisses Madero and his revolution as quixotic (146), the revolution "was one of the last old-fashioned, pre-industrial wars, in which modern techniques and machinery had only an occasional role to play. It was a war of epic battles and mythical warrior-heroes, two of whom—Pancho Villa and Emiliano Zapata—have achieved fame throughout the world" (Rutherford 213).

In McCarthy's Border Trilogy the revolution comes to represent the peasant's kindness in the face of continued oppression. The foreign ownership of places like *La Babícora* by men like William Randolph Hearst and the corruption of Captain Rául, who imprisons the old man Orlando at Encantada are continually opposed by the basic human kindness of the workers, those very people the revolution should have freed from oppression. It is a country, Travis tells Billy and the other cowboys, where the goodness of the people contrasts with the reality of the historical moment:

I was a cattlebuyer for Spurlocks. . . . I rode all over northern Mexico. Hell, there wasnt no cattle. Not to speak of. Mostly I just visited. . . . I liked the country and I liked the people in it. I rode all over Chihuahua and a good part of Coahuila and some of Sonora. I'd be gone weeks at a time and not have hardly so much as a peso in my pocket but it didnt make no difference. Those people would take you in and put you up and feed you and feed your horse and cry when you left. You could of stayed forever. They didnt have nothin. . . . You could see that the revolution hadnt done them no good. A lot of em had lost boys out of the family. Fathers or sons or both. Nearly all of em, I expect. They didnt have no reason to be hospitable to anybody. Least of all a gringo kid. That plateful of beans they set in front of you was hard come by. But I was never turned away. Not a time. (COP 90).

As I have shown elsewhere, the Mexican Revolution is an overt presence in each book of the trilogy.[8] It appears in *All the Pretty Horses* with Luis's story of Huerta, and Luis and Antonio's continued subjection to Don Héctor reveals the failure of the revolution to effect social reform or increased independence for the peasants. The failure of Madero's revolution is a prominent theme in both Dueña Alfonsa's and Don Héctor's conversation. The revolution is even more prominent in *The Crossing*, historically the earliest of the novels with its beginning in 1939 during Cárdenas' presidency. In his travels, Billy encounters such characters as the young female revolutionary and her mother-in-law and the blind revolutionary who tells him his story. The *corrido* about "El güerito" that Billy hears on his return from the U.S. seems to cast Boyd as a hero for the oppressed, a revolutionary fighting against the "patrón's men" (381). But, more importantly, as Dirk Raat has said, "*corridos* function as barometers of the Mexican's attitudes towards events. The *corrido* is a kind of collective diary, an ethnohistorical document containing facts about society and history. Most *corridos* depict the Mexican as either victim or hero and often have themes of intercultural conflict. Many express frustration and anger over Anglo and North American dominance, and are, at times, a call to action" (48). Even Quijada admits the *corrido* "tells about him. . . . The corrido is the poor man's history" (*Crossing* 386). The *corrido* allows those not in power to lament their oppression and to rail against that oppression. In essence, then, the *corrido* offers hope. The Mexican people needed a hero because they lacked power.[9] They may have gained certain agrarian reforms, but absentee landowners still dominated Mexico. The living circumstances of the Munoz family and of the indian Quijada, who works for Hearst's *La Babícora*, reiterate the failure of the revolution, land reform, and the continued presence of foreign ownership of Mexican resources.

The revolution may have had little effect on the distribution of power and income in Mexico, but America's reaction to it helped reshape fundamental aspects of the American military and attitudes about war. While the United States never officially entered the Mexican Revolution, America invaded Vera Cruz in 1914, and after Pancho Villa's attack on Columbus, New Mexico, the government mobilized 40,000 National Guardsmen on the border near El Paso by June 18, 1916 (Vanderwood and Samponaro 10; 12). Even though America technically maintained its neutrality, the mobilization of so many troops gave the army a chance "to test new equipment and to train personnel, to hone its command structure and modernize its supply and support services. . . . Because of its Mexican venture, the U.S. Army finally became a twentieth-century fighting force, in large part due to Pancho Villa" (Vanderwood and Samponaro 186). Pershing's foray into Mexico chasing Pancho Villa specifically helped the Army develop tank warfare and redefine troop supply from mule and train dependencies to vehicular supply. In essence, America's training along the border helped the troops' preparedness for World War I.[10]

Perhaps most importantly, though, the Army's pre-World War I presence in the Southwest influenced its return to the Southwest to prepare for World War II. If the first World War showed America's willingness to involve itself in Europe's problems, the second World War created the American Superpower mystique. The atomic bomb, a creation with its heart in the Southwest, fundamentally changed the face of war in the modern world. No longer would two opponents meet on the field and battle trench to trench. The technological wizardry that eliminated human contact with the enemy heightened the brutality of war. Glanton's gang is animalistic, but they see the value of human life. Modern warfare removes the human(ity) from war, creating apathy and devaluing the warrior's knowledge of his enemy's life, hence his own. In essence, the atomic bomb made it easier to kill both from a technological standpoint and from a psychological standpoint. The effects extend beyond the battlefield. As Robert L. Holmes asserts in *On War and Morality*, the "paradox of contemporary civilization is that beyond a certain point the individual's security begins to vary inversely with the power embodied in the systems meant to ensure that security" (3).

Mr. Johnson's "[w]ars and rumors of wars" hold in them not just the history of civilization, a contention that would agree with Judge Holden's theories on war; these wars he hears on the radio (probably Korea and possibly the Egyptian Revolution) carry with them the threat of total annihilation of all countries because of the destructive power of the atomic bomb. War is nothing new, as Mr. Johnson says,[11] and that war dominates the discourse is nothing new to McCarthy readers. The epigraphs that open *Blood Meridian* point to the violence inherent in mankind. However, the Border Trilogy is not just about violence; it is about the inevitability of war, the inability to survive peacefully. At times, war seems god, or at least (as Kundera claims), war offers unity. Holmes argues that

Since originating an estimated forty thousand years ago, war has consumed more wealth, demanded greater sacrifice, and caused more suffering than any other human activity. In shaping history it has eclipsed even religion, in whose service it has so often been enlisted. But although war has brought out the worst in man, it has also brought out the best. While it cannot be said to have done much for music, it has inspired literature and poetry and brought advances in science, medicine, and technology that otherwise might have been long in coming. Ruskin claims that it has been essential to art as well. It has sometimes been the cohesive force that has brought together divided peoples to form strong and durable societies. (12)[12]

This would seem to be the case in the Mexico of the Border Trilogy. Travis' account of his trips to Mexico as a cattle buyer mirrors moments both John Grady and Billy experience in their trips to Mexico. John Grady, on his way back to the *Hacienda de Nuestra Señora de la Purísima Concepción*, gets a ride with some farmworkers "[a]nd after and for a long time to come he'd have reason to evoke the recollection of those smiles and to reflect upon the good will" of the men in the truck (*APH* 219). Similarly, Billy and Boyd both receive assistance from the peasants and workers in *The Crossing*. The kindness of the Mexican people is contrasted and perhaps fostered by the oppressive world in which they live. The *hombres del país* who take the handcuffed captain are men of the country, not men of the government (*APH* 281). They instinctively know that John Grady is telling the truth about his horses and require no retribution for his actions in kidnapping a man of the government. Boyd's immediate popularity after "kill[ing] the manco in a gunfight" and the worker's shout that "[h]ay justicia en el mundo" (*C* 317–8; there's justice in the world) also signal the underlying dissatisfaction of the Mexican populace. Billy's later encounter with the drunk patriot further subverts the docility of the populace and points to the potentially violent anti-American sentiment in the country (*C* 356). McCarthy's continual references to the Madero revolution accentuate the dichotomy between the revolution's goals and its achievements. These are people who have no reason to offer kindness, especially to *gringo* kids, but who do so despite the false hope created by a revolution eventually institutionalized and adopted by the dominant political machine of the country.

Much like the revolution in Mexico, World War II created false hopes in America. When Billy returns to America, he tries to enlist because "I dont have anyplace to go" (*C* 341), but the army will not take him because of his heart. Dianne C. Luce contends that "Billy's attempts to enlist in the armed services come to stand for his only sustained effort to live among men in *The Crossing*, and this enterprise is doomed, too" (211–2).[13] However, Billy's desire to join the community by entering the army is ironic: the institution he tries to join is a primary cause of the increased alienation and isolation he and John Grady feel. These are boys "disinherited by war and war's machinery" (COP 204). After trying to enlist multiple times, Billy works on a line camp, and, in a scene that mirrors his later encounter with the Mexican patriot, he goes to a bar in Winslow and orders a beer. In a second bar, where he meets a soldier and a bartender, his reticent stoicism causes problems. The bartender claims the "[u]niform dont mean nothin to him" (C 349). He follows this accusation with a bit of patriotic fear-mongering, telling the soldier that Billy would care if a uniform with "that risin sun on the collar . . . was comin down Second Street" (C 349). The patriotism is tempered by the location of the patriot: an empty bar in Winslow, Arizona, where a soldier drinks alone. Billy later drifts across the Southwest where "[b]y the spring of the third year of the war there was hardly a ranch house in all of that country that did not have a gold star in the window" (C 350). The Southwest has "had it pretty rough. . . . Pretty rough," Mr. Sanders tells Billy (C 351). There is little talk of the glory of war on Billy's wanderings.

Nevertheless, the war was a boon for the Southwest. Despite the gold stars and rough times for the families, war transformed the West economically.[14] However, the economic benefits did not match the loss of life and hope that McCarthy infuses into his World War II veterans. Billy's encounter with the American patriot takes place in an empty bar. John Grady's father returns from war a broken, dying man. As John Grady and Billy are talking about their respective trips to Mexico, Billy tells John Grady "this country aint the same. Nor anything in it. The war changed everthing. I dont think people even know it yet" (COP 78). World War II was a war that robbed America of joy in victory. Unlike in previous, imperialistic wars, America gained no land; and unlike World War I, this was not the war to end all wars. After World War I, Americans listened

> to network radio shows. . . . [S]educed by the imagery of advertising and the cinema, encouraged to ride out of familiar, stable locations in search of the unfamiliar or for the sheer experience of movement, Americans became a part of a distinctively modern, discontinuous and anonymous culture: a culture that was, and is, not specifically tied down to any individual locality, state, region—or, indeed, to any particular nation. (Gray 50)

This seduction by technology became less pleasurable after World War II and Hiroshima. America suffered heavy losses and inflicted even greater losses by dropping the bomb, a move that stunned the world. More obvious, though, was the effect on servicemen returning to America. John Grady's father, a former P.O.W. and survivor of the Bataan Death March, returns not "the same" despite his son's assertion that he is the same "inside" (*APH* 12). On their last ride, he looks "over the country with those sunken eyes as if the world out there had been altered or made suspect by what he'd seen of it elsewhere. As if he might never see it right again. Or worse did see it right at last" (*APH* 23). John Grady's father may be wracked by pneumonia (many Bataan survivors returned with fatal pneumonia or other deadly infectious diseases), or he may have cancer or emphysema promoted by the cigarettes and lighters distributed to American soldiers.

Much like John Grady's father, Troy returns from the war isolated. After his discharge from the Army, he "wandered all over this country" (*COP* 22), he tells Billy—right after telling him about a driving trip to Amarillo with Gene Edmonds, when the "front of the car . . . was just packed completely full of jackrabbit heads . . . all lookin out, eyes all crazy lookin" (*COP* 22). Troy's story highlights the post-war industrial world. While it is still possible to hit jackrabbits driving in West Texas at night, the likelihood has diminished somewhat as the rabbits have grown used to cars. Gene Edmonds' "brand new Olds Eighty-eight" (21) roaring down the highway is America in the twentieth century. The trip from El Paso to Amarillo (around 418 miles) in ten hours is a modern miracle in 1949. (Compare Troy's trip to that of John Grady and Lacey Rawlins, who ride from San Angelo to Eldorado, 43 miles, in one day, in *All the Pretty Horses*.) The speed of the trip, however, is countered by the hellish grill "covered with blood and rabbit guts" (22). The death and ghoulish appearance of these rabbits is classic McCarthy; it is also a classic confrontation between technology and nature. America's new-found love affair with the American automobile, with dynamic movement, creates gothic images of morbidity.

Shortly after John Grady and his father discuss the selling of the ranch, poker, and John Grady's grandfather, his father sees a newspaper and wonders, "How can Shirley Temple be getting divorced?" (*APH* 13).[15] Shirley Temple's divorce signifies the passage of time and the loss of innocence. To John Grady's father, the death of the grandfather and Shirley Temple's divorce both represent the death of pre-World War II values and life; in some respects, the divorce symbolizes the failure of World War II to fulfill the promise of peace, prosperity, and world-wide democracy. The end of the war in

> 1945 brought both euphoria and a rush to fulfill the promise of the myth of return. ... The nation that emerged from the war, and to which the veterans returned, was not the place they had left.... But the most profound gap between the expectation and the reality of victory was opened by the breakdown of the wartime alliance between the United States and the soviet [sic] Union. Whatever else victory was supposed to mean, the establishment of permanent peace and a rational world order was the irreducible minimum. (Slotkin 329, 332)[16]

Shirley Temple's divorce, the grandfather's death, and the loss of the ranch do not exactly offer order. Paradoxically, according to Alex Hunt, the splitting of the atom, a moment of supreme Cartesian physics, created disunity and "challenges our anthropocentric view of the relationship between humanity and the natural world" (31). As Hunt says, Billy's tears at the end of *The Crossing* "mourn the violence of humanity and humanity's ultimate alienation from nature through its appropriation of nature's power" (37).

Isolation and alienation seem at the heart of McCarthy's novels; however, the alienation of the individuals comes at a time when America has exponentially increased its world-wide involvement in other countries' affairs. The very creation and use of the atomic bomb virtually forced America into a universal role as a Big Brother peacekeeper, making isolation impossible to maintain. Wars and rumors of wars will always intrude; the technology of the twentieth-century delimits John Grady's desire to live on "a little spread up in the hills" where he can kill his own meat and remove himself from the world below (*COP* 77). What John Grady and Billy learn is that "each of us has a secret frontier within him, and that is the most difficult frontier to cross because each of us hopes to find himself alone there, but finds only that he is more than ever in the company of others" (Fuentes 161). Essentially, isolation and alienation are never complete because technology subverts the ability to remain alone. World War II acts as a moment of aporia for these boys: the alienation and isolation of the individual is deconstructed by the ever growing communal responsibility and intrusion.

The governmental intrusion upon the lives of the ranchers in the Southwest signifies this communal growth. Lurking in the background of *Cities of the Plain* are the army surveyors sent to "find the sorriest land they" can

(11). This land will become part of the militarized Southwest that includes Fort Bliss and the White Sands Missile Range. Increased military presence began during the Mexican Revolution and continued as America created its nuclear arsenal. The transition from privately-owned land did not always go smoothly, though. While McGovern recognizes that "the army's goin to take this place," the only way Mr. Prather will "leave [is] in a box" (264, 62). When John Grady interrupts Mr. Johnson as he listens to the radio, we get a short history of New Mexico. Mr. Johnson tells John Grady that "Oliver Lee always said he come out here because the country was so sorry nobody else would have it and he'd be left alone. Of course he was wrong. At least about bein left alone" (61). The army will "take the whole Tularosa basin. . . . Folks will piss and moan about it. But they dont have a choice. They ought to be glad to get shut of it" (62). Oliver Lee was wrong on both accounts, it seems. Not only would he not be left alone, something John Grady must also learn, but he has moved to land that people do want. The army's takeover was just another in a long history of land wars that includes the Mexican Revolution, the Lincoln County Wars, and the expansion of White Sands Missile Range.[17] Even before the military takeover of the land, Lee was involved in the Lincoln County wars in New Mexico. This battle over land and water rights "attracted desperados from all parts of New Mexico, Texas, Colorado and south of the Rio Grande" ("White Sands" sect. 3). The most famous participant was, of course, Billy the Kid.

When Mr. Johnson tells John Grady he is listening to "[w]ars and rumors of wars," he echoes our experience reading McCarthy's Border Trilogy. These three novels are replete with allusions and direct references to the wars that dominate the American Southwest and northern Mexico's past. Even those who fail to participate directly in the wars are affected, and the wars themselves are products of earlier wars. This constant revolution of war and violence sits at the heart of the trilogy. More importantly, though, that history affects everyone, without distinction. John Grady and Billy cannot reverse the world by running to Mexico or returning the wolf to her natural habitat. Instead, these conflicts hold within them the sense that what "is constant in history is greed and foolishness and a love of blood and this is a thing that even God—who knows all that can be known—seems powerless to change" (APH 239). John Grady and Billy are left "disinherited by war and war's machinery" (COP 204); yet "[t]he world of our fathers resides within us" (COP 281). The paradoxical country whose technology both alienates and unifies becomes a world within which John Grady Cole can not survive. His knife fight with Eduardo, the challenge made by honking a car horn, is emblematic of the dichotomy of the modern world after World War II.

The kindness Billy encounters as the trilogy ends is subverted by the circular nature of the novel. Billy's room off Betty's kitchen returns us to the opening of *The Crossing*. In a sort of postmodern looping, we are returned to the time of Billy's childhood before he leaves to return the wolf to Mexico. In essence, we return to the Parham family's move out of Grant County (named for Ulysses S. Grant) to Hidalgo County (named for Guadalupe Hidalgo, the father of Mexican independence). It is this looping back to war and war's referents that defines McCarthy's Border Trilogy. The history of the region and those who live there is shrouded in war. John Grady and Billy become men unified by war and violence, and this war creates a map of existence for each person, a map both distinct and overlapped with the maps of others.

Notes

1. Leo Daugherty sees in *Blood Meridian* (1985) the "warrior judge's work to achieve dominion—to be the realized . . . archon of *this* Anaretic planet" (164), and Rick Wallach makes an apt comparison between the martial codes of *Beowulf* and *Blood Meridian*, contending that the "structured social systems that justify and promulgate conflict, represent violence as craft, and conventionalize destructive activity in a craftsmanly way" (113). Robert L. Jarrett, in his *Cormac McCarthy*, argues that the judge "articulates an ideology of conquest that defends unlimited war as the supreme arbiter of the conflict between . . . wills (81), and that *Blood Meridian* "forces its readers . . . to confront the history of violence and the unicultural rhetoric of the antebellum period of Manifest Destiny" (93). War and *Blood Meridian* seem to go hand in hand (or perhaps hand to hand), and while we cannot necessarily call Judge Holden the novel's spokesman, he does do the most speaking about war:

> This is the nature of war, whose stake is at once the game and the authority and the justification. Seen so, war is the truest form of divination. It is the testing of one's will and the will of another within that larger will which because it binds them is therefore forced to select. War is the ultimate game because war is at last a forcing of the unity of existence. War is god. (249)

2. For discussions of history in *Blood Meridian*, see John Sepich, *Notes on Blood Meridian* (Louisville: Bellarmine College P, 1993); and Dana Phillips, "History and the Ugly Facts of Cormac McCarthy's *Blood Meridian*," *American Literature* 68.2 (1996): 433–60.

3. Edwin T. Arnold, in "The Mosaic of McCarthy's Fiction," contends that "the ending of *Blood Meridian* looks forward, the beginning of *Pretty Horses* looks backward, and they meet at a point where text joins text" (19).

4. See Américo Paredes, *"With His Pistol in His Hand": A Border Ballad and its Hero*. Paredes contends, "It was the Treaty of Guadalupe that added the final element to Rio Grande society, a border. The river, which had been a focal point, became a dividing line. Men were expected to consider their relatives and closest neighbors, the people just across the river, as foreigners in a foreign land" (15).

5. Juárez's victory represented "a triumph of anti-colonialism in an age of dominant empires. As such, it anticipated the struggles of the mid-twentieth century in an exemplary manner" (Hamnett xii). The Treaty of Guadalupe Hidalgo separated El Paso del Norte between the two countries. Named after Benito Juárez in 1888, Juárez gained its notoriety during the Revolution of 1910–1920. The city was crucial to Francisco Madero's early volley to overthrow Díaz, providing access to American arms and other goods. See my article, " 'Mexico para los Mexicanos': Revolution, Mexico, and McCarthy's Border Trilogy," in *Myth, Legend, Dust: Critical Responses to Cormac McCarthy*, ed. Rick Wallach (Manchester: Manchester UP, 2000), 249–55, for a more complete discussion of Juárez and the Border Trilogy. See Hamnett's *Juárez* for biographical information on Benito Juárez and his fight for Mexican autonomy from France.

6. There is, of course, historical precedent for the army's purchase of McGovern's ranch. In 1941–42, when the government began the Los Alamos project (the atomic bomb), they intended to lease the land from ranchers. After testing the bombs, fearing radiation fallout, the government offered to buy the ranches or extend the leases. If ranchers did not agree to either of those terms, the army would file a "condemnation suit" ("White Sands" sect. 4). As late as 1982, the Dave McDonald family was still protesting the army's rancher payment program. McDonald contended that the army did not follow the lease agreement. For more information about land issues, see "White Sands Missile Range—A Regional History," and Ferenc M. Szasz, *The Day the Sun Rose Twice: The Story of the Trinity Site Nuclear Explosion, July 16, 1945* (Albuquerque: U of New Mexico P, 1984).

7. Gail Moore Morrison argued in 1992 (before the completion of the trilogy) that the revolutionary tales put John Grady's disappointments in perspective and transform him into a man of action (191). I would agree that the tales are important, but John Grady seems already a man of action in *All the Pretty Horses*. In fact, he would do well to be less action oriented and more thoughtful. These tales also do not, it is revealed in *Cities of the Plain*, teach John Grady much about Mexico. Even after his trip to Mexico in *All the Pretty Horses*, he still asks Billy, "Dont you think if there's anything left of this life it's down there?" (COP 218). Unlike Billy, who seems to understand that Mexico does not provide an answer ("I concluded my business down there a long time ago"), John Grady still sees Mexico as a panacea for the dying ranch life.

8. For extended discussion of the historical Madero and his presence in the trilogy, see my "Whose Story Is It? History and Fiction in Cormac McCarthy's *All the Pretty Horses*," *Southern Quarterly* 36.2 (1998): 103–10. For more comprehensive historical explication of the trilogy's many references to the Mexican Revolution, see my " 'Mexico para los Mexicanos': Revolution,

Mexico, and McCarthy's Border Trilogy," in *Myth, Legend, Dust: Critical Responses to Cormac McCarthy*, ed. Rick Wallach (Manchester: Manchester UP, 2000).

9. See Américo Paredes, *With a Pistol in His Hand*, for the best discussion of *corridos*. See also Merle E. Simmons, *The Mexican Corrido as a Source for Interpretive Study of Modern Mexico* (Bloomington: Indiana UP, 1957), for an impressive collection of *corridos* arranged by subject.

10. Michael D. Carman writes that "[t]he Army's chief of staff and inspector general reported that the entire Army had benefited from the mobilization" (48). See also Clarence C. Clendenen, *Blood on the Border: The United States Army and the Mexican Irregulars* (London: Macmillan, 1969), for a discussion of Pershing's pursuit of Villa and American preparation for World War I. Vanderwood and Samponaro also contend that the U.S. army was ranked behind Germany and Japan at the turn of the century. The American Air Force was in worse shape. Because the government moved the training ground to the Southwest border and trained pilots in Mexico (188), the plane the gypsies move in *The Crossing* (401–02) could be an American Air Force plane used during training.

11. Two of John Grady Cole's uncles "were killed in Puerto Rico in eighteen ninety-eight" (*APH* 7). Most likely, they were killed in the Spanish/American War.

12. I should point out that Holmes' work focuses on the inherent immorality of any war, arguing against philosophers like Augustine who contend that war can be just (morally correct). Holmes quotes those who support war as useful to art and science, including an interesting passage from Adolf Hitler's *Mein Kampf*: "Mankind has grown great in eternal struggle . . . and only in eternal peace does it perish" (qtd. in Holmes 13). Hitler's claim sounds similar to something Judge Holden would say.

13. Luce writes that Billy's damaged heart suggests "his shortcoming is more in courage than in the capacity for understanding" (212). I would add a secondary reading of the scene as a commentary on the absurdity of the army and war. Billy's own logical observation "If I'm goin to die anyways why not use me" (*C* 341) shows both the subtle humor in McCarthy and the silliness of an army that recognizes "You aint got noplace else to go" (*C* 337) but refuses to allow him to enlist.

14. See Gerald D. Nash, *The American West Transformed: The Impact of the Second World War* (Bloomington: Indiana UP, 1985) for a discussion of World War II's impact on the American economy. Obviously, World War I changed the American economy as well: "from a debtor nation [the United States] had been transformed into a creditor nation, with loans to Europe worth $13,000,000,000" (Gray 50).

15. Temple's divorce was reported on page one of the *San Angelo Daily Standard* on December 5, 1949.

16. Slotkin's *Gunfighter Nation* is an excellent look at the myth of the West and its development in film and politics. The passages quoted above discuss John Ford's *Ft. Apache* (1948), a film in which an adult Shirley Temple appears. Interestingly enough, Slotkin points out that between 1947 and 1949 Hollywood produced approximately 150 Westerns, many of them either propaganda/patriotic films or anti-war films detailing transgressions by American armed forces.

17. While Mr. Johnson's story of Oliver Lee and Colonel Fountain seems odd intermixed with army intrusion, his story reinforces the violence of the Southwest, representing "one of the last old-West killings" in the region ("White Sands" sect. 3). Lee, along with William McNew, was accused of "defacing" a brand on a steer belonging to W. A. Irwin of El Paso. Albert J.

Fountain served as a Special Prosecutor for the case. On January 31, 1896, Fountain and his eight-year-old son disappeared while returning home from Las Cruces. The bodies were never recovered. See William Keleher, *The Fabulous Frontier: Twelve New Mexico Items* (Sante Fe, NM: Rydal P, 1945), for a more comprehensive discussion of Lee and Fountain. Interestingly, Fountain fought with Benito Juàrez at one time.

Works Cited

Arnold, Edwin T. "The Mosaic of McCarthy's Fiction." Hall and Wallach 17–23.

Arnold, Edwin T., and Dianne C. Luce, eds. *Perspectives on Cormac McCarthy*. Rev. ed. Jackson: UP of Mississippi, 1999.

Bingham, Arthur. "Syntactic Complexity and Iconicity in Cormac McCarthy's *Blood Meridian*." *Language and Literature* 20 (1995): 19–33.

Carman, Michael Dennis. *United States Customs and the Madero Revolution*. El Paso: Texas Western P, 1976.

Daugherty, Leo. "Gravers False and True: *Blood Meridian* as Gnostic Tragedy." Arnold and Luce 159–74.

Fuentes, Carlos. *The Old Gringo*. Trans. Margaret Sayers Peden and Carlos Fuentes. New York: Farrar, 1985.

Gray, Richard. *American Poetry of the Twentieth Century*. Longman Literature in English Series. Ed. David Carroll and Michael Wheeler. New York: Longman, 1990.

Hall, Wade, and Rick Wallach, eds. *Sacred Violence: A Reader's Companion to Cormac McCarthy*. El Paso: Texas Western P, 1995.

Hamnett, Brian. *Juárez*. New York: Longman, 1994.

Holmes, Robert L. *On War and Morality*. Princeton: Princeton UP, 1989.

Hunt, Alex. "Right and False Suns: Cormac McCarthy's *The Crossing* and the Advent of the Atomic Age." *Southwestern American Literature* 23.2 (1998): 31–37.

Jarrett, Robert L. *Cormac McCarthy*. New York: Twayne, 1997.

Kundera, Milan. *The Art of the Novel*. Trans. Linda Asher. New York: Grove P, 1987.

Luce, Dianne C. "The Road and the Matrix: The World as Tale in *The Crossing*." Arnold and Luce 195–219.

McCarthy, Cormac. *All the Pretty Horses*. New York: Vintage, 1993.

———. *Blood Meridian or The Evening Redness in the West*. New York: Vintage, 1992.

———. *Cities of the Plain*. New York: Vintage, 1999.

———. *The Crossing*. New York: Vintage, 1995.

Morrison, Gail Moore. "*All the Pretty Horses*: John Grady Cole's Expulsion from Paradise." Arnold and Luce 175–94.

Paredes, Américo. *"With His Pistol in His Hand": A Border Ballad and Its Hero*. Austin: U of Texas P, 1958.

Parrish, Tim, and Elizabeth A. Spiller. "A Flute Made of Human Bone: *Blood Meridian* and the Survivors of American History." *Prospects* 23 (1998): 461–81.

Pilkington, Tom. "Fate and Free Will on the American Frontier: Cormac McCarthy's Western Fiction." *Western American Literature* 27.4 (1993): 311–22.

"Porfirio Diaz, Remarkable President of Mexican Republic." *San Angelo Daily Standard* 7 Mar. 1911: A2.

Raat, W. Dirk. "The Mexican Pet and Other Stories: Folklore and History." *Twentieth-Century Mexico*. Ed. W. Dirk Raat and William H. Beezley. Lincoln: U of Nebraska P, 1986. 44–54.

Rutherford, John. "The Novel of the Mexican Revolution." *The Cambridge History of Latin American Literature*. Vol. 2. *The Twentieth Century*. Ed. Roberto González Echevarría and Enrique Pupo-Walker. Cambridge: Cambridge UP, 1996. 213–25.

Slotkin, Richard. *Gunfighter Nation: The Myth of the Frontier in Twentieth-Century America*. New York: Atheneum, 1992.

Vanderwood, Paul J., and Frank N. Samponaro. *Border Fury: A Picture Postcard Record of Mexico's Revolution and U.S. War Preparedness, 1910–1917*. Albuquerque: U of New Mexico P, 1988.

Wallach, Rick. "From *Beowulf* to *Blood Meridian*: Cormac McCarthy's Demystification of the Martial Code." *Southern Quarterly* 36.4 (1998): 113–20.

"White Sands Missile Range—Regional History." *Public Affairs Office White Sands Missile Range*. 8 May 1998. <http://www.army.mil/paopage/Pages/reghis.htm>.

"AS OF SOME SITE WHERE LIFE HAD NOT SUCCEEDED"

Sorrow, Allegory, and Pastoralism in
Cormac McCarthy's Border Trilogy

―――――◆◆◆◆◆―――――

George Guillemin

The pastoralism of Cormac McCarthy's Border Trilogy most likely constitutes the three novels' most overlooked aspect, and this not despite the novels' relative accessibility, but because of it. The simplicity of their quest stories, their generic proximity to the Western, and the conventionality of their plot structures as heroic journeys apparently have caused the novels' complexity to go largely unacknowledged. Interpretations that confine themselves to the realistic façades of *All the Pretty Horses*, *The Crossing*, and *Cities of the Plain* do not necessarily constitute misreadings, yet they ignore the novels' multiple layers and the very essence of their meanings. The argument to follow will therefore concern itself with this stylistic, structural, and semantic complexity and demonstrate in what ways allegory and melancholia join forces in redefining pastoralism within the Border Trilogy.

What can be salvaged from a mimetic reading for the present purpose are certain formal aspects, among them the circumstance that all three of the novels are open-ended, episodic narratives told by an amorphous narrator while the narrative point of view rests with protagonists John Grady Cole and Billy Parham throughout (except for subchapters in *Cities of the Plain* where Magdalena provides the point of view). *All the Pretty Horses* and *The Crossing* are structured as picaresque initiation quests, and the journey motif principally structures their plots. Moreover, it is important to note that despite all realistic detail *The Crossing* goes even further than *All the Pretty Horses* in creating a fabular cosmology at odds with any authentic location. Rather than real-life Mexico, the novel stylizes an anachronistic pastoral world whose distinguishing feature is that it is not the United States, perhaps because American pastoralism needs "as the century ends, an older and darker Arcadia in which to be enacted" (Hass 41). The genre of the Western—rating among "the allegories of the twentieth century" (Owens 230)—is modified in *All the Pretty Horses* and *The Crossing* into tales of inverted frontier life, the frontier being not the beachhead of civilization in a howling wilderness but a last stronghold against civilization. Mythological topoi dramatized include the ones of the dispossessed yeoman and Jeffersonian agrarianism, of the last cowboy and the frontier, of the New Adam and rugged individualism.

The foregoing observations may grace even the most mimetic readings of *All the Pretty Horses*, and this in spite of the fact that myth and the picaro are signs not of mimetical but of stylized, heteroglot writing.[1] As self-contained as the novels' plot level discourse is, we must wonder why the trilogy's patent striation into narrative and meta-narrative by an allegorical discursivity has never been thoroughly analyzed. Among the indications of the existence of a meta-narrative are certain less-than-realistic elements, which neither the plot progression nor the story proper calls for and which run the danger of placing these tales in the category of melodramatic quests. Why, for instance, is Dueña Alfonsa's tale interpolated at great length in *All the Pretty Horses*; the tales of the Mormon, the blind veteran and the *gitano* in *The Crossing*; and those of old Mr. Johnson, the blind maestro and the vagrant in *Cities of the Plain*? Why do the novels refer the reader time and again to the sadness of other characters, such as Alejandra, John Grady's father, Boyd, Magdalena, Mac, Socorro? And why from the start do they immerse John Grady and Billy—at least in the first two novels—in a despondency that is disproportional and atypical for young picaresque heroes, and that exceeds its functionality as an element of romance? Why make the denouement of their stories (returning to the U.S. from Mexico) anticlimactic when the text has more or less prepared for a happy ending of sorts (justice at home)? Why does John Grady's melancholia persist even in the face of auspicious prospects and eventually bring about his death? And why is it that Billy chooses a nomadic, ascetic lifestyle over the recovery of his inheritance or settled life both in *The Crossing* and *Cities of the Plain*?

Along with these incongruities, which are hard to account for within the parameters of the respective plots, certain decontextualized moments and the paratactic quality of the narrator's language refer us to the structural complexities of the novels and the existence of discursive layers. Despite a certain consensus among critics as to the existence of a deeper level of meaning in the case of *All the Pretty Horses*, some hesitancy to define this subsurface semantics seems to linger. In her very early study of the novel, Nancy Kreml goes so far as to show how the author "establishes a transparent style, with little limitation of interpretation, against which he plays a secondary, more highly constrained foregrounded style; further, he uses the elements of the foregrounded style to signal a thematic shift, an intrusion of another level of meaning" (138). Having identified this discursive striation and catalogued its linguistic, structural, and semantic specificities, however, Kreml forgoes drawing any further conclusions. What makes her observation important here, however, is that discursive striation constitutes the hallmark of allegorical texts.

Allegorical discourse is structured by the dialogic tension between a parabolical surface meaning and alterior levels of meaning. Fairy tales, for instance, resemble virtually pure allegories insofar as their surface meanings are complete in themselves and perusable without recourse to their intrinsic meta-narratives. That the story of *All the Pretty Horses* remains perfectly intelligible even if the secondary style is ignored must be considered the secret of the novel's success, because there is reason to believe that many readers may take *All the Pretty Horses* for little more than an unconventional Western. The option of restricting oneself to a superficial reading oblivious to the correlated layers of allegorical meaning is clearly not as available to readers of *Outer Dark*, and this might explain both why *Outer Dark* did *not* sell half a million copies and why McCarthy was so uneasy about the fact that *All the Pretty Horses* did.[2]

The hypotheses ventured here then are, firstly, that a homogenous narrative voice grounds the novels in a profound melancholia and effects something like a "melancholy gaze"; secondly, that this same amorphous narrator conveys the melancholia with the help of an underlying allegorical metadiscourse; and thirdly, that the loss of the pastoral vision of harmony between man and nature constitutes the subject of the narrator's allegoresis. Moreover, the novels seem to reconceptualize literary pastoralism along posthumanist, ecopastoral lines. Although all three of the novels are pastoral tales in their own right, it could be argued that, taken together, they form an overarching structure composed of the three traditional pastoral motifs: escape into the pastoral realm, immersion into pastoral harmony, and purified return to urban civilization. The pastoralism thematized disagrees with literary convention insofar as wilderness is rated as the ideal pastoral space of nature, and insofar as the foregoing motifs are altered into the quest for a pastoral lifestyle (*All the Pretty Horses*), the journey through a pastoral world (*The Crossing*), and the foreclosure of the pastoral vision anywhere (*Cities of the Plain*). Rather than mourning the demise of Arcadian nature, the trilogy's narrative voice develops a deep-seated nostalgia for a pastoral lifestyle closely associated with the southwestern wilderness and clearly recognized as being anachronistic. It modifies traditional pastoralism into an existentially egalitarian commitment of the characters to the materiality of both nature (pastoral landscape) and discourse (storytelling), and this out of a survivalist intentionality which defies the narrator's melancholia at the same time it is inspired by it.

Melancholia

Allegory and melancholia mutually complement each other because both are concerned with what is absent, lost, or part of the past, "the meaning constituted by the allegorical sign" being the repetition "of a previous sign with which it can never coincide, since it is of the essence of this previous sign to be pure anteriority" (De Man 209–10), melancholia being insistent in its grief over a loss that can neither be remembered nor forgotten since the melancholy self is subject to "an Other who precedes and possesses me, and through such possession causes me to be" (Kristeva, *Power* 10). As the subsequent argument will bear out, melancholia and allegory work in sync in the Border Trilogy, one functioning as a semantic conditioner and mood, the other as a literary device for verbalizing it (with a certain feedback to take into account).

Assuming that something like a so-called "melancholy gaze"[3] constitutes the perceptual mode inducing allegoresis, we could start by identifying the curiously emphasized melancholia in the texts. The first of the novels, *All the Pretty Horses*, commences with the wake for John Grady's late grandfather, the opening pages introducing every one of the aesthetic devices listed above (pastoral, allegory, melancholia): there is the death-centered gaze in John Grady's reported words at the deathbed, "That was not sleeping. That was not sleeping" (*APH* 3); there is a pastoral motif in the allegorical invasion of the rural location by the train John Grady watches "boring out of the east like some ribald satellite of the coming sun howling and bellowing" (3); there is a *vanitas*-motif in his outdoor meditation "like a man come to the end of something" (5); a *memento mori*-motif in his contemplation of "an old horseskull" (6). Steeping the text in sadness from its very inception, these stock emblems of allegoresis are offered before the real trouble has even started, and a portentous opening it makes.

By the end of the first novel there will have been sorrow enough to go around. John Grady will have lost the ranch, his father, his lover Alejandra, his mother substitute Abuela. He will find himself estranged from his mother, his former girlfriend, his friend Rawlins, and Don Héctor, the one employer who put faith in him. He will have witnessed Blevins' being killed, and he will have killed a man himself. *The Crossing*, the novel's sequel, continues in this vein because Billy in turn loses both of his parents, his brother, their patrimony (in the form of the horses), and the hope to reintegrate himself into mainstream American life (failure to enlist, failure to return to the parental homestead). At the end of *Cities of the Plain*, John Grady will have lost his wife-to-be and his very life to their suicidal *amour fou*; Billy is reduced to an introverted drifter. Despite the melodramatic hardships on the plot level, however, there is reason to believe that the melancholia felt by the protagonists actually precedes these hardships and is even conducive to their occurrence through a sense of premonition, like a self-fulfilling prophecy. As shall be seen later in more detail, it is in fact the narrator's underlying melancholia that stylizes the narrative events into allegorical tales of fate.

The first novel's inventory of sorrow prompts Gail M. Morrison to observe, "Like virtually all of McCarthy's work to date, *All the Pretty Horses* is permeated with a sense of loss, alienation, deracination and fragmentation" (175). Interestingly, these terms—loss, alienation, deracination, fragmentation—catalogue the very sources of melancholia. When the Dueña in *All the Pretty Horses* suggests that "[b]etween the wish and the thing the world lies waiting" (238), she allegorically situates the melancholic's alienated existence between the loss of the "thing" and the obsessive preoccupation with its impossible restoration. The abject subject's sepia vision, its "melancholy gaze," as it were, thus assumes the function of a universal paradigm:

The abjection of self would be the culminating form of that experience of the subject to which it is revealed that all its objects are based merely on the inaugural *loss* that laid the foundations of its own being. There is nothing like the abjection of self to show that all abjection is in fact recognition of the *want* on which any being, meaning, language, or desire is founded. (Kristeva, *Power* 5)

But how could such a psychic profile be applicable to John Grady's character, or that of Billy? Teenage boys would seem unlikely to set out on pastoral quests across the boundaries of country, culture, and age if they were caught up in the catatonic state of melancholia. What is more, John Grady and Billy, whose persistent misfortune may be exceptional but is hardly atypical for either a picaresque novel or a Western, remain true *picaros* of the cowboy tradition—restless, resourceful, and independent—even after everything that *can* take a turn for the worse has done so. Still, evidence for a melancholy state of mind surfaces on the very first pages of the first novel, and the problem at the bottom of the trilogy's melancholia is summed up in the statement that John Grady "felt wholly alien to the world although he loved it still" (*APH* 282). The passage goes on to expand John Grady's grief over having lost Alejandra into an allegorization of the melancholic's dilemma of being caught between compulsive thanatopsis and a simultaneous attachment to the material world:

He thought that in the beauty of the world were hid a secret. He thought the world's heart beat at some terrible cost and that the world's pain and its beauty moved in a

98 Sorrow, Allegory, and Pastoralism

relationship of diverging equity and that in this headlong deficit the blood of multitudes might ultimately be exacted for the vision of a single flower. (282)

Other instances reflecting on the protagonists' alienation read almost like the clinical symptoms of melancholia, such as the following:

He felt something cold and soulless enter him like another being and he imagined that it smiled malignly and he had no reason to believe that it would ever leave. (APH 254)

He lifted his face and stood by the roadside and his thoughts were that other than wind and rain nothing would ever come again to touch him out of that estrangement that was the world. Not in love, not in enmity. The bonds that fixed him in the world had become rigid. Where he moved the world moved also and he could never approach it and he could never escape it. He sat in the roadside weeds in the rain and wept. (C 279).

When he rode into the yard it was raining lightly and he could see them all at supper through the rainbleared glass of the kitchen window.... He thought it was like seeing these people in some other time before he'd ever come to the ranch. Or they were like people in some other house of whose lives and histories he knew nothing. Mostly they all just seemed to be waiting for things to be a way they'd never be again. (COP 233–34)

At the risk of stating the obvious, we must acknowledge that the meditations ascribed to the protagonists' points of view in these passages are clad in rhetoric beyond their intellectual scope (for instance, a phrase like "diverging equity"). If nothing else, this observation encourages us to note the discrepancy between the sober chronicling of dynamic action and the somber voice transmitting static, melancholy thought. Although the surface discourse is realistic and disinterested enough to give a plausible account of John Grady's or Billy's outer progress, the true commitment of the narrative is obviously to the non-mimetic meta-discourse on their inner states. In fact, the plot progression seems to be principally motivated by the desire to contextualize the contents of the secondary discursive strain which is inherently melancholy, allegorical, and therefore neither mimetic nor disinterested. But if narration of the journey from the protagonists' point of view serves essentially to set the stage for a meta-discourse beyond their intellectual scope, we have to localize this meta-discourse on the narrational plane and conclude that the melancholia permeating the texts is in fact projected onto protagonists, landscape, and rhetoric all. So while it is safe to say that John Grady's and Billy's alienation is captured in the meta-narrative, it is even more appropriate to say inversely that the melancholia of the meta-narrative—which is the narrator's—couches itself in the allegorical enactment of the boys' alienated existence.

What is realized in turn on the level of the meta-narrative (and perhaps by the narrators of the interpolated tales too, but not on the plot level) is the therapeutic effect of melancholy discourse to restore a sense of the lost self through the very performance of its discursive lamentation: telling one's tale of rue becomes an antidote against one's very ruefulness. Melancholy allegoresis reveals the affirmative flipside to its own sorrow whenever the allegorization of unspeakable loss "endows the lost signifier with a signifying pleasure, a resurrectional jubilation even to the stone and corpse, by asserting itself as coextensive with the subjective experience of a named melancholia—of melancholy jouissance" (Kristeva, *Sun* 102). Rather than merely presaging the end of John Grady, the Dueña's projection that "[t]hose whom life does not cure death will" (*APH* 238) contains this ambiguous nature of allegory. It suggests that, while nothing will terminate delusion and melancholia except either death itself or the allegorical *naming* of death, the naming, storytelling option does constitute a viable alternative. Because it procures an identity for the melancholy subject by lending a voice to speechless sorrow, the death-centered vision of allegory generates a mode of discursive survival and opens onto a restored vitality of sorts. It is in this sense that the "product of the corpse, seen from the point of death, is life" (Benjamin, *Ursprung* 194).[4]

Allegory

Among the various passages in *All the Pretty Horses* that combine melancholy mood with allegorical mode, the following instance reads virtually like a classic *vanitas*-motif of the lone watcher on the hill:

He slept that night in a field far from any town. He built no fire. He lay listening to the horse crop the grass at his stakerope and he listened to the wind in the emptiness and watched stars trace the arc of the hemisphere and die in the darkness at the edge of the world and as he lay there the agony in his heart was like a stake. (256)

Instances such as this one, while containing enough personal sorrow to account for the textual melancholia, bespeak a rhetorical excessiveness in their reiteration of sorrow that transcends the personal narratives and identifies this melancholia as meta-narrational. As said earlier, it is in fact the narrator's underlying melancholia that stylizes the narratives and their events into allegorical tales of fate. The foregoing conclusion that the protagonists' portraiture is compromised by their infusion with the melancholia of the meta-narrative is corroborated by the texts' inclusion of other saturnine figures besides them, such as John Grady's father, Alejandra, and the Dueña Alfonsa in *All the Pretty Horses*; such as Boyd, the hermit, the blind man, the *gitano* in *The Crossing*; and such as Magdalena, Mac, old Mr. Johnson and Socorro in *Cities of the Plain*.

Yet the meta-narrational melancholia is moreover suggested by recurrent emblems of pastoral loss that occur quasi-independently of the protagonists' sorrow. One of these emblems, in *All the Pretty Horses*, is the "lost nation" of the Comanches which John Grady envisions as "nation and ghost of nation passing in a soft chorale across that mineral waste to darkness bearing lost to all history and all remembrance like a grail the sum of their secular and transitory and violent lives" (5). Passages of this sort—of which there are many in the trilogy—form pure allegories of the pastoral vision lost. Even within the context of the grief on the plot level they seem excessive, and they would make the texts appear hopelessly melodramatic were they read in any way other than allegorically. For the melancholy narrator, however, they are the one means to enunciate his pastoral nostalgia at all. To say it once more, melancholia (both as a semantic conditioner and psychoanalytical symptom) and allegory complement each other. In the present context, Jacques Lacan's dictum that "the unconscious is structured in the most radical way like a language" (234) can arguably be rephrased to state that the melancholy unconscious is structured in the most radical way like allegorical discourse, for allegories—while signifying the reiterated absence-qua-presence of anterior allegories—always also signify ultimate absence, the nothingness or void of death itself. It is in truth the deferred enunciation of the inenunciable meaning of death that renders allegory the privileged discursive vehicle for melancholia. Kristeva identifies this significatory potential of allegory "as lavishness of that which *no longer is*, but which regains for myself a higher meaning because I am able to remake nothingness" (*Sun* 99).

But Kristeva's words on allegory's higher meaning that remakes nothingness capture another aspect of allegory which will be instrumental in our reading of the Border Trilogy. Kristeva in effect refers us to the surplus meaning of allegory, the semantic excess characterizing its signifying of ultimately inenunciable meaning, such as the meaning of loss. Allegory's negative aspect of continuously deferring meaning to typological antecedents is compensated by the automatic ordering of these back references into syntagmatic sequence. While reiterating his internal predicament, the melancholic's allegorical discourse always also aligns the external world and its history with his melancholy gaze, which in an act of discursive self-empowerment subordinates the outer macrocosm to the inner microcosm of his stunted self.

As a case in point, Billy perceives his own biography in a moment of dejection quasi-posthumously, as a tale already told:

> He seemed to himself a person with no prior life. As if he had died in some way years ago and was ever after some other being who had no history, who had no ponderable life to come. (C 382)

His impression of being a relict from the past is confirmed by the reaction of other people when he passes on horseback through the town of Deming, after returning from his second trip to Mexico (although this specific articulation of their reaction originates, of course, with the narrative voice):

> The few cars that passed gave him all the berth that narrow road afforded and the people looked back at him through the rolling dust as if he were a thing wholly alien in that landscape. Something from an older time of which they'd only heard. Something of which they'd read. (334)

Similarly, John Grady's view of his own past after losing Alejandra becomes melancholy and allegorically selective: "He saw very clearly how all his life led only to this moment and all after led nowhere at all" (APH 254). John Grady's observation harks back to the Dueña's notion of predetermined fate and her consequent lack of "sympathy with people to whom things happen. It may be that their luck is bad, but is that to count in their favor?" (240). As will become clearer in the course of the argument, the notion of fate—

which is allegorical in its prescriptive dynamics—is shared by characters, intratextual storytellers, and the narrative voice itself. The Dueña's view of history, for one, is subsumed under the narrativity of the amorphous narrator and serves primarily to lend to the narrative perspective the authority of alleged historical truth (as it places the events of the main narrative in intertextual sequence with the historical account).[5]

Benjamin suggests that the (allegorizing) storyteller reads personal biographies as well as history in a retrospective manner because "death is the sanction of everything the storyteller can report. From death he has borrowed his authority" (Benjamin, *Illuminationen* 396).[6] He illustrates his proposition by writing that "a man . . . who died at thirty-five will appear to *remembrance* at every point of his life as the man who dies at the age of thirty-five" (402). And indeed, what with its tales, parables, dreams, and general melancholia of past things remembered, the trilogy seems to presuppose death as the semantic structuring principle par excellence. Stories are grounded in death insofar as their dynamic remembrance bases itself on the static, no longer dynamic, image of their subject as perceived in moments past. The erstwhile agency of the story's subject becomes the agency of the storyteller so that it is not except posthumously that "the lamented dead person begins to resemble himself" (Blanchot 82). What this means is exemplified by a character in *The Crossing* who has internalized the retrospective mode of remembrance so thoroughly that he inadvertently reverses its order into the compelling logic of people anticipating their specific ends:

He said that moreover it could not be otherwise that men's ends are dictated at their birth and that they will seek their deaths in the face of every obstacle. (379)

Another case in point is Billy's sense of self in the following passage:

He passed back north through the small mud hamlets of the mesa, through Alamo and Galeana, settlements through which he'd passed before and where his return was remarked upon by the poblanos so that his own journeying began to take upon itself the shape of a tale. (331)

Like a corpse (at the same time no longer and still the person remembered), stories as well as visual images are inherently allegorical in their references to death and mortality, and hence inherently melancholy. Even more than stories, photographs—like those collected by the *gitano*'s father in *The*

Crossing—remember people from the point of death, even if their deaths have not been consummated. Seen so, stories and photographs become straight allegories of the passage of time and of deaths foretold rather than authentic remembrances, as the following passage suggests:

> Every representation was an idol. Every likeness a heresy. In their images they had thought to find some small immortality but oblivion cannot be appeased. (C 413)

Seen as *memento mori* images, stories and pictures capture "the anterior future that the past bequeaths to the present" (Schleifer 330), and they may thus inspire the notion "that there is no order in the world save that which death has put there" (C 45).

In order to flesh out this supposition regarding the nature of the narrator's retrospective allegorization even of present events—and of his usurpation of the protagonist's point of view—let us take a look at the scene in *All the Pretty Horses* where John Grady witnesses the photo session of a newly-wed couple:

> ... they stood on the steps for their photograph to be taken and in their antique formalwear posed there in front of the church they already had the look of old photos. In the sepia monochrome of a rainy day in that lost village they'd grown old instantly. (284)

Clearly, the melancholy gaze that reads moribundity into a wedding scene, of all moments, emanates from the amorphous narrator, not John Grady, who even as he functions as perceptual medium cannot possibly testify to the "sepia monochrome" quality of the photos right after they have been taken. Having seen not the picture, but only the scene it records, John Grady cannot engage in such a nostalgic reflection, whereas the narrator's plaintive eye translates the photographic *re*-presentation into a quasi-posthumous recollection of lives that *will have* passed.

Moreover, the photo scene indicates that not only the protagonist's perceptual autonomy is compromised by its subjection to the narrator's melancholy allegoresis, but the overall representation of the material world and its history as well. The appropriation of John Grady's sorrowful state by the narrative point of view, and the persistence of his sorrows—for him unrelieved by the allegorical naming of it—beyond the first novel's ending and up to his death in the third, indicate that the trilogy is not concerned with the allegorization of personal grief alone, even as it does make John Grady—more than Billy—the principal carrier of it. Rather, the characters' melancholy tales read as allegorical pieces in a mosaic, an overall allegory which ultimately serves to contextualize pastoral nostalgia with a melancholy view of history. As the following passage testifies, this observation identifies an essential feature of allegory:

Allegorical repetition—the relationships among signs in a typological allegorical narrative—is a temporal process assuming difference as well as resemblance but denying the possibility of any complete identification. The language of allegory is then purely figurative; it is not based upon perception. (Madsen 139)

As a result of being placed in allegorical sequence, stylization of things past causes these very memories to become depersonalized and generic. Thus, the legend of Boyd as retold in the *corrido*, the song Billy keeps hearing throughout his third trip to Mexico, represents but a variation on the theme of the revolutionary hero:

It tells what it wishes to tell. It tells what makes the story run. The corrido is the poor man's history. It does not owe its allegiance to the truths of history but to the truths of men. It tells the tale of that solitary man who is all men. (C 386)

Projecting a static picture of history, "allegory superinduces a vertical or paradigmatic reading of correspondences upon a horizontal or syntagmatic chain of events" (Owens 208). To read reality and history alike as a chronicle of sequential events implies a shift away from a descriptive to a prescriptive mode of discourse. While being dramatized (and titled) as spatial crossings of borders between societies, John Grady's and Billy's quests resemble in effect journeys through time (from mid-twentieth century to ever more antiquated societal structures). The various *vanitas*-moments at the beginning of *All the Pretty Horses* (Native Americans, horse skull, John Grady's disproportional sorrow) seem incongruous less because they are out of place, but because they are out of time, so to speak. They make perfect sense, however, within the context of the allegorical concept of history as an atemporal correspondence of past with present.

Unlike standard historiography, which approaches the historical record with a plethora of models and methods, the allegorical chronicle fails to make the distinction between history and myth, seeing history not as an evolutionary progress involving cause and effect but as recurrent enactments of the ever same drama whose individual events are highlighted as exemplary moments within the set course of history.[7] The chronicler makes it his task to place the course of history in line with a metaphysical truth, history for him being "essential only in the stages of its decay" (Benjamin, *Ursprung* 145). We find both of these alternative concepts in the rival versions of the Rochas' family history in *All the Pretty Horses*. Whereas Don Héctor's account (144–46) takes an historiographical approach, an allegorical interpretation defines the Dueña's chronicling of history and its logic:

For me the world has always been more of a puppet show. But when one looks behind the curtain and traces the strings upward he finds they terminate in the hands of yet other puppets, themselves with their own strings which trace upward in turn, and so on. In my own life I saw these strings whose origins were endless enact the deaths of great men in violence and madness. (231)

By structuring history as a ritual succession of stops and starts—a strategy which finds its parallel in the parataxis and elision of allegorical discourse—the allegorist's interpretation of history reflects his melancholy desire to read a metaphysical continuity into human existence that defies its transitory and discontinuous nature. In other words, "the insight into the transience of things, and the concern to rescue them for eternity, is one of the strongest motives in allegory" (Benjamin, *Ursprung* 199). For if allegory concerns itself with typological "projection—either spatial or temporal or both—of structure as sequence" (Owens 207), the allegorist can self-consciously instrumentalize it like a heuristic device not only to highlight past and presence according to his own melancholy memory, but also to force future events into line with that memory. An example of such an arbitrarily-imposed typology is given in the fatalism grounding the Dueña's father's "great sense of the connectedness of things" and in the parable he uses to elaborate it:

He claimed that the responsibility for a decision could never be abandoned to a blind agency but could only be relegated to human decisions more and more remote from their consequences. The example he gave was of a tossed coin that was at one time a slug in a mint and of the coiner who took that slug from the tray and placed it in the die in one of two ways and from whose act all else followed, cara y cruz [face and reverse]. No matter through whatever turnings nor how many of them. Till our turn comes at last and our turn passes. (*APH* 230–31)

To the melancholy gaze, the past—yet another allegory—presents itself primarily as distance to its inception, its consummation, and the present. In general, "allegory designates primarily a distance in relation to its own origin, and, renouncing the nostalgia and the desire to coincide, it establishes its language in the void of this temporal difference" (De Man 210). In allegory the past functions as a temporally-removed preview of the present (which in this sense is already part of the past), and so allegory is essentially catastrophic because it subjects to its retrospection even those deaths that have not yet occurred (i.e., the readers' deaths).

The past carries with it a secret index by which it is referred to redemption. Are not we ourselves grazed by a breath of the air that surrounded those previous? do not the voices to which we lend our ears contain an echo of those now silent? do the women we court not have sisters who did not live to know them? If this is so, then there is a secret agreement between past generations and ours. Then our coming was expected on earth. (Benjamin, *Illuminationen* 251–52)

Seen this way, it is the ritual impetus of storytelling—which is inherently allegorical—that turns the discontinuity of human lives (temporality) into continuity (immortality) through an incremental (discontinuous) and spiral (continuous) rhythm of remembrance: each generation passing on an update of the inherited legacy of stories. An example of such generational remembering is given in the collective memory of a truly pastoral culture in *The Crossing*:

The Tarahumara had watered here a thousand years and a good deal of what could be seen in the world had passed this way. Armored Spaniards and hunters and trappers and grandees and their women and slaves and fugitives and armies and revolutions and the dead and the dying. And all that was seen was told and all that was told remembered. (192)

Memory is preserved here because the Tarahumaras' is an oral culture, given to storytelling. A negative textual instant, where memory fails to be passed on because it has taken the form of pictures rather than stories, is also given in *The Crossing*:

These likenesses had value only to the living who had known them and with the passage of years of such there were none. . . . What he came to see was that as the kinfolk in their fading stills could have no value save in another's heart so it was with that heart also in another's in a terrible and endless attrition and of any other value there was none. (412–13)

Proceeding in a cumulative rather than an ordering manner, the melancholy gaze of allegory translates historical progression into a ritual process. The *vaqueros*' tales "of the cattle and the horses and the young wild mares in their season and of a wedding in La Vega and a death at Víbora" (*APH* 227) are not inherently melancholy but are rendered melancholy by the implication of storyteller and audience as anticipated parts in the endless succession of tales (and by the paratactic sentence structure of their re-presentation in the novel). They become reiterations of other, identical tales, allegories of the forever incomplete, fragmentary, ruinous; and "ruins thus stand for history as an irreversible process of dissolution and decay, a progressive distancing from origin" (Owens 206). That the narrative voice of the trilogy does in fact perceive history as a chronicle of variations of parallel tales of sorrow is suggested by the regular interpolation of tales: such as that of the Dueña in *All the Pretty Horses*; the tales of the Mormon, the blind veteran, and the *gitano* in *The Crossing*; and those of old Mr. Johnson, the blind maestro and the vagrant in *Cities of the Plain*, all of which tales are intrinsically melancholy. The human lives represented are ultimately nothing more nor less than discourse anthologized within the chronicle of a world that is itself allegorical text:

For this world also which seems to us a thing of stone and flower and blood is not a thing at all but is a tale. And all in it is a tale and each tale the sum of all lesser tales and yet these also are the selfsame tale and contain as well all else within them. So everything is necessary. Every least thing. (C 143)

As circumscribed in this quote, typological history signifies nothing so much as anteriority itself, and in the pastoralism of the trilogy the nostalgia for forever anterior and lost pastoral origins becomes the vanishing point of its allegoresis and melancholia both: an imaginary wound that will not heal and keeps calling for rhetorical ointment. Ultimately, the protagonists have to be read as allegorical agents, re-enacting the old new tale of pastoral quest and failure. And ultimately, it is loss itself, of course, that functions as the sole referent of allegory in the trilogy because other objects lost besides the pastoral way of life are mourned: lovers, family, friends or animals

108 Sorrow, Allegory, and Pastoralism

gone. This general sense of loss is affirmed by old Mr. Johnson's answer to John Grady's question of what the hardest lesson in life might be:

I dont know. Maybe it's just that when things are gone they're gone. They aint comin back. (COP 126)

As shall be seen, versions of the pastoral old and new are placed in a typological sequence that terminates in the ever same melancholia in the Border Trilogy.

Pastoralism

Allegory in general contains instructions for its own interpretation as well as "the ideological value which is attached to interpretation as a means of perceiving some ideal or absolute value manifest in an interpreted world" (Madsen 144). As argued, the patent striation of the trilogy into narration of plot action on the one hand and allegorical meta-narratives on the other serves to situate a melancholia felt over the loss of the pastoral vision, entirely in keeping with pastoral convention. What complicates the matter is that the trilogy simultaneously uses its allegorical cosmology to develop an alternative pastoral vision out of traditional pastoralism by replacing cultivated nature with wilderness as the pastoral ideal. From Arthur Ownby's incarceration in *The Orchard Keeper*, to the foreclosure on Lester Ballard's farm in *Child of God*, to the protagonists' escapist endeavors in Mexico in the Border Trilogy, McCarthy's work has time and again addressed the datedness of the traditional pastoral cosmology at the same time as it keeps invoking it. It is by including, rather than denying, the earlier cosmologies and placing them in sequence that the trilogy creates the conditions for rewriting them as well as for infusing the rewritten cosmology with a new pastoral ethos.

Thus, what is retained from traditional pastoralism is, for one thing, the utopian quest for a simpler way of life in nature, and perhaps the joint reading of nature, ruin, and corpse as allegories of loss: "if nature is always already moribund, then it is always already allegorical as well" (Benjamin, *Ursprung* 145). The gist of McCarthy's pastoralism may well be captured in the traditionally pastoral and traditionally melancholy epigraph of *Et In*

Arcadia Ego, engraved into Judge Holden's rifle (BM 125): "I, death, am also in Arcadia." Moreover, the congruence between the implied narrator's and the protagonist's perspective is far from new but a familiar feature of pastoral allegory:

> ... there is a complicated interaction between events, the implications of the familiar symbolic landscape, and the protagonist's shifting, all but irremediably ambivalent state of mind. The work of mediation enacted in the "plot" is even more strenuously undertaken within the protagonist's mind. (Marx 56)

Morrison could not be more right when writing, "Landscape remains, in *All the Pretty Horses*, a central character and a characterizing agent" (178), for both John Grady and the land figure as allegorical agents in the elaboration of the overarching pastoral theme, however innovative or traditional the latter may be.

What is altered in McCarthy's pastoralism is that landscape and characters share their fate (the negative materiality of death) and status (the positive materiality of life) as existential equals due to the erasure of all previous utopian pastoral hopes. Nature in McCarthy's pastoralism still comes across as containing allegorical meaning but without any promise of transcendence, as being "cosmic without being metaphysical" (Phillips 447). While the romantic view of the world and its "[s]alvation history, which understands the natural world and man's travails in it as symbols of the spirit, has long since been played out" (Phillips 448), the romantic turn toward material nature is intensified into a literally materialist world view in exclusion of all dramatic tension between human characters and natural setting. In fact, the trilogy establishes a post-humanist approach in the sense that it thinks of the cosmos in terms of a non-anthropocentric materialism. This concept is elucidated in the penultimate scene of *All the Pretty Horses* when John Grady's view of the cosmos in a moment of nearly total abjection at Abuela's grave includes nature in a meditation on the world's indifference and obliviousness to human categories of meaning such as age, race, class, gender, and life itself:

> ... for a moment he held out his hands as if to steady himself or as if to bless the ground there or perhaps as if to slow the world that was rushing away and seemed to care nothing for the old or the young or rich or poor or dark or pale or he or she.

Nothing for their struggles, nothing for their names. Nothing for the living or the dead. (APH 301)

Voiding nature of all humanly-inferred cognition and agency, the narrative perspective, which speaks through John Grady's point of view here, erases traditional models of pastoral harmony which subject nature to man's humanizing order. The melancholy gaze, whose sole structuring principle is the reiteration of loss, thereby introduces an egalitarian model of pastoral harmony that grounds itself in the recognition that all things human and non-human are implicated in the universal experience of loss.

That pastoralism then as now defines itself primarily as a compositional literary mode is indicated by the fact that, although the trilogy resolves the tension between retrospective pastoral nostalgia and a forward-looking ecopastoral ideology, it retains the distinctive elements of the pastoral mode. Before we identify the specific aspects of pastoralism in the trilogy, the term "pastoral" calls for a definition, and we shall borrow it from an ecocritical source:

"Pastoral" is used in an extended sense, familiar to Americanists, to refer not to the specific set of obsolescent conventions of the eclogue tradition, but to all literature—poetry or prose, fiction or nonfiction—that celebrates the ethos of nature/rurality over against the ethos of the town or city. This domain includes for present purposes all degrees of rusticity from farm to wilderness. (Buell 23)

In order to define the pastoral elements in the Border Trilogy, let us follow the order of "relatively constant features of pastoralism" listed by Leo Marx as "the intricate interplay between the tripartite topography (urban, middle, wild); the narrative or conceptual structure; and the sequence of the protagonist's or speaker's states of mind and feeling" (54). John Grady's transition from different states of nature is easy to trace in *All the Pretty Horses*, and equally easy to trace are his preferences. During his single visit to the city to watch his mother perform at the San Antonio theater, he manages to dispel his fear that he may have underrated the essence and protocol of urban culture. Having naïvely expected an alternative existential paradigm rather than mere amusement, his wariness of city life is only heightened when he finds new meaning neither in the theater as a cultural institution nor in the representation of that culture by the play's microcosm:

He'd the notion that there would be something in the story itself to tell him about the way the world was or was becoming but there was not. There was nothing in it at all. (21)

John Grady's trip to San Antonio serves merely to confirm his preconceptions about the realm of the city, and so it is without surprise, regret, or delay that he heads straight back to the ancestral ranch. Eluding the ranch's imminent sale, he and his friend Rawlins literally cross the border into a *terra incognita*, as suggested by the oil company map they use, which shows "roads and rivers and towns on the American side of the map as far south as the Rio Grande and beyond that all was white" (34). The place they come to after some hardship is a pastoral paradise of the traditional cut, an almost mythical *locus amoenus*:

The Hacienda de Nuestra Señora de la Purísima Concepción was a ranch of eleven thousand hectares situated along the edge of the Bolsón de Cuatro Ciénegas in the state of Coahuila. The western sections ran into the Sierra de Anteojo to elevations of nine thousand feet but south and east the ranch occupied part of the broad barrial or basin floor of the bolsón and was well watered with natural springs and clear streams and dotted with marshes and shallow lakes or lagunas. In the lakes and in the streams were species of fish not known elsewhere on earth and birds and lizards and other forms of life as well all long relict here for the desert stretched away on every side. (97)

The closing line of the quote introduces the third topological variety at issue here, which is wilderness, and consequently we will dispense with a third quote to document the textual occurrence of it. After all, desert constitutes the prevailing landscape for large tracts of the entire trilogy.

Instead, let us move on to those narrative elements clearly supporting a pastoral reading of the novels. To summarize the general line of Marx's argument, the narrative structure of the pastoral is closely tied to the protagonist's (more or less picaresque) progress through the three consecutive stages of disengagement, quest, and reintegration. The typical pastoral plot therefore narrates how the hero departs from social circumstances too constraining, complex, or hierarchical, how he seeks out a simpler, independent way of life either among country people or alone, and how he eventually comes to terms with the established order and returns to civilization, having matured in the process (due to either enlightenment or disillusion). Marx focuses on three kinds of recurrent episodes that typify both the pastoral plot and the pastoral protagonist, one of these episodes being the "moment when the protagonist enjoys a sense of ecstatic fulfillment, a feeling of calm selfhood and integration with his or her surroundings sometimes including a lover or companion" (56). Down to the details of lover (Alejandra) and companion (Rawlins), the definition matches exactly John Grady's situation at the *hacienda* before falling into disgrace and being arrested. The fulfillment in his new profession of breaking in and breeding wild mustangs is verbalized in the monologues he addresses to the stallion "in spanish in phrases almost biblical repeating again and again the strictures of a yet untabled law. Soy comandante de las yeguas, he would say, yo y yo sólo" (128; I am the commander of the mares . . . I and I alone). This state of pastoral bliss is unparalleled in *The Crossing* and *Cities of the Plain*, and unsurprisingly Mexico retains its air of a pastoral dreamworld for John Grady only. Even years later, when working as a ranch hand on Mac McGovern's ranch, John Grady fantasizes about returning to live there. His idea that "if there's anything left of this life it's down there" prompts Billy to observe "I damn sure dont know what Mexico is. I think it's in your head" (COP 218). Billy's experiment with pastoral escape fails to produce anything as romantic as John Grady's life at the *hacienda* but rather marks the beginning of a nomadic lifestyle that continues through the end of the trilogy altogether, and it is in the self-subsistent life of the nomad that Billy finds pastoral sustenance.

The moment consummating the pastoral dream traditionally precipitates a contrary, anti-climactic experience of the pastoral hero, designed to impel the latter to retrace his steps and reconsider his place in nature:

Another decisive moment is the protagonist's thrilling, tonic, but often traumatic and finally chastening encounter with wildness: some aspect, external or internal, of unmodified, intractable, seemingly hostile nature. The hero may meet a wild beast, a cannibal, a savage; in a storm or on a mountaintop he may be made aware of the brutal indifference and immensity of Not-Man. In these texts wildness also has its psychic counterpart: the potential loss of impulse control. The upshot of this episode, accordingly, also is to set limits to the initial, centrifugal impulse. To keep going in the direction of unmodified nature, the hero senses, is to risk another, more dire loss of selfhood: a merging with the nonhuman whose ultimate form is death. (Marx 57)

The entire third chapter of *All the Pretty Horses* arguably represents this stage of the pastoral narrative. John Grady's dream of a bucolic life at the *hacienda*—working with horses with his best friend, finding the friendship of the simple rustic ranch hands, riding a full-blooded stallion through a romantic landscape, romancing the *hacendado*'s daughter—suffers a first disillusionment when he is arrested, is shattered during his imprisonment, and finds its seemingly final destruction in the death of the hired assassin he kills in self-defense there. Rather than finding his way back into the society he has quit (as Marx's model would suggest) and returning with Rawlins to Texas, however, John Grady crosses into his home country as if trespassing, and he does so solely in order to restore Blevins' horse to its rightful owner. At least in this first installment of the trilogy he deviates markedly from the conventional course outlined by Marx insofar as he does not back away from the brutal indifference of Not-Man, does not check his pastoral impulse, but commits himself to it for good when retracing his steps back into the wilderness, "into the darkening land, the world to come" (302). As his meditation at Abuela's grave on the world's indifference exemplifies, he succumbs fully to the moment of truth and takes his cue from its alienating aspect rather than from Rawlins' attempt at resocializing him. But it is for the narrator as much as for John Grady that the Dueña's pessimistic parable on the idealist's limbo between fact and fiction speaks true:

In the end we all come to be cured of our sentiments. Those whom life does not cure death will. The world is quite ruthless in selecting between the dream and the reality, even where we will not. Between the wish and the thing the world lies waiting. (238)

That the alienating impulse within the pastoral context emanates less from the wildness of nature itself than from the ruthlessness of humans becomes even clearer in *The Crossing*, for here it is wilderness incarnate in the wolf, and not a quest for a supposedly more pastoral territory, that inspires the protagonist's journey. Nowhere does the shift of the ideal pastoral space from that of the cultivated landscape to that of untouched wilderness become more apparent than in the emblem of the wolf, an emblem that is picked up again in *Cities of the Plain*.[8] But the very fact that the wolf herself needs protection because the wildness she represents is threatened by the even more ferocious order of human civilization signals the imminent loss of even this latter-day pastoral ideal.

Before we consider the role of John Grady and Billy as pastoral protagonists, let us consider a third type of pastoral episode, one instrumental in enhancing their pastoral impulse while transforming them into ecopastoral heroes. Quintessential for Marx's argument, because he introduces it as being inherently American and having no precedent in classic pastoral literature, is the episode of the pastoral realm's being abruptly invaded by "a machine or some other manifest token of the dynamism of modern industrial society" (57). Marx considers this literary phenomenon, alluded to by his previous book title *The Machine in the Garden* (1964), essential for understanding the ideological implications of contemporary pastoralism:

> What this episode accomplishes, indeed, is to invert the "representative event" of the dominant, progressive ideology. So far from being an occasion for an optimistic vision of history, the sudden intrusion of the machine upon the native landscape evokes feelings of dislocation and anxiety. It reactivates the alienation that had initially provoked the pastoral impulse. (57)

To illustrate his point regarding the machine, Marx argues that "[n]o image caught the mood better than the familiar Currier and Ives prints of locomotives hurtling across the western prairie" (37), and so it may not be incidental that in the very opening scene of *All the Pretty Horses* we find John Grady watching a train in what constitutes in effect an allegory of industrial invasion of pastoral space:

> It came boring out of the east like some ribald satellite of the coming sun howling and bellowing in the distance and the long light of the headlamp running through the tangled mesquite brakes and creating out of the night the endless fenceline down the dead straight right of way and sucking it back again wire and post mile on mile into the darkness after where the boilersmoke disbanded slowly along the faint new horizon and the sound came lagging and he stood still holding his hat in his hands in the passing groundshudder watching it till it was gone. (3–4)

Other instances of machines entering pastoral environments in the trilogy include the train that whisks Alejandra away forever, her father's airplane which connects the pastoral realm of the *hacienda* with the metropolitan energy field of Mexico City, the explosion of the atomic bomb at the end of *The Crossing*, and the Army's takeover not just of Mac's ranch but of the entire valley in *Cities of the Plain*. Seen in the light of this third episodic type, John Grady and Billy's action is marked less by deviation from the parameters of the American pastoral, than by a continuation of it. What is more, the melancholia, the nostalgic view of history, and the allegorical impulse that inform the narrative point of view finally fall into place, for they function as the discursive symptoms of the pastoral alienation Marx associates with the machine's interruption of the idyll. Yet whereas for Marx the pastoral protagonist yields to the sensibility of restoring himself to society when "the new machine technology is made to seem the irreversible motive force of history itself" (57), the trilogy cultivates images of the machine in the garden from the start in order to allegorize the pastoral protagonist's alienation and melancholia as terminal and as tied to the alienation and melancholia of nature itself. Relevant moments, which are to be found throughout the novels, are usually presented within melancholy contexts. What qualifies the melancholia and alienation of this third type of episode as terminal and irremediable in these texts is a rather novel aspect which renders the escapist intentionality of pastoralism itself obsolete:

> The machine-in-the-landscape episode marks the emergence of a distinctive industrial age variant of pastoralism. In the symbolic topography that had previously lent expression to that ancient world view, the locus of power, wealth, hierarchy, sophistication—of the complex world—had been fixed in space . . . : the realm of urbane social life here, the countryside (and wilderness) there. But the new machine power figured forth a fundamental transformation in relations between society and nature. . . . Potential invaders of all sectors of the environment, the forces represented by the new technology necessarily blur (if they do not erase) the immemorial boundary lines between city, countryside, and wilderness. By threatening to take dominion everywhere, they intensify—at times to the point of apocalyptic stridency—the dissonance that pastoralism always had generated at the junction of civilization and nature. (Marx 58)

The machine's allegorical transgression and obliteration of boundaries in American pastoralism gives us a pretty good idea of why John Grady finds no sustenance in Rawlins' observation that rural Texas "is still good country," for John Grady is forced to admit "it aint my country," explaining vaguely, "I dont know what happens to country" (*APH* 299). Insofar as in the larger context of the trilogy *Cities of the Plain* actually shows that the machine has come to stay in the garden in a copresence of urbanized with pastoral space (the Army owns the land, cowboys drive around in trucks), Robert Jarrett could not have been more correct when he wrote, before the publication of *Cities of the Plain*, that "As a series title, The Border Trilogy supersedes the titles of the individual narratives, implying a larger historical continuity or other essential link that presumably connects *All the Pretty Horses* to *The Crossing* as phases of a single, larger narrative" (97). As it patently arranges its plots as quest for a pastoral life (*All the Pretty Horses*), journeys through a pastoral world (*The Crossing*), and the foreclosure of the pastoral vision anywhere (*Cities of the Plain*), the trilogy as a whole tacitly acknowledges the obsolescence of utopian pastoralism. At the same time it retains the escapist element in its tales as well as the nostalgia for a pastoral ideal that is wilderness rather than garden. To McCarthy's pastoral heroes applies what Marx writes about *The Great Gatsby*, to wit, that "pastoral hope is indicted for its deadly falsity, but the man who clings to it is exonerated" (59).

To understand the shift in pastoral thinking at bottom of the trilogy's pastoralism, that is, the shift from cultivated to wild landscape as the ideal pastoral space, one has to consider the conceptualization of the protagonists' and narrator's states of mind. The repercussions of the machine-in-the-garden motif affect the narrative structure only insofar as they reinforce the logic of the protagonist's return to a civilizationally-sanctioned way of life, but they affect his psychic economy in a manner so negative that it contrasts starkly with his positive, reconciliatory reaction to the traumatizing-nature episode.

As suggested earlier, the traditional pastoral protagonist has been identified from the very inception of pastoralism as a mediator, "a 'liminal figure' who moves back and forth across the borderland between civilization and nature" (Marx 43) and whose "liminal position accounts for his superior grasp of metaphysical reality" (Marx 44). This dictum alone could be brought to bear on the protagonists of the Border Trilogy who travel back and forth between the closed frontier of Texas or New Mexico and the still wild world of northern Mexico in an essentially nomadic way: homeless, migratory horsemen at home in neither world. It could well serve as a description of John Grady and Billy when Marx describes the pastoral hero as

something of an ascetic; he is independent, self-sufficient, and, like Henry Thoreau or the rugged western hero of American mythology, a man singularly endowed with the qualities needed to endure long periods of solitude, discomfort, and deprivation. In his character and behavior this liminal figure combines traits that result from his having lived as both a part of, and apart from, nature; from his having lived as both a part of, and apart from, society. (43)

This dual implication of the pastoral is another aspect McCarthy's protagonists have in common with classic pastoral literature. They, too, betray, at least initially, an ambivalent state of mind induced by the problem of balancing the realms of nature and civilization while maintaining their pastoral position (John Grady more than Billy, as it turns out). And like the classic American pastoralist, they set out on their quests not so much out of necessity but out of their own volition and a boyish craving for adventure. Unlike the country people of Mexico whom they encounter and depend on for sympathy and advice, John Grady and Billy at no point become unselfconscious enough to forget the cultural background they stem from and to cease reflecting on the distance they have put between it and themselves. In this sense the protagonists of the trilogy, like those of other American pastorals, are marked by a "double consciousness." Their escapist journeys and quests originate in a conscious thought process which is motivated by their increasing alienation at home, which moreover accounts for their persistent melancholia, and which terminates in their intellectual and emotional development into an alternative pastoral type, namely into the so-called ecopastoral hero, or eco-hero.

Placing him within the tripartive narrative structure of the heroic, Tim Poland derives the term "eco-hero" from the traditional figure of the mythical hero. Poland redefines the heroic self—achieved as the hero's boon for his community rather than for himself in the course of his quest, trial, and atonement—as "a synthesis of . . . [the] image of the heroic Self with the image of the relational Self emergent in deep ecology, or *ecosophy*. . . ."[9] Poland summarizes the term "ecosophy" as follows:

Suffice it to say that, unlike mainstream ecological perspectives focusing on the preservation of resources and natural beauty for the use and pleasure of the human community, ecosophy is an ontological perspective that rejects the traditional Western view of "man-in-environment." It favors a world view that situates humanity "in integrity," that perceives humanity as part of, not separate from, all living forms, that sees humanity in relation to the ecosphere, not upon it. In addition to the central concept of existence as relational rather than individual, ecosophy recognizes all components of the ecosphere as having intrinsic value for their own sake. This stance, accordingly, seeks and nurtures diversity and complexity and fights against all forms of pollution, class hierarchy, and outside threats to bioregional autonomy. (196)[10]

Essentially, the eco-hero translates into that pastoral figure of recent western American writing who has come to adopt an "ecocentric Self" (Poland 197) in place of the egocentric self, and to cultivate in his dealings with nature a relational quality that identifies and aligns the human self with its environment instead of imposing the former upon the latter. Morrison's notion of landscape as character in *All the Pretty Horses* (178) does not begin to unfold its full meaning until contextualized with this ecopastoral world view and the attendant change of the pastoral self-image "from 'man the conqueror' of the ecosphere to 'man the biotic citizen' of it" (Poland 196). Remarkable about the figure of the eco-hero is that it has developed not in American pastoralism in general but in *western* American pastoralism, that is, in narratives involving virtually uninhabitable wilderness as nature's last stronghold against man. Taking its survivalist cues from the Native American way of life, the western hero (including the gunslinger) has always stood out by his ability to adapt to, and survive in, terrain hostile to man, to live off the land, to cover his tracks, to leave the places visited as undisturbed as possible. The western eco-hero differs from the traditional hero of the Western only insofar as he affects this existential acclimatization not out of an individual but a collective survival instinct. In short, the emergence of the western eco-hero essentially boils down to the addition of an ecological dimension to the concept of the traditional western hero.

As careful interaction with the land constitutes the condition for survival in the desert, it is not despite the bleakness of the desert landscape of the West, but because of it, that western American pastoralism dispenses with the anthropocentric idea of man's colonizing and self-authorized cultivation of wilderness into a garden. The regional reinterpretation of the meaning of pastoralism evidently turns on a changed attitude toward the concept of wilderness. The term "wilderness" generally associates environments defiant of human habitation, as epitomized in the desert landscape. In conjunction with the progressive destruction of nature for the exploitation of resources, that is, the very process that has brought about the ongoing revival of the pastoral mode in contemporary writing, the pastoral domain appears to have moved from Marx's center position of wilderness-turned-garden and "rural landscape as the locus of stability and value" (Love 203) to wilderness itself. This development cannot come as much of a surprise, for American pastoralism contained from the start a "gap between scrabbling actuality and picturesque Jeffersonian ideal, according to which the ethos of farming empowers, not frustrates, the pursuit of culture," so that starting with Thoreau "[p]astoral hedonism becomes an indictment of the deadening pragmatism of agrarian economy" (Buell 12). The ideological shift in pastoralism was anticipated all along, but not realized until the firm establishment of ecology within the natural sciences. Germinating the old seed of pastoral self-doubt, recent ecological concern and the adjacent fear of an impending environmental holocaust have exploded traditional pastoralism from within and "radicalized the pastoral experience" (Love 203) through a fundamental reconsideration of wilderness as a space of precarious equilibrium rather than a barren wasteland.

The ideology behind this pastoral radicalism suggests that pastoralism today needs to be understood not merely as a mediating way of life in harmony with both the natural and the societal environments, but as a state of metaphysical awareness as well. The pastoral ethos has undergone an analogous shift from an anthropocentric view of nature as a material stockpile to a post-humanist, materialist view of man and nature as being equal and codependent. The ecopastoralist writes not from outside but from inside the natural world, having reduced the man–nature hierarchy to a zero level of shared materiality. In *All the Pretty Horses*, the demise of the old pastoralist vision is allegorically captured in the aspect of John Grady's moribund father (who no longer even lives on the Grady ranch) when they ride together one last time:

Looking over the country with those sunken eyes as if the world out there had been altered or made suspect by what he'd seen of it elsewhere. As if he might never see it right again. Or worse did see it right at last. See it as it had always been, would forever be. (23)

Situating John Grady within our ecopastoral reading in turn, the new egalitarian view of the world "as it had always been, would forever be" is allegorized in the novel's man-horse theme, invoking a metaphysical unity between John Grady and horses. The supposition that the man-horse relationship represents its central theme is borne out by John Grady's centaur-like, "half-man, half-horse" quality (Morrison 181), by the closing image of John Grady and his horse as "their long shadows passed in tandem like the shadow of a single being" (302), and by the image of John Grady contrasting with that of his father (quoted above):[11]

The boy who rode on slightly before him sat a horse not only as if he'd been born to it which he was but as if were he begot by malice or mischance into some queer land where horses never were he would have found them anyway. Would have known that there was something missing for the world to be right or he right in it and would have set forth to wander wherever it was needed for as long as it took until he came upon one and he would have known that that was what he sought and it would have been. (23)

Resembling something like a pastoral apotheosis, the image functions as a mere prelude to a number of rather unconventional instances of John Grady's communicating with horses, instances in which the progressive intensification of the boy-horse relationship illustrates (on the plot level) the thematic development (on the secondary level). His patronizing if fair behavior in the early horsebreaking scenes is still characterized by the master-subject relationship of traditional animal husbandry. When we read that "he did not stop talking to the horse at all, speaking in a low steady voice and telling it all that he intended to do " (103–4), that he "talked to it just as if it were neither crazy nor lethal" (106), that "[h]e thought the horse had handled itself well and as he rode he told it so" (125), or that he talks to the purebred stallion "softly in spanish" (126), these monologues go hardly beyond the baby talk susurrus commonly addressed to domestic animals. John Grady's reverence for horses in the pastoral, though not ecopastoral, realm of the *hacienda* is yet of a degree shared by the Mexican hands and foreman ("like John Grady he would talk to the horse and often make promises to him and he never lied to the horse" [127]). So while this reverence prepares us for the impending shift in pastoral world view, it is not until later in the novel that John Grady's revelations to or about horses acquire a fantastic touch and begin to read like allegorical monologues on the relational quality characterizing the ecopastoral ethos.

The moment patently launching John Grady's transition from pastoral to ecopastoral world view seems to occur during a campfire conversation of the young horsemen with the oldtimer Luis. The latter, a veteran cavalryman, assumes the role of John Grady's guide in introducing him to the mystical notion that "the souls of horses mirror the souls of men more closely than men suppose" (111). Poland points out that the allegorical hero is traditionally guided during his quest by an advisory figure (like Dante being guided by Virgil and Beatrice), and that "[t]he guide's obligation is to show the hero the way to the inclusive vision and the acquisition of the boon, not to bestow it upon him" (203). Analogously, John Grady's ecopastoral cosmology evolving later in the narrative seems to come as the result of a mental process triggered by Luis's disquisitions. Even his dream of a heaven of horses (161) seems to recall Rawlins' question "if there was a heaven for horses," in answer to which Luis "shook his head and said that a horse had no need of heaven" (111). In an ecosophical reformulation of Donne's words that "any man's *death* diminishes *me*, because I am involved in *Mankinde*" (441), Luis elevates the horse to an emblematic manifestation of the oversoul:

> Lastly he said that he had seen the souls of horses and that it was a terrible thing to see. He said that it could be seen under certain circumstances attending the death of a horse because the horse shares a common soul and its separate life only forms it out of all horses and makes it mortal. He said that if a person understood the soul of the horse then he would understand all horses that ever were. (111)

Even at this point John Grady appears to be aware of environmental destruction and lost continuity, because he asks Luis in his own parabolic manner "if it were not true that should all horses vanish from the face of the earth the soul of the horse would not also perish for there would be nothing out of which to replenish it . . ." (111). The very real concern underlying this question,[12] and the fact that Luis passes it off as a moot issue tantamount to blasphemy, suggest an incipient fissure between the old man's traditional pastoralism and John Grady's nascent ecopastoral awareness.

But the alternative relational quality of the eco-hero does not fully manifest itself in John Grady's mentality until after the structural anticlimax which is constituted by the incidents in prison, the conference with the Dueña, and the loss of Alejandra. The final chapter contains the following example:

> Blevins' horse was breathing with slow regularity and his stomach was warm and his shirt damp from the horse's breath. He found he was breathing in rhythm with the

horse as if some part of the horse were within him breathing and then he descended into some deeper collusion for which he had not even a name. (266)

The observation that John Grady cannot name this "deeper collusion" recalls the inenunciable continuity discussed in the context of melancholia: a continuity which precedes our existence, which is abjected during the formation of the self, and which defines the Lacanian "real." While the psychoanalytical model of never-remembered-because-never-forgotten loss is itself an allegorical construct and a reconstruction of the workings of allegoresis, it enters into this allegory on John Grady's continuity with the horse which cannot be named. The continuity thus allegorized invokes the lost harmony between man and nature. Another dream image may serve to corroborate this reading of the horse as a fable creature, heraldic of the ecopastoral vision:

. . . in his sleep he dreamt of horses and the horses in his dream moved gravely among the tilted stones like horses come upon an antique site where some ordering of the world had failed and if anything had been written on the stones the weathers had taken it away again and the horses were wary and moved with great circumspection carrying in their blood as they did the recollection of this and other places where horses once had been and would be again. Finally what he saw in his dream was that the order in the horse's heart was more durable for it was written in a place where no rain could erase it. (280)

Nicely capturing allegory's timeless rewriting of anterior texts, this allegorical dream image circumscribes how the human master plan inscribed on the stones of the natural, pastoral world has been eroded over time, whereas the horse as an equine emblem of nature's self-renewing continuity remains impervious to erosion. Half domesticated and half wild, the horse here prefigures the mediating world view of ecopastoralism. To sum up the implications of the horse-man theme, we may conclude that the contrastive profiles of father and son early in *All the Pretty Horses* herald this generational shift from traditional to ecosophical pastoralism. The passage is immediately succeeded by the *ubi sunt*-allegory of an abandoned domain of the old agrarian order:

In the afternoon they passed through the ruins of an old ranch on that stony mesa where there were crippled fenceposts propped among the rocks that carried remnants of a wire not seen in that country for years. An ancient pickethouse. The wreckage of an old wooden windmill fallen among the rocks. (23)

The context of this melancholy motif reintroduces our earlier conclusion that melancholy and allegorical elements in the trilogy are superimposed on the text proper in the form of a meta-narrative, and that this meta-narrative manifests itself most clearly in certain pastoral emblems usurping the protagonists' points of view while originating with the narrative voice. These emblematic allegories can now be said to form a figurative, typological arc comprising images of pastoral harmony as well as of pastoral loss. For example, when John Grady and Rawlins set out on their pastoral quest, an allegory stylizes the episode into a liturgic ascension to a prelapsarian paradise of mystical, redemptive quality:

They . . . rode out on the round dais of the earth which alone was dark and no light to it and which carried their figures and bore them up into the swarming stars so that they rode not under but among them and they rode at once jaunty and circumspect, like thieves newly loosed in that dark electric, like young thieves in a glowing orchard, loosely jacketed against the cold and ten thousand worlds for the choosing. (30)

Eventually, however, the land they traverse (allegorized as a garden, the pastoral ideal) comes across as the garden fallen along with mankind, fallen not because of man's religious failings but strictly because of his secular ones. In the metaphysics of ecopastoralism—which implicates not nature in man's fate, but nature and man in the same, shared fate—original sin returns as man's hubris of claiming the earth for his own exploitation. Within a non-anthropocentric universe, evil emanates not from a serpent tempting man to become like God, but from man instructed by God to "replenish the earth, and subdue it" (Genesis 1.28). Predictably, the novel contains images that thematize the obsolescence of traditional pastoralism in allegorizations of the New Adam, his ruined garden, and their joint melancholia:

He rode through a grove of apple trees gone wild and brambly and he picked an apple as he rode and bit into it and it was hard and green and bitter. . . . He rode past the ruins of an old cabin. . . . There was a strange air to the place. As of some site where life had not succeeded. The horse liked nothing about it. . . . (225–26)

What makes this image allegorical is the typological back reference to anterior *pre*-texts involving gardens lost and mourned. While referring us to something explicitly absent—here, the former beauty of the garden—the allegory also refers us to the implicit presence of the pastoral dream as a notion always already subjected to erasure through the melancholy gaze. Unlike comparable *ubi sunt*-motifs in pastoral literature, the garden is shown here in its moment of erasure as a truly utopian vision no longer even desirable. The passage speaks of classic pastoralism itself as of some discursive site where life never has succeeded and never will.

The ecopastoral alternative is suggested in such surrealistic dream images as the following passage on the heaven of horses:

That night he dreamt of horses in a field on a high plain where the spring rains had brought up the grass and the wildflowers out of the ground and the flowers ran all blue and yellow far as the eye could see . . . and there was nothing else at all in that high world and they moved all of them in a resonance that was like a music among them and they were none of them afraid horse nor colt nor mare and they ran in that resonance which is the world itself and which cannot be spoken but only praised. (APH 161–2)

This and the previous example both constitute melancholy allegories, one being informed by an apocalyptic cosmology, that is, a *vanitas*-vision of a lost pastoral past; the other by a utopian cosmogony, that is, a redemptive vision of a celestial world ordered to suit an equally utopian ecopastoral ideal. The dream image makes for an allegory of an ecopastoral, rather than a just plain pastoral, utopia because John Grady runs among the horses as their equal, not their master. Both the allegorical character of the vision and its underlying melancholia testify to the fact that its object, namely pastoral harmony between man and nature, "cannot be spoken" and is thus discursively unattainable. Here as elsewhere in the trilogy the narrator's melancholy gaze stylizes nature into an icon of loss. Much in the same way, baroque literature treats nature as an allegory in itself, implicated in the human fall from grace and therefore inherently sorrowful and as silent as the already quoted passage on the world's indifference renders it. In the context of allegoresis—baroque or contemporary—pastoralism works two ways: At the same time that the retreat out of a corrupt civilization into pastoral nature is motivated by *Weltschmerz* (the sorrow felt over a world gone to ruin), nature itself induces melancholia firstly because the pastoral ideal of the *locus amoenus* defies reification, and secondly because the pastoral dream itself is always already subject to the pastoral break, that is, the intrusion of death, of evil, or—in American pastoralism—of the machine in the garden. In the trilogy, the grief in nature is caused less by original sin than by the inherent futility of all pastoralist quests, including ecopastoral ones.

Among the emblems of pastoral loss that recur quasi-independently of the protagonist's sorrow is John Grady's vision of the Comanches "like a dream of the past" (APH 5). As he admits to Magdalena, the vision of the Native Americans—to be understood as representatives of a pastoral way of life—occurred regularly during his boyhood:

... the ghosts of the Comanches would pass all about him on their way to the other world again and again for a thing once set in motion has no ending in this world until the last witness has passed. (COP 205)[13]

Even more sorrowful is the allegorization of the wolf's soul into the spirit of wilderness in *The Crossing* (127), more sorrowful for the reason that wilderness constitutes nature's ideal state within the context of ecopastoralism and hence the last natural sanctuary altogether. In *Cities of the Plain*, the motif is picked up again when old Mr. Johnson recounts the last time he heard a wolf, and the metaphysical implication of the motif is made explicit:

But I guess I was always what you might call superstitious. I know I damn sure wasnt religious. And it had always seemed to me that somethin can live and die but that the kind of thing that they were was always there. I didnt know you could poison that. I aint heard a wolf howl in thirty odd years. I dont know where you'd go to hear one. There may not be any such a place. (126)

Finally, Boyd himself is stylized into an allegorical, emblematic figure of loss both on the plot level (having become a legend that merges with earlier such legends in the *corrido*) and on the narrative level. He appears in Billy's dreams even in *Cities of the Plain*, and his memory connotes a loss that goes beyond Boyd's death. Even before his death Boyd is stylized as his own double, a typological figure of melancholy thanatopsis:

He looked like his own reincarnation and then his own again. Above all else he looked to be filled with a terrible sadness. As if he harbored news of some horrendous loss that no one else had heard of yet. Some vast tragedy not of fact or incident or event but of the way the world was. (C 177)

In *Cities of the Plain*, even the dream that the still relatively pristine wildness of Mexico might make for a pastoral haven is given up for lost when Billy dismisses Mexico as "in your head" (218). Moreover, the ecopastoral vision is also subjected to erasure and melancholia, not only because its intratextual avatar, John Grady, loses his life, but because other allegorical representatives of ecopastoralism, such as Native Americans, are shown not as avatars but as epigonal relicts of the past:

> ... late in the day he passed in his riding a scattered group of their wickiups propped upon that scoured and trembling waste.... They had no curiosity about him at all. As if they knew all that they needed to know. They stood and watched him pass and watched him vanish upon that landscape solely because he was passing. Solely because he would vanish. (APH 301)

Whether or not indians camped out in West Texas as late as the 1950s, these figures are essentially a mirage, a self-referential allegory on a defunct ecopastoral way of life, "lost to all history and all remembrance" (APH 5). By implication, the image identifies John Grady's ecopastoral status as equally allegorical, melancholy, and anachronistic.

The environmental critique contained in the Border Trilogy goes hardly beyond a negative assessment of all pastoralism "as of some site where life had not succeeded" because its ecological statement consists of little more than a metaphysical flirt with nature. Indeed, McCarthy's ecopastoral allegoresis may well exhaust itself in reinstating nature as a literal fact and liberating it from its anthropocentric reduction to an object of human appropriation.[14] While ecopastoral writing in general seems "to have provided a growing contemporary audience with that sense of an ecological reality check they do not find elsewhere" (Love 204), the trilogy does little more than ground man and nature equally in the absolutely indifferent and absolutely shared materiality of existence. But the lack of ecosophical commitment can hardly be the point, for the pastoral genre has been, and continues to be, culturally constructed as an imaginary or poetic escapism and not as an effective ideology. Even ecopastoralism cannot be discussed except as an exclusively literary construct, and it would be "a mistake to think of pastoralism as chiefly concerned with the defense of physical nature itself" (Marx 66).

Palimpsest

It is in this way, then, that the compositional unity of the Border Trilogy manifests itself. Pastoral subject, melancholy mood, and allegoresis interact closely on the narrative plane to reconceptualize traditional American pastoralism along ecosophical lines and to subject it simultaneously to the same typological nostalgia that characterizes all antecedent forms of pastoralism. Stylistically, the trilogy approximates the quality of a palimpsest since allegoresis serves as the primary aesthetic principle, so that—read in this context—McCarthy's offhand remark that "books are made out of books" (Woodward 31) refers us to the novels' rhythmic erasing and rewriting of antecedent meanings and pre-texts, the de- and recontextualizing of their own back references. The subsuming of contemporary ecopastoralism under the melancholia of traditional pastoralism, and the allegorical form chosen for this subsuming, make for the truly unique aspect of the trilogy. Rather than losing itself in a vaguely activist commitment, the trilogy reconnects to the pastoral melancholia of *The Orchard Keeper* and to its mythic animism. What remains here as there in the form of epiphanic moments are the narratives themselves, the smaller tales they contain, and the act of storytelling as such, both as dramatized *in* the novels and as practiced *by* the novels. Thus the trilogy mediates between the positive force of pastoral identification and the negative force of compulsive thanatopsis by advancing two solutions, one answering to the alienation of being a discontinuous part of a cosmic continuity, the other answering to the alienation of the pastoral subject. One is the extension of picaresque wanderlust beyond the novel's ending in what amounts to the heroes' nomadic existence grounded in relational identification with the cosmos: the strictly secular teleology of ecopastoralism. The other solution is that of the storyteller who literally comes to terms with his melancholia by allegorizing it and thus attains omnipotent control over his internal world of sorrow. More than in *All the Pretty Horses*, these alternatives, the nomad's drifting and the storyteller's work of memory, figure in *The Crossing*, what with Billy Parham's triple journey and the number of interpolated tales. And while John Grady succumbs to his pastoral pipe dreaming in *Cities of the Plain*, Billy takes his cue by remaining a nomad and a storyteller. Perhaps it is in this sense that the reader is to understand the Dedication concluding the trilogy: "*The story's*

128 Sorrow, Allegory, and Pastoralism

told / Turn the page" (COP 293), meaning, turn to other stories of pastoral dreaming and you will hear an identical tale of sorrow and solace.

Notes

1. Interestingly, the picaresque genre is allegorical by nature. *The Adventures of Huckleberry Finn*, for instance, becomes a psychogram of antebellum southern society if one reads the novel allegorically.
2. See Woodward for details about McCarthy's scepticism toward the success of *All the Pretty Horses*.
3. "Melancholy gaze" is to be understood here both in the Benjaminian sense of a visual automatism translating all objects contemplated into allegories on death, and in the Lacanian sense of a scopic manifestation of the death effects governing the psychic economy.
4. This and other citations of Benjamin are my translations from the German editions listed.
5. We find instances of allegorical vision of the past even on the plot level, such as in the killing scene in prison, where the narrative perspective projects a typological sequence—ceaseless repetition of always the same—directly into the killer's eye:

> He looked deep into those dark eyes and there were deeps there to look into. A whole malign history burning cold and remote and black. . . . [T]he figure moved with incredible speed and again stood before him crouching silently, faintly weaving, watching his eyes. They were watching so that they could see if death were coming. Eyes that had seen it before and knew the colors it traveled under and what it looked like when it got there (APH 200).

6. In *All the Pretty Horses*, the sanctioning of discourse by death is taken so far that the dead Blevins comes to John Grady in his dream to talk "of what it was like to be dead and Blevins said it was like nothing at all and he believed him" (225).
7. The argument owes its gist to the passage in "The Storyteller" differentiating "between him who records history, the historian, and him who narrates it, the chronicler. The historian is instructed to explain the occurrences he is occupied with in one way or another; under no circumstances can he resign himself to passing them off as model pieces of the world's course. The chronicler, however, does precisely this . . ." (Benjamin, *Illuminationen* 397). Benjamin traces the origin of the genre of historic tragedy back to the fact that baroque theory "paid no heed to the separation between legend and history in the analysis of tragedy" (Benjamin, *Ursprung* 101).
8. Old Mr. Johnson nostalgically recalls the last time he heard wolves howl (COP 126).
9. Poland relies for his concept of the eco-hero on Joseph Campbell's definition of the mythological hero in *The Hero With a Thousand Faces* (1949).
10. Perhaps the clearest articulation of an ecopastoral stance in McCarthy's work outside the trilogy is found in *Blood Meridian*, where the spirit of ecopastoralism is neatly captured in the phrase "optical democracy" (247).
11. The contrast between John Grady's pastoral idealism and his father's resignation may ex-

plain why the protagonist is never referred to by his patronym but is called John Grady after his maternal line of ancestors throughout the trilogy.

12. The same notion underlies old Mr. Johnson's observation regarding the spirit of the wolf (COP 126).

13. Another such instance is the twilight scene concluding *All the Pretty Horses*, which strikes a note of pastoral nostalgia by stylizing a bull (strongest of the domesticated beasts) who is lost in, and incompatible with, the drought-plagued desert landscape into an allegory on the demise of traditional pastoralism:

> In the evening a wind came up and reddened all the sky before him. There were few cattle in that country because it was barren country indeed yet he came at evening upon a solitary bull rolling in the dust against the bloodred sunset like an animal in sacrificial torment. The bloodred dust blew down out of the sun. (302)

14. In *All the Pretty Horses*, the aggressively exploitative attitude toward nature is exemplified by the "oilfield scouts' cars parked along the street that looked like they'd been in a warzone" (11), cars that help to implement a land management along lines of maximum efficiency.

Works Cited

Benjamin, Walter. *Illuminationen*. Frankfurt/Main: Suhrkamp, 1977.
———. *Ursprung des deutschen Trauerspiels*. Frankfurt/Main: Suhrkamp, 1978.
Blanchot, Maurice. "Two Versions of the Imaginary." *The Gaze of Orpheus and Other Literary Essays*. Barrytown: Station Hill P, 1981. 79–89.
Buell, Lawrence. "American Pastoral Ideology Reappraised." *American Literary History* 1. 1 (1989): 1–29.
De Man, Paul. "The Rhetoric of Temporality." *Critical Theory Since 1965*. Ed. Hazard Adams and Leroy Searle. Tallahassee: Florida State UP, 1986. 199–222.
Donne, John. "Meditation XVII." *The Complete Poetry and Selected Prose of John Donne*. Ed. Charles M. Coffin. New York: Random, 1952. 441.
Hass, Robert. "Travels with a She-Wolf." *New York Times Book Review* 12 June 1994: sec. 7: 1+.
Jarrett, Robert L. *Cormac McCarthy*. New York: Twayne, 1997.
Kreml, Nancy. "Stylistic Variation and Cognitive Constraint in *All the Pretty Horses*." *Sacred Violence: A Reader's Companion to Cormac McCarthy*. Ed. Wade Hall and Rick Wallach. El Paso, Texas Western P, 1995. 137–48.
Kristeva, Julia. *Power of Horrors. An Essay in Abjection*. New York: Columbia UP, 1982.
———. *Black Sun. Depression and Melancholia*. New York: Columbia UP, 1989.
Lacan, Jacques. *Écrits. A Selection*. New York: Norton, 1977.
Love, Glen A. "Et in Arcadia Ego: Pastoral Theory Meets Ecocriticism." *Western American Literature* 27. 3 (1992): 195–207.
Madsen, Deborah L. *Allegory in America: From Puritanism to Postmodernism*. London: Macmillan, 1996.

Marx, Leo. "Pastoralism in America." *Ideology and Classic American Literature*. Ed. Sacvan Bercovitch and Myra Jehlen. Cambridge: Cambridge UP, 1987. 36–69.

McCarthy, Cormac. *All the Pretty Horses*. New York: Vintage, 1993.

———. *Blood Meridian or the Evening Redness in the West*. New York: Vintage, 1992.

———. *Cities of the Plain*. New York: Vintage, 1999.

———. *The Crossing*. New York: Vintage, 1995.

Morrison, Gail M. "*All the Pretty Horses*: John Grady Cole's Expulsion from Paradise." *Perspectives on Cormac McCarthy*." Ed. Edwin T. Arnold and Dianne C. Luce. Rev. ed. Jackson: UP of Mississippi, 1999. 175–94.

Owens, Craig. "The Allegorical Impulse: Toward a Theory of Postmodernism." *Art After Modernism: Rethinking Representation*. Ed. Brian Wallis. New York: New Museum of Contemporary Art, 1984. 203–35.

Phillips, Dana. "History and the Ugly Facts of Cormac McCarthy's *Blood Meridian*." *American Literature* 68. 2 (1996): 433–60.

Poland, Tim. " 'A Relative to All That Is': The Eco-Hero in Western American Literature." *Western American Literature* 26. 3 (1991): 195–208.

Schleifer, Ronald. "Walter Benjamin and the Crisis of Representation: Multiplicity, Meaning, and Athematic Death." *Death and Representation*. Ed. Sarah W. Goodwin and Elisabeth Bronfen. Baltimore: Johns Hopkins UP, 1993. 312–33.

Woodward, Richard B. "Cormac McCarthy's Venomous Fiction." *New York Times Magazine* 19 Apr. 1992: 28–30+.

THE WORLD ON FIRE

Ethics and Evolution in Cormac McCarthy's Border Trilogy

Jacqueline Scoones

The fear of you and the dread of you shall be upon every beast of the earth, and upon every bird of the air, upon everything that creeps on the ground and all the fish of the sea; into your hand they are delivered.

—Genesis 9.2

Wake up and piss, he said. The world's on fire.
Let the son of a bitch burn.
Come on and give me a hand.
Billy shoved the hat back from his face and looked up. All right, he said.

—*Cities of the Plain* 175

One of the predominant Border Trilogy themes is that the human story, our world, is only a fragment of the earth's history—yet one increasingly influential and dangerous for many of earth's inhabitants. For in the Border Trilogy, McCarthy portrays a variety of extinctions both past and possible:

the extinction of families and homes, customs and beliefs, governments and nations, civilizations, salt seas, the fish that once swam in them, grey wolves and, by inference, all living things. The uncontrolled violence of nature and its sometimes-inexplicable processes is juxtaposed with the increasingly potent trajectory of violence wrought by men. The cycles of life and death that occur as part of natural processes, the apparently unaccountable disasters, both large and small, which result from the forces of nature, are contrasted with the ways humans have harnessed and directed natural forces during the twentieth century.[1] In the trilogy, McCarthy gives accounts of extraordinary human cruelty, violence, and disasters, connecting technological development to the improved efficiency of warfare. McCarthy reminds us, without nostalgia, of the costs of our discoveries and progress, and he notes the failures and limitations of our knowledge.[2] Perhaps most significantly, McCarthy illustrates the magnitude of sovereign power governing humanity, and explores the ways individual life is embedded in a system that controls the collective "naked life" of all.[3] Ultimately, the three novels comprise a meditation on the history of the relationship between sovereign power, its extraordinary technology, and the capacities of human hearts.

Since the explosion of the first atomic bomb in 1945, the world has faced the possibility that vast conflagrations could extirpate entire nations. Before the end of the century, the long, bloody history of men, their weapons, their laws, and their wars reached the point at which it became possible for humanity to doom itself, and many other forms of life, to total extinction.[4] Embedded in the Border Trilogy are haunting questions: Does humanity possess the ability to control what it has wrought? Can we avert biopolitical catastrophe in the twenty-first century? McCarthy's interrogations of these issues do not lead to neat conclusions, and the trilogy's ending does not, as it cannot, provide answers to these particular queries. Yet, McCarthy does provide, rather uncharacteristically, a kind of final instruction.[5] The third trilogy novel, *Cities of the Plain*, ends with a dedication, located on the face page of the Epilogue's final lines. The Dedication is not addressed to a particular person, and its purpose seems larger than simply to signify respect or affection for an unknown reader or readers. The term *dedication* derives from the Latin *dedicare*, meaning *to proclaim*, and McCarthy's proclamation directs all readers to commit (or to dedicate themselves) to an action, for it finishes with the phrases, *"The story's told/Turn the page"* (293). The position of the Dedication on the recto page is obviously important, as a reader customarily closes a book after reading the final line of the text and reaching the final period. McCarthy's decision to place the Dedication at the end of the trilogy instead of at the beginning, as is customary, suggests that the movement away from the story and into the actual is not a closing off but rather a continuing, a turning to. The reader makes a visual leap from the last period of the Epilogue across blank space to the type of the Dedication, a leap re-enacted when we turn the Dedication page and find ourselves re-entering the visual space of our actual world. The Dedication is a type of opening, or threshold, a simultaneous showing of the told story, now a "monument," and of the way we are both of and apart from it. The story told is in our hands, in the form of the book and in the realm of our imagination. The world into which we turn when we have completed this reading is also in our hands. McCarthy establishes a continuum between the pages of text and the texture of our lives; there is little closure in his conclusion, and when we eventually close the book it is with the recognition that just as this virtual story was made, so is the actual story we inhabit a process of making. A dedication establishes a special relationship between the self and what has been made and the act of dedication is an act of consecration; something is set apart for special use, or for special purposes, and thus is made sacred. The Border Trilogy's dedication reminds us of our physical being in the physical world; if this physical world is the basis of our story then it, too, requires dedicated hearts and hands, as do those with whom we dwell.

The Dedication is a form of witnessing, for it observes and refers to the world in the text and to the world in which the text exists:

> *I will be your child to hold*
> *And you be me when I am old*
> *The world grows cold*
> *The heathen rage*
> *The story's told*
> *Turn the page.* (COP 293)

In the Border Trilogy, McCarthy represents civilization's controlling forces as heathen constructs, as systems of laws and practices that ignore the laws of the world itself.⁶ The term *rage* derives from the Latin *rabere*, meaning *to be mad*, and so "*The heathen rage*" alludes not only to the explosive hostilities prevailing in the world but also suggests a derangement.⁷ To order the world purely in human terms, to ignore the world's laws, is an insanity, one reflecting (and creating) a profound disorder. The world, neglected, is out in the cold, because the "heathen," whose faith in their own constructs is ever increasing, have lost all sense of their place within the world.

The directions McCarthy provides in the Dedication point to a way beyond the rage. These directions are not a guide nor a map, as they do not locate nor attempt to find a specific path.⁸ Instead, the directions put each reader in an unsited place of multiple, fluid relations: to this book and its author, to other readers and their stories, and to the world in which all dwell.⁹ This place of relations is a place of motion and it is also, significantly, a place of contact, of touching and being touched with care. To hold and then to be held suggests a pattern of consideration, of faithfulness, a holding to, and it is finding this faith, in this context, that seems crucial to McCarthy. To turn the page becomes a means of turning to that is not simply turning over a new leaf, not simply a crude means of establishing sequential relationships between text and reader and world. To turn the page is a way of inhabiting the world, a "turning-itself-towards" that respects or esteems all that is present in the world. In his translation of the *Anaximander Fragment*, Heidegger describes this "turning-itself-towards" as "reck" or "care" which "tends to something so that it may remain in its essence" (46). Heidegger traces the derivation of the term *reck* (the Middle High German *ruoche*) and concludes that we should speak of it as that care, or solicitude, that corresponds to order. The heathen are reckless and thus the "*world grows cold,*" rather than remaining present in its essence. In Heidegger's translation of the *Anaximander Fragment*, "order and thereby also reck belong to one another (in the surmounting) of disorder" (57). It is this way of being present in the world to which McCarthy directs us through the threshold of the Dedication. Heathen rage, the reckless abandonment of the world, inevitably leads to human extinction.¹⁰ McCarthy's Dedication suggests that at the beginning of a new century, we turn the page and attend to the world. Through the Border Trilogy, McCarthy illustrates how biological life and political existence have become indistinguishable, yet he also portrays the continuing existence of a specific type of consecrating action, evidence of a faith that perpetually consecrates the world.

One of the primary means through which McCarthy explores the range of sovereign power, its technology, and its effect on naked life is through his portrayal of the ways place has been transformed to site, thus rendering environments and the living things dwelling within them biopolitical entities. McCarthy does not limit his concern to human life, but constructs his interrogations in terms of the earth and all its inhabitants. In fact, his depictions of landscapes and animals superbly illustrate the disordering effects of sovereign power. Animals inhabit particular places in specific ways; by transforming place into site, nature as a place independent of the human no longer exists but is reconceived as a series of sites within the human domain. In *The Fate of Place*, Edward Casey traces the philosophical history of Western concepts of place, describing how place was gradually "deprived of its dynamism" as it was superseded by concepts of space. Casey explains that as space became characterized by "pure extensionality" and its relation to time, place was gradually transformed into nothing more than "site." Casey's stated purpose is to "rediscover the special non-metric properties and unsited virtues of Place" (201). Modernity, he explains, aims to subordinate "all discrete phenomena to the *mind*" (203), and yet the fact that place is inhabited by our bodies "is momentous in its consequences" (239). In his final chapter, on place as theorized by late-twentieth century philosophers, Casey describes how place has been redefined in terms of the human body by Husserl and Merleau-Ponty, for whom "the world of places is densely sedimented in its familiarity and historicity and its very materiality while, at the same time, it is animated and reanimated by the presence of the lived body in its midst. In the end, both factors . . . are required . . . for a full determination of place" (241). Place, Casey concludes, is "something in process, something unconfinable to a thing. Or to a simple location" (337).

McCarthy constructs his Border Trilogy settings as processes rooted in land, and inherent in landscapes is perpetual change. Yet, while Casey argues that we now see place as a process, his statement does not account for the ways places are, in fact, still and increasingly conceived and charted in terms of their positions on global economic and military maps. McCarthy portrays the effects of modernization on landscapes, and his representations are not as reassuring as Casey's vision. For when place as process is a process of rapid change increasingly dictated by distant forces and demands, the lives of inhabitants are disrupted and the results are disorienting.[11] Survival requires re-orienting through adaptation and in many cases this proves impossible. Illustrated through the Border Trilogy are some of the failures.[12]

McCarthy is renowned for his portrayals of extraordinary brutality, and his novels are sometimes critiqued in terms of the ways he portrays vicious killings. Yet, there is a notable difference between McCarthy's graphic depictions of individual deaths and his understated, even subtle allusions to the demise of entire species and civilizations. McCarthy hints at the logic of this distinction in the epilogue to *Cities of the Plain*, when Billy Parham discusses with the narrator the slight but crucial distinction between the Spanish words *desvanecerse* and *desaparer*; that which is vanished, disappeared, or expelled versus that which is missing or, in a tertiary meaning, extinct. In the Border Trilogy McCarthy develops an increasingly violent trajectory of destruction in the basic action of the three novels, beginning in *All the Pretty Horses* with the connection he establishes between the presence of the railroad and the ghosts of the annihilated Comanche civilization, moving to the detonation of the first atomic bomb in the New Mexican desert at the conclusion of *The Crossing*, and ending with the invocation of nuclear missiles through Billy's misrecognition of a radar tracking station in the epilogue of *Cities of the Plain*. In earlier novels McCarthy often depicted gruesome human deaths and was sometimes criticized for his stupendous displays of human barbarism. In the Border Trilogy, McCarthy writes beyond the horrific by invoking the realm of the unspeakable. When portraying the history of cruelty, McCarthy's detailed descriptions compel readers to confront past practices of appalling human violence without the emotional buffers of sentimentality or simplistic sensationalism. That which has happened, McCarthy does not veil. In terms of the extinctions he invokes in the Border Trilogy, what McCarthy does not describe cannot, in fact, be described because it is inexpressible. For as the Epilogue's narrator explains to Billy, "Pero desaparecido? He shrugged. Where do things go? . . . In such a case one can come upon no footing where even to begin" (*COP* 278).

McCarthy's means of exploring the unspeakable *desaparecido* laces virtually all of the action in the three Border Trilogy novels, but is perhaps most profoundly evident in his delineation of place. The three novels, *All the Pretty Horses*, *The Crossing*, and *Cities of the Plain*, reveal the profound correlations between the ways in which humans construct their relationships with the natural world and the manner in which they construct their relationships to each other. McCarthy tells the stories of various systems of power that shape civic and personal relationships as they shape individual relationships to the land, revealing the powerful geometry that maps individual lives as it seeks to define responsibilities, obligations, borders, histories, and nations. The trilogy specifically portrays how rapid destruction is inherent in rapid construction. While natural forces shape mountains and plains, rocks and river beds over the course of many centuries, humankind now has the ability to blast a mountain apart in a moment—making easier the construction of railroads and multi-lane highways, the process of mining, and the building of cities. McCarthy's portrayal of the accompanying development of the U.S. military industrial complex during this period, the installation of military centers and technology in the southwestern United States, is connected to both local and international damage. The disintegration of individual lives is an effect of battles fought by nations in the name of those individual lives and the communities they inhabit.

The journeys of John Grady Cole and Billy Parham, their efforts to emplace themselves both in narratives and in terrains, reflect our struggles to define our relationship to places—not sites—at the end of the twentieth century. For the difference between living at a particular site and dwelling in a particular place reflects the difference between inhabiting the world in a way that demarcates lines and points, that neatly defines the self and its relationship to the surface of the world around it, and a mode of existence that sustains a process, a continual redefinition of self as place-productive, as a multiplicity of relationships. As John Grady and Billy cross borders, stray from expected courses, rove beyond the limits of accustomed places, their very digressions, their deviations from domesticity and their flight from encroaching technology, are structured in the form of classic quests. These quests map the ethical structures of human relationships to the places they inhabit, revealing the dangers inherent in forgetting that place is a process, not a point.[13]

McCarthy demonstrates this danger specifically, and perhaps most poignantly, in *The Crossing*, through the story of a lone pregnant wolf who, having lost her mate, roams north from Mexico across the border into New Mexican cattle country in search of other wolves. Knowing she will eventu-

138 *Ethics and Evolution*

ally be trapped and shot for bounty, the young Billy Parham traps the wolf and attempts to return her to the mountains of Sonora. His trip is a tragic failure; the land on which the wolves once roamed still exists as site, but it is now animated by different bodies, defined in different terms by cattle and fences, humans and law. After the wolf's death, Billy wanders through the mountains where she once might have, surveying the land:

> The scrub juniper that grew along the rim leaned in a wind that had long since passed. Along the face of the stone bluffs were old pictographs of men and animals and suns and moons as well as other representations that seemed to have no referent in the world although they once may have. He . . . looked out over . . . the broad barranca of the Bavispe and the ensuing Carretas Plain that was once a seafloor and the small pieced fields and the new corn greening in the old lands of the Chichimeca where the priests had passed and soldiers passed and the missions fallen into mud and the ranges of mountains beyond the plain . . . where the terrain lay clawed open north and south, canyon and range, sierra and barranca, all of it waiting like a dream for the world to come to be, world to pass. . . . He saw the smoke of a locomotive passing slowly downcountry over the plain forty miles away. (C 135)

Although the stone bluffs on which Billy sits seem static, the passage illustrates the continuing process of change, ranging from the geological to the technological. The wind that shaped the juniper also shaped the bluff; the seafloor, once home to fish long extinct, evaporated into cornfields; the passing and present humans who, like the wind, shaped land as they passed through; the boy on horseback now watching a train disappear away from him as the sun passes overhead, marking yet another day in his life.

This passage provides a pertinent example of how, in the trilogy novels, the presence of humans in a place inevitably defines that place in terms of a process rife with political implications. The references to missionaries and soldiers, given McCarthy's representation of Mexico's history as nearly seamless conflict, is an obvious reminder of colonization and nation building. Although the significance of terrain "clawed open" is ambiguous and could simply be a powerful description of the natural forces shaping the earth, there also exists a possible reference to mines and the brutal mining industry in which predominantly Indian laborers still work. The "clawed open" land resonates more strongly through later associations, for in the next series of paragraphs Billy dreams of "wild men" who warn him of their work, men "Chiseling in stone with stones those semblances of the living world they'd have endure and the world dead at their hands" (C 135–6). Men, like nature, open the earth, but the purposeful clawing of men produces different effects. At the end of *The Crossing* Billy witnesses the test explosion of the atomic bomb in the desert near Alamogordo; the wild men chiseling invoke the work of the Manhattan Project, and the mines connote the uranium later used in nuclear weaponry. Thus, this isolated place where Billy dreams is connected to the rest of the earth in both time and place, including specifically the U.S. military industrial complex and all the terrains on which World War II was fought. The allusion refers, in particular, to Japan, where two atomic bombs were exploded, and to the impending development of the U.S. Southwest as the venue for exploration, discovery, and testing of new weaponry. It also invokes the Philippines, where John Grady's father was in the Bataan Death March. Past conquests and future annihilations merge through the images, and the rapacity of death is present in the figure of the vulture "hanging motionless in some high vector" over all (135). In this paragraph, McCarthy weaves past through present into future; the impact of the atomic bomb is suggested not only in human terms but also in terms of nature, for "The country seemed depopulate and barren and he saw no game and saw no birds and there was nothing about but the wind and the silence" (C 134).

Near the end of the novel, Quijada, a Yaqui Indian (one not working in the mines but managing a sector of William Randolph Hearst's huge Mexican ranch, *La Babícora*) tells Billy, "The world cannot be lost. We are the ones. And it is because these names and these coordinates are our own naming that they cannot save us. That they cannot find for us the way again (C 387). In his construction of space and place, McCarthy simultaneously represents the "pure extensionality of space" and the "densely sedimented" particularity of places occupied by bodies—bodies both alive and dead. The world will be lost to us if we do not save ourselves, but the world will not necessarily cease to exist. Life much older and stronger than humans may adapt and survive. Through young male protagonists, McCarthy explores the process of mapping the self, of locating oneself within a landscape while constructing a landscape of self within. His central protagonists have no clear understanding of their directions and destinations; John Grady and Billy are part of larger narratives they only partially recognize and understand, narratives of history, of politics, of laws and their construction of the borderlands as sites. Robert Jarrett notes, "Reading, narrating, mapmaking, and questing—these are activities that are no longer innocent but reveal our desire to project a fixed structure on a world whose chaos resists such interpretations" (103). The narratives constructing John Grady and Billy, as Jarrett notes, invoke and critique this desire for structure. Through the portrayal of its constant frustration, the perpetual lack of meaning, direction, and even the "nihilism" which is sometimes ascribed to McCarthy, we are reminded of the impossibility of mapping the immensity of space and time. In *After Virtue*, Alisdair MacIntyre argues that "man is essentially a story-telling animal" and that the way in which we learn to understand the society in which we exist is to understand the narratives in which we are embedded and to position ourselves within these narratives (216).[14] Jarrett suggests that John Grady and Billy are unable to participate in any such narratives, that both heroes are "anachronisms" (99). Yet, as the young men try to orient themselves through stories and through travel, we are also made conscious of the nature of place as a process defined by human occupation. The narratives of John Grady and Billy define places—even as it becomes increasingly apparent that places are impossible to concretize, to define. Through McCarthy, we see the concepts of both site and place amply illustrated in their differences; the indeterminacy of space, the arbitrary mapping of sites, and the animation of place through the presence of the body. In the Border Trilogy, we "rediscover the special non-metric and unsited virtues" associated with place (Casey 201).

Just as the names and coordinates on our maps cannot locate us, the arbitrary names and coordinates of our laws and religion are often equally incapable of giving direction, and we are, in fact, frequently misguided by them. In the Border Trilogy, McCarthy's construction of implicit ethics, concepts that exist outside human law, reflect an ecological sense of right and wrong. McCarthy writes of cranes who fly their paths, "Their hearts in flood" (C 388); the ardent-hearted John Grady and the broken-hearted Billy search unsuccessfully for a place in which to dwell and a story to inhabit there. The image of the cranes flying their paths together represents the instinctive behavior that ensures survival of the species, a law above the laws of men.[15] The reference to cranes in this context suggests Jeremiah 8.7: "Even the stork in the heavens knows her times; and the turtledove, swallow, and crane/keep the time of their coming; but my people know not the ordinance of the Lord." The implication is that having turned away from God's laws to those of their own creation, men have lost the proper course. The cranes "obey" unwritten laws while human laws, which redefine and represent the natural in human terms, inadequately direct us.

McCarthy distinguishes between the predatory nature of animals and that of men; animals kill to ensure survival, while men too often kill because they can. The inherent cost of killing for human convenience is most obviously exemplified through the story of the female wolf Billy tries to return to Mexico in *The Crossing*. The image of wolves appears again in *Cities of the Plain*, through the story old Mr. Johnson tells young John Grady about seeing, long ago, six dead wolves hanging on a fence, killed with strychnine baits by a government trapper. Johnson continues:

A week later he brought in four more. I aint heard a wolf in this country since. I suppose that's a good thing. They can be hell on stock. But I guess I was always what you might call superstitious. I know I damn sure wasnt religious. And it had always seemed to me that somethin can live and die but that the kind of thing that they were was always there. I didnt know you could poison that. I aint heard a wolf howl in thirty odd years. I dont know where you'd go to hear one. There may not be any such a place. (126)

Wolves have become the *desaparacido*, in both literal and political terms. In the interest of cattle ranching and its economic concerns, the U.S. government "disappeared" the wolves, which were also trapped in Mexico for bounty money. There is nothing inherently unnatural about a species becoming extinct but again McCarthy suggests that we do not know enough about what is lost to the world when we extinguish aspects of it, and our various poisons forever change our experiences of the places in which we dwell. McCarthy reminds us that there is no possible return to what was. John Grady and Billy literally have no homes to which they can go back, any more than John Grady can ride "to where I couldnt find a single day I ever knew" (COP 232). We cannot escape the present we inhabit, a present formed by all that is and is past. That we can shape the present to meet our needs, that laws give us the right to do so, does not mean that such actions are "right." Humans cannot divine the value of those things permanently lost to the world and should be careful in exercising what are apparently divine rights over the earth.[16]

McCarthy often equates the past with the lost, but the losses McCarthy enumerates are not tinged with sentimentality, and he leaves little room for regret. Characters who suffer loss do so not with operatic grief, but with intensely private pain. Mr. Johnson's mourning for his dead daughter, Margaret, one of the trilogy's few public displays of loss, does not take the form of a reasonable sadness, for his loss cannot be reasoned, and is thus depicted as a confused anguish. Mr. Johnson's daughter should have lived to inherit his ranch, but that possibility is lost just as the possibility of hearing wolves howl has been lost to Mr. Johnson's world. McCarthy's central characters suffer anguish alone, and their anguish is often specifically related to matters of inheritance. Billy and Boyd Parham lose not only their family but also their horses, which are their only inheritance. In the opening pages of *All the Pretty Horses* (and the trilogy), McCarthy equates the death of John Grady Cole's grandfather, the planned sale of his ranch, and the gradual demise of the American prairie not only with John Grady's status as a disinherited cowboy, but with the larger history of nations, their changing landscapes, and deaths of men in wars. A train passing through from east to west is juxtaposed with the image of Cole holding the skull of a horse; a reference to the spirits of Comanche warriors, passing on the old war trail and carrying stone age tools, serves simultaneously as background and foreshadowing for the many evocations of Mexico's ongoing civil unrest and World War II in each of the trilogy novels.[17] McCarthy constructs a vision of a rapidly diminishing way of life, the futile hopes of young cowboys in the southwestern borderlands during the middle of this century, with World War II and the atom bomb explosion as background, perpetual violence in Mexico as a continuous thread, and the threat of nuclear armament and annihilation looming in the future-present. Throughout the three volumes, McCarthy maintains the thematic connections between technological development, war, changing landscapes and the stories we tell about our past, the changes we have wrought, and the future we cannot see.

After reading the Border Trilogy, it is clear that the opening section of *All the Pretty Horses*, deeply resonant with references to the past, is profoundly central to McCarthy's thematic concerns and, in fact, introduces through rich imagery most of the important ideas McCarthy will explore through the ensuing thousand pages of narrative. Through the description of John Grady's viewing of his grandfather's body, his attendance at the funeral, his movements in and out of doors, to and from the ranch and between the town and the city, McCarthy frames his concerns with place, history, technological change, representation, and the cycles of violence and sorrow inherent in human life. Telescoped into the first thirty pages of the novel, McCarthy introduces aspects of the conflicts he ultimately portrays among faith, law, justice, and forgiveness. He also portrays the comforts and costs of love, and sets all in a landscape to which John Grady is extraordinarily attentive.

The trilogy begins: "The candleflame and the image of the candleflame caught in the pierglass twisted and righted when he entered the hall and again when he shut the door" (APH 3). This line introduces a pattern of central images McCarthy constructs about the relationship between fire and humans. The candleflame, lit by John Grady's mother to honor her father is, in this context, a sign of worship. Connected to the "ticking of the mantel clock" John Grady hears, and "twisted" by the force of the air John Grady moves by opening and shutting the door, the flame is associated with both the fragility and inevitable extinguishing of human life. The flame moves and is shaped by man, just as John Grady's life is shaped by unseen human forces. The unattended flame, associated with the comforting warmth of worship, campfires, and illumination of the dark, is also connected with the forces of destruction, the evil done by firelight, and the harnessing of fire's power to wreak havoc on the earth. In one of the most important of the trilogy's symbols, Billy captures the wolf by baiting a trap set in a firepit, harnessing the forces of god and man together as instructed in order to achieve his goals. What he achieves is beyond his control, however, and the analogy to the work of the Manhattan Project, the harnessing of natural forces to achieve ends with unforeseeable consequences, is clear.[18]

In this opening sentence, McCarthy also immediately establishes the important relationships among action, reflection, perspective, and representation by showing us not only the small flame, the votive, but also the flame's reflection in the pier glass. This reflection is a small, first instance of the "infinitude of alternate being and likeness" that McCarthy invokes specifically in the epilogue to *Cities of the Plain* through the sceptre carried by a member of the troupe of men in the traveler's dream (275),[19] and through the many other reflective surfaces glimmering in the trilogy. In the next paragraph, the corpse itself becomes an example, when John Grady says of his dead grandfather, "You never combed your hair that way in your life" (*APH* 3). The concept of "alternate being and likeness" is also portrayed through theatrical performances, operas, carnivals, and the photographs hanging in the cold corridor behind John Grady as he stands looking at the dead body of his grandfather. These photographs of "forebears only dimly known to him" (*APH* 3) are linked to the images Billy Parham sees of a family not his own in the trilogy's epilogue. The glass photograph plate at which Billy looks is broken and "puzzled back together," and its "slightly skewed geometry" emphasizes the fragmentary nature of our perspectives and our interpretive processes by "[a]pportioning some third or separate meaning to each of the figures seated there. To their faces. To their forms" (*COP* 290). The fragmented images of a family, noted in sentence fragments, reflect the Border Trilogy's engagement with our inevitably fragmented relationships to each other, to our stories, and to the places in which we dwell at the end of the twentieth century. However, the evidence of effort to "puzzle back together" the pieces connotes the attempt we still make to apportion meaning to our past and our connections to others.

The trilogy ends with an image of an aged Billy sleeping in a small room, cared for by a young woman and her family. The bodies of the two old men are thus equated, one at opening and one at end, and between them circles the narrative. As he looks at his grandfather's dead body, John Grady thinks, "That was not sleeping. That was not sleeping" (*APH* 3). We know that although Billy still lives, still sleeps and dreams, he too will soon become something he never was, and will never sleep again. Death is not and does not resemble sleeping. After viewing his grandfather's corpse John Grady walks outside and in the distance hears a calf bawl into the cold and windless night. The animal cry, occurring when we might expect some emotional display from the human character, is not necessarily a symbolic substitute for John Grady's grief but is perhaps a symbol of universal need combined with the uselessness of grief uttered in the empty dark. A young animal cries into the darkness and goes unanswered; John Grady stands alone "like some supplicant." Then the train passes through, "howling and bellowing in the distance and the long light of the headlamp running through the tangled mesquite brakes and creating out of the night the endless fenceline down the dead straight right of way and sucking it back again wire and post mile on mile into the darkness." John Grady "stood still holding his hat in his hands in the passing ground-shudder watching it till it was gone" (APH 3–4).

The calf's bawl becomes a locomotive's bellow, a living, iron animal streaking through the landscape with only a bit of the track ahead illuminated in the darkness. It glimpses only the narrow frame of life illuminated before it as it passes into the dark distance, beyond view. The image of a narrow beam lighting the way of a moving vehicle is repeated later in *Cities of the Plain*, when Billy drives a Ford truck through the roads of west Texas. In both instances, McCarthy depicts the limited range of view that is possible looking "down the dead straight" in the night. The train signifies both the passing of life and life past, for within a few pages we learn that the plains through which it bellows were once inhabited by Comanche and Kiowa, most of whom died facing an encroaching railroad that made possible the existence of cattle ranches and the "endless fenceline." They, too, have left traces of their passages as they moved through the land, "the constant drag of the travois poles in the sand like the passing of some enormous serpent" (APH 5). The ground shudder John Grady feels from the train echoes the shudders caused by all things passing through that land, the ancient roads replaced by tracks which will, in turn, be augmented at the end of the century by a vast network of interstate highways and a mammoth trucking industry, and by jet planes cracking through the sky.

The opening scene ends with Luisa, the Mexican woman who manages the house, bringing John Grady sweetrolls, hot from the oven, the first of many such scenes we see enacted between women and young men in kitchens throughout the trilogy. After giving John Grady his roll and butter, Luisa "touched the back of his head with her hand before she returned to the stove" (APH 4). The simple gesture is repeated in the final scene of the trilogy when Betty offers Billy comfort as he wakes from his dream of long-dead Boyd and she reaches out to pat his hand (COP 291). The cycle enacted through the trilogy, which Edwin Arnold masterfully describes in his reading of the Epilogue, is firmly cemented by this gesture.[20] Different figures are substituted in the cycle but, in fact, that is the point. It is the gesture of a woman's hand reaching out to comfort, the hand reminding through touch that we are not alone, that McCarthy uses both to open and to close the trilogy.[21]

The density of intertextual allusion in the first two pages is profound.

When first published, *All the Pretty Horses* was met by some McCarthy readers with dismay, for it seemingly lacked the depth and complexity of his previously published works.[22] With the publication of *Cities of the Plain*, however, the scope of the trilogy's structure has become clear and *All the Pretty Horses* must now be recognized as its superbly crafted first volume.[23] At the grandfather's funeral, "the preacher's words were lost in the wind," and "the weather was all sideways," blowing the mourners' chairs among the tombstones (APH 4). At the end of the trilogy we learn that John Grady will be buried in this graveyard, and the image of the empty, tumbling canvas chairs is not simply laden with the specter of death for all, but is now haunting in specific terms. For Billy tells John Grady in *Cities of the Plain* that John Grady will go back to San Angelo "One of these days" (181).[24] After his grandfather's funeral, John Grady rides "where he would always choose to ride," on the ancient road "where the painted ponies and the riders of that lost nation came down out of the north with their faces chalked and their long hair plaited and each armed for war which was their life" (APH 5). John Grady's presence here clearly foreshadows his eventual return to this road by the only means possible—as one among the warrior ghosts. When John Grady is described, at the end of his ride, "like a man come to the end of something" (5), we recognize that this is, in fact, where his remains end. The paragraph portrays not only the end of John Grady's way of life, but the end of all lives and the histories of those lives with them.

The conclusion of the trilogy, the epilogue to *Cities of the Plain*, functions as a bookend to the opening sequences of *All the Pretty Horses*, first situating an aged, virtually empty-handed Billy Parham under a freeway somewhere in Arizona, overland trucks bound both east and west over his head, near the beginning of the next century. In the novel's concluding pages, Billy believes for a moment that he sees to the west a Spanish Mission, but he has incorrectly substituted this image for what is actually a radar tracking station. As Jarrett notes, McCarthy reveals in his narratives that our "national myth of historic progression from nature to civilized domination of nature . . . is an interpretive projection and illusion"(139). For the "civilizing" efforts of man, through missionary work, western expansion, the growth of border economies and the development of space exploration and defense systems, are portrayed as inevitable processes with increasingly catastrophic effects.

The image of the radar tracking station resonates profoundly, both in terms of the Epilogue's immediate action and in terms of all four of McCarthy's western novels. The presence of the station signifies the evolution of our weaponry and our wars, most notably the expansion and relocation of battlegrounds into the space above the earth and, as a result, the separation between a source and its target. McCarthy tracks the development of innovative weaponry and its impact on environments first in *Blood Meridian*, through the introduction of the rifle and the Colt revolver and, sequentially in the Border Trilogy novels, through the shift away from personal combat to the bombs and missiles of atomic and nuclear weaponry. Juxtaposed with the increased distance between antagonists and the apparent depersonalization of violence is, of course, the exponentially increased impact of that violence. The violence and battles McCarthy describes in the Border Trilogy are actually far less graphic than the images he portrays in *Blood Meridian* and, ironically, the scenes of personal violence McCarthy explicitly describes in the trilogy all incorporate the relatively basic weaponry of fist, knife, and gun. The ramifications of the advanced weaponry to which McCarthy alludes in the trilogy but which he does not describe, is all the more horrifying precisely because the violence of advanced weaponry seems so remote and impersonal. McCarthy's descriptions of beatings, torture, eye-sucking, knife fights, firing squads, and even his reference to the "Death March" (presumably the Bataan Death March in the Philippines during World War II) all include an element of the personal: men, face to face, engage for the express purpose of hurting or killing one another. The white dome of the radar tracking station, which Billy briefly believes is "one of the ancient spanish missions" (COP 289), represents the modern religion of science and our belief that through such advanced technology either we will no longer have to face each other in direct, bloody confrontation, or possibly that the existence of such systems may prevent war altogether.

Billy also believes he sees, in the overcast moonlight

> a row of figures struggling and clamoring silently in the wind. They appeared to be dressed in robes and some among them fell down in their struggling and rose to flail again. He thought they must be laboring toward him across the darkened desert yet they made no progress at all. They had the look of inmates in a madhouse palely gowned and pounding mutely at the glass of their keeping. (COP 289)

In the morning, Billy realizes that the figures are "rags of plastic wrapping hanging from a fence" (COP 289), but the vision of the tracking station and the lunatics beyond serve as McCarthy's closing commentary on the nature and power of technology. Billy's vision could be variously interpreted as a symbol of what we have wrought, as a warning omen, as a glimpse of the past or even of another history, and as an example of how sometimes what we see is not what we make of it. The latter interpretation is particularly compelling because we trust the technology of the radar tracking station and other similar devices (such as satellite photographs) to tell us what is there, to make sense by giving us data which we then interpret and draw conclusions.

In the paragraph immediately following, McCarthy portrays Billy at a spring, "leaning to bow his mouth and suck from the cold silk top of the water." He then sees "a tin cup on a stob" and he holds it in his hands "as had thousands before him unknown to him yet joined in sacrament" (COP 290). The juxtaposition of the tracking station and the tin cup, the mitigated experience of the world and the immediacy of sensation, the labor of war with the practice of communion, are connected to the stranger's narrative of the conclusion of his dream. The stranger says that he woke and found "all I had forsaken I would come upon again." Billy asks, "What had you forsaken?" and the traveler replies:

> The immappable world of our journey. A pass in the mountains. A bloodstained stone. The marks of steel upon it. Names carved in the corrosible lime among stone fishes and ancient shells. Things dim and dimming. The dry sea floor. The tools of migrant hunters. The dreams enchased upon the blades of them. The peregrine bones of a prophet. The silence. The gradual extinction of rain. The coming of night. (COP 288)

McCarthy constructs the history of humanity in a paragraph of fragments. The images are rhetorically related to the photographs, both whole and fragmented, placed in many of the trilogy settings. They provide snippets of evocative, yet unfathomable meaning. The stranger's words refer to human presence in the world: the history of journeys and explorations; religion, sacrifice, and war; representation of meaning and meaning lost, together with lost creatures. The natural world and its dimming, the end of an era, is linked to hunters, tools, and the dreams the tools were made to achieve.

The bones of the prophet, "peregrine," perhaps connote the way Christianity spread throughout the Americas and wasted away here, and perhaps suggest the endangered bird itself, an endangered traveler. The final phrases, progressively emptied of sound, motion, and light, reverse the act of creation. A cycle ends. The stranger has said that the dreams and acts of men are "driven by a terrible hunger" to "meet a need which they can never satisfy, and for that we must be grateful" (COP 287). The tin cup helps to meet the basic need of thirst, is a shared thing that shares the world. The radar tracking station and the dreams it signifies reflect man's ambition but also an abandonment of the world, even though the purpose of its existence is to save us.

Billy, too, was once a tracker, and the image of him juxtaposed with the station in the desert moonlight encapsulates not only the magnitude of technological progress in the latter half of the twentieth century, but also its resulting limitations and dangers. Billy's tracking abilities, learned from his father, stem from an immediate engagement with nature, an engagement in which his perceptions are unfiltered by any mediating technology. When tracking, Billy is the technology; his success depends upon his sensitivity to the environment, his physical proximity and mental attentiveness to his surroundings. What he seeks, specifically, are visual signs of disorder.[25] He is able to find a den of puppies in the rocks above a flood plain because he notices long grass where the den area has been protected from cattle grazing. Billy tells John Grady, in jest, that he can "track lowflyin birds" (COP 171), and this remark echoes strangely when we eventually see him facing the tracking station that does, in fact, have the ability to track flying things that not only leave no evidence of their passing on the ground, but are perceived before they even arrive. Equally telling is Billy's humorous bragging that he is a "trackin fool" (171), for when he goes from the plains into the city on a far more urgent mission, he is unable to track John Grady through Juárez. In the chaos of the streets it is impossible for Billy to find signs of John Grady's movement, and Billy misses him somewhere in the urban terrain. When Billy goes to The White Lake to seek information about John Grady, the pimp Eduardo says, "No one knows this country" (COP 241). Eduardo is specifically referring to the fact that Mexico cannot be known and, at least in Billy's case, he is accurate. For Eduardo's statement applies not only to Mexico as metaphor and as structure, but literally to the landscape of the city through which Billy cannot track John Grady, and to the Mexican landscape through which he has not been able to track his brother Boyd. The capacities of the "trackin fool" rely largely on his sensory perceptions of the world and in this way he is closer to the animals he tracks than to the technological version of the tracker. When tracking animals, Billy is attentive to the natural processes of places and gleans signs from variations in these processes. Earlier in their conversation Eduardo describes Billy as "half wild," and the description is not untrue (240).[26] Billy knows something of the way the wild behaves and something of the way men behave, and he is both of and apart from both.

In Mexico, Billy travels from point to point looking for the young men he loves in order to protect them. He does not study the processes of the places through which he passes with an aim to finding what he seeks, for he can not distinguish the visible evidence of their passing from that of other men passing. Billy must rely on the eyes of others, on indirect information, to help him find Boyd and John Grady and by the time he does, it is far too late to help either of them. The radar tracking station can track moving targets beyond the range of vision by projecting radio waves. Individual stations are connected to a radar netting center that receives and exchanges data among other radar tracking stations, thus forming a radar netting system. The system is a matrix, one designed to protect against incoming missiles. It is the product of a sovereign power that has transformed all places and all people into potential targets, a power that harnesses the world's elements and exerts control through a vast electronic network. The system is evidence that all places in the world have become part of a system of sites, and it is evidence of a dream of vast power. Yet the radar tracking system, like the "mission" Billy believes it to be, also symbolizes a longing for safety and for peace.[27]

McCarthy's invocation of the silent, still, darkness of the world is a potent omen. Yet, his powerful constructions of the permanence of places and the continuity he establishes between acts of "turning-itself-towards" others and the things of the world, reaffirm the necessity of faithfully consecrating the presence of life. The humorous, nearly innocuous exchange between John Grady and Billy used as epigraph for this essay in fact encapsulates some of the deepest issues at stake in the Border Trilogy: "The world's on fire" and yet, while dangerous blazes threaten, most wait in sleep.[28] Having been awakened, Billy's retort reflects both the desire to avoid disturbance, involvement and responsibility, as well as his possible desire to see the world scorched as it has seared him, to see it consumed by fire as it consumed those he loved. In the book of *Genesis*, God said, "Let there be light" and the world formed out of chaos. Billy's "Let the son of a bitch burn" signifies both man's appropriation of the world in his image and man's undoing—both tacitly and explicitly—of what has been created. John Grady's instruction to "Come on and give me a hand," urges Billy to move, to act, to join another man working in the face of possible loss, possible disaster. "All right," Billy says, and we know this is the truly "right" choice. For a short while later, John Grady and Billy are together able to accomplish what initially appears foolish, useless, and impossible, moving a huge rock "up out of its resting place these thousand years" (COP 176) in order to save wild orphan puppies. John Grady's ingenuity and improvised technology have been employed to rescue pups whose mother, one of a pack of wild dogs killing and eating cattle, was killed by a group of ranchers, including John Grady and Billy themselves.[29] John Grady reaches into the ground to rescue most of the puppies, but it is Billy whose long arm brings the last one to the surface. Together, through combined efforts, the young men enact, albeit on a very small scale, the possibility that hearts and hands can join in harnessing technology in the aim of saving life, not destroying it. And when John Grady dies, Billy takes the pup they have rescued together for his own. The hands of humans into which the world has been delivered entire—either through a god's creation or man's creation of atomic weapons—can, in fact, attend to the things of the world with care. Whether there are enough of these hearts and hands remains the question.[30]

Notes

1. McCarthy's portrayals of humankind reflect the ideas of Aldo Leopold, one of the first Western scholars to articulate human moral responsibility to the environment in the context of the modern technological era. In his essay "The Land Ethic," Leopold points out that history is a product not only of human enterprise but also of "biotic interactions between people and land" (205). Leopold notes that evolution is a natural process of elaborating and lengthening the pyramid of life, but that human intervention in this process through the development of

tools has resulted in changes of "unprecedented violence, rapidity, and scope" (217). Leopold's primary concern is that the effects of these changes may be "more comprehensive than is intended or foreseen" and he raises two fundamental questions: "Can the land adjust itself to the new order? Can the desired alterations be accomplished with less violence?" (218). Leopold was particularly concerned about the American southwest, and his questions are fundamental to the Border Trilogy. In the epilogue to *Cities of the Plain*, the stranger declares to Billy, "This story like all stories has its beginnings in a question. . . . Where all is known no narrative is possible" (277). Leopold's questions are McCarthy's beginning.

2. The advances and limitations of human knowledge are a prevalent McCarthy concern, one that he explores in myriad ways. In his western novels, McCarthy examines our ability to make and to understand meaning, and thus knowledge, through any type of narrative construct or visual representation. In each of these novels, acts of creation and attempts to construct meaning are implicitly connected to human desires to "know" about god and the possibility of preordained fate. McCarthy characters explicitly discuss whether there is a god and, if so, what god's interest in the world might be. In this essay, I am specifically addressing two aspects of these larger issues: the advances and limitations of our technologies, and our ability to predict how these technologies affect the world. One important, recurring example that simultaneously portrays the progress and limits of our technologies is McCarthy's depictions of the limits of medical technology. Throughout the trilogy and in *Blood Meridian*, disease and difficult childbirths defeat the capacities of doctors. The deaths of men that McCarthy portrays are usually directly caused by other men (John Grady's father and grandfather are the notable exceptions), while most of those who die prematurely from other causes are women. Modern technology may have given the modern woman certain conveniences, but it can't necessarily save her life. Men have improved their killing capacities, but they still can't guarantee that their wives and daughters will survive the process of bringing life into the world.

3. In *Homo Sacer*, Giorgio Agamben asserts that we do not sufficiently grasp the degree of violence evident in modern biopolitics (113). Expanding the ideas Foucault presented on biopolitics in *The History of Sexuality: An Introduction, Volume I*, Agamben argues that life itself has become the center of State politics, for all lives are sacred to the State and yet all lives can be killed without sacrifice. Life, embodied, "is always already caught in a deployment of power . . . is always already a biopolitical body and bare life" (187). The "sacred man" through which sovereign power is constituted is simply evidence of the capacity to be killed, Agamben declares, and exists solely as a site of value (153). Agamben states that the body is the site at which law, fact, juridical rule and biological life appear "as a threshold of absolute indistinction" (187). "The very body of homo sacer is, in its capacity to be killed but not sacrificed, a living pledge to his subjection to a power of death" (99). The Border Trilogy narrative reflects Agamben's ideas, particularly in the sense that in the trilogy, sovereign power—manifested through weaponry and global electronic matrixes—has achieved absolute power over life on earth through the laws of nations. McCarthy, like Agamben, is interested in the relationship between law and violence, how men construct laws in order to control human nature, and the ways in which laws justify deaths in the name of life.

4. In an essay on McCarthy's first western novel, *Blood Meridian* (which is essentially a prequel to the Border Trilogy), Leo Daugherty states, "the entire novel makes clear . . . that the human world is, and has always been, a world of killing." In a discussion of the novel's pivotal character, Daugherty argues that when the judge names his gun *Et in Arcadia Ego*, this name "stands

not for his gun and not for himself, but rather for murderous humankind on this very real killing planet" (165). Daugherty notes that in an early passage of the novel, McCarthy uses the phrase "planet Anareta" as a simile for earth, and Daugherty explains (citing the OED) that during the Renaissance Anareta "was believed . . . to be 'the planet which destroys life,' and 'violent deaths are caused' when the 'malifics' have agents in 'the anaretic place.' " Thus, Daugherty claims, McCarthy intends to portray "our own Earth [as] Anaretic" (163). The Border Trilogy maintains and, in fact, expands this grim view of the human world in specific terms, but the trilogy's earth is one that through natural geological and biological processes gradually extinguishes certain life forms as others are created. Within the long post-Big Bang journey to eventual destruction, there is in the natural world a necessary balance between destruction and creation, which the actions of men threaten to destroy.

5. In his article "The Last of the Trilogy: First Thoughts on *Cities of the Plain*," Edwin T. Arnold explains that in all his novels, "McCarthy's conclusions are ambiguous and open-ended, mysterious shifts into alternate realities or into parables implying secret truths or gnosis." The epilogue of *Cities of the Plain* is, according to Arnold, "the most elaborately conceived of these endings, for it concludes not only the novel but the trilogy itself and, moreover, comments on the totality of McCarthy's work. . . . [T]his epilogue may be read as a deliberate meditation on the nature of artistic creation, the responsibilities and limitations of the creator, and the independent existence of that which is created" (239). Robert Jarrett also notes McCarthy's "inconclusive conclusions," and suggests that for McCarthy, as for Kurt Vonnegut, "novelistic endings are arbitrary, merely convenient stopping points" (106). My reading of the epilogue is obviously indebted to these interpretations.

6. I am not suggesting that McCarthy creates a dichotomy between nature and civilization, for he clearly evokes an all-encompassing nature that humans can only perceive in part, a nature to which humans have only a very limited access, not a nature that is simply non-city and thus easily visited, witnessed, and understood. The fact that our direct perceptions of nature are swiftly waning (in part because we have developed so much of nature for human use) as we gain more knowledge of natural phenomena is one of McCarthy's concerns. In the Border Trilogy, despite the fact that cities are often the source of conflict, evil, and tragedy, and that nature is more frequently a happy setting for the young male protagonists, McCarthy makes great effort to demonstrate that the nature/civilization dichotomy is false. Cities are part of nature and are subject to natural forces. Uncontrolled civilizing forces are still firmly embedded in the world of nature.

7. The term *rage* also connotes desire, or passion. After killing Eduardo, John Grady explains to Billy that when he saw Magdalena's corpse, "I just wanted him. Bud, I wanted him" (COP 259). The rage of the world is embodied in these sentences; the fact that John Grady's desire to kill Eduardo is not a fit of anger but a self-destructive passion is obviously significant. The madness of his act is not refuted by his statement that he "didnt care to live no more" and that the end of his life "come almost as a relief to me" (259). It is precisely this that constitutes madness, a kind of deep emotional disturbance that simultaneously excuses John Grady from the act he has committed (the plea of insanity is used to avoid taking legal responsibility for a crime) and indicts him, for it is he who says to Magdalena that the only unforgivable thing in the world is "desesperación," a hopeless despair, suicide (COP 206). (The Spanish word can also connote that something is maddening or infuriating.)

8. The limitation of mapping, of finding direction in the world, is a prominent trilogy theme and is cogently discussed by Robert Jarrett in chapter 5 of *Cormac McCarthy*.

9. Arnold discusses the Dedication in similar terms. He suggests that through the final scene of the Epilogue, McCarthy emphasizes "the 'matrix' . . . of flesh and earth" and "closes the circle of humanity" (243). The Dedication that follows "speaks to us all," Arnold states, and he connects the shifts between the "I" and the "you" in the Dedication to the stranger's statement to Billy in the Epilogue: "Every man's death is a standing in for every other. And since death comes to all there is no way to abate the fear of it except to love that man who stands for us. . . . That man who is all men and who stands in the dock for us until our own time come and we must stand for him" (COP 288). Arnold concludes, "The 'Dedication' thus positions us all with a sweetness and a gentleness that astonishes" (244).

10. The title of the final trilogy novel, *Cities of the Plain*, refers most obviously to the ancient cities of Sodom and Gomorrah. The biblical accounts of the cities indicate that God destroyed them in punishment for the "unnatural sins" of the inhabitants, and the depictions portray God's wrath as a just response to unrepentant sin. Sodom and Gomorrah are believed to have been located under what is now the Dead Sea and the correlate cities in the novel, El Paso and Juárez, are located on the plain of what was once a huge salt sea. God destroyed Sodom and Gomorrah by sending fire and brimstone from heaven. Brimstone, or sulfur, is an essential element of combustion used in matches, gunpowder, and photography, which are all specifically relevant to the trilogy. El Paso and Juárez are, of course, located approximately forty miles from the White Sands missile testing range, approximately sixty miles from Alamogordo and the White Sands National Monument, site of the first atomic bomb test explosion, and approximately 300 miles from Los Alamos, where the Manhattan Project designed the atomic bomb and where research is currently conducted on nuclear weaponry. It seems possible to develop a loose correlation between the "unnatural sins" (engaging in intercourse without the purpose of procreation) of the Sodom and Gomorrah inhabitants and the potential for literally undoing nature itself through the explosion of atomic and nuclear weapons, acts of desire committed in the name of creating something—peace, safety, new borders, etc.—but which literally undo that which has been created.

11. The speed of human technological change is not inherently unnatural, as Frederick Turner notes in "The Invented Landscape." Turner, in fact, defines nature as "acceleration," a process beginning with the "Big Bang" and falling "onward into more and more conscious, beautiful, tragic, complex, and conflicted forms of existence, away from the divine simplicities and stupor of the primal energy field" (44). Turner argues that human technological development is a logical part of this acceleration. However, Turner also makes an important distinction between "good technology" and "bad technology" and states that he is not necessarily "advocating a continuous indiscriminate acceleration of our activities" (44). Turner's basic definition of "good technology" is that which "respects the existing technology of nature" and "increases and does not decrease the organized complexity of the world." Bad technology, according to Turner, "is technology that destroys technology, whether in the form of the bodies of animals and plants, or in the form of our own rich material and mental culture" (50). The point here is that evolution, in nature and in human technology, is a normal and sometimes rapid process, but that natural evolution leads to more adaptation and complexity while "bad technology" is purely destructive. (Other portions of Turner's essay, which suggest that humans should become environmental artists by increasing "*the scope, power, beauty, and depth of technology*" (49) in order to serve God, including the ecotransformation of other planets, are rather problematic.)

12. Mr. Johnson, for example, is described as having adapted to extraordinary technological

changes, but not to the death of his daughter: "In his time the country had gone from the oil lamp and the horse and buggy to jet planes and the atomic bomb but that wasnt what confused him. It was the fact that his daughter was dead that he couldnt get the hang of" (COP 106). Margaret died apparently of cancer, and it is tempting to consider a possible correlation between her disease and her close proximity to the atomic testing sites. The relationship among progress, loss, and value is clear.

13. Jarrett discusses the travels of John Grady and Billy as "contemporary versions of the Childe Roland version of the quest" (105).

14. Arran Gare discusses MacIntyre's examination of the relationship among narrative, tradition, and ethics in the article "MacIntyre, Narratives, and Environmental Ethics." Gare neatly summarizes the essence of MacIntyre's argument: "The narrative of one life is part of an interrelated set of narratives, defining the individual as a member of a number of interrelated institutions.... While the narratives constituting these institutions are already there before people are inducted into them, and they are being lived before they are recounted, individuals are not merely ciphers for these stories. As members of communities, individuals are engaged in the quest for a successful life. It is in this context that virtues must be understood. Virtues are those dispositions which sustain practices and enable people to achieve the goods internal to those practices and, most importantly, sustain people in the relevant kind of quest for the good. ... The quest is not separate from forms of community" (5–6). Dianne Luce's observations in "The Road and the Matrix" about McCarthy's interest in and construction of matrixes of stories that give meaning to human existence reflect MacIntyre's position.

15. Laws, of course, now also govern space; a basic example is that pilots must obey international law regarding the boundaries of fly zones. Migratory birds are also subject to the laws of the nation they fly over and in which they stop; a migratory bird declared protected or endangered in one nation does not necessarily receive protection in another.

16. The importance of considering the distinctions between what one can do and what one should do with that potential ability is made explicit early in *The Crossing*, after Boyd and Billy encounter the Indian who will later slaughter their parents. He demands they bring him supper. Boyd asks Billy if they are going to feed the Indian and Billy responds, "Yes. We can do that I reckon." Boyd comments, "Everthing you can do it dont mean it's a good idea" (9). The ambiguity of this act reflects a complicated mix of motives and values: the boys have disrupted the Indian's attempt to find food; Billy attempts both to rectify this and to offer hospitality to a stranger; Billy may also be trying to assuage the Indian's anger to ensure that he and Boyd will escape this encounter unscathed. The act and the discussions the two boys have about it relate to the complex reasoning underpinning the creation and use of certain technologies that are designed to achieve good purposes, but that do not always produce expected results. As Boyd says later, "We ought not to of gone out there to start with.... Ought we." To which Billy replies, "No." Boyd then queries, "Why did we?" and Billy responds, "I dont know" (12–13). This is further underscored later in the novel when the *ganadero* tells the boys "What act does not assume a future that is itself unknown?... You do not know what things you set in motion.... No man can know. No prophet foresee. The consequences of an act are often quite different from what one would guess. You must be sure that the intention in your heart is large enough to contain all wrong turnings, all disappointments. Do you see? Not everything has such a value" (202). McCarthy's point is that in this dark world we cannot see past our justifications.

17. In each of the novels, McCarthy refers to several large-scale civil and international conflicts, during different historical periods, ranging from the clashes among the Native American tribes, battles between the Spanish Conquistadors and the indigenous people, wars between the Native Americans and the settlers, the conflicts and war between the U.S. and Mexico, and the two World Wars. In *Cities of the Plain*, McCarthy alludes to the Korean War and, through his portrayal of a dream of human sacrifice, to the Aztecs. The layering of specific allusions is very dense, and cannot be adequately addressed in this essay. One example, however, is that the village Casas Grandes, in Chihuahua, Mexico, central to much of the action in *The Crossing*, was the location of what may be the second largest massacre (between one and two thousand people) that ever took place in the prehistoric Southwest. According to archeologists, "everyone in the community was killed" (LeBlanc 252). Furthermore, the Casas Grandes site is linked to similar communities in Hidalgo County, New Mexico—the location of the Parham home and the place where the Indian massacres the Parham parents. LeBlanc explains, "Some 80 miles . . . north of Casas Grandes was a cluster of sites in Hidalgo County and extreme southeast Arizona. . . . That they interacted with Casas Grandes is clear; whether they were a competing polity is not clear" (LeBlanc 254). LeBlanc notes that archeologists have found evidence of burning at two of these sites, Clanton Draw and Box Canyon, which "lie 2.5 miles apart along Animas Creek" (343). While LeBlanc cautions that it is difficult to interpret the nature of the information obtained from these particular sites, he notes that "the defensive aspect of the sites is still detectable, and there is still ample evidence of warfare" (337). The sites were abandoned.

18. Billy writes a "letter" of warning about the trap to the *vaqueros* who use the fire by "etching" with a stick in the earth. The message is written in Spanish, but Billy's father points out (in one of the last phrases he utters to Billy) that there "Aint no guarantee" the *vaqueros* can read (C 50–1). McCarthy underscores the possibility that sometimes we cannot recognize warning signs even when they are directly before us and, furthermore, that even if we see such signs we may not be capable of interpreting them.

19. The full passage reads: "He carried a sceptre on the head of which was his own likeness and the likeness carried also such a sceptre in miniature and this sceptre too in what we must imagine to be some unknown infinitude of alternate being and likeness" (COP 275). The sceptre, emblem of authority, becomes a *mise en abyme* signifying simultaneously the continuity of sovereign power and the limited life of the sovereign. The authority invoked also seems to suggest the power of the author as creator, perpetuating the stories-within-stories that are the lives of humankind. Representation is both being and likeness.

20. Most pertinent here is Arnold's observation that Betty "acts as mother to the child, and the trilogy ends in the place of lullabies, which takes us back to the title of the first book of the trilogy" (243). See also n9.

21. Throughout the trilogy, there are many instances in which McCarthy's depictions of human hands and their gestures are heavily symbolic. Two are particularly pertinent here, not only because they connect male and female hands and hearts precisely at the moment when a specific hope is extinguished, but also because they are embedded in specific types of witnessing. The trilogy's action is launched immediately after John Grady says good-bye to his former girlfriend, Mary Catherine, whom he leaves looking after him as he walks away from her: "He didnt look back but he could see her in the windows of the Federal Building across the street standing there and she was still standing there when he reached the corner and stepped out of

the glass forever" (*APH* 29). The image of the Federal Building window—its frame reflecting not just Mary Catherine and her choice to leave him but the customs and laws of the land and life John Grady will never have—allows us to view Mary Catherine watching John Grady as he watches her reflecting on his leaving. Mary Catherine is not connected to the land nor to horses, but to town life, cars, sidewalks, and social niceties; a world composed of reflected images. Offering friendship with her hand, Mary Catherine epitomizes the pretty future John Grady does not desire. Within a page, he and Rawlins ride out of town into the dawn, "at once jaunty and circumspect, like thieves newly loosed in that dark electric" (30). Having stolen a backwards look at his ex-girl, John Grady steals into Mexico; when he next watches a girl's reflection it will be his first sighting of Magdalena (another Mary) in the bar-mirror of a Juárez whorehouse. When John Grady last reaches out to a girl, it will be to touch the cheek of her corpse (*COP* 229).

22. As noted by Arnold in his review of *Cities of the Plain*, "Horseman, Ride On," *World & I* 13 (Oct. 1998): 259–67.

23. In "The Last of the Trilogy," Arnold explains that McCarthy had written a screenplay "Cities of the Plain" sometime during the early 1980s, and that in terms of basic action the screenplay and the novel are closely related. Arnold traces the similarities and differences between the two pieces and explores how McCarthy then created background histories for the two protagonists in the first two trilogy novels.

24. The brief exchange, part of a longer conversation between the young men, begins with Billy's question:

> You think you'll ever go back to that country?
> I doubt it.
> You will. One of these days. Or I say you will. If you live. (*COP* 181)

The exchange is significant in several ways, for not only will John Grady return only in death, but Billy is, once again, simultaneously correct and incorrect. John Grady lives in order to die and, thus, to return to San Angelo. He does not, however, return as the "you" to whom Billy speaks. It is also worth noting that John Grady's body is buried in a place he has declared "aint my country" (*APH* 299). Due to space considerations, McCarthy's interest in the relationship among nation, earth, death, and burial must necessarily be addressed elsewhere.

25. Eyesight is highly problematic in the Border Trilogy, which is laced with examples of the failure of eyes to "see" and the ability of the various blind characters to "know" significant things beyond the world of sight. In "The Road and the Matrix," Dianne Luce describes McCarthy's concept of the world as matrix, noting that McCarthy's unpublished screenplay "Whales and Men" and *The Crossing* illustrate that "For wolves and whales, the matrix of the world in which they are embedded is comprised of and accessed through physical sense" (the wolf's ability to smell and the whale's ability to hear). Luce then discusses how the "comparable physical sense for humans is usually assumed to be eyesight," but she notes the crucial distinction that "eyesight is curtailed by physical . . . proximity in ways that the wolf's sense of smell or the whale's sense of hearing transcends, nor does it provide man an immediate apperception of the world sufficient to compensate for his tendency to replace the world with language." As Luce notes about *The Crossing*, we come to understand in the Border Trilogy that "the world itself is not perceptible through eyesight" (208).

26. It might be argued that Billy resembles the "wolf-man" and John Grady the "bandit," the

158 Ethics and Evolution

"Friedlos" or "man without peace" of ancient Germanic law who is "banned from his city." Agamben describes the life of the wolf-man, the bandit, as "not a piece of animal nature without any relation to the law and the city. It is, rather, a threshold of indistinction and of passage between animal and man, *physis* and *nomos*, exclusion and inclusion: the life of the bandit is the life of the *loup garou* . . . who is precisely *neither man nor beast* and who dwells paradoxically within both while belonging to neither" (104–5). Agamben explains, "What has been banned is delivered over to its own separateness and, at the same time, consigned to the mercy of the one who abandons it . . ." (110). Billy and John Grady reflect the modern condition in which through the banishment of sacred life we have been made free, and yet we are at the mercy of sovereign power that places life "at the center of State politics" (111). Alex Hunt also discusses Billy as a figure of both the wilderness and the city in his unpublished paper "Mapping the World Between: Cormac McCarthy's *The Crossing*." Hunt states that Billy's experience with the wolf "has cast him into a liminal relation to the human realm from which he views it as the outlaw wolf wandering through alien terrain. At the same time, society views him as something foreign and unassimilable" (8). Drawing upon the theories of Deleuze and Guattari, Hunt's argument focuses on the way McCarthy "remaps" concepts of "civilization" and "wilderness" revealing, in the process, that these are "imposed categories on a borderless space" (8).

27. Electrical impulse, electricity, does not always function as expected, as McCarthy illustrates through lightning flashes, the firing synapses in Magdalena's brain, and the light hanging in Mac's barn. The electrical "failure" of the light, which inconsistently shocks the cowboys when they turn it on, is not just a humorous device, but also represents how we are not always safe from the things we have invented and that we trust to work. Throughout the trilogy, McCarthy lightly traces the development of electronics and its rapid spread throughout the world, noting the power of radio to broadcast across national boundaries in *All the Pretty Horses*, the power of the atomic bomb in *The Crossing*, and (among many other images of electronic technology) the presence of a television in a hotel lobby at the end of *Cities of the Plain* (264)—a bookend to the hotel lobby John Grady occupies while watching his mother in San Antonio. In perhaps the most poignant juxtaposition of electric light imagery, McCarthy opens *Cities of the Plain* with images of the "gaudy red and green . . . neon signs" reflected in the rain puddles and the faces of cowboys viewed in "bloodred barlight" (3); he closes the novel with the image of the kitchen light Betty leaves on for Billy in the Epilogue's final scene (291).

28. In the epilogue to *Cities of the Plain*, the stranger tells Billy that the world is also revealed in dreams, but that "it is the narrative that is the life of the dream while the events themselves are often interchangeable. The events of the waking world on the other hand are forced upon us and the narrative is the unguessed axis along which they must be strung. It falls to us to weigh and sort and order these events. It is we who assemble them into the story which is us. Each man is the bard of his own existence. This is how he is joined to the world. For escaping from the world's dream of him this is at once his penalty and his reward" (283).

29. The scene of the hunt is possibly the most gruesome in the novel. It is necessary for the ranchers to execute the dogs in order to protect cattle, but when Billy and John Grady simultaneously rope a dog and its head explodes in a cloud of blood between the two, "[s]omething evoked out of nothing and wholly unaccountable," it is clear that we are meant to associate the uncontrolled aggression of the hunt with larger forces (COP 167). The responses of the characters are significant: Joaquín laughs, John Grady "coiled his rope" and went after

the "lone remaining dog," while Billy exclaims "Goddamn," stops, wipes the blood off his hands, and sits watching them ride away. The last dog killed is a nursing bitch, and Billy does not take part in her death (perhaps a reference to the pregnant wolf he tried to save in *The Crossing*). Had the others quit after the explosion the mother would have lived, and there would be no need to save the puppies. It is, significantly, Joaquín who kills the mother. John Grady later tries to remedy the act, but Billy does not engage in the action in the first place.

30. In "Whales and Men," an unpublished screenplay about how men have hunted the whale to near extinction and about a doomed effort to save a specific whale, McCarthy explicitly makes this point several times. One of the characters, Guy, refers to an interview in which Mother Theresa was asked about the futility of her endeavors. Guy says, "all she does is deal with hopeless poverty and terminal disease. And she seemed puzzled by the question and . . . she said: He [God] didn't call upon me to be successful. He just called upon me to be faithful" (24). Later in the screenplay, Kelly echoes this sentiment. In an argument with her boyfriend John, she declares, "It's beneath us, this excuse that we're beset with the greatest woes ever to face mankind." John replies, "You dont think that's true?" Kelly states, "That's not the point. Giving up is the point. I cant know the future. You cant. But I can live this life I've been given with grace and dignity and honor" (123). John eventually undergoes a change of mind and heart and, at the end of the screenplay, he writes a letter to Kelly and his friend Peter (now married to each other) in which he states: "I believe we are arks of the covenant and our true nature is not rage or deceit or terror or logic or craft or even sorrow. It is longing. I know that we are lost but I no longer believe that we are doomed" (130). Although Cormac McCarthy wrote these lines well before he wrote the Border Trilogy (see Luce 216 n13), it is perhaps to these sentiments, this active faith and hope, that McCarthy suggests we turn when we "Turn the page" into the dimming world.

Works Cited

Agamben, Giorgio. *Homo Sacer: Sovereign Power and Bare Life*. Stanford: Stanford UP, 1998.
Arnold, Edwin T. "The Last of the Trilogy: First Thoughts on *Cities of the Plain*." Arnold and Luce 221–47.
Arnold, Edwin T., and Dianne C. Luce. *Perspectives on Cormac McCarthy*. Rev. ed. Jackson: UP of Mississippi, 1999.
Casey, Edward S. *The Fate of Place: A Philosophical History*. Berkeley: U of California P, 1997.
Daugherty, Leo. "Gravers False and True: *Blood Meridian* as Gnostic Tragedy." Arnold and Luce 159–74.
Gare, Arran. "MacIntyre, Narratives, and Environmental Ethics." *Environmental Ethics* 20.1 (1998): 3–21.
Heidegger, Martin. *Early Greek Thinking*. Trans. David Farrell Krell and Frank A. Capuzzi. San Francisco: Harper Collins, 1984.
Hunt, Alex. "Mapping the World Between: Cormac McCarthy's *The Crossing*." Unpublished ms. [Presented in part, Association for the Study of Literature and the Environment Third Biennial Conference, Kalamazoo, MI, 2–5 June, 1999].
Jarrett, Robert T. *Cormac McCarthy*. New York: Twayne, 1997.

LeBlanc, Steven A. *Prehistoric Warfare in the American Southwest.* Salt Lake City: U of Utah P, 1999.

Leopold, Aldo. *A Sand County Almanac and Sketches Here and There.* New York: Oxford UP, 1949.

Luce, Dianne C. "The Road and the Matrix: The World as Tale in *The Crossing.*" Arnold and Luce 195–219.

MacIntyre, Alasdair C. *After Virtue: A Study in Moral Theory.* 2nd ed. Notre Dame: U of Notre Dame P, 1984.

McCarthy, Cormac. *All the Pretty Horses.* New York: Vintage, 1993.

———. *Cities of the Plain.* New York: Vintage, 1999.

———. *The Crossing.* New York: Vintage, 1995.

———. "Whales and Men." Unpublished ts. Cormac McCarthy Papers, Southwestern Writers Collection, Albert B. Alkek Library, Southwest Texas State U, San Marcos.

Turner, Frederick. "The Invented Landscape." *Beyond Preservation: Restoring and Inventing Landscapes.* Ed. A. Dwight Baldwin, Jr., Judith De Luce, and Carl Pletsch. Minneapolis: U of Minnesota P, 1994. 35–66.

Wilson, Edward O. "The Little Things That Run the World." *Conservation Biology* 1.4 (1987): 344–46. Rpt. in *Environmental Ethics: Divergence and Convergence.* Ed. Richard G. Botzler and Susan J. Armstrong. 2nd ed. Boston: McGraw, 1998. 32–34.

The Vanishing World of Cormac McCarthy's Border Trilogy

Dianne C. Luce

Early in *Cities of the Plain*, when Billy and Troy are driving late at night, returning to the McGovern ranch that is about to be taken over by the government, Billy rounds a curve and collides with a large owl, which dies "cruciform" on the shattered windshield "like an enormous moth in a web" (34). It is one of those moments in which life veers, a moment as unexpected as anything in the Border Trilogy. Troy is visibly shaken, and the seemingly irrelevant event settles him in his decision not to return to his boyhood home. Billy appears less affected, reassuring Troy that it was "just a owl" (35). But his reverence for the creature and his understanding of the import of its death are communicated in his actions and in the narrative perspective that conveys them:

> The owl was all soft and downy. Its head slumped and rolled. It was soft and warm to the touch and it felt loose inside its feathers. He lifted it free and carried it over to the fence and hung it from the wires.... (34)

The imagery echoes the scene in which Billy as hunter shoots a rabbit in order to feed himself and the wolf in *The Crossing*: "he pooled it up all warm and downy in his hands with the head lolling and carried it out through the woods till he could find a windfall tree" (77). But here the dead owl is an image of the natural world crucified at the hands of man, the truck and the fence manifestations of the imposition of his mechanized world on the world of nature. The owl's death reprises in miniature the death of the she-wolf in *The Crossing*—diminished like so much in *Cities of the Plain*. If Billy does not allow himself to react, it is because he has learned not to feel so deeply his pain at the extermination of the Mexican wolf in the Southwest, the incursion of technology and government into the terrain of his youth, the vanishing of the cowboy and his way of life . . . or to acknowledge it consciously.

The collision with the owl is prefigured in Troy's grotesque story of the many jackrabbit heads he collected on the grill of Gene Edmonds's Oldsmobile, driving at night to a rodeo after the war. Pushing the car to a hundred and ten, Troy was aware that he was hitting the rabbits, but neither he nor Gene cared until confronted with the image of their heads and innards stuck in the grill of the car. Troy makes it black comedy, with a woman screaming as if Gene has exposed himself (which in a sense he has) and the rabbit heads "lookin out, eyes all crazy lookin. Teeth sideways. Grinnin" (COP 22). "I cant tell you what it looked like" Troy says, "I come damn near hollerin myself." Billy quietly listens to this story of carnage, which has been prompted by their own hitting a jackrabbit frozen in their headlights. If he finds it humorous, he gives no such indication, and he must certainly recognize their own implication in the destruction of the rabbits (over-plentiful though they may be[1]), just as he will accept his complicity in the killing of the owl later that night. Billy and Troy are cowboys and horsemen, but they have accepted the cars and roads of the modern world and the resulting destruction of wildlife.[2]

Together, these two incidents bring into focus the ecological vision of the Border Trilogy that is most explicit in the first section of *The Crossing* and that links the trilogy with McCarthy's unpublished screenplay "Whales and Men" (and even with his earliest novel, *The Orchard Keeper*). In bringing the trilogy to closure, *Cities of the Plain* foregrounds both the domestic concerns of John Grady Cole, with his quest for home and love and his identification with the horse (the wild creature domesticated), and the ecological and spiritual concerns of Billy Parham, whose totem is the wolf (the predator who must remain wild if she is to exist at all). The accomplished shape of the trilogy reveals that all along it has considered the relationship of wildness to domesticity, the predatory nature of man and his drive for civilization, and the "wildness within" (APH 60) that Western man denies to his own destruction (concerns that are also obviously central to *Blood Meridian*).

The world of the Border Trilogy is a vanishing world, beginning with the death of John Grady's grandfather and ending with the death of John Grady himself and the implied death of Billy beyond the last page of *Cities of the Plain*. From the title of *All the Pretty Horses* to the dedication of *Cities of the Plain*, the trilogy is a lullaby singing to sleep the vanishing cowboy (Luce, "Heroism" 156; Arnold 243). John Grady's vision of the vanished Comanches early in *All the Pretty Horses*—"nation and ghost of nation ... bearing lost to all history and all remembrance like a grail the sum of their secular and transitory and violent lives"—is reciprocated at the end of that novel with the indians' premonition of his own passing: "They stood and watched him pass and watched him vanish upon that landscape solely because he was passing. Solely because he would vanish" (5; 301). John Grady rides into the sunset at the end of his novel and into "the world to come" (302): the world of the 1950s and the eradication of the kind of life he has so ardently sought. Billy's novel ends with the false dawn of the atomic bomb, signalling the dominance of man's predation over both nature and his fellow man in the name of "civilization." Both novels suggest, however, some deeper persistence of the world itself in the rising of the "right and godmade sun" in *The Crossing* (426) and in the assurance of a "world to come" in *All the Pretty Horses*.[3]

The storyteller Billy encounters in the epilogue of *Cities of the Plain* reminds him that his life "vanishes at its own appearance. Moment by moment. Until it vanishes to appear no more" (273), but later he makes a distinction between vanishing and disappearing: "Lo que se desvanece es simplemente fuera de la vista. Pero desaparecido? [What vanishes is simply out of sight. But disappeared?] He shrugged. Where do things go?" (278). The storyteller's words distinguish crucially between the merely unseen and the essentially eradicated, reinforcing the idea explored in *The Crossing* that the world itself persists outside of time and outside our time-bound sensory perception of it.[4] One of the clearest images of this in *The Crossing* is the narrator's vision of the dead wolf which "already ran among the mountains at once terrible and of a great beauty" and "which cannot be held never be held and is no flower but is swift and a huntress and the wind itself is in terror of it and the world cannot lose it" (127). Not "the world must not lose it" but "the world cannot lose it." The great terror and beauty manifested in the world's creatures are evanescent, while the world itself endures. This consolation is conveyed through the trilogy's narrators and the storytellers who speak to Billy, but it remains elusive to John Grady, Billy, and the other cowboys whose beloved world vanishes moment by moment. Old Mr. Johnson articulates this grief and uncertainty when he confides to John Grady:

> I aint heard a wolf in this country since [1917]. I suppose that's a good thing. They can be hell on stock. But I guess I was always what you might call superstitious. I know I damn sure wasnt religious. And it had always seemed to me that somethin can live and die but that the kind of thing that they were was always there. I didnt know you could poison that. (COP 126)[5]

And indeed, the trilogy is an elegy for the evanescent world of the Southwest and a celebration of the great hearts of those who live alienated within "[t]he world [grown] cold" (COP 293) and who mourn or honor the passing of the wolves, the indian, the cowboy.

"Vanish" is a word repeated over and over throughout the trilogy, sometimes in passages of portent but more often in mundane contexts which reduce vanishing to a mere fact of life and in which the persistence of the vanished is never called into question, as if McCarthy would remind us of the simple faith in the persistence of objects learned in our early childhood. For example, "the deer in the bajada leapt away and vanished in the dusk and the little doe lay kicking" (APH 282); "Then [the wolf's white bandage] too vanished and he closed the gate and turned toward the house" (C 72); "they still could see nothing at all on the far shore of the lake where the rider had vanished" (C 175); "The doctor levered the big wooden steering wheel to the left and the headlights swung away and the figures vanished once more into the indenominate dark of the Mexican night" (C 302); "The single taillight had a short in the wiring and it winked on and off like a signal until the truck had rounded the curve and vanished" (COP 33); "He . . . tested the air with his nose but the smell had passed and vanished"

(COP 153).[6] The significance of such images is sometimes considerably darker, however, as when Jimmy Blevins is walked into the ebony grove to face assassination: "The other man walked behind them carrying the rifle and Blevins disappeared into the ebony trees hobbling on one boot much as they had seen him that morning coming up the arroyo after the rain in that unknown country long ago. . . . John Grady watched the small ragged figure vanish limping among the trees with his keepers" (APH 177). Death is never far away in the Border Trilogy, and the most crucial vanishings are permanent, becoming what Jacqueline Scoones calls "the unspeakable *desaparecido*" (136).

Most notations of evanescence close paragraphs, sections, or chapters, and all of them of course involve witnessing. Thus through repetition and emphasis, they take on the significance of an incantation. Indeed, just before the final vanishing of John Grady witnessed by the remaining indians at the end of *All the Pretty Horses*, McCarthy accumulates a sequence of such scenes in which John Grady rides off and vanishes, witnessed by men on whom he has made some impression: the men at Langtry, Texas, to whom he seems "some apparition out of the vanished past" ("they both stood watching until he turned the corner at the cafe and there was nothing more to see"); the judge in Ozona (John Grady "raised his hand and the judge raised a hand back and he rode out down the street from pool to pool of lamplight until he had vanished in the dark"); and Rawlins (Rawlins "stood holding his horse while the rider turned and rode out and dropped slowly down the skyline. He squatted on his heels so as to watch him a little while longer but after a while he was gone" [APH 287, 294, 300]). The cowboy hero's riding off at the end of the story is, of course, a stock device, but McCarthy uses such images throughout the trilogy, typically conjoining them with the implication of evanescence. After their encounter on the road, the diva watches Billy and Boyd ride off, following them out of sight with her opera glasses: "As if she might better assess them in that way where they set forth upon the shadowbanded road, the coming twilight. Inhabiting only that ocular ground in which the country appeared out of nothing and vanished again into nothing, tree and rock and the darkening mountains beyond, all of it contained and itself containing only what was needed and nothing more" (C 231). John Grady and Billy each stand within the border world "like a man come to the end of something" (APH 5; similar line at C

291), and their feats within that vanishing world are no more foregrounded in the trilogy than is the transience of their world.

Many images of vanishing point to the evanescence of the natural world. John Grady stands on a bridge in San Antonio and watches "the snow vanish in the river"(APH 20) in a passage that foreshadows Don Arnulfo's comparison of the wolf to the snowflake (C 46). And John Grady speculates about the vanishing of the horse, asking the Mexican *mozo* "if it were not true that should all horses vanish from the face of the earth the soul of the horse would not also perish for there would be nothing out of which to replenish it" (APH 111). In Billy's troubling dream of wolves after he has heard the story of the blinded revolutionary,[7] they stand in a crescent about him, their eyes "like footlights to the ordinate world and then they turned and wheeled away and loped off through the snow and vanished smoking into the winter night" (C 295). Both here in his unconscious dream and earlier in his waking vision of the she-wolf before he has captured her, Billy has a sense of the spirit or the essence of the wolf that persists outside of its physical manifestation in the "ordinate" world. Indeed, his waking vision of the wolf echoes John Grady's waking vision of the Comanche nation quoted above: "wolves and ghosts of wolves running in the whiteness of that high world as perfect to their use as if their counsel had been sought in the devising of it" (C 31). And Billy's collision with the owl on the road receives further implied commentary when John Grady and Héctor drive back toward the ranch house after dark from the little cabin John Grady is preparing for Magdalena, and they too come across owls:

> Two owls crouching in the dust of the road turned their pale and heartshaped faces in the trucklights and blinked and rose on their white wings as silent as two souls ascending and vanished in the darkness overhead. (COP 201)

This emphasis on the barn owls as spirit recalls the crucifixion imagery associated with the owl struck by Billy.[8] At the same time, the two owls here prefigure the deaths of John Grady and Magdalena, while retroactively identifying Billy himself with the lone crucified figure. This linking of wildlife and human life suggests the kinship and sanctity of all life that is one of the central concerns of the Border Trilogy.

The imagery of evanescence receives its most pointed and focused treatment in the story of the blind revolutionary in *The Crossing*, for here is set forth the notion of the world as illusion (and indeed all three of the long interpolated stories in *The Crossing* address the problem of the vanishing world). The blinded man's wife tells Billy that her husband's ruined eyes "dried and wrinkled and the cords they hung by dried and the world vanished," becoming an "estrangement" (277; 279). Early in his blindness, the revolutionary can access the world only in his dreams. He "dreamt of the country through which he'd ridden in his campaigns in the mountains and the brightly colored birds thereof and the wildflowers and he dreamt of young girls barefoot by the roadside in the mountain towns whose own eyes were pools of promise deep and dark as the world itself" (277). In his despair because "the world and all in it had become to him but a rumor," he attempts to drown himself, believing that "the blind had already partly quit the world anyway" (282). His witness offers the consolation that "Si el mundo es ilusión la perdida del mundo es ilusión también" (283; If the world is illusion the loss of the world is illusion also). Initially the blind man accepts this notion of the world as illusion but rejects the intended consolation: "He said that it was not a matter of illusion or no illusion.... He said that the light of the world was in men's eyes only for the world itself moved in eternal darkness and darkness was its true nature" (283). Gradually, though, he comes to see that as he moves through the vanished world meeting people on the road—people who offer him gifts and tell him "of the sorrows in their lives"—"The world unfolded to him in a way it had not before in his life" (285). Although his dreams and even his visual memories have vanished, he is compensated with a truer perception of the world itself:

He said that like every man who comes to the end of something there was nothing to be done but to begin again. No puedo recordar el mundo de luz, he said. Hace muchos años. Ese mundo es un mundo frágil. Ultimamente lo que vine a ver era más durable. Más verdadero. (291; I cannot remember the world of light. It was long ago. That world is a fragile world. Finally what I came to see was more enduring, truer)

This passage links the blind man with John Grady and with Billy, other young men come to the end of something. He has learned something akin to what the old indian tells Billy when he urges him to return to the world of men (C 134). "To move is to abut against the world" the blind man says. "Sit quietly and it vanishes.... He said that in his blindness he had indeed lost himself and all memory of himself yet he had found in the deepest dark of that loss that there also was a ground and there one must begin" (291–92). The blind man's consolation, that his blindness has enabled him to see the world itself in its truer and more enduring form, that to live and move means continually abutting against the "vanished" world,[9] stands opposed to the palpable despair he felt at losing his eyesight; and it is counterposed against the concrete and prevailing imagery of the vanishing world in the Border Trilogy. It is no accident that much of that imagery is conjoined with the falling of darkness at day's end. Nightfall and sunrise are the rhythmic reminders of the evanescence and paradoxical persistence of the world in the Border Trilogy, and the blind man's experience is an intensified parable of the cowboys' confrontation with the vanishing of their world.

If the trilogy offers such consolation as the Platonic notion of the material world as illusion, yet McCarthy's prose here, as in his earlier works, valorizes the concrete world of nature and of man's crafts. It is this vanishing world that John Grady and Billy love and that their texts invite readers to mourn. And the core image of the vanishing world in the trilogy is the vanishing *loba*—the Mexican grey wolf virtually exterminated by the 1950s. In McCarthy's hands she comes to represent not only the material world of nature destroyed by man, but the very spirit of wildness and of the eternal world itself, a swift huntress that the world cannot lose. The wolf, like the whale in McCarthy's screenplay "Whales and Men," is made the way the world is made; and while these related works often imply that the material world is illusion, they as often suggest the immanence of spirit within these creatures.

Where the wolf is concerned, reference to such immanence of spirit is not uncommon in the ecological works that the trilogy engages, particularly in Aldo Leopold's *Sand County Almanac*, Barry Lopez's *Of Wolves and Men*, or in those such as James Burbank's *Vanishing Lobo* that denounce the extermination of the Mexican grey wolf and the work of the field agents (such as Echols) responsible for its eradication.[10] Billy's forbearing to kill the she-wolf he has trapped and his doomed endeavor to return her to the mountains of Mexico are radical acts for a young man of his generation and upbringing. They spring from insight similar to that which transformed Aldo Leopold into one of America's earliest and most influential environmentalists. As a young man who had just earned a Master's degree in Forestry from Yale, in 1909 Leopold was employed by the U.S. Forest Service on the border between New Mexico and Arizona and assigned to work with J. Stokely Ligon, a Texan seventeen years his senior, who was to become one of the Southwest's most renowned wolf hunters (Flader 9; Burbank 100–01). The two "shared a mutual love for hunting and their passion for observing wildlife" (Burbank 102), and they would eventually co-write a book "Southwestern Game Fields" that Leopold abandoned before publication (Flader 19, 60). Their project was to eradicate the Mexican wolf to protect livestock and preserve game for hunting. By 1912 Leopold was promoted to supervisor of northern New Mexico's Carson National Forest, and by 1915 he was devoting almost all his time to game and fish management in the Southwestern District (Flader 9, 11). In the same year Ligon was appointed inspector for New Mexico's Predator and Rodent Control (PARC) program (Burbank 102–3). Both men met with hunters and ranchers to gather support, and the wholesale and methodical slaughter of the Mexican grey wolf (*Canus lupus baileyi*) went forward (Flader 12; Burbank 102). Leopold was not himself a wolf-hunter, nor was he the "most vehement advocate of extermination" according to biographer Curt Meine. "But as designated propagandist, Leopold enthusiastically railed against 'vermin,' 'varmints,' and the 'skulking marauders of the forest' " (Meine 155). Years later Leopold would write, "In those days we had never heard of passing up a chance to kill a wolf" (130). But it was precisely his experience of killing a wolf that Leopold would come to represent as symbolic of the radical reversal in his ideas about the wolf's role in nature and man's, teaching him that "Only the mountain has lived long enough to listen objectively to the howl of a wolf" (Leopold 129).

In his essay "Thinking Like a Mountain" in *Sand County Almanac* (1949), Leopold writes that one day, eating lunch on a rimrock, he and his companions saw a creature swimming in the river below. At first they thought it was a doe, but when it climbed the bank facing them, they saw it was a she-wolf, whose grown pups rushed from the willows "in a welcoming mêlée of wagging tails and playful maulings" (130). Instantly the men were shooting excitedly into the pack, scattering them and wounding one pup and the she-wolf. They descended to finish the business:

> We reached the old wolf in time to watch a fierce green fire dying in her eyes. I realized then, and have known ever since, that there was something new to me in those eyes—something known only to her and to the mountain. I was young then, and full of trigger-itch; I thought that because fewer wolves meant more deer, that

no wolves would mean hunters' paradise. But after seeing the green fire die, I sensed that neither the wolf nor the mountain agreed with such a view. (130)

In her study of the evolution of his conservationist ideas, Susan Flader points out that "Thinking Like a Mountain" was written in response to criticism from Leopold's former student and illustrator H. Albert Hochbaum, who felt that Leopold's book-in-progress "breathed too deeply of regret and of aloof sourness or self-righteousness toward man's despoliation of nature." Hochbaum reminded Leopold, "It is only by accepting ourselves for what we are, the best of us and the worst of us, that we can hold any hope for the future," and he suggested that Leopold acknowledge his earlier role in promoting the eradication of the wolf in the Gila area of New Mexico (Flader 3–4). Flader has concluded that Leopold's essay, drafted in 1944, "compressed into one dramatic moment a realization that had required years. It was a realization that grew . . . out of his lifelong experience with the management of deer on wolfless range. . . . Man with his arrogance and his engines of violence now presumed, in his solicitude for deer and cattle, to lop the large carnivores from the apex of the [biotic] pyramid, making food chains shorter and less complex and thus disorganizing the system. Because the wolf stood at the apex of the pyramid, it became Leopold's symbol of the pyramid itself, of land health" (2). As an ecologist writing of his experience twenty-odd years earlier, Leopold expresses his objection to the extermination of the wolf, citing the burgeoning of the deer herds, the over-browsing of the mountain and the starving of the deer: "I now suspect that just as a deer herd lives in mortal fear of its wolves, so does a mountain live in mortal fear of its deer" (132). The environmental consequences were dire on the ranches as well: "The cowman who cleans his range of wolves does not realize that he is taking over the wolf's job of trimming the herd to fit the range. He has not learned to think like a mountain. Hence we have dustbowls, and rivers washing the future into the sea" (Leopold 132). Such consequences are hinted to be one of the reasons for the failure of the dry and unproductive McGovern ranch in *Cities of the Plain*, where a wolf's howl has not been heard since 1917 (126).[11]

But what Leopold claims to have seen in the green fire of the wolf's eyes the day he killed her is not the ecological consequences of the eradication of the wolf. He would understand that only gradually and much later. Instead, he asserts her value as a creature of the wilderness rather than as an object to be possessed and controlled. And he avers that his new vision of her moved him toward his mature philosophy of an "ethical relation to land" that cannot exist "without love, respect, and admiration for land, and a high regard for its value . . . in the philosophical sense" (223). In the mythic representation of his experience, Leopold's vision of the dying wolf leads him to understand "Thoreau's dictum" that "In wildness is the salvation of the world" (133). Finally, he understands that the "Ability to see the cultural value of wilderness boils down . . . to a question of intellectual humility" (200).[12]

Leopold's rejection of killing the wolf, a species endangered by hunting, amounts to a curbing of the hunting spirit in himself in favor of protecting the hunted species. His work shows interesting compatibility with Spanish philosopher José Ortega y Gasset's *On Hunting*, published in English translation in 1972, and which also provides useful context for interpreting the hunting of wolves and of dogs in the Border Trilogy.[13] Ortega defines hunting as "*what an animal does to take possession, dead or alive, of some other being that belongs to a species basically inferior to its own.*" It is "precisely the series of efforts and skills which the hunter has to exercise to dominate with sufficient frequency the countermeasures of the animal which is the object of the hunt" (57). Ortega stresses that while "killing is not the *exclusive* purpose of hunting" (53), the activities that comprise the hunt cannot occur without the serious life-and-death stakes implied in taking possession of the animal "dead or alive" (thus he rejects as effete the notion of hunting with a camera [106–10]). The hunt's end is signaled by the hunter's taking possession of the prey, usually by killing it, but that is not the goal of hunting. Rather, for Ortega, the goal is the exercise of the predator's efforts and skills that can be practiced only in hunting a wily prey who might realistically evade the hunter. Hunting is not something done to the game by the predator, but it is rather an activity called forth from the inherent "venatic relationship" between two species that "find themselves a very specific distance apart on the zoological scale. . . . [O]ne does not hunt a superior or an almost equal, but neither does one hunt the excessively inferior, because then the latter cannot use his wiles" (58), and in that case there is by definition no hunt. When man hunts, he "opens this margin to the beast deliberately and of his own free will. He could annihilate quickly and easily most animal species, or at least precisely those that he delights in hunting. Far from doing that, he restrains his destructive power, limits and regulates it—the veto *par excellence* is the closed season; he strives to insure the life of the species, and, above all, in the venatic dealing with animals he leaves them, in effect, free to play their own 'game' "(58).

In his parable "Thinking Like a Mountain," Aldo Leopold's rash killing of the she-wolf is not hunting according to Ortega's definition (and Leopold would surely agree), but it is a manifestation of the predatory instinct in man. Ortega describes a similar scene in which a carload of hunters driving to a game reserve saw two wolves cross the road in front of them and pause "with unusual tranquility . . . a few yards from the vehicle. An intense tumult was instantly produced in each one of the travelers" (137). They screeched to a halt and frantically dove for their rifles. They had not been hunting, Ortega emphasizes. Since they were heading to a reserve, their weapons were encased and stored out of their hands. But for Ortega the event is illustrative:

all that sudden uproar shows the automatic discharge of the predatory instinct which survives in modern man as a rudiment. In this case since the men are hunters, it means that the archaic and suffering instinct, nourished by exercise, has been notably rehabilitated in them. . . . The hunters, of course, see the two wolves as "game"— that is, as creatures with regard to which the only adequate behavior is to hunt them. It is a question of reflex and not of deliberation. . . . It is not man who gives to those wolves the role of possible prey. It is the animal . . . which demands that he be considered in this way, so that to not react with a predatory intention would be anti-natural. . . . [H]unting . . . is a relationship that certain animals impose on man, to the point where not trying to hunt them demands the intervention of our deliberate will. . . . It should not be said, then, that the hunters . . . are exceptionally destructive beings that annihilate whatever comes into their view. Not at all; they see the wolves as what they really are—creatures gifted with marvelous powers of evasion, to the point where they are, essentially, "that which escapes," the unsubmissive, the surly, the fugitive, which is generally hidden, absent, unobtainable, wrapped in solitude. (137–38).

Like the hunters Ortega describes, Leopold acts instinctively. He has not been hunting, though he was a hunter whose predatory instinct had been nourished and heightened. His killing this particular wolf, as Leopold himself acknowledges, is simply the exercise of one species' superior technological skill to ambush a member of an "inferior" species encountered by chance. Leopold's youthful conception that killing the wolf preserved the deer, the game species of choice, might place his act within the context of deer-hunting activities except that, as Leopold later came to understand, the deer species needed no protection from the wolf, whereas the wolf species itself needed protection from man. Ortega's definition of hunting excludes the coordinated efforts to expunge the Mexican wolf from the Southwest, in that they were expressions of man's superiority over the wolf with killing as the primary goal. Assassination and genocide (as Burbank refers to wolf-hunting) are not hunting at all in Ortega's sense.

Yet some wolf hunters to a modest extent exercised deliberate will in curbing their destructive powers for the sake of the hunt. And Leopold curbed even his hunting instinct itself for the sake of the environmental matrix, with the goal of preserving all species and leaving them free to "play their own 'game' " (Ortega 58). Their restraint, meager or profound, illuminates Billy's decisions concerning his relation to the *loba*.

Billy is in a unique position to see the wolf. Growing up in Hidalgo County, New Mexico, in the 1930s (he would be ten in 1934), he lives in the ancient runway of the Mexican wolf at a time when they were all but extinct elsewhere in the Southwest.[14] In *The Wolf in the Southwest*, David E. Brown[15] writes, "Only in Hidalgo County's Animas, Peloncillo, and San Luis mountains did wolves persist into the 1930s—their constantly depleted ranks continually refurbished by new recruits crossing the Mexican border along long-established runways . . ." (25). The wolves crossed into Hidalgo County "between the Guadalupe and Peloncillo mountains and between the Peloncillo and Big Hatchet ranges"—the areas from which W. C. Echols took most of his wolves (Brown 75). As the northern extension of Mexico's Sierra Madres, the last natural habitat of the Mexican wolf, the Animas Mountains near the Parhams' homestead "provided a natural travel route for lobos coming in from Mexico" (Brown 77; C 3). Billy's she-wolf crosses "the international boundary line . . . and . . . crossed the old Nations road a mile north of the boundary and followed Whitewater Creek west up into the San Luis Mountains and crossed through the gap north to the Animas range and then crossed the Animas Valley and on into the Peloncillos as told." Then she circles west through Cochise County in Arizona and back east to the Animas Plains where she comes across the first trap set for her by Billy and his father (C 24–26).

In the nineteen-teens and early 1920s, the Mexican wolf had been perceived as a serious threat to livestock (unnecessarily, according to Burbank) and deer (its natural prey). But because of the energetic pursuit of their extinction by trappers such as "Stoke" Ligon, by 1925 wolves had ceased to present any significant problem to ranchers except for the occasional *lobos* that crossed into the United States from Mexico (Brown 71). In the mid-twenties, PARC agents developed the preventive strategy of patrolling the few remaining habitats in the U.S. and posting their most effective wolfers along the border to greet any crossing wolves with hasty annihilation. No other measures were thought necessary (Brown 73, 81). W. C. Echols, whose traps and matrix Billy uses to hunt the she-wolf, was assigned to border patrol in Hidalgo County at the OK Bar Ranch near Cloverdale to hunt wolves in the Animas Mountains (Brown 67, 73, 86). In some years, such as 1932, no wolves were killed in New Mexico except for those taken by Echols on the border (Brown 83, 85), indicating both the success of the government's campaign to eliminate the wolf and Echols's proficiency as a wolf-hunter. He killed about four wolves a year until 1933, when the lessening of "American livestock interests in Old Mexico" and Mexico's discontinuance of its wolf control efforts led to increases in its wolf population and consequently in those that crossed into the United States.[16] Between 1933 and 1943, Echols took between six and nineteen wolves every year except one (Brown 83–86).

When Billy wakes to the sound of wolves howling in his first winter in Hidalgo County, he is hearing the remnant of a nearly extinguished species. He does not react with the alarm that a cattleman in the Southwest might have felt a decade or two earlier or even in the 1930s in Hidalgo County. Billy's first vision of wolves thus has more in common with Aldo Leopold's enlightened recognition of the "green fire" in the she-wolf's eyes than it does with the traditional attitudes of the ranchers or the PARC agents. He responds to the wolf aesthetically and spiritually:

> They were running on the plain harrying the antelope and the antelope moved like phantoms in the snow and circled and wheeled and the dry powder blew about them in the cold moonlight and their breath smoked palely in the cold as if they burned with some inner fire and the wolves twisted and turned and leapt in a silence

Dianne C. Luce 175

such that they seemed of another world entire. . . . He could see their almond eyes in the moonlight. He could hear their breath. He could feel the presence of their knowing that was electric in the air. (C 4)

The boy's reverence is implied in the imagery and diction of the passage describing his vision and in the terse comment that "He never told anybody" (5) what he has seen. But when he has this experience Billy is a child and still quite responsive to the authority of his father (even though his furtive night-time excursion to see the wolves anticipates his sneaking food to the vagabond indian and partially causes his disobedience of his father in returning the wolf to Mexico). When Will Parham determines to trap the she-wolf, Billy naïvely accepts the project with an interest consistent with his childhood fascination with the *lobo*. Indeed, when he begins to track her, he invites the vision again, like Aldo Leopold, "thinking like a mountain": "He closed his eyes and tried to see her. Her and others of her kind, wolves and ghosts of wolves running in the whiteness of that high world as perfect to their use as if their counsel had been sought in the devising of it" (31). Billy's vision of the wolves and his willingness to help his father kill her (and perhaps even his own hunting instinct) are in tension from the beginning of *The Crossing*, and this tension is explored through the contrasting views of the wolf implied in Echols's hunting, which Billy's father endorses, and in Don Arnulfo's comments on the nature of the *lobo*: in his community's admiration for Echols's ability to track the elusive wolf and in Don Arnulfo and Billy's own intuition that the wolf is an indispensable manifestation of the world itself.

In most respects, McCarthy's references to Echols are based in fact. The historical W. C. Echols was the premier wolf hunter on the Hidalgo County/Mexico border until his retirement in 1943 (Brown 86). (Though his absence from his cabin is of considerable duration in *The Crossing*, the cabin is still set up for wolf-hunting, and there is no reference to his having retired.) As Mr. Sanders of the SK Bar Ranch (McCarthy's fictionalized version of the OK Bar Ranch where Echols had his cabin) says, "He's about half wolf hisself" (C 19). Echols used traps rather than the strychnine poisoning favored by some wolf killers, and he was essentially a tracker who read sign left by wolves and then placed his traps strategically to outsmart the animals. They were difficult to take, as they had become wary of man and traps over years of being hunted. Simply tracking the wolf down was ineffective because, as Echols wrote in his accounts of 1927, "They cover 40 miles of country to my personal knowledge on the States side, and probably more in Mexico," so his method was "to place my traps in the most likely passways for them and await results" (Brown 76). A particularly trap-shy wolf might quit the trails altogether, taking to rocky country where tracking was impossible. "When a wolf quits traveling trails," Echols wrote, "anyone familiar with them knows the job of taking one of this character" (Brown 78). Echols had particular difficulty tracking one wolf that came into the Animas Mountains only "at intervals, and does not make the same round at each visit following along the roughest part of the range" (Brown 81). What's more, the wolf often detected the traps: "a large female wolf came up my trapline from the Spur toward OK Ranch, and located and went around every trap. On the following day, I rearranged, or re-set, every trap moving them some and fixed the places where I took them up back just as if the traps were still there" (Echols, quoted in Brown 77). Cattle might blunder into the traps, or coyotes might respond to the lure before wolves did, as in *The Crossing* (28, 39; Brown 162, 81). Or a large wolf capable of dragging a trap some distance might occasionally pull out of a trap entirely (Brown 78, 82). As Will Parham sets the traps, he tells Billy, "Echols used to pull the shoes off his horse. Then he got to where he'd tie these cowhide slippers he'd made over the horse's hooves. Oliver told me he'd make sets and never get down. Set the traps from horseback" (C 23). In a 1925 letter to Stokely Ligon, his supervisor, Echols related that he set his traps with "a small light pole, spiked at the end for this purpose, and never dismounted from my horse unless [the] trap was sprung." He would cover his traps with "the largest piece of dry cow manure I could find." Even then he considered himself "fortunate, as the wolves did not come along until my scent was all gone from setting the traps" (Brown, 73–74). McCarthy also draws on Brown's account of wolf-hunter Roy McBride's quest in 1970 for an elusive she-wolf named Las Margaritas for some of the details of the Parhams' pursuit of the she-wolf in *The Crossing*:

[McBride] made three blind sets in a narrow cow trail in the gap of a mountain, convinced that the wolf would not go to any baited site. . . . McBride had stepped from his horse to a steer hide while setting the traps, the dirt had been removed by a sifter, and the traps had been boiled in oak leaves. The trap could not have been better concealed. Nonetheless, the wolf [left the trail above the first set and] returned to the trail without being caught and approached the second set on the other side of a pine tree that had fallen across the trail. Again the wolf left the trail and went around the trap. As it neared the third trap, the wolf left the trail before getting to the trap site. On trailing up the trap, McBride later found a coyote in it. (162; cf. C 22, 39)

Echols was a hired assassin, but in the practice of his trade he also functioned as a hunter of the wolf in Ortega's sense. His rejection of poisoning, a handicap not embraced by every PARC agent, meant that he must hone his skills of detecting and tracking the wolf. His accounts of his hunts, or at least Brown's excerpts from them, stress the difficulty of outsmarting the wolf and the very real possibility that a wolf might elude him, and they downplay or omit descriptions of the kill.[17]

Echols's traps were probably the double-spring Number $4^{1}/_{2}$ Newhouse favored by most of the Southwest's wolf trappers from 1912 through the 1930s and even later (Brown 34). These are the traps Boyd finds in Echols's cabin that Billy thinks, with good reason, look like bear-traps (C 18). In fact, the $4^{1}/_{2}$ Newhouse weighed $5^{1}/_{4}$ pounds with a jaw spread of $8^{3}/_{4}$ inches (Brown 33).[18] Brown includes no direct reference to Echols's having used scent to lure wolves, and many trappers were more concerned with the placement of their sets than with baiting the traps. One veteran, Bill Castro, said, "I want to get a wolf to step automatically into the trap *before* he has time to think about the bait" (Brown 36). But enough trappers used scent posts to justify Brown's assertion that they were "an important factor in wolf trapping" (36). A basic recipe called for

eight coyote glands (or wolf)
$^{1}/_{4}$ liver with gall
1 kidney
black coyote or wolf dung (black from eating meat diet). (Brown 36)

The glands were ground together and placed in a glass jar in a warm place "until well rotted." Then the dung was dissolved in water or wolf or coyote urine and added to the rotted glands. Another recipe used more of the wolf's body parts, urine, and drops of asafetida, anise oil, tonquin musk and Canton musk rather than dung (Brown 36–37). McCarthy's novel emphasizes the wolf's acute sense of smell as her primary means of perception of the world (see Luce, "Road" 207–10); thus it is appropriate that he makes scent-posting part of Echols's wolf-trapping strategy. The matrix that the Parhams find in Echols's cabin causes Billy's father to whisper, "Good God" when he sniffs it, and to refuse to let Boyd smell it (C 17); but ironically, the matrix made of the glands and urine of dead wolves causes the she-wolf—who "might have left the country altogether if she had not come upon the scent of a wolf just below the high pass west of Black Point"—to stop "as if she'd walked into a wall." She "was moving out of the country not because the game was gone but because the wolves were and she needed them" and she "wore a haunted look" (C 25–26). Social scent is used against her in country where wolf society no longer exists, and the bait keeps her there until she too is trapped. The Parhams do not know what is in Echols's matrix, but the narrator does, and the passage comments on the extinction of the wolf by man, and, significantly, on the extinction of the wolf-trapper himself:

In the jars dark liquids. Dried viscera. Liver, gall, kidneys. The inward parts of the beast who dreams of man and has so dreamt in running dreams a hundred thousand years and more. Dreams of that malignant lesser god come pale and naked and alien to slaughter all his clan and kin and rout them from their house. A god insatiable whom no ceding could appease nor any measure of blood. The jars stood webbed in dust and the light among them made of the little room with its chemic glass a strange basilica dedicated to a practice as soon to be extinct among the trades of men as the beast to whom it owed its being. (C 17)

It was a brutal endeavor. Beyond the scent and the traps, there were the "numbing club" (Brown 37) and the guns used to finish the wolf down to the last one and to put the wolf-hunter finally out of business. As Ortega says, "If man did not [restrain his superiority over his prey] he would not only destroy animals, he would also destroy, coincidentally, the very act of hunting which fascinates him" (58–59). Ortega means that the essence of hunting is voided in such circumstances, but McCarthy's text applies the metaphor of the individual hunt to mankind's relationship to the hunted species, pointing to the end result of man's irresponsible hunting even when hunting is conceived as an expression of man's essential nature, as in Ortega. It implies that however much Echols may participate in the mystery of the hunt, he is ultimately involved in a process that is not hunting at all because it does not take precautions to preserve the venatic relationship, but rather has killing—even eradication of the species—as its true goal. Even Brown, whose dispassion Burbank finds objectionable, writes, "Wolves were killed by any means feasible, not for fur or sport, but simply to 'clean them out'" (32).

Of course Billy is not thinking of this as he pursues the she-wolf. Hunting her using Echols's methods and tools, Billy reawakens his childhood vision of the wolves and confirms and extends his abilities as a tracker. (Years later he takes the lead as he and John Grady search for the den of the wild dogs in *Cities of the Plain*, and he only half-jokingly claims to be "a trackin fool" [171].) He tracks the wolf with the heart of a hunter rather than a killer: his mind is on the challenge of the hunt for the worthiest of opponents. At this point, Billy is unconscious of his desire to preserve the wolf, and his lack of awareness allows him the illusion and the pleasure of the genuine hunt that can only end in the possession of the animal, dead or alive, that Ortega admires. He is, in effect, taking a vacation from the drudgery of his daily routine and escaping into nature, into the "absolute *outside*," which Ortega defines as the essential appeal of sport hunting (139; 152). Billy hears Mr. Sanders tell of Echols's uncanny instinct for finding the wolf: "He'd put down a trap someplace and there wouldnt be the first sign of anything usin there and I'd ask him why he was makin a set there and half the time he couldnt answer it. Couldnt answer it" (C 27). Echols has achieved what Ortega describes as "that mystical union with the animal, a sensing and presentiment of it that automatically leads the hunter to perceive the environment from the point of view of the prey, without abandoning his own point of view" (142). Together with his own failure to trap the wolf, Billy's awareness that Echols has a knowledge he does not is what sends him to Don Arnulfo in Animas, a seven-hour ride north of Cloverdale. Billy asks for a new scent, but he really hopes to hear something about the wolf that will enable him to track her more successfully.

However, what Don Arnulfo tells him undercuts Echols's endeavor, and even though Billy does not recognize it at first, the old man reinforces Billy's early intuition of the value and mystery and spirit of the wolf. Don Arnulfo denies that Echols knows what the wolf knows: "El lobo es una cosa incognoscible. . . . Lo que se tiene en la trampa no es mas que dientes y forro. El lobo propio no se puede conocer. Lobo o lo que sabe el lobo. Tan como preguntar lo que saben las piedras. Los arboles. El mundo" (C 45; The wolf is an unknowable thing. What is caught in the trap is no more than teeth and fur. The wolf itself cannot be known. The wolf or what the wolf knows. Like asking what the stones know. The trees. The world).[19] Further, he warns Billy that the wolf cannot be trapped, that if he catches her, he will have nothing:

> You want to catch this wolf. . . . Maybe you want the skin so you can get some money. . . . You can do that. But where is the wolf? The wolf is like the copo de nieve. . . . You catch the snowflake but when you look in your hand you dont have it no more. Maybe you see this dechado [example]. But before you can see it it is gone. If you want to see it you have to see it on its own ground. If you catch it you lose it. And where it goes there is no coming back from. Not even God can bring it back. (46)

If Don Arnulfo is right that "The wolf is made the way the world is made," to catch her is impossible, for the world "is made of breath only" (46); but to vanquish the wolf from the world is to alter the world beyond the remedy even of God. His paradox stresses both the spiritual nature of the wolf and the irremediable loss of a species pursued to extinction. Both lead to Billy's break with his father and community when he decides to save the wolf instead of killing her. His close and appreciative observation of her as he tries to return her to her kind in Mexico is his naïve and futile attempt to approximate seeing the wolf "on its own ground."

When Billy returns to Cloverdale after hearing Don Arnulfo speak of the mystery of the wolf, he turns off the road "for no reason at all" and finds where the wolf has been digging in the ashes of the *vaqueros*' fire. He sets new traps in the ashes, "but his heart was not in it" (C 49).[20] A crucial shift has already taken place in the tension between his education as a rancher's son and his own intuition about the wolf. Suddenly, Billy achieves intuitive "knowledge" of her movements such as he has admired in Echols, but he no longer cares if he traps the wolf, perhaps because what Don Arnulfo has told him, in meshing so precisely with his earlier spiritual vision of her, elevates her in his mind to the position of an equal—something that Ortega points out makes the hunt impossible, and that Leopold and Burbank, with their ecological visions, would approve. Billy still goes through the motions of hunting her, but when he resets his traps in the ashes of the *vaqueros*' campfire, "He didnt even bother to put on the deerskin gloves" to mask his scent (C 50). When he actually succeeds in trapping her, however, the hunt is rejuvenated precisely because he decides neither to destroy the wolf nor to obey his father's directive to leave the wolf in the trap and fetch him when she is caught. Billy has his father's rifle with him, and it would be no greater disobedience if Billy were simply to kill the wolf as Echols would do than it is for him to take her home with him. His decision to trap her again—to rope her in such a way as to free her from the steel trap but disable her deadly teeth—re-engages him in the essential activities of the hunt and allows him to "take possession" of her more fully than killing her would do (though ultimately and paradoxically he will agree with Don Arnulfo that he does not possess her at all [C 90]).[21] The choice presents greater challenges to his skill and ingenuity than even tracking her has, for in tracking her he has had the help of his father and the model of Echols, but in tying and gradually forging a relationship with this wild creature (not taming her) he has no precedent and almost no sympathy from others. His actions evoke the reader's admiration, however, partly because in Billy's acts we discern an extension and creative improvement on the true "hunt." Ortega ends his meditation on hunting by pointing out how frequently Plato and Saint Thomas Aquinas invoked hunting as a metaphor for their own philosophical striving: "for him [Plato] defining is always like capturing the thing. . . . Like the hunter in the absolute *outside* of the countryside, the philosopher is the alert man in the absolute *inside* of ideas, which are also an unconquerable and dangerous jungle. As problematic a task as hunting, meditation always runs the risk of returning empty-handed" (151–52). Billy's quixotic gesture towards taking the wolf home with him (as if he will ask his parents, "Can I keep her?") postpones his conscious acknowledgment of a decision he has already made in his heart. Billy is a hunter, but not a killer. He has no wish for the wolf to disappear from the world. Instead, he has the philosopher's desire to know the wolf herself, even to grasp what Don Arnulfo has said is essentially unknowable. Further, he moves from the role of bounty hunter to that of steward. He tells the Mexican horsemen "that the wolf was the property of a great hacendado and that it had been put in his care that no harm come to it" (C 90).

Although Billy knows of no precedent for taking a wolf alive and he invents the strategy as he goes along, McCarthy's scene builds on naturalist and artist Ernest Thompson Seton's story "Lobo, King of the Currumpaw," first published in *Scribner's* in 1894 and collected in *Wild Animals I Have Known*.[22] In 1893, Seton had accepted a job offer from a friend, Louis Fitz-Randolph, to reduce the predation on his Currumpaw Ranch near Clayton in northern New Mexico. "[M]y job was to hunt and destroy wolves, and show the cowboys how to do the same" Seton wrote in his autobiography (*Trail* 238). However, though Seton undertook the project in good faith, his biographer, H. Allen Anderson writes that "[g]iven his humanitarian philosophy toward animals, it is not easy to imagine him in the role of a hired wolf hunter." He speculates that Seton accepted the job because he "saw this experience as a golden opportunity to expand his knowledge of wolves and other wildlife in a region of North America he had never seen. In his journal, he analyzed the behavior of local species, and these notes were used in many of his later publications" (54–55). In his story of Lobo, Seton represents himself as the unreflective wolf-hunter, but he writes in the introduction to *Wild Animals I Have Known*, "The life of a wild animal *always has a tragic end*" and asserts that the moral of his book is that "we and the beasts are kin. . . . Since, then, the animals are creatures with wants and feelings differing in degree only from our own, they surely have their rights. This fact, now beginning to be recognized by the Caucasian world, was first proclaimed by Moses and was emphasized by the Buddhist over two thousand years ago" (12–13). In fact, this classic animal story, the first to avoid anthropomorphizing animals, "came to symbolize the extermination of wolves from the southern plains" (Anderson 56) and is a literary antecedent to Leopold's repudiation of wolf-hunting.[23] Anderson writes that for Seton, "the Indians in Canada and, to a lesser extent, the cowboys in New Mexico represented a collective ideal in that both groups demonstrated how men could live in harmony with other men and with their wilderness environment. In that respect, Seton identified more with the utopians and less with [Frederick Jackson] Turner—yet [in the story] he had cast himself as a heroic wolfer with a job to fulfill" (57).

According to Seton's story, Lobo was particularly crafty,[24] and he had evaded all attempts to take him until his mate Blanca was killed and her body's scent used as a lure. He lingered in the area where Blanca was taken, howling his dismay every night until he was captured himself. With traps on all four feet, Lobo lay injured for two days before Seton found him, "Yet, when I went near him, he rose up with bristling mane and raised his voice, and for the last time made the cañon reverberate with his deep bass roar.... How his huge ivory tusks did grind on those cruel chains [of the traps], and when I ventured to touch him with my rifle-barrel he left grooves on it which are there to this day. His eyes glared green with hate and fury, and his jaws snapped with a hollow 'chop,' as he vainly endeavored to reach me and my trembling horse" (*Wild* 50). Like Billy, however, when the moment came to kill Lobo, Seton could not follow through. As Seton and a friend began to choke Lobo to death with their lassos, "[s]omething like compunction" came over him and he decided to take the wolf back to his camp in a manner that anticipates Billy's:

He was so completely powerless now that it was easy to put a stout stick through his mouth, behind his tusks, and then lash his jaws with a heavy cord which was also fastened to the stick. The stick kept the cord in, and the cord kept the stick in so he was harmless. As soon as he felt his jaws were tied he made no further resistance, and uttered no sound, but looked calmly at us and seemed to say, "Well, you have got me at last, do as you please with me." And from that time he took no more notice of us.

We tied his feet securely, but he never groaned, nor growled, nor turned his head.... His breath came evenly as though sleeping, and his eyes were bright and clear again, but did not rest on us.

Chained in a pasture, Lobo ignored the food and water Seton placed near him: "He lay calmly on his breast, and gazed with those steadfast yellow eyes away past me down through the gateway of the cañon, over the open plains—his plains—nor moved a muscle when I touched him. When the sun went down he was still gazing fixedly across the prairie." In the morning, Lobo was dead (51–53).

Setting aside biographical context and judging only from the story, it would appear that, like Leopold's, Seton's experience with Lobo contributed to his repudiation of his old way of relating to animals.[25] Billy's decisions and strategies for saving the she-wolf thus place him in the literary tradition of at least two wolfkillers who repudiated their acts and wrote to encourage others in a more enlightened ecological vision.[26] He understands as he watches the wolf in the light of his night fire that

When those eyes and the nation to which they stood witness were gone at last with their dignity back into their origins there would perhaps be other fires and other witnesses and other worlds otherwise beheld. But they would not be this one. (C 74)

Disturbingly, however, Billy's and more especially John Grady's acts as they hunt down the wild dogs preying on McGovern's cattle in *Cities of the Plain* echo Seton's portrait of his initial brutality in his pursuit of wolves. By Ortega's definition the wild dog hunt is so debased as to comprise no true hunt. Though the dogs have turned feral, they have "no experience as quarry" (COP 162) and they are too easy prey to challenge the men's hunting skills. Ortega writes that "wolves, by nature, count on an 'ideal' hunter. Before any particular hunter pursues them they feel themselves to be possible prey, and they model their whole existence in terms of this condition. Thus they automatically convert any normal man who comes upon them into a hunter" (138). But the wild dogs, bayed by Travis's hunting hounds, howl back in response. In disgust Billy calls them "ignorant sons of bitches" (COP 160). They know no evasive tactics and simply run ahead of the horses as if they can outpace them. The men set out to exterminate these dogs, and though he initially joins his fellows with good cheer, Billy especially seems to have little expectation of any true venatic relationship between the men and the dogs they pursue: "Dogropers, called Billy. I knew it'd come to this." When he and John Grady set off after Joaquín, who calls out "Adelante, muchachos," they correct him, coining the labels "Perreros" and "Tonteros," identifying themselves not as cowboys but as "Dog-boys" (with perhaps a pun on *perrería*—a colloquialism for "dirty trick") and "Fool-boys" (164). The dog-chase is a debasement of the hunt, and the men's reactions of disgust and brutality parallel the wolves' reaction to hunting cattle, who also have no experience as prey: "the ignorance of the animals was a puzzle to them.... The ranchers said they brutalized the cattle in a way they did not the wild game. As if the cows evoked in them some anger. As if they were offended by some violation of an old order. Old ceremonies. Old protocols" (C 25).

Lopez describes this violation of an old ritual, which occurs when the predator hunts a domesticated animal:

> I [call] this exchange in which the animals [predator and prey] appear to lock eyes and make a decision the conversation of death. It is a ceremonial exchange, the flesh of the hunted in exchange for respect for its spirit. In this way both animals, not the predator alone, choose for the encounter to end in death. There is ... a sacred order in this.... And it ... happens only between the wolf and his major prey species. It produces, for the wolf, sacred meat.

Imagine a cow in the place of the moose or white-tailed deer. The conversation of death falters noticeably with domestic stock. . . . They have had the conversation of death bred out of them. They do not know how to encounter wolves. . . .

What happens when a wolf wanders into a flock of sheep and kills twenty or thirty of them in apparent compulsion is perhaps not so much slaughter as a failure on the part of the sheep to communicate anything at all—resistance, mutual respect, appropriateness—to the wolf. The wolf has initiated a sacred ritual and met with ignorance. (94–95)

Though roping and dragging the dogs to death is an efficient means of killing them without risk of shooting one another, John Grady's double-roping the yellow dog with Billy and tearing it apart elevates his cruelty, hinting not only at his status as frustrated predator but also at the anger that underlies his pursuit of these animals that threaten his way of life. In *Wild Animals I Have Known*, Seton writes of his similar method of killing a trapped wolf (Lobo's mate Blanca, in this case) so as to preserve the hide:

Then followed the inevitable tragedy, the idea of which I shrank from afterward more than at the time. We each threw a lasso over the neck of the doomed wolf, and strained our horses in opposite directions until the blood burst from her mouth, her eyes glazed, her limbs stiffened and then fell limp. (46)

Seton repudiates the cruelty of this technique when he applies it to Lobo. John Grady's act shocks Billy out of his complacency despite the fact that he is offended at the degradation of the hunt. Though he never sees the wild dog as the equal of the wolf he has earlier hunted, he is clearly sobered at his complicity in its inhumane death. John Grady coolly retrieves his rope from the feet of the headless dog and then sets out with the gleeful Joaquín after the last of the dogs (who is, ironically, the mother of the pup John Grady will later insist on rescuing and adopting). Billy, on the other hand, remarks to John Grady in the taciturn way he always employs when he is most moved, "Damn. . . . I didnt know you was goin to do that. . . . Son of a bitch." Then he sits coiling his rope, wiping the blood from his hands, and watching silently as John Grady and Joaquín chase after the spotted dog. After Joaquín ropes it and drags it to its death, Billy rides to the rim-rock, lights a cigarette, "and sat looking out over the country to the south" (COP 168)—a gesture that recalls Troy's unnerved reaction to their sudden collision with the owl. At some level Billy must remember his image of the wolf's death by dragging in *The Crossing*: "he suddenly saw as in an evil dream the specter of the horse at full gallop on the plain with the wolf behind at the end of the rope and the dogs in wild pursuit and he snatched the rope from about the saddlehorn just as the reins broke and the horse wheeled and went pounding" (64).[27] Such scenes in the trilogy represent moments of awareness of an essential aspect of man's tragic place within the world—his complicity, even with the best of intentions, in the destruction of the world he loves. Don Arnulfo has said that Billy should seek to recognize the place where God "conspires in the destruction of that which he has been at such pains to create" (C 47), and the trilogy demonstrates that Billy need not look far since man himself, with his predatory instinct, perverted because it is denied, sublimated in "civilization," is the created agent of that destruction.

Indeed, finally Billy kills the very wolf he has saved, and with her the pups she carries in her womb. His choice not to attempt saving the unborn cubs is troubling as it seems a repudiation of his impulse to save the wolf and as it might seem to link him with PARC agents who killed both adults and wolf cubs, engaging in "denning" or the tracking of the dens and destroying the young (although Burbank reports that wolf hunters "often let pups go during denning to assure a reliable crop of animals for future extermination activities, assuring their continued livelihood" [99]). Billy's act is the reverse of John Grady's when he enlists Billy's help to back-track the wild dogs to their den and pups. Both men are thus engaged in paradoxical and self-contradictory behaviors with regard to these wild creatures.

McCarthy's screenplay "Whales and Men" casts light on Billy's decision to let the unborn wolf cubs die with their mother, as his decision is prefigured twice in the choices made by the marine biologist Guy Schuler and ultimately endorsed by the play's other characters. The play begins with a scene of beached whales, which several young people move among compassionately but helplessly while the more experienced Schuler euthanizes them. He has devoted his life to studying and saving whales, and he has come to accept the impossibility of saving every individual. His act is repeated late in the screenplay when he convinces the heart-broken Kelly McAmon (who in many ways adumbrates Billy in her valuing of the whale) that they must kill an orphaned whale before it is torn apart by gathering sharks. This scene parallels Billy's shooting the she-wolf rather precisely, as he recognizes that the dogs being set upon the wolf, apparently limitless in number, will eventually kill her. Billy reaches his decision to turn back and shoot her himself after some time of riding under a "half moon . . . cocked in the east over the mountains like an eye narrowed in anger" (C 121)—a delicate echo of Aldo Leopold's notion of "thinking like a mountain." Similarly, the scene in "Whales" suggests that Billy recognizes the world he might choose to bring the cubs into as one that will pursue them to their deaths as well since it is a world in which men act out the wildness within, all the while denying it and repudiating wildness itself. As much as he has come to respect the wolf, Billy's act is one of acquiescence in the unchangeable darkness of the world, a recognition that his enterprise is "Doomed" (C 129). His new vision is reflected in his ritual shooting of the hawk and watching as it "vanished beyond the cape of the mountain" (C 129). When he finds a drop of its blood, he cuts his hand and mingles his own blood with the hawk's on the stone in a gesture that affirms his brotherhood with the predator on the altar of the world itself.[28] The bow and arrow with which Billy shoots the hawk are fashioned to enable him to hunt for food. When he decides to return to civilization, he commits the bow to the river in a parallel ritual, leaving behind him this "Legacy of some drowned archer, musician, maker of fire" (137), a gesture that hints the ambiguity of his competing but conjoined instincts as both hunter and agent of culture.

Paradoxically, Billy's impulse to save the wolf and her pups can be fulfilled only by helping them to die with a minimum of pain and indignity—as Guy Schuler does with whales in irremediable circumstances. Some of the characters in McCarthy's screenplay, particularly those trained in science like the lapsed doctor John Western and the marine biologist Guy Schuler, intermittently retreat into the "objectivity" of analysis or pure science in response to their horror at the extermination of whales by men who seem no more evil than others.[29] At the end of "Whales and Men," however, its educated and articulate characters, especially Kelly and Peter Gregory, are moved by their witnessing of and complicity in the death of the infant whale to take action to save the species—somewhat like Seton's, Leopold's and Lopez's efforts as teachers or writers to bring mankind to an enlightened view of the wolf and the wilderness. The play ends with Kelly's husband Peter Gregory addressing the Irish Parliament on behalf of the whale, a "nation" which "Because it spoke an alien tongue . . . was given no hearing.

Not in the world's courts and not in mens' [sic] hearts" (133). The wolf, too, is referred to as an alien "nation" in *The Crossing* (74)—as are, of course, the eradicated indians (*APH* 5). The reference is to a well-known passage from another work of ecological vision, Henry Beston's *The Outermost House* (1928), which Guy Schuler quotes from memory in "Whales and Men" (94). In that work, subtitled *A Year of Life on the Great Beach of Cape Cod* and loosely modeled on Thoreau's *Walden*, Beston pleads for "a wiser and perhaps a more mystical concept of animals." Our view of them is distorted because we live "by complicated artifice" and "Remote from universal nature." "And therein we err" he writes:

For the animal shall not be measured by man. In a world older and more complete than ours they move finished and complete, gifted with extensions of the senses we have lost or never attained, living by voices we shall never hear. They are not brethren, they are not underlings; they are other nations, caught with ourselves in the net of life and time, fellow prisoners of the splendour and travail of the earth. (24–25)[30]

Peter Gregory's appeal to Parliament echoes the voices of deep ecologists who "have stressed the link between listening to the nonhuman world (i.e., treating it as a silenced subject) and reversing the environmentally destructive practices modern society pursues" (Manes 16), and it adumbrates the storyteller's question of Billy in the epilogue of *Cities of the Plain*: "Do you love him, that man [who stands in the dock for us]? . . . Will you listen to his tale?" (288–89). The trilogy asks the same of us in regard to the wolf and all the endangered creatures of the border (men and women included). Billy is not articulate and does not fully formulate even his own tale, but he does listen—to wolves and to men. In that, he is our surrogate.

Billy spends his last days in eastern New Mexico, outside of Portales. He has made a vigil to De Baca County to look for the grave of his sister near Fort Sumner (*COP* 289), also, ironically, the burial place of Billy the Kid. But Billy never returns to Hidalgo County, where Boyd has his final resting place. Were he to do so, he would find a world partly restored to the wild and vanishing one of his childhood. For in the Peloncillo and Animas areas of Arizona and New Mexico where Billy trapped the wolf, the Malpai Borderlands Group, a non-profit coalition of ranchers, was formed in 1993 with the goal of restoring "the natural processes that create and protect a healthy, unfragmented landscape to support a diverse, flourishing community of human, plant, and animal life in our Borderlands Region" (J. Page 55). One of its first co-executive directors was rancher Bill McDonald, who in 1998 joined Cormac McCarthy as a MacArthur Fellow. McDonald was concerned that ranchers "were losing ground socially and politically, seen to be raping the land," and the group wanted to demonstrate that they could restore the health of the environment and at the same time preserve the ranching way of life (J. Page 55). Through carefully planned and controlled burns and thoughtful regulation of their cattle's movements on the ranges so as to rest the pastureland, the group has rejuvenated the grasslands, protected endangered species and even witnessed the reappearance of the jaguar.

Central to the group's efforts is the Gray Ranch, a 321,000-acre tract of land in the bootheel of New Mexico that is bisected by the Animas Mountains and that includes the San Luis Pass. The ranch is a single land-holding that had had absentee landlords since the 1880s (J. Page 53, 56). Thus, in all likelihood, this tract includes the land rented by the Parhams in *The Crossing*. When rumors were afloat in the late 1980s that the government was to buy the ranch and create the Animas National Wildlife Refuge, local citizens were distressed at the thought of as many as 65,000 visitors a year descending on the area (J. Page 53). In 1984, proponents of wolf reintroduction were alarmed to hear that the Fish and Wildlife Service and Animal Damage Control agents had instructions to bring in any wolves sighted on the Gray Ranch "dead or alive." And there were also rumors that ranchers were covertly killing wolves in the area (Burbank 154).[31] Then in 1990 the Gray Ranch was purchased by the Nature Conservancy just as it began rethinking its practice of buying up "Last Great Places" and "sequestering them as fenced-off refuges" (J. Page 53). Shortly before the formation of the Malpai Borderlands Group, one of its participating ranchers, Drum Hadley, formed the Animas Foundation, which arranged to purchase the Gray Ranch from the Nature Conservancy (J. Page 56).

For years ranchers and then the Forestry Service had quickly extinguished grassland fires started by lightening strikes, but Hadley and other ranchers of the Malpai Group had come to understand that fire was a vital natural process that was needed to burn away woody and scrub growth such as cholla, mesquite, snakeweed and turpentine bush and allow the regrowth of the native grasses. When Drum Hadley gained control of the Gray Ranch, he fenced cattle out of a 1,662-acre pasture including a former Pleistocene

Lake near San Luis Pass until enough grass returned to support a lightening fire. Within three years, the burned lake bed was lush with grass (J. Page 56).

None of this recent land history appears in the pages of the Border Trilogy, but it is implicit in the location of the Parham ranch. When Boyd and Billy gather wood and Boyd rides in the travois, he watches to the west "where the sun simmered in a dry red lake under the barren mountains" (C 5). Later, he dreams of a "big fire out on the dry lake" and troubled child that he is, he dreams that people are burning in the fire (35), just as he has seen his own fate in the indian's eyes: "Eyes in which the sun was setting. In which the child stood beside the sun" (6). The burning lake is undeniably Dantean and clearly resonates with the apocalyptic detonation of the bomb on the White Sands Missile Range near Alamogordo, New Mexico, with which *The Crossing* ends.[32] But that false dawn is followed by a true one, the rising of the "right and godmade sun" (426). What Boyd cannot envision is the burning lake that signals renewal of the range. And Billy, with his vision of the matrix of life, does not return to Hidalgo to see the cooperation of the ranchers with the environment to preserve them both, which Billy would happily have joined had he been born later, and which he might have led, like Bill McDonald, had he not retreated from his vision in despair of finding in others any "likeness to his own heart" (C 120).

Notes

1. The jackrabbit is not endangered. "The creature's population increases dramatically and plunges just as suddenly. The breeding potential is so high that heavy hunting, disease and an endless array of predators apparently have little effect on jackrabbit numbers.... While expanding human populations have destroyed the habitat of many animals, the transformation of timberland into cropland has increased the food readily available for jackrabbits." Tularemia epidemics periodically reduce the populations, but never wipe them out. Ranchers' attitudes toward the overabundant jackrabbit are indicated in the facts that until fairly recently some western states offered bounties for them, and drives to herd the hares into a tightening circle and then beat them to death with clubs were organized. Now there is more awareness of the natural cycle of population control among the jackrabbits, and ranchers allow nature to take its course (Curtis 11–12).

2. Indeed, Peter Coates writes that revisionist historians of the West have recently pointed to the cowboy as one of the causes of ecological trouble in the Southwest: "the cowboy who has

for so long sheltered behind the image of the Marlboro Man at large in settings of pristine natural beauty is in the firing line as the ultimate contemporary eco-villain and varmint. Cowboys and cattlemen are in trouble not only for opposing the wolf's return but because their bovines denude the public lands, squeezing out wildlife by hogging grazing and water" (246).

3. In his essay-review skeptically assessing New Western History, Coates cites the *longue durée* of Donald Worster, whom he singles out as the best of these new historians. Coates summarizes Worster's position that despite outrageous economic and ecological imperialism evident in the history of the West, "human conquest is an illusion. Nature bats last and will strike back. . . . His [Worster's] triumphant cry that nature will prevail 'too wild really to tame, too old to change, too large to reduce to a mere human scale' echoes Ernest Hemingway's stance in that archetypical 'lost generation' novel, *The Sun Also Rises* (1926), which its huntin' and fishin' author characterized as a human tragedy with the earth living on, taking his cue from Ecclesiastes 1:4 'one generation passeth away and another generation cometh; but the earth abideth forever. The sun also rises' " (253). See also my discussion of the ending of *The Crossing*, with its echoes of Ecclesiastes and Hemingway in "The Road and the Matrix" (Arnold and Luce 212, and esp. 218 n24).

4. For full discussion of the concept of the timelessness of the world itself and its treatment in the gypsy's tale and elsewhere in *The Crossing*, see my chapter, "The Road and the Matrix: The World as Tale in *The Crossing*" (Arnold and Luce 195-219).

5. In "Whales and Men" Guy Schuler says, "If I dont know what the whale is how can I talk about his nonexistence. What is it that doesnt exist? There are times when . . . I get a fleeting vision of the pure platonic whale and I have a sense that what we are after, the whaleness of the whale, does exist as an idea, but an idea with which we are inadequate to deal. . . . I think Melville is right. It's like killing God. *That* whale's existence is the whale I cant deal with. . . . I wont know in this world where that whale will have gone when the last whale is slaughtered and hauled from the sea. But that there can be no whale seems a sort of monstrous paradox" (25).

6. See similar passages, some with variant phrasing, in *All the Pretty Horses* (58, 94, 149, 173); *The Crossing* (190, 371); and *Cities of the Plain* (137-38).

7. Billy's visions are diminished after the death of the she-wolf, but this one occurring in his dreams is prompted by the story told him by the blind man and his wife. It is as if he unconsciously accepts the advice that the *sepulturero* (gravedigger or sexton) has given the blind man's wife not to forget the faces of her lost family even though this keeps her sorrow alive: "while it was true that time heals bereavement it does so only at the cost of the slow extinction of those loved ones from the heart's memory which is the sole place of their abode then or now. Faces fade, voices dim. Seize them back, whispered the sepulturero. Speak with them. Call their names. Do this and do not let sorrow die for it is the sweetening of every gift" (C 288).

8. The barn owl, with its heart-shaped face and its pale feathers, is endangered in several states because of the reduction of grasslands and meadowlands which are its chief hunting habitats (Mooney 42). The large owl Billy hits with the truck is more likely a great horned owl, whose coloration is more moth-like. The great horned owl is not an endangered species.

9. See my "The Road and the Matrix: The World as Tale in *The Crossing*" for discussion of the *gitano*'s complementary consolation that time and loss are illusory and that the world itself is eternal.

10. Burbank and Lopez both stress the differences between Native American views of the wolf and those of Europeans and Anglo-Americans. For example, Lopez writes, "most Indians respected the wolf's prowess as a hunter, especially his ability to always secure game, his stamina, the way he moved smoothly and silently across the landscape. They were moved by his howling, which they sometimes regarded as talking with the spirit world. The wolf appears in many of their legends as a messenger in fact, a great long-distance traveler, a guide for anyone seeking the spirit world. . . . The wolf as oracle, as interlocutor with the dead, is an old idea" (102–03).

Coates points out that "For the average preservationist, . . . the wolf's supreme value resides in how it symbolizes a prelapsarian wilderness that was once the entire continent" (241). While McCarthy's work obviously encompasses this view, his emphasis on the enduring nature of the wolf and of the world itself modifies without undermining his conservationist stance. While it expresses the ethics of deep ecology, the trilogy also encompasses a transcendence of eco-tragedy.

11. The causes are complex, however. The riparian habitat of the Rio Grande river valley has now been reduced by 95 percent due to clearing of land for agricultural and other development and the building of dams, which have disrupted the flood cycles that once watered the large streamside trees (Monks 24). Paradoxically, the increase in winter precipitation in the area resulting from global warming and the heating of the Pacific Ocean has promoted the growth of cool-season active weedy and woody vegetation and contributed to the squeezing out of the warm-season active grasses. Thus, according to ecologist James Brown, "You've got the strange situation . . . where more moisture is leading to what appears to be desertification" (Page 60). Largely due to man's interventions, the border grasslands are dying.

Interestingly, according to Flader it was Leopold's two visits to the Mexican state of Chihuahua in 1936 and 1937 that contributed most strongly to his new ideas concerning the contributions of diverse species to the health of the biotic community. In his essay "Conservationist in Mexico" Leopold wrote: "It is ironical . . . that Chihuahua, with a history and a terrain so strikingly similar to southern New Mexico and Arizona should present so lovely a picture of ecological health, whereas our own states, plastered as they are with National Forests, National Parks and all the other trappings of conservation, are so badly damaged that only tourists and others ecologically color-blind, can look upon them without a feeling of sadness and regret." There he found deer thriving among their natural predators in a ratio that had been stable for centuries. Flader concludes, "Leopold's trip in the Chihuahua sierra marked his first clear realization that deer and predators could coexist in relative equilibrium in an uncontrolled environment. . . . [I]t was the trip to Mexico that finally made him appreciate the function of predators in maintaining the health of the system—or indeed let him see what health was" (153–54).

12. Leopold continues: "The shallow-minded modern who has lost his rootage in the land assumes that he has already discovered what is important; it is such who prate of empires, political or economic, that will last a thousand years" (200). In the Border Trilogy, the pimp Eduardo is the individual who best exemplifies this attitude, with his buying and selling of women and his boasting to John Grady that "we will devour you, my friend. You and all your pale empire" (COP 253). But implicit in the trilogy is also McCarthy's criticism of the machinery of American imperialism and its rage to dominate foreign lands, peoples, and the very environment. The narrator of *Cities of the Plain* comments on John Grady's childhood that he

was nurtured like a "young lord. As if he were never to be disinherited by war and war's machinery" (204).

13. Meine indicates that Leopold read works in conservation philosophy by Ortega in the early 1930s (296).

I am grateful to Jacob Rivers for calling my attention to Ortega's *On Hunting* and to Ernest Thompson Seton's *Wild Animals I Have Known*.

14. An occasional wolf was still to be taken in Grant County, just north of Hidalgo County, in the late 1920s (Brown 74–75). The Parham family moves from Grant County to Hidalgo County (C 3).

15. My use of Brown was anticipated by Sean K. Robisch in his paper, "The Trapper Mystic: Werewolves in *The Crossing*" delivered at the conference, Cormac McCarthy: An International Colloquy, El Paso, Texas, October 1998, and subsequently published in *Southwestern American Literature* 25.1 (1999) 50–54.

16. Brown explains:

> From 1934 to 1940, during Lazaro Cárdenas's presidency, many large estates in Mexico were broken up and small plots of land given to peasants. Many of these large ranchos in Chihuahua and Sonora had been owned or operated by Americans. The portioning of these lands and the generally poor economic conditions caused professional predator trappers, mostly gringos, to leave the country.
>
> These measures undoubtedly resulted in a few years of reduced pressure against the wolf and led to concern about wolves along the border (101).

17. The tally of wolves taken is always included, however, which prompts James Burbank to write in *Vanishing Lobo*, "For those who want to quantify and measure the extent of wolf eradication in the Southwest, I recommend David L. [sic] Brown's book, *The Wolf in the Southwest*, which provides all the figures, charts, documentation, and statistics one might wish for, along with a well-developed discussion of wolf-killing methodologies. Let those who wish to quantify the eradication of the wolf do so" [106]. Brown regrets the extermination of the wolf, but there is admiration for the wolf-hunter's skill in his accounts of Ligon and Echols's successes in the field.

18. For a photograph of this large and formidable-looking trap, see Brown 34. Lopez prints a photo of the Newhouse Number 14 wolf trap, which was developed later. With toothed jaws, it was designed to hold the wolf more securely (190).

19. Adumbrating Don Arnulfo's lesson to the Western boy and to McCarthy's Western readers, Lopez writes, "The mistake that is made . . . with consistency, it seems, only by educated Western people, is to think that there is an ultimate wolf reality to be divined, one that can only be unearthed with microscope and radio collar." The indian does not share this misconception: "The animal is observed as a part of the universe. Some things are known, others are hidden. But it is not a thing to be anxious over" (80).

20. Again, McCarthy borrows details from McBride's capture of Las Margaritas: "At times, McBride noticed that Las Margaritas had investigated a campfire along the road where log truck drivers would stop and cook. He decided to set a trap near a road that the wolf was sure to come down if it continued to kill in this pasture. He built a fire over the trap and let it burn out. At the edge of the ashes he placed a piece of dried skunk hide. . . . [T]he wolf came down the road, winded the ashes and skunk hide, and walked over to investigate. Las Margaritas was

caught by the crippled foot and the trap held" (Brown 163; cf. C 50, 52). See Brown 160 for a photograph of Las Margaritas taken by McBride after he had killed her.

21. In his historical analysis of European and Anglo-American attitudes about the wolf, Lopez points out that René Descartes "articulated the belief that not only were animals put on earth for man's use but they were . . . without souls and therefore man incurred no moral guilt in killing them. This was a formal denial of a 'pagan' idea abhorrent to the Roman Church at the time: that animals had spirits, that they should not be wantonly killed, and that they did not belong to men" (147).

22. Lopez also summarizes Seton's story in *Of Wolves and Men* (192–93).

23. As a schoolboy, Leopold read Seton's works and at Yale he attended a lecture series that included Seton (Meine 16, 52). It is plausible to think that when he met Hochbaum's challenge to write of his own renunciation of wolf-killing, Leopold may have drawn on Seton's account of killing Lobo.

24. Anderson points out that Seton "ascribed to Lobo the adventures of several individual wolves observed or reported in the Clayton area . . . before narrating the events leading to the old marauder's capture" (56).

25. In another account of his time in the Southwest, Seton also repudiated the extermination of canids. According to Anderson, Seton was supposed to have hit upon a method of taking two coyotes every night. But in "Four Months in New Mexico" Seton wrote, "I have changed from a coyote killer to a coyote protector; and the devilish secret of destruction shall perish with me" (Anderson 51).

26. Lopez is clearly part of this tradition although he does not depict himself as a wolf-hunter in the same way as do Seton and Leopold. Lopez chronicles his own conversion experience, which like Billy's involved a repudiation of the male role models he had been raised to emulate:

> Hunting is an ingrained male activity, especially in rural America, where few male children grow up not wanting to hunt. I hunted as a boy and I remember very clearly the first time I thought there was something wrong with the men I admired, something fundamentally backward about the kind of hunting that was held out to me as what men were supposed to do. . . . I was reading a book about big game animals in which Jack O'Connor, then the gun editor of *Outdoor Life*, described suddenly coming on seven wolves on a river bar in the Yukon. O'Connor . . . opened fire. 'With considerable expenditure of ammunition,' he wrote, he killed four of them, and then said he was sorry he'd done it for two reasons. 'For one it was August and the hides were worthless. For another, my shooting spooked an enormous grizzly bear.'
>
> I couldn't get over that.
>
> . . . [O'Connor] never questioned his own role as a predator, nor his right to kill another predator, like the wolf, in pursuit of its game." (160)

Lopez's accounts of wolf hunters include other instances of their "ambivalence." For example, he quotes Alaskan trapper Lawrence Carson, whose remorse sounds remarkably like those of Seton and Leopold:

> Lobo died as he had lived, in defiance of all things that would dare to conquer him. His bloody career was ended, but even in death his fiery eyes and truculent jaws opened in a look of unremitting hate. Lobo, king of his domain—and rightly a king he was called—was dead. . . .

As I looked at his lifeless form, a feeling of condonation came over me. Even though he had been a wanton destroyer of wild life and ill-deserving of mercy, somehow I felt sorry that he was gone. I wondered if the great mountains and deep silent valleys that had been his range would miss him. I wondered if at night, when the moon hung low like a great ball of fire, the dark, shaggy spruce trees would miss his wild, deep-throated call. Something has [sic] been taken away that would never be put back in the scheme of things. Somehow I felt as if there was an irrepairable loss. (163)

27. Barry Lopez describes an even more brutal wolf-killing that occurred in Texas a few years before the writing of his book on wolves:

... three men on horseback rode down a female red wolf and threw a lasso over her neck. When she gripped the rope with her teeth to keep the noose from closing, they dragged her around the prairie until they'd broken her teeth out. Then while two of them stretched the animal between their horses with ropes, the third man beat her to death with a pair of fence pliers. (152)

28. Edwin Arnold has suggested to me the relevance of Robinson Jeffers's "Hurt Hawks," in which the speaker reluctantly gives "the lead gift" to a crippled hawk, noting that "The wild God of the world is sometimes merciful to those / That ask mercy, not often to the arrogant." Acknowledging kinship with the predator, the speaker says, "I'd sooner, except the penalties, kill a man than a hawk; but the great redtail / Had nothing left but unable misery. . . ." When he gives the hawk freedom,

What fell was relaxed,
Owl-downy, soft feminine feathers; but what
Soared: the fierce rush: the night-herons by the flooded river
cried fear at its rising
Before it was quite unsheathed from reality. (198–99)

The poem resonates with several of the trilogy's instances of animals (especially predators) killed at the hands of man out of either mercy or cruelty: Billy's killing of the she-wolf and her apotheosis in the mountains, his shooting the hawk (out of quite a different impulse), and his hitting the owl with the truck.

29. In "Whales and Men" John Western infers that Schuler stopped trying to save the whales after he spent some time on a whaler:

He found the men likable, generous. Many of them seemed to have a feeling for the whales. He thought if he could find out why men kill whales it would help him to stop it. Instead this question led him into mazes in the human psyche from which he felt fortunate to escape with his soul intact. (82)

Similarly, Barry Lopez writes, "It is easy to criticize Western man for his wholesale destruction of the wolf and to forget the milieu in which it was effected. The men I have met who killed wolves at one time or another for a living were not barbarians. Some were likable, even humble men; others were insecure, irresponsible" (144).

Later in "Whales and Men" Kelly observes to Guy that he was not faithful in his attempts to protect the whales, and he agrees with her, explaining:

> I pretended it was a matter of keeping an emotional distance from the whales so that I could do the work. But . . . I saw where the sort of commitment I contemplated could take me. That there could come a point somewhere where I would have to choose. Between whales and men. That I could be called upon to take sides in some irrevocable way and that ultimately it could mean taking human life. And I knew that if I did I was lost. (115)

30. In "The Road and the Matrix," I discuss the matrix of value and meaning accessed through the human capacity for narrating the world and treat in this context the images of the net of life and time, and the web of the world woven by God. But the metaphor of the web or net of life is common in ecological writing as well. Indeed, this passage from Beston serves as epigraph for Barry Lopez's *Of Wolves and Men* (1978).

31. According to Richard Woodward, who interviewed McCarthy in 1992, McCarthy was acquainted with writer and radical environmentalist Edward Abbey, and he met with him shortly before Abbey's death in 1989 to discuss a covert program to reintroduce wolves to southern Arizona (30). Abbey's manifesto of environmental activism, the novel *The Monkey Wrench Gang* (1975), describes the ecologically corrupt cities of the West and their demand for technology and hydraulic power in terms that are relevant to McCarthy's Border Trilogy, especially its final volume:

> Thickets of power cables, each strand as big around as a man's arm, climbed the canyon walls on steel towers, merged in a maze of transformer stations, then splayed out toward the south and west—toward Albuquerque, Babylon, Phoenix, Gomorrah, Los Angeles, Sodom, Las Vegas, Nineveh, Tucson, the cities of the plain. (27)

32. See Jacqueline Scoones's article in this volume, "The World on Fire: Ethics and Evolution in Cormac McCarthy's Border Trilogy" (n18) for discussion of archaeological evidence of the burning of this place in ancient warfare.

Works Cited

Abbey, Edward. *The Monkey Wrench Gang*. New York: Avon, 1992.

Anderson, H. Allen. *The Chief: Ernest Thompson Seton and the Changing West*. College Station: Texas A&M UP, 1986.

Arnold, Edwin T. "The Last of the Trilogy: First Thoughts on *Cities of the Plain*." Arnold and Luce 221–47.

Arnold, Edwin T., and Dianne C. Luce. *Perspectives on Cormac McCarthy*. Rev. ed. Jackson: UP of Mississippi, 1999.

Beston, Henry. *The Outermost House: A Year of Life on the Great Beach of Cape Cod*. New York: Holt, 1988.

Brown, David E., ed. *The Wolf in the Southwest: The Making of an Endangered Species*. Tucson, U of Arizona P, [1983].

Burbank, James C. *Vanishing Lobo: The Mexican Wolf and the Southwest*. Boulder: Johnson Books, 1990.

Coates, Peter. "State of the Art: Chances with Wolves: Renaturing Western History." *Journal of American Studies* 28.2 (1994): 241–54.
Curtis, William. "He's All Ears!" *National Wildlife* 17 (Feb.–Mar. 1979): 10–13.
Flader, Susan L. *Thinking Like a Mountain: Aldo Leopold and the Evolution of an Ecological Attitude Toward Deer, Wolves, and Forests.* Columbia: U of Missouri P, 1974.
Jeffers, Robinson. *The Selected Poetry of Robinson Jeffers.* New York: Random, 1959.
Leopold, Aldo. *A Sand County Almanac and Sketches Here and There.* New York: Oxford UP, 1949.
Lopez, Barry Holstun. *Of Wolves and Men.* New York: Scribner's, 1978.
Luce, Dianne C. "The Road and the Matrix: The World as Tale in *The Crossing*." Arnold and Luce 195–219.
———. " 'When You Wake': John Grady Cole's Heroism in *All the Pretty Horses*." *Sacred Violence: A Reader's Companion to Cormac McCarthy.* Ed. Wade Hall and Rick Wallach. El Paso: Texas Western P, 1995. 155–67.
Manes, Christopher. "Nature and Silence." *The Ecocriticism Reader: Landmarks in Literary Ecology.* Ed. Cheryll Glotfelty and Harold Fromm. Athens: U of Georgia P, 1996. 15–29.
McCarthy, Cormac. *All the Pretty Horses.* New York: Vintage, 1993.
———. *Cities of the Plain.* New York: Vintage, 1999.
———. *The Crossing.* New York: Vintage, 1995.
———. "Whales and Men." Unpublished ts. Cormac McCarthy Papers, Southwestern Writers Collection, Albert B. Alkek Library, Southwest Texas State U, San Marcos.
Meine, Curt. *Aldo Leopold: His Life and Work.* Madison: U of Wisconsin P, 1988.
Monks, Vicki. "Bordering on Extremes." *National Wildlife* 37 (June/July 1999): 22–29.
Mooney, Rick. "Helping a Heartland Hunter." *National Wildlife* 26 (June–July 1988): 40–44.
Ortega y Gasset, José. *On Hunting.* Trans. Howard B. Wescott. New York: Scribner's, 1972.
Page, Jake. "Ranchers Form a 'Radical Center' to Protect Wide-Open Spaces." *Smithsonian* 28 (June 1997): 50–61.
Scoones, Jacqueline. "The World on Fire: Ethics and Evolution in Cormac McCarthy's Border Trilogy." *A Cormac McCarthy Companion: The Border Trilogy.* Ed. Edwin T. Arnold and Dianne C. Luce. Jackson: UP of Mississippi, 2001. 131–60.
Seton, Ernest Thompson. *Trail of an Artist-Naturalist: The Autobiography of Ernest Thompson Seton.* London: Hodder and Stoughton, 1951.
———. *Wild Animals I Have Known.* New York: Grosset & Dunlap, 1926.
Woodward, Richard B. "Cormac McCarthy's Venomous Fiction." *New York Times Magazine* 19 Apr. 1992: 28–31+.

COWBOY CODES IN CORMAC MCCARTHY'S BORDER TRILOGY

Phillip A. Snyder

I

Where's the all-american cowboy at?

—*Cities of the Plain* 3

This question, uttered by Billy Parham in the second paragraph of Cormac McCarthy's *Cities of the Plain* in reference to John Grady Cole, circumscribes the central issue around which all three volumes of the trilogy revolve: the shifting locus of American cowboy identity and the displacement of the vocation within which that identity and its attendant values once flourished. The settings of the Border Trilogy volumes, not to mention their writing, are far removed from the thirty-year post-Civil War heyday of the cowboy and the cattle industry and thus connect themselves mostly to the legend that remains, despite their authentic and realistic textures. As David Dary writes in his epilogue to *Cowboy Culture*,

The golden age of the real cowboy in the American West was gone as the twentieth century dawned. Yet a cowboy culture was still glowing brightly in the minds of Americans. While this culture still permeates our society, it is not the culture of the real nineteenth century cowboy. Rather it is a blend of fact and imagination.... (332)

Operating in the midst of the twentieth century and endangered by habitat loss and familial dislocation, McCarthy's cowboys must adapt to a new western environment or die, particularly after their attempts to relocate themselves in Mexico, the original, centuries-old site of cowboying in the Americas, prove to be instructive and evocative but ultimately unsuccessful. Although unrivaled in its stylistic excellence and thematic complexity, the Border Trilogy shares with other modern and contemporary western texts a hard-edged nostalgia for the cowboy past tinged with a persistent advocacy of cowboy virtues in the present, particularly as invested in the materiality of cowboy culture. For example, much like the contemporary rodeo, through which largely anachronistic ranch skills have found a rationale and locus for being quite apart from their original practical necessity in earlier ranch culture, the Border Trilogy preserves such traditional cowboy codes as "riding for the brand" exhibited in such traditional cowboy tasks as breaking horses and checking range cattle. These tasks are now seriously imperilled as essential western activities, even in contemporary cattle production. As cowboy codes continue to assert their influence on contemporary American culture, literary and otherwise, the cowboy occupations out of which they came are becoming increasingly archaic. In *Cowboys of the Americas*, Richard W. Slatta describes the Anglo cowboy of the late nineteenth-century American West as an ambiguous figure whose essential qualities as described by contemporary observers depended greatly on the circumstances of their observation—mostly on whether the cowboy was at play or at work: "Writers who saw cowboys in town, letting off steam after months on the trail or range, saw only lawlessness and debauchery in the cowboy's life. The few observers who actually spent time on the range with working cowhands formed an entirely different and positive view" (47–48). John Baumann's laudatory 1887 assessment, for example, focuses entirely on the cowboy character as embodied in the cowboy vocation: "He is in the main a loyal, long-enduring, hard-working fellow, grit to the backbone, and tough as whip cord;

performing his arduous and often dangerous duties, and living his comfortless life, without a word of complaint about the many privations he has to undergo" (qtd. in Slatta 47). From the beginning, then, the myth of cowboy virtues depended directly on the reality of vocational cowboy performance.

To sustain its exploration of the ambiguous space between the myth and reality of the modern West, the Border Trilogy depends primarily on its two young protagonists, both of whom possess a visceral loyalty to a vanishing lifestyle and a stubborn persistence in quest completion. *All the Pretty Horses* chronicles sixteen-year-old John Grady Cole's 1948 American disinheritance and his subsequent Mexican search to recover the familial ranching dream from which he has been and will continue to be distanced. As a parallel initiation story, *The Crossing* charts sixteen-year-old Billy Parham's tripartite Mexican journey toward an integration of personal freedom and individual responsibility as expressed first in his obsession to trap and then free a she-wolf; second in his and his younger brother Boyd's attempt to recover his family's stolen horses; and third in Billy's quest to find his lost brother. Both texts reenact the traditional western male initiation pattern—as exemplified in such diverse texts as Charlie Siringo's autobiographical *A Texas Cowboy* and Jack Schaefer's fictional *Monte Walsh*—in which the initiate-protagonist escapes the confines of home, finds sufficient vocational mentors for guidance, and undergoes the requisite series of physical and spiritual trials out of which he emerges tried and true to the developmental ideal of the western man: self-determined, self-contained, self-assured, and self-evident. However, McCarthy also keeps the efficacy and relevance of such western initiation open to question, especially in *Cities of the Plain*, set in 1952 and featuring more vocational cowboy activity than the other two volumes. The novel continues to trace the initiation denouement, or unraveling, of John Grady and Billy, each of whom still refuses to relinquish his essential cowboy self-identity—John Grady as the mythic cowboy in search of a lost homestead and Billy as the loyal saddle pard in search of a balance between the demands of idealism and pressures of reality. Both face the positive/negative polarities that seem inherent in each of their archetypal cowboy qualities, but only Billy, the trilogy survivor, displays enough flexibility and pragmatism to compromise rigid cowboy ideals, even though he ends up as a stand-in substitute for his former cowboy self as a movie extra, an old drifter, his saddle long since sold and his separation from his self-identifying cowboy vocation almost complete. McCarthy consistently undercuts the ideological and pragmatic foundations of the *bildungsroman*, a genre committed to the articulation of the fulfillment of a developmental human ideal: a mature character who comes to be at home in the world. While still investing his two protagonists with the heroic stature and admiration traditionally due them, he suggests that both of their choices—John Grady's dying young with little compromise and Billy's living old with much accommodation—amount to essentially the same thing in the end. Neither choice delays the inevitable changes in the twentieth-century West both protagonists see coming. Neither choice ends in the completion of their respective quests; neither choice settles their drifting wanderlust; and neither choice leaves anything of much substance beyond their individual narratives, which are, however, very substantial.

Thus McCarthy critiques and renovates, at the same time as he reaffirms, the cowboy codes which structure the behavioral patterns of John Grady and Billy. These cowboy codes also embody ideals which signify well beyond their western borders, reflecting national notions of a fundamental American identity and revealing an essentially American anxiety over the apparent instability of that identity. As Henry Nash Smith observes in *Virgin Land* with reference to Frederick Jackson Turner's frontier thesis, Americans may still see themselves as having been formed by the call of the West and the requirements of extending the border between civilization and frontier westward across the country. Writing around the same time period in which the Border Trilogy is set, Smith calls this frontier notion a "massive and deeply held conviction" (4), and it remains a pervasive cultural myth today regardless of its historical validity. In short, we, along with John Grady and Billy, want to believe in the pragmatic sufficiency of a mythic ideology. This may be the most significant border McCarthy explores in the trilogy—the one that lies in the gap between the ideal and the real, a wild zone in which often conflicting elements are given play to produce a shifting relation of theory and practice characterized by a deferral of closure and marked by a continuous accommodation. In the last paragraph of his conclusion to *Gunfighter Nation*, a rich exploration of the frontier myth in twentieth-century America, Richard Slotkin addresses the dynamics of mythic discourse and stresses the necessity of such deferral and accommodation in producing and transmitting that discourse:

Myth is not only something *given* but something *made*, a product of human labor, one of the tools with which human beings do the work of making culture and society. The discourses of myth are, and have been, medium as well as message: instruments of linguistic and ideological creativity as well as a constraining grammar of codified memories and beliefs. We can use that instrument to reify our nostalgia for a falsely idealized past . . . or we can make mythic discourse one of the many ways we have of imagining and speaking truth. By our way of remembering, retelling, and re-imagining "America," we too engage myths with history and thus initiate the processes by which our culture is steadily revised and transformed. (559–60)

Slotkin's privileging here of myth-making as purposeful production rather than as naïve consumption underscores the importance of our taking responsibility for our mythic discourse and the ideology underlying it, particularly by encouraging its continuous revision, because only by such revision can we call ourselves and our mythic discourse into question. This revisionary calling into question opens up the possibilities for multiple sites and modes for truth-telling within our mythic discourse and also may ensure the existence and viability of a counter-discourse which mediates against the totalizing effects of mainstream mythic discourse.

Accordingly, McCarthy's articulation of cowboy codes eschews closed interpretations of simplistic singularity and instead celebrates their function as open dialogic figures capable of suggesting an ambient and infinite signification within the gaps present in even their most essential aspects. McCarthy's cowboy codes may be represented productively as binary figures—such as independence/integration for the paradoxical cowboy character—whose deconstruction produces borderline meanings which subvert, rather than assert, the code's hegemonic hierarchy. Further, for John Grady and Billy, these binary codes function within the larger unity/multiplicity social figure which Jacques Derrida describes in the following passage as the site for self/other interaction. Here Derrida argues that individuals, like societies, are defined fundamentally by their capacity to be different from themselves, which difference constitutes the ground of the ethical relation within society, calling self-identity into question by bringing it into relation with another identity:

[D]econstruction . . . insisted not on multiplicity for itself but on the heterogeneity, the difference, the disassociation, which is absolutely necessary for the relation to the other. The privilege granted to unity, to totality, to organic ensembles, to community as a homogenized whole—this is a danger for responsibility, for decision, for ethics, for politics. . . . [T]he identity of a culture is a way of being different from itself. . . . Once you take into account this inner and other difference, then you pay attention to the other and you understand that fighting for your own identity is not exclusive of another identity, is open to another identity. . . . That is what I tried to demonstrate in the book called *The Other Heading*: in the case of culture, person, nation, language, identity is a self-differentiating identity, an identity different from itself, having an opening or gap within itself. (13–14)

In other words, Derrida argues that cultures and individuals escape totality, or closure via the unity of homogenized wholeness, by definition, because the very identity of cultures and individuals *is* to be self-differentiating and therefore open to the other. In addition, the tension inherent in these cultural or individual openings or gaps creates an ethical responsibility to account for the binary figure's dissonance and to defer its closure, especially in relation to the self and the other. In fighting for their own identities, for example, John Grady and Billy must engage other identities, as well as the binary cowboy codes, in ethical terms, because the cowboy culture in which they operate is not a unified totality but an infinite heterogeneity whose codes insist on privileging figures which are different from themselves. While we may structure many such possible figures, the following five binary codes will suffice to demonstrate the basic status of cowboy codes in the Border Trilogy as essentially heterogeneous and thus ethically grounded: independence/integration, dominance/dependence, rivalry/respect, survival/hospitality, and action/eloquence.

II

Son, not everbody thinks that life on a cattle ranch in west Texas is the second best thing to dyin and goin to heaven.

—*All the Pretty Horses* 17

Independence/Integration. This figure represents the duality of self-sufficiency and teamwork in cowboy culture as manifested, for example, in such standard notions as "top hand" and "riding for the brand" or "saddle-pards," and may be the most pervasive defining figure in the construction of cowboy character, literary and otherwise. While individual excellence and independence may be at the center of cowboy identity, that identity also depends on relationships forged in vocational and familial communities; western individuality would be incomplete without its integration into communal activities which demand cooperation and loyalty. Even a drifting cowboy like Monte Walsh, independent and proud of his vocational status long after he has become an anachronism, still exhibits tremendous loyalty to his former partner, Chet Rollins, who, like Billy, accommodates himself to the changing West; although individually unmatched as a cowboy, Monte forges his cowboy identity and achieves most of his greatest cowboy exploits as part of the Slash Y cowboy crew. The central relationship around which Larry McMurtry's *Lonesome Dove* quartet[1] revolves is the partnership of Woodrow Call and Augustus McCrae who, despite their vastly different temperaments, form a decades-long union that nothing can break. For instance, after McCrae's Montana death at the end of *Lonesome Dove*, Call fulfills his partner's last request and singlehandedly takes McCrae's body on an epic journey back to Texas for burial, stubbornly rejecting any consideration except his promise to his partner. Likewise, Mackey Hedges's *Last Buckaroo*, a semi-autobiographical first novel by a working cowboy, explores the dynamics of cowboy partnership in depicting the evolving relationship between Tap McCoy, an old buckaroo[2] and Dean McCuen, a dude intent on becoming a cowboy, as they drift from outfit to outfit. At first, Dean is hired on only because Tap won't work without him, but as the novel progresses, Dean's skills develop from his growing experience while Tap's skills diminish because of age, bringing about a generational reversal as Tap is hired on only because of Dean. The main plot of Louis L'Amour's *Conagher* centers on the title character's refusal to desert the outfit for which he works and his willingness to put everything, including his life, on the line in his persistent defense of the ranch against rustlers. L'Amour's *Hanging Woman Creek* features winter line camp partners, Pronto Pike and Eddie Holt, doing much the same thing in protecting the Bar J cattle in their charge. Written in the same tradition as these foregoing texts, the Border Trilogy explores the interaction between its protagonists' penchant for self-orientated isolation and their attraction for other-oriented duty as integral, if somewhat paradoxical, aspects of their respective initiations. McCarthy's protagonists try to accept responsibility and to enact justice for the other, which relation with the other, according to Emmanuel Levinas, actually constitutes subjectivity rather than opposes it: "Responsibility in fact is not a simple attribute of subjectivity, as if the latter already existed in itself, before the ethical relationship. Subjectivity is not for itself; it is, once again, initially for another" (96). John Grady and Billy's sense of partnership and their obsession with recovering and returning that which has been lost, whether horses or people or lifestyle, reflect this Levinasian sense of subjectivity because they can approach self-realization only by supporting the other. In short, John Grady and Billy are top hands who ride for the brand.

All the Pretty Horses partakes of all the traditional heroic cowboy codes and sets the tone for the entire trilogy as an exploration of their efficacy in the modern world. The novel begins with what Gail Moore Morrison describes as John Grady's "expulsion from paradise" in the loss of the family ranch, sold by John Grady's mother on her father's death, despite the boy's own efforts to preserve it—a loss which makes him as disenfranchised as the Comanches from whom the ranch was taken originally: "The last of his grandfather's line with its generations-deep commitment to the land, [John Grady] is certainly as powerless to protect it against foreign encroachment . . . as was the Comanche nation he envisions as he rides out along their ancient war trail . . . after his grandfather's funeral" (Morrison 176). This disenfranchisement, of course, sets up the novel's heroic archetypal journey, which Morrison discusses as a profound and productive rite of passage, which moves John Grady toward his final journey back home, "the naif no longer, but a man considerably deepened and enriched by the experience" (191). Nevertheless, McCarthy's Comanche comparison suggests that while John Grady's epic journey may evoke a noble western tradition, it may also be as doomed to failure as the Comanches' because of the loss of the community and culture in which his individual excellence thrives. Dianne C. Luce takes up many of the same issues as Morrison in her analysis of heroism in the novel, delving beneath John Grady's superficial heroic traits and exploits (dismissed by some critics and reviewers as improbable and excessive) to explore his movement from romantic to realistic notions of the world: "[H]e is the romantic dreamer who gradually awakens to reality . . . and who responds by abandoning his quest for dominance and courageously embracing instead a quest for truth and understanding. This is his true heroism"

(155–56). Writing before the publication of *Cities of the Plain*, which may suggest some modification of their claims for a completed initiation in *All the Pretty Horses*, both Morrison and Luce stress the individuality of John Grady's development in his quest to recover somehow his lost ranching paradise in a fallen world, and they both argue for the ultimate efficacy of that quest, at least in his self-actualization, but only Luce stresses fully the significance of his self-development as a function of his relation to others: "The consequences of his actions together with others' assessments of him ... gradually teach him to honor reality over fantasy, truth over expediency, courage over avoidance" (159–60). However, the judgment of others is only one aspect of John Grady's self-other relationships that figures predominantly in the novel; the self's call to responsibility for the other may be far more significant. Jimmy Blevins, for example, the lightning-spooked boy outlaw who wants to join up with John Grady and Lacey Rawlins in Mexico "Cause I'm an American" (45), represents more than a test of John Grady's pragmatism; rather, Blevins represents a test of John Grady's ethics and his willingness to take responsibility for the other, however troublesome or guilty or destructive or evil Blevins may turn out to be. Further, John Grady does not have a choice between naïvete and maturity, or between romance and reality in accepting responsibility for Blevins; rather, his choice is between enacting his idealistic cowboy codes or not, for these codes have meaning only as they are enacted within a communal context in the real world. While Rawlins rightly predicts dire consequences from their association with Blevins and justifiably says, "I aint takin no responsibility for him" (69), John Grady simply says, "I dont believe I can leave him out here afoot" (71), even though Blevins—near-naked and horseless—is entirely responsible for his own predicament. The notion of partnership, even their marginal one with Blevins, pervades the novel for good and for ill: paradoxically, it not only saves John Grady and Rawlins in prison as they fight together for survival because they use the money Blevins slips them just before his execution for necessary bribes, but it also attaches them to Blevins and his guilt, which attachment puts them into prison in the first place.

The Crossing parallels *All the Pretty Horses* in its exploration of the problematics of partnership and of integrating the isolate into the community, all within the heroic *bildungsroman* tradition; but it examines even more fully the destructive aspects of either taking or not taking individual responsibility for the other. Although many of the same generalizations made about *All the Pretty Horses* by such critics as Morrison and Luce could apply in some ways to *The Crossing*, reading it simply as a more developed version of *All the Pretty Horses* would ignore its own particular character. Billy, for example, operates not so much as a double for John Grady but more as his fraternal twin—his *cuate*, translated from Spanish as buddy or twin—because, while Billy shares many of John Grady's qualities as well as a similar Mexican initiation, he remains his own man, much more isolated and pragmatic and full of wanderlust, for instance, than his future saddle partner. They certainly share, however, a deep capacity for enduring loyalty, whether or not they have a brand for which to ride, and their respective initiations share a tragic archetypal quality. As the priest says to the old man in the long story told to Billy by the heretical hermit in *The Crossing*: "Ultimately every man's path is every other's. There are no separate journeys for there are no separate men to make them. All men are one and there is no other tale to tell" (156–57). Billy's three journeys to and fro across the American-Mexican border may be described thus as one journey along the border between the conflicting impulses of independence and integration that drive him from home and then call him back again. Because Billy always seems to be destined to live along this independence/integration border, he may indeed fulfill the prophetic warning of the old Indian sage near the end of Billy's first journey:

He told the boy that although he was huérfano still he must cease his wanderings and make for himself some place in the world because to wander in this way would become for him a passion and by this passion he would become estranged from men and so ultimately from himself.... He said that while the huérfano might feel that he no longer belonged among men he must set this feeling aside for he contained within him a largeness of spirit which men could see and that men would wish to know him and that the world would need him even as he needed the world for they were one. Lastly he said that while this itself was a good thing like all good things it was also a danger. (134)

The sage's proleptic and insistent designation of Billy as *huérfano*, or orphan, despite Billy's protests to the contrary, underlines the veracity of the entire passage, for it is probable that Billy's parents, unbeknownst to him, have already been murdered. In addition, Billy's largely inexplicable abandonment of his family to restore the she-wolf to the Mexican mountain wilderness out of which she came must relate somehow to this wanderlust passion and estrangement from men of which the sage speaks. Finally, Billy's subsequent behavior as chronicled in both *The Crossing* and *Cities of the Plain* demonstrates the good and the danger inherent in the "largeness of spirit" for which the world would seek him. His brother Boyd's partnership with him certainly partakes of both good and danger, reflecting many aspects of the John Grady–Rawlins partnership, with Boyd occupying the more idealistic John Grady role and Billy occupying the more pragmatic Rawlins role. Like John Grady, Boyd tends to lead out in determining such courses of action as, for example, giving a horse and money to the girl they rescue, while Billy, like Rawlins, inevitably goes along with his partner, even when acting under protest. Such faith in one another is mutual and completely understood as befitting one of the most sacred of western bonds—partnership. Their reunion conversation on Billy's return from his initial Mexican journey illustrates the fundamental depth of this understood faith in each other, with Billy stating, "I reckon you thought I was dead" and Boyd responding, "If I'd of thought you was dead I wouldnt be here" (171). Boyd meets Billy's next question, "Are you ready to go?" with "Yeah . . . Just waitin on you" (171), agreeing implicitly with Billy's unspoken but understood decision to avenge their parents' deaths and recover their stolen horses. Their earlier decision not to tell their parents about the Indian drifter who coerces them into giving him food and information on their place, of course, has contributed directly to their parents' murder and underscores the negative aspects of their partnership, not to mention the destruction that follows in the wake of their decision to follow the trail of the killers instead of staying at home and rebuilding their lives there; but they are willing and able to take the bad with the good according to the western code of partnership.

In *Cities of the Plain*, John Grady and Billy's mutual association with Mac McGovern's Cross Fours Ranch—even though its future remains bleak—satisfies the latent sense of longing that pervades the previous two volumes for the union of such nonpareil cowboys within a cattle outfit worthy of them. Indeed, their relationship seems so balanced, with Billy's mature pragmatism and John Grady's tenacious idealism tempering one another, that their success as partners seems assured. Certainly their sense of loyalty has earlier been well tested—perhaps best represented by John Grady's refusal to cease his courtship of Alejandra, a betrayal of Don Héctor; by Billy's persistent care for his brother, an ultimate failure; and by their respective recoveries of their lost horses—but their capacities for loyalty and ethical conduct are tried even more severely in *Cities of the Plain*. Their early initiations complete, they must act out a drama that reiterates earlier figures and events and underscores McCarthy's critique of the *bildungsroman* as a productive developmental mode for ensuring individual maturation and survival in the world. Both seem destined by their stubborn adherence to their cowboy codes to ignore earlier lessons and repeat past decisions, all in an effort to do what they perceive as their duty. John Grady's fatal attempted rescue of Magdalena parallels both his foiled romance with Alejandra and Boyd's ill-fated rescue of the unnamed Mexican girl; Billy's reluctant support of John Grady's naïve plan to purchase Magdalena parallels his willingness to help Boyd and the Mexican girl, even while questioning the wisdom of Boyd's attachment to her; and Billy's inability to save either his brother or his partner from themselves and their cavalier heroism illustrates the insufficiency of pragmatism when operating in the face of idealism. As Billy tells John Grady, "Most people get smacked around enough after a while they start to pay attention. More and more you remind me of Boyd. Only way I could ever get him to do anything was to tell him not to" (*COP* 146). Nevertheless, their integrity, a curious blend of impracticality and action in support of each other and the Cross Fours, remains largely intact throughout the novel and allows them to experience genuine cowboy life on the ranch, which, although in decline, represents a good brand for which to ride, a kind of cowboy utopia with its combination of rich family heritage, good bosses, a good cook, and good cowboys, all of whom work well together with camaraderie and good humor. For John Grady it represents a replacement for the familial inheritance he lost with his mother's sold birthright and suggests the possibility of recovering his dream of marriage and family ranching. It is no wonder he refuses even temporary work at another spread, even though he could use the extra money, for, as he explains in paraphrasing the cowboy motto of riding for the brand, "I guess I dont know how to work for but one man at a time" (51). Mac acts as a surrogate father for him, understanding implicitly his desire to make a little homestead for himself and Magdalena at Bell Springs, despite the difficulty of the enterprise. Mac's generous offer of his late wife Margaret's wedding ring to John Grady betokens his possible inheritance of Mac's good fortune to have married a good ranch woman who, unlike John Grady's mother, valued the land and culture as much as he did. In fact, Margaret's absence haunts the Cross Fours and its inhabitants, who continue to feel both her loss and her continuing influence on the ranch. It is no wonder Billy decides to stay on after her death, even though his wanderlust must have been calling him to leave, and to continue riding for her family brand. Billy even understands to a certain degree why living at Bell Springs with Magdalena appeals so much to John Grady, although Billy's earlier dream of so living himself has changed, and his comments to John Grady reflect his cynicism. "I used to think rawhidin a bunch of bony cattle in some outland country would be just as close to heaven as a man was likely to get," he tells John Grady. "I wouldnt give you much for it now" (77). Nevertheless, neither Billy nor John Grady will quit on the Cross Fours or on each other as long as there exists some hope of their mutual preservation.

III

Maybe it's like Mac says. Ever man winds up with the horse that suits him.

—*Cities of the Plain* 14

Dominance/Dependence. This figure represents an analogous articulation of the independence/integration duality but with even more emphasis on ethical and reciprocal relationships as, for example, between cowboy and horse, a partnership most central to working cowboy culture. Even famous popular television or film cowboys and other westerners are linked inextricably with their equally famous mounts, so much so that we can hardly think of one without the other: Roy Rogers and Trigger, Dale Evans and Buttermilk, Gene Autry and Champion, the Lone Ranger and Silver, Tonto and Scout, Tom Mix and Tony, Hopalong Cassidy and Topper, Rex Allen and Ko-Ko, and so forth. These fictional human-equine partnerships, though quite fanciful in their depiction of impossibly intelligent horses responding magically to their riders' every command, still reflect genuine human-equine partnerships that can exist outside Hollywood in the real world, particularly in defining these partnerships as fundamentally dependent on a mutually beneficial cooperation between rider and horse.[3] While horses must be "broken" to the will of the cowboy, for instance, the best cowboys engage this domestication with the prime directive of not "breaking the horse's spirit," although, as McCarthy puts it in *All the Pretty Horses*, they are initially "trussed up . . . with the voice of the breaker still running in their brains like the voice of some god come to inhabit them" (105) to ensure their attachment to their breakers rather than their herd. Monte Roberts, a famous horse trainer and best-selling author, describes this domestication process as "joining up" and, like McCarthy, stresses its ethical dimensions as both cowboy and horse give up the urge for individual dominance in favor of mutual dependence. Although this method has been practiced by some horse trainers for centuries, its widespread popularity today may be unmatched in previous years. Each edition of *Western Horseman* features articles on and advertisements by real life "horse whisperers" such as Buck Brannaman, Craig Cameron, Bill and Tom Dorrance, Ray Hunt, John Lyons, Buster McLaury, Pat Parelli, and Dennis Reis, among others, all of whom work with real horses and real riders in the real world to establish an honest, dependable relationship between horse and rider without doing damage to either. In his article on real-life horse whisperers, Robert M. Miller reviews the history of famous "horse tamers" to the present day in an effort to describe "the scientific reasons why natural horsemanship . . . works so dramatically well," arguing that "I see no place for such obscure and supernatural 'horse whispering.' I can do these things and so can any person willing to learn" (85).

In cowboy culture, the bond between cowboy and horse is particularly strong because it forms a working partnership that makes possible the safe and successful execution of their fatiguing and sometimes dangerous vocational pursuits day-in and day-out. Indeed, the quality of that partnership reflects both individual and mutual excellence, as illustrated in the old cowboy aphorism that "the best man rides the best horse," in the traditional trail drive practice of having the foreman and top hands pick their string of horses from the remuda before the lesser cowboys, and in the contemporary rodeo practice of designating each year the top rodeo horses in each event as well as the top rodeo cowboys. Excellent cow or cutting horses are trained to respond instinctively to situations and not to depend solely on their riders' instructions, so they must exhibit a certain independence from their human partners to be effective; poor cow or cutting horses, on the other hand, are trained to await those instructions, so their human dependence teaches them to be uncertain and therefore ineffective. Great cowboy-cow horse teams work with a smooth precision that makes them as one even though each plays an entirely different role—as illustrated, for example, in the dog-roping episode from *Cities of the Plain*, an impressive exhibition of roping skill. The bond between cowboy and horse is considered to be so sacred, in fact, that riding another man's horse without permission constitutes a breach of conduct so serious as to be likened to sleeping with another man's wife. This comparison of horse and wife, while often ridiculed as a derogatory reduction of women, reflects instead the seriousness with which cowboys take their horses and their wives and the high value they place on their relationships with them both. A good horse, like a good wife, represents a real "certitude," as J. Frank Dobie eloquently notes in the following, an epitaph to good cow horses everywhere:

All the old-time range men of validity whom I have known remembered horses with affection and respect as part of the best of themselves. After their knees begin to stiffen, most men realize that they have been disappointed in themselves, in other men, in achievement, in love, in whatever they expected out of life; but a man who has had a good horse in his life—a horse beyond the play world—will remember him as a certitude ... amid all the flickering vanishments. (306)

McCarthy's cowboys, John Grady and Billy, both value their horses in this way—as certitudes and as parts of the best of themselves.

John Grady in particular illustrates this ethical joining up of cowboy and horse in his repeated demonstrations of his "natural horsemanship," ranging from his amazing feats of riding to his unwillingness to turn on the barn light at night because it "bothers the horses" (*Cities* 41). McCarthy establishes this cowboy/horse connection as a fundamental motif in the trilogy early on as he describes John Grady and his father taking their last ride together:

The boy who rode on slightly before him sat a horse not only as if he'd been born to it which he was but as if were he begot by malice or mischance into some queer land where horses never were he would have found them anyway. Would have known that there was something missing for the world to be right or he right in it and would have set forth to wander wherever it was needed for as long as it took until he came upon one and he would have known that that was what he sought and it would have been. (APH 23)

Here McCarthy undercuts the ubiquitous nature-or-nurture conundrum by his double simile which, while giving a brief acknowledgment to nurture in John Grady's cowboy identity ("as if he'd been born to it which he was"), develops around a hypothetical proposition to give nature more than its just due ("he would have known that that was what he sought"). Nevertheless, neither nature nor nurture dominates here but are mutually dependent, incomplete without the other, just as John Grady would have been incomplete without horses. The final passage of the novel further reflects this absolute integration of cowboy and horse as John Grady rides off into the sunset with Redbo and the Blevins bay horse: "horse and rider and horse passed on and their long shadows passed in tandem like the shadow of a single being" (302). Although McCarthy describes the relationship between John Grady and horses as almost mystical, he keeps that relation grounded in reality and refuses either to anthropomorphize horses or make John Grady a part of the horse herd; he and horses may have a relationship, but they remain discrete and disassociated. For example, when John Grady is breaking the wildest horse in La Purísima's string, a "bucketheaded . . . grullo" (105), to demonstrate the practical effectiveness of his horse-breaking ideology to a skeptical Rawlins, his success depends not on domination or identification, but on relation. In reply to Rawlins's question regarding the efficacy of "sacking out"[4] the horse before saddling it to familiarize it with being touched, John Grady responds, "I dont know. . . . I aint a horse" (106), emphasizing his unwillingness to subsume the horse within the self, or the other within the same, by pretending he understands what a horse thinks or feels. In fact, he notes his ignorance of horses by observing to Oren that "When I was a kid I thought I knew all there was to know about a horse. Where horses are concerned I've just got dumber and dumber. . . . If a man really understood horses he could just about train one by lookin at it" (COP 53–54).

John Grady may not be a horse or fully understand them, but he knows how to have a productive conversation with one and, in addition, how to train it to be useful to other riders besides himself, in obvious refutation of the myth that a one-cowboy horse should be preferred over one who will accept different riders. For instance, the once-wild *grullo*'s thorough training and gentleness are clearly evident: "the horse was patiently walking the enclosure with three children astride it and another leading it and yet another hanging on to its tail" (APH 245). John Grady's work with horses in practice thus reflects well his theories about horses, particularly the notion of establishing a relationship with a horse that does not violate the horse's sense of being, as he expresses in his conversation with Oren about horse training:

> I think you can train a rooster to do what you want. But you wont have him. There's a way to train a horse where when you get done you've got the horse. On his own ground. A good horse will figure things out on his own. You can see what's in his heart. He wont do one thing while you're watchin him and another when you aint. He's all of a piece. When you've got a horse to that place you cant hardly get him to do somethin he knows is wrong. He'll fight you over it. And if you mistreat him it just about kills him. A good horse has justice in his heart. I've seen it. (COP 53)

This acknowledgment of the horse's sense of integrity and the necessity of establishing a just relationship forms the basis of John Grady's theory and practice of "natural horsemanship" and is echoed by many successful horse trainers today. John Grady and Billy risk death to recover their stolen horses, in part because they must keep the faith with them and not violate their sense of justice. In true cowboy fashion they call their horses by name—Redbo, Bird, Keno, Niño, and so forth—and often address them as "partner," talking to them almost as they would to one another; they take care of their horses' needs before their own; and they mourn their horses' loss or injuries. Further, they believe the horses reciprocate their attention to the ethical cowboy-cow horse relation; even Billy, the skeptic, believes in John Grady's notion that horses can distinguish between truth and lies by knowing what lies in the human heart:

You think a horse knows what's in your heart?
Yeah. Dont you?
Billy didnt answer. After a while he said: Yeah. I do. (COP 84)

If their hearts are true in this sense, cowboys can form a partnership with their horses that enacts justice by respecting their horses' individual integrity and by never asking their horses to do anything wrong. John Grady and Billy have horses well-suited to them because they value only horses that reflect back their own ethic of horsemanship.

IV

[The Indian] looked into the eyes of the boy. The boy into his. Eyes so dark they seemed all pupil. Eyes in which the sun was setting. In which the child stood beside the sun.

He had not known that you could see yourself in others' eyes nor see therein such things as suns. He stood twinned in those dark wells with hair so pale, so thin and strange, the selfsame child. As if it were some cognate child to him that had been lost who now stood windowed away in another world where the red sun sank eternally. As if it were a maze where these orphans of his heart had miswandered in their journey in life and so arrived at last beyond the wall of that antique gaze from whence there could be no way back forever.

—*The Crossing* 5–6

Rivalry/Respect. This figure encompasses the symbiotic adversarial relationship between enemies: because the self must be defined primarily through difference, the enemy other, in whatever form it takes, helps to make that self possible. The quality of the western self depends on the quality of the adversaries it successfully engages, whether they be natural or human. The westerner, as a man to match the Rocky Mountains, views himself at the most basic level as the product of a harsh environment populated with hostile beings, a survivor whose stature relates directly to the extremity of the conditions he has endured and to the lethal capacity of the enemies into whose eyes he has gazed. Fictional western heroes reflect this formula for self-formation in virtually every aspect of their beings, and the narrative tension of virtually every western novel or film revolves around an adversarial relationship that builds toward a climax consisting of a final good versus evil confrontation which usually ends with the hero dispatching his antagonist and, in so doing, enhancing his own heroic stature and reifying the power of good. This basic protagonist/antagonist figure, however, often features structural and thematic variations which move it beyond the cliché, even in the most popular venues, to allow for different explorations of the rivalry/respect binary. For instance, in *Hondo*, L'Amour's first published novel, the title character's relationship with the Apaches, his main antagonists, is ambivalent to say the least. Hondo values the Apache way of life, having once lived and taken a wife among them, but he nevertheless works as an army scout against their interests. Vittorio, the Apache chief, spares Hondo's life, in part because of the white man's experience with Apache culture as well as his demonstration of individual courage so valued in that culture. This adversarial relationship ends not with a violent confrontation, but with Vittorio letting Hondo live to help raise Vittorio's adopted white son as long as he refuses to scout for the army. When L'Amour's novels do end in violent confrontation, they sometimes feature a similar adversarial ambivalence, as in *Shalako*, which climaxes with the title character's hand-to-hand combat with the nonpareil Apache warrior, *Tats-ah-das-ay-go*, or the Quick-Killer. As the Apache falls off a precipice to his death, Shalako looks him in the eye and cries out to him in Apache, "Warrior! Brother!" (167). Contemporary revisionist Western writers make a particular point of undermining traditional expectations regarding this protagonist/antagonist cliché and the notion that good always triumphs over evil. In McMurtry's *Lonesome Dove*, for example, the seemingly inevitable final confrontation between the Texas Ranger captains Call and McCrae and the renegade Blue Duck, literally decades in the making, never takes place: Blue Duck is captured and goes to the gallows because a lucky shot by a fat deputy named Decker cripples the outlaw's horse. In the sequel, *Streets of Laredo*, Call kills Mox Mox, the manburner, and his men, but he fails to kill Joey Garza, the boy sniper, who wounds Call thrice, a failure that haunts Call horribly. Pea-Eye, a marginally competent fighter and a reluctant hero, wounds Garza, and Gordo, the butcher, finishes him off. However, in all these variations on this dominant western theme, the pervasive threat of death constitutes the Western's essential aesthetic. As Jane Tompkins observes: "The imminence of death underwrites the plot, makes the sensory details of the setting extraordinarily acute, and is responsible for the ritual nature of the climax: a moment of violence formalized, made grave and respectable, by the thought of annihilation" (24). She adds that death's presence brings comfort and reassurance as well as horror (27). Indeed, she argues that death may be the ultimate western destination: "To go west, as far west as you can go, west of everything, is to die" (24). Tompkins's observations on death work well with McCarthy's Westerns. While Judge Holden of *Blood Meridian* may be the preeminent enemy other and harbinger of death in McCarthy— "What joins men together . . . is not the sharing of bread," he tells the kid, "but the sharing of enemies. . . . Our animosities were formed and waiting before ever we two met" (*BM* 307)—the Border Trilogy features many rival relationships which are tinged also with respect and mutual necessity. John Grady and Billy's adversarial relationships, even with their deadliest enemies, display an intriguing interaction within this rivalry/respect binary, which creates a curious intimacy unique to adversaries. Many of their adversaries, in fact, serve as would-be mentors for them. The most significant exchanges in McCarthy often occur between enemies.

In *All the Pretty Horses*, for example, John Grady's relationship with Dueña Alfonsa turns on their respective love and concern for Alejandra, which also sets them at odds with one another despite their obvious affinity and places John Grady both in and out of harm's way. Their chess games serve as an obvious symbolic counterpart to their conversations, which fluctuate continuously along the rivalry/respect border and reflect the Dueña's superiority in determining the most effective overall strategy and in pursuing the chess moves it generates. In their early conversations, as in their early chess games, she measures John Grady's discourse skills in much the same way as the unnamed prison assassin and the pimp Eduardo later measure his knife-fighting skills, so that she can ascertain how best to checkmate him rhetorically. She concludes their first conversation by making clear exactly what is at issue and who determines it, refuting John Grady's appeal to justice: "No. It's not a matter of right. You must understand. It is a matter of who must say. In this matter I get to say. I am the one who gets to say" (137). She concludes their second conversation, which includes a long autobiographical account of her life remarkable for its intimate detail, by making clear exactly what constitutes their relationship: "I've been at some pains to tell you about myself because among other reasons I think we should know who our enemies are" (240–41). In *The Crossing* this kind of adversarial knowing forms the basis of Billy's plan to catch the she-wolf. He believes he must learn how to think like a wolf to catch a wolf, so he consults the wolf experts, beginning with his investigation of Echols's wolf-trapping paraphernalia in his uninhabited cabin on the SK Bar ranch, especially the vial of wolf-bait labeled #7 Matrix. In his later interview with Don Arnulfo, Billy comments that Echols has the reputation of knowing the wolf well: "El señor Sanders me dice que el señor Echols es medio lobo el mismo. Me dice que él conoce lo que sabe el lobo antes de que lo sepa el lobo" (45; Mr. Sanders tells me Mr. Echols is half wolf himself. He tells me he knows what the wolf knows before the wolf knows). Don Arnulfo responds that "no man knew what the wolf knew": "El lobo es una cosa incognoscible. . . . Lo que se tiene en la trampa no es mas que dientes y forro. El lobo propio no se puede conocer. Lobo o lo que sabe el lobo" (45; The wolf is an unknowable thing. What one has in the trap is no more than teeth and fur. One cannot know the true wolf. Neither the wolf nor what the wolf knows). Billy's rescue of the she-wolf after he has trapped her reflects his eagerness to engage, as well as his reluctance to kill, this traditional enemy of cattlemen, as if he and his world would be diminished by her extinction. Her fate somehow allied with his, she becomes a *doppelgänger* who haunts him for his inability to save her once he takes responsibility for her, as well as an other in whose gaze he sees another world, a world which, according to Don Arnulfo, is ordered by death (45). Billy wants to preserve this world, and perhaps his own, from annihilation by saving the wolf in whose eyes he perceives it: "When those eyes and the nation to which they stood witness were gone at last with their dignity back into their origins there would perhaps be . . . other worlds otherwise beheld. But they would not be this one" (74). In *Cities of the Plain* Billy and Eduardo form an unusual union of pragmatists whose antipathy for one another is balanced by their mutual disapproval of John Grady's courtship of Magdalena and is tinged with a certain degree of respect. In his first meeting with Eduardo, Billy attempts to press his friend's suit even though it is clear he agrees with Eduardo's assessment of the situation, which agreement Eduardo draws out of the reluctant Billy several times during their conversation with pointed questions regarding Billy's own beliefs:

What can he offer this girl? Why would she leave?
I dont know. I reckon he thinks she's in love with him.
Heavens, said Eduardo. Do you believe such a thing?
I dont know.
Do you believe such a thing?
No. (133)

Their conversation culminates in a discussion of John Grady's delusion, his "irrational passion" (134), as Eduardo calls it, which constructs a happy story of what his future will be with Magdalena, a story Eduardo critiques because it is false, saying, in reference to men who create such stories in their minds, "The world may be many different ways for them but there is one world that will never be and that is the world they dream of" (134). He asks Billy for his concurrence, which Billy grants grudgingly because of his loyalty to John Grady, replying, "I just dont like to say it. . . . It seems like a betrayal of some kind" (134). While Billy may articulate it differently, he says basically the same thing to John Grady as Eduardo says to him, making him and the pimp some kind of allies in their attempts to dissuade John Grady from his planned course of action. John Grady's duel with Eduardo—like Billy's earlier conversations with him on John Grady's behalf—provides evidence of Eduardo's willingness to spare John Grady and to mentor him toward survival, although Eduardo's capacity for death-dealing remains undiminished. Eduardo underscores the adversarial intimacy of this duel-to-the-death confrontation with a sexual metaphor as he urges, "We must make a beginning. It is like a first kiss" (248). In McCarthy's West such curious adversarial intimacy rivals even that of partnership in forging the heroic self because it is the enemy gaze that reflects that self most dramatically.

V

> De todos modos el compartir es la ley del camino, verdad? [At any rate, sharing is the law of the road, true?].
>
> —*Cities of the Plain* 267

Survival/Hospitality. Another reconciliation of self-interest and duty to the other, this figure parallels independence/integration and dominance/dependence in its privileging of individuality operating for the benefit of community. Levinas frames the site of this figure within a face-to-face encounter with the other which includes an inherent ethical demand for responsibility: "The tie with the Other is knotted only as responsibility . . . whether accepted or refused, whether knowing or not knowing how to assume it, whether able or unable to do something for the Other. To say: here

I am" (97). For Levinas this sense of responsibility and welcome comprises the foundation of selfhood and society, the *a priori* assumption on which his ethical philosophy is built, even though we can never actually meet the demands of responsibility and thereby free ourselves from it. Any attempt to do so by some action, however well intended, such as donating food and clothing to refugees for example, would do violence to the other by reducing the other in a totalizing gesture, arrogantly communicating, "I know what you need and will provide it." This is not to say, however, that we should not make such generous contributions or extend our best hospitality to those in need; the point is that our contributions and hospitality cannot relieve us of our responsibility. We meet our responsibility for the other most ethically with a simple face-to-face welcome, unattached to any concrete demands or offers, one that says "here I am" and thus preserves an infinite sense of our relation to the other. Many of the encounters in McCarthy are of this kind and are characterized by hospitable gestures of welcome. While existence in the often inhospitable environments of the Border Trilogy requires a certain degree of survival instinct, the hospitality that also pervades these environments may play as crucial a role in defining them. That great generosity of spirit and sustenance can flourish in such environments embodies the McCarthian sense of grace, made more intense within a western setting where strangers are welcome at the campfire or hearth because, on the frontier, individual survival has always depended on mutual hospitality. In Siringo's *A Texas Cowboy* and Schaefer's *Monte Walsh*, itinerant cowboys riding the grub line looking for work are always welcome to a couple ranch or cow camp meals and an overnight stay whether or not there are jobs available, demonstrating the pervasiveness of cowboy hospitality in fact and in fiction. In *Hondo*, Angie Lowe welcomes the Apaches to water at her springs in partial exchange for an uneasy peace with them and nurses the injured Hondo back to health, who reciprocates by cutting firewood and making needed repairs around her ranch. In *Lonesome Dove*, Clara Allen takes in July Johnson's infant son abandoned by his mother, Ellie, and eventually July himself; she later adds Lorena Wood, a former whore and rival for McCrae's attentions, to her household with similar acceptance and generosity. In *Streets of Laredo*, Lorena, now married to Pea Eye Parker and the mother of his five children, reiterates Clara's hospitality by adopting the orphaned Garza children and the crippled Call, demonstrating at the end of the *Lone-*

some Dove saga that hospitality endures over violence and death. Thus individual survival, instead of being opposed to hospitality, becomes dependent on it, according to the frontier contract for building community, the breach of which defines the degenerate and the outlaw within that community, who, in violating the welcome of hospitality, becomes an ignominious exile, like the nameless Indian who repays the Parham boys for their hospitality by killing their parents.

Instances of hospitality abound throughout the Border Trilogy, particularly in the first two volumes, as multiple manifestations of its dominant motif: the wandering stranger being taken in and cared for. In *All the Pretty Horses*, John Grady is picked up every time he tries to hitch a ride regardless of the weather or other circumstances; he, Rawlins, and Blevins are taken in, fed, put up overnight, and packed a lunch the next day by a family at a small *estancia* who refuse any payment; two girls get them cigarettes at their request when they are prisoners and cry about their probable fate; John Grady buys the knife that saves his life from his fellow prisoners, Faustino and the Sierra León Indian; and, after his escape, he is spared by three "Men of the country" (281) who, instead of robbing him of his goods and horses, give him a *serape* because he does not have one. *The Crossing* features instances of hospitality extended at almost every turn of its plot: the *vaqueros* sharing their lunch with Billy on the range; the rancher from Cloverdale, New Mexico, whose wife and ranch hands doctor the she-wolf and equip Billy for his trip to Mexico; the American border guard who lends Billy money; the numerous Mexicans and Indians who feed and house Billy and Boyd in their travels, especially the Muñoz family, who also care for Boyd after he is wounded; the doctor who treats Boyd without requiring payment; the American waitress who feeds Billy breakfast for free; and the gypsies who heal the wounded Niño horse. Billy's later commentary to Troy in *Cities of the Plain* on the Mexican hospitality he received and feels honor-bound to reciprocate by helping the Mexican farm workers repair their flat tire, bears witness to hospitality's power to replicate itself and reflects the paradox inherent in the survival/hospitality binary—that to be secured survival must be risked through hospitality. Billy cannot make an adequate response to Troy's question, "How come you had to stop back there?" beyond "I just did" without recourse to a personal narrative recounting the hospitality he has just repaid:

It's just that the worst day of my life was one time when I was seventeen years old and me and my bud—my brother—we was on the run and he was hurt and there was a truckload of Mexicans just about like them back yonder appeared out of nowhere and pulled our bacon out of the fire. I wasnt even sure their old truck could outrun a horse, but it did. They didnt have no reason to stop for us. But they did. I dont guess it would of even occurred to em not to. That's all. (36)

Travis's commentary later in the novel on his post-revolutionary Mexican experience verifies Billy's and thus demonstrates the pervasiveness of the hospitality ethic in Mexico, as well as the necessity of personal narrative in accounting for that hospitality:

Those people would take you in and put you up and feed you and feed your horse and cry when you left. You could of stayed forever. They didnt have nothin. Never had and never would. . . . They didnt have no reason to be hospitable to anybody. Least of all a gringo kid. That plateful of beans they set in front of you was hard come by. But I was never turned away. Not a time. (90)

John Grady adds his own witness as he and Billy discuss Mexico sitting on their horses from the vantage point of a Jarilla mountain pass: "I came out of there on the run. Ridin at night. Afraid to make a fire. . . . Been shot. Those people would take you in. Hide you out. Lie for you. No one ever asked me what it was I'd done" (217). In their respective testimonies Billy and Travis and John Grady attempt to put into language the Levinasian notion of welcome by refusing to reduce their Mexican experiences to some obvious label or easy definition, choosing instead to let their experiences speak for themselves as much as possible in their narratives, emphasizing not so much what was done for them as the "here-I-am" spirit in which it was done.

VI

You dont talk much, do you? he said.
Not a whole lot.
That's a good trait to have.

—*All the Pretty Horses* 19

Action/Eloquence. This figure typifies the notions that in the West actions speak louder than words and that the truth distinguishes itself from the lie essentially by behavioral evidence; in short, we expect cowboys to reflect the strong silent stereotype of the western hero. In *Last Buckaroo*, for instance, Tap, the first-person narrator, assesses Dean's progress in his development as a cowboy, delineating at the same time those characteristics which mark the real buckaroo—industrious work habits, authentic dress and tack, excellent horsemanship, solid farrier skills, good humor, and a certain verbal reticence: "He'd gotten to where he didn't talk so much" (43). In *Lonesome Dove*, Call's laconic demeanor reflects his no-nonsense, all-business approach to life and contributes to his aura of extreme competence and near invincibility, while McCrae's loquaciousness at first undermines our sense of his capabilities because we do not take him as seriously as we do Call until we see McCrae in action, pistol-whipping an insolent bartender and rescuing Lorena from Blue Duck and his band. When Call speaks, his words have a hefty eloquence in their directness, their brevity, their understatement, and their connection with reality, as when he explains the near-fatal beating he gives an army scout by saying, "I hate a man that talks rude. . . . I can't abide it" (741), or when he carves an epitaph for Josh Deets: "SERVED WITH ME 30 YEARS. FOUGHT IN 21 ENGAGEMENTS WITH THE COMMANCHE AND KIOWA. CHERFUL IN ALL WEATHERS, NEVER SHERKED A TASK. SPLENDID BEHAVIOUR" (808). Thus, while language must be distrusted in the Western, it must also be valued, as Tompkins points out in the following:

> Time and again they set up situations whose message is that words are weak and misleading, only actions count; words are immaterial, only objects are real. But the next thing you know, someone is using language brilliantly, delivering an epigram so pithy and dense it might as well be a solid thing. (49)

In McCarthy's borderlands, language bears the same weight of reality as do physical performance and natural phenomena, his style aspiring to achieve a tangible substance to match the reality of his plot and setting. His protagonists weigh words in much the same manner, for although John Grady and Billy may not be loquacious, they are eloquent both in action and in discourse, particularly when that discourse is tied to behavior. John Grady's meditations on horsemanship and Billy's hospitality narratives, for example, embody a linguistic aesthetic that attempts to bridge the inevitable gap between signifier and signified by making their words as concrete as their referents. Billy's father believes this signifier/signified link should be one reality, inviolate, the one determining the other; as he berates Billy for being late without accepting his excuse, he says there is only one reason people have for being late: "It's that their word's no good. That's the only reason there ever was or ever will be" (C 51).

Although action and language signify equally well for McCarthy, behavioral performance may be privileged over verbal. In *All the Pretty Horses* John Grady differentiates between the values of "reasonable" discourse and loyal behavior in responding to Rawlins's I-told-you-so speech after they are arrested because of their association with Blevins: "I know you did [tried to reason with me.] But some things aint reasonable. . . . You either stick or you quit and I wouldnt quit you I dont care what you done" (155–56). Later, when the captain tries to undermine his story, he says, "There aint but one truth. . . . The truth is what happened. It aint what come out of somebody's mouth" (168). In matters of life and death, action certainly counts more than language. As Eduardo accurately prophesies just before his duel with John Grady begins, "I think you will find that often in a fight the last one to speak is the loser" (COP 248). In fact, during their fatal confrontation, John Grady speaks only five sentences: "I come to kill you. . . . I come to kill you or be killed. . . . I didnt come to talk. . . . You dont need to worry about my youth. . . . You're a liar" (247–49). He utters all but the last one before the duel begins and, with that exception, is absolutely silent throughout Eduardo's deadly monologue. John Grady's silence reveals his inexperience as a knife-fighter, while Eduardo's loquaciousness suggests his confidence. But it is the perfectly timed blow, like the perfectly articulated word, that speaks most profoundly as John Grady kills Eduardo with a desperate thrust to the jaw, a blow that closes Eduardo's mouth once and for all. This is not to say, however, that ordinary speech, more abundant in *Cities of the Plain* than in the previous two volumes, lacks profundity, as illustrated in the following conversation between John Grady and Billy near the end of the novel:

John Grady nodded. What would you do if you couldnt be a cowboy?
I dont know. I reckon I'd think of somethin. You?
I dont know what it would be I'd think of.
Well we may all have to think of somethin.
Yeah. (217)

Harkening back to Billy's initial question regarding the location of John Grady, the "all-american cowboy," this passage also evokes the thematic sense of loss present throughout the Border Trilogy. In the ordinary speech of extraordinary cowboys, McCarthy articulates the simple dilemma of cowboys facing a vanishing culture: what to do? His epilogue to *Cities of the Plain*, set some fifty years later, reinforces this sense of its inevitable loss and suggests that the only balm available to assuage its attendant grief may be narration and the ethical relation it implies. As they part company underneath a freeway overpass, the itinerant stranger, the last of the trilogy's many mysterious sages and philosophers, asks seventy-eight-year-old Billy the following questions, referring metaphorically to the man whose death stands in for our own: "Do you love him, that man? Will you honor the path he has taken? Will you listen to his tale?" (288–89). Betty, the ranch woman who welcomes the wandering Billy into her family, seems to represent a direct reply to these questions. When Billy tells her, "I'm not what you think I am. I aint nothin. I dont know why you put up with me," she replies, "Well, Mr Parham, I know who you are. And I do know why" (292). She speaks as if for all of us, reaffirming the value of the cowboy codes McCarthy explores throughout the trilogy and particularly the value of the cowboys who embody them, John Grady and Billy. Because their deaths stand in for our own, we love them, we honor the path they have taken, and we listen to their tales.

Notes

1. The publication order is as follows, with the order of the novels' time settings noted in brackets: *Lonesome Dove* (1985) [3], *Streets of Laredo* (1993) [4], *Dead Man's Walk* (1995) [1], and *Comanche Moon* (1997) [2].
2. Buckaroo, from the Spanish word *vaquero*, depicts the Great Basin (Nevada, western Utah, eastern Oregon, southern Washington, northern California) cowboy, who is distinguished from cowboys of other regions by his particular dress and tack and cowboying techniques, adapted to meet the different environmental requirements of his region.
3. Michele Morris notes that the cowboy-horse relationship "is not quite as romantic as the movies portray. Trigger and Silver were well-groomed sidekicks practically wedded to Roy and the Ranger. In reality, a cowboy thinks of his horse as a well-trained tool as much as a loyal partner. 'I always figured that if someone offered me more for my horse than I thought he was worth, I'd sell him,' said one old cowboy. But a lot of sentimental guys would disagree. They

put the old horses out to pasture and let them die natural deaths. That's why cowkids often learn to ride on Grandpa's old gelding" (115–16).

4. Mike Kevil writes, "The term *sacking out* probably originated when cowboys long ago would take a gunny sack and rub it all over a colt to get him accustomed to the feel of being handled. In the old days, many colts ran loose on the range until they were four or five years old. Except when they were branded and/or gelded [castrated], they were never touched until the horse breaker ran them in and started working with them. Because they had never been handled, it was important that they get used to the feel of something being rubbed against them, and a gunny sack was handy to use" (64).

Works Cited

Dary, David. *Cowboy Culture: A Saga of Five Centuries*. Lawrence: U of Kansas P, 1989.
Derrida, Jacques. *Deconstruction in a Nutshell: A Conversation with Jacques Derrida*. Ed. John D. Caputo. New York: Fordham UP, 1997.
Dobie, J. Frank. *The Mustangs*. Boston: Little, Brown, 1952.
Hedges, Mackey. *Last Buckaroo*. Salt Lake City: Gibbs-Smith, 1995.
Kevil, Mike, and Pat Close. *Starting Colts*. Colorado Springs: Western Horseman, 1990.
L'Amour, Louis. *Conagher*. New York: Bantam, 1969.
———. *Hanging Woman Creek*. New York: Bantam, 1964.
———. *Hondo*. Greenwich, CT: Fawcett, 1953.
———. *Shalako*. New York: Bantam, 1962.
Levinas, Emmanuel. *Ethics and Infinity: Conversations with Philippe Nemo*. Trans. Richard A. Cohen. Pittsburgh, PA: Duquesne UP, 1985.
Luce, Dianne C. " 'When You Wake': John Grady Cole's Heroism in *All the Pretty Horses*." *Sacred Violence: A Reader's Companion to Cormac McCarthy*. Ed. Wade Hall and Rick Wallach. El Paso: Texas Western P, 1995. 155–67.
McCarthy, Cormac. *All the Pretty Horses*. New York: Vintage, 1993.
———. *Blood Meridian or The Evening Redness in the West*. New York: Vintage, 1985.
———. *Cities of the Plain*. New York: Vintage, 1999.
———. *The Crossing*. New York: Vintage, 1995.
McMurtry, Larry. *Lonesome Dove*. New York: Pocket, 1985.
———. *Streets of Laredo*. New York: Simon and Schuster, 1993.
Miller, Robert M. "Horse Whisperers: Who Are They and Where Did the Term Come From?" *Western Horseman* 63.4 (1998): 80–85.
Morris, Michele. *The Cowboy Life: A Saddlebag Guide for Dudes, Tenderfeet, and Cowpunchers Everywhere*. New York: Fireside, 1993.
Morrison, Gail Moore. "*All the Pretty Horses*: John Grady Cole's Expulsion from Paradise." *Perspectives on Cormac McCarthy*. Rev. ed. Ed. Edwin T. Arnold and Dianne C. Luce. Jackson: UP of Mississippi, 1999. 175–94.
Roberts, Monte. *The Man Who Listens to Horses*. New York: Random, 1997.
Schaefer, Jack. *Monte Walsh*. Lincoln: U of Nebraska P, 1963.

Siringo, Charles A. *A Texas Cowboy, or Fifteen Years on the Hurricane Deck of a Spanish Pony—Taken from Real Life*. Lincoln: U of Nebraska P, 1978.
Slatta, Richard W. *Cowboys of the Americas*. New Haven: Yale UP, 1990.
Slotkin, Richard. *Gunfighter Nation: The Myth of the Frontier in Twentieth-Century America*. New York: Atheneum, 1992.
Smith, Henry Nash. *Virgin Land: The American West as Symbol and Myth*. Cambridge: Harvard UP, 1950.
Tompkins, Jane. *West of Everything: The Inner Life of Westerns*. New York: Oxford UP, 1992.

BOYS WILL BE BOYS AND GIRLS WILL BE GONE

The Circuit of Male Desire in Cormac McCarthy's Border Trilogy

―――◆◆◆◆◆―――

Nell Sullivan

"What are you? . . . You are nothing."
—Tiburcio, *Cities of the Plain* 183

"I'm not what you think I am. I aint nothin."
—Billy Parham, *Cities of the Plain* 292

Published separately over a span of six years, the three volumes of Cormac McCarthy's Border Trilogy constitute an intricately woven text, not only through the use of common protagonists, but through the common themes and images resonating in all three. One of the most striking patterns to emerge is the narrative expulsion or containment of women. Two textual moments bracketing the action of the Border Trilogy suggest the uneasy place that women hold within it. In *All the Pretty Horses* (1992), the first volume, Lacey Rawlins tries to rein in John Grady Cole's self-destructive desire for women, telling him, "She aint worth it. None of em are," referring ostensibly to the Barnett girl but also to John Grady's mother, who has symbolically betrayed him by divorcing his father and selling his grandfather's ranch.[1] Yet John Grady does not defer to Lacey's wisdom; after pausing for a moment, he replies, "Yes they are"(10). Near the end of *Cities of the Plain* (1998), Billy cradles John Grady's corpse in his arms and calls on God to witness the destruction wrought by women:

Goddamn whores, he said. He was crying and the tears ran on his angry face and he called out to the broken day against them all and he called out to God to see what was before his eyes. Look at this, he called. Do you see? Do you see? (261)

The narrative between these two scenes in the Border Trilogy witnesses the systematic expulsion of women, affirming Tiburcio's appraisal of Magdalena as "nothing," a cypher, and confirming that the Western, even its twilight incarnation in *Cities of the Plain*, remains what Jane Tompkins calls a "womanless milieu" (*West* 44).

Each novel in the trilogy ultimately excludes the potentially significant female characters as part of a process of the obviation of women. Some forty years ago, Leslie Fiedler described the classic American novel as featuring a "strategy of evasion" of heterosexuality, because heterosexuality leads inexorably "to the fall to sex, marriage, and responsibility" (xx–xxi). While Robert Jarrett notes that the trilogy's commercial appeal is based in part on "significant elements of heterosexual romance" (99), under this thin veneer is a very different kind of love story, one much more consistent with Fiedler's *hierogamos* (or sacred marriage), "the peculiar American form of innocent homosexuality" (Fiedler 349, 531). Jarrett's recognition that John Grady Cole and Billy Parham experience "a loss of an initially stable identity based on a mythicized past" (105) might be extended, or rather, refined to reveal one facet of that loss: the destabilization of gender roles in the context of a Western narrative, in which gender roles are usually very clearly defined. While women are systematically eliminated from the narrative in the trilogy, the feminine itself remains and is ultimately "performed" by biologically-male characters. Even *Cities of the Plain*, the most overtly heterosexual volume of the trilogy, symbolically repeats but does not resolve gender issues raised in the first two volumes. By divorcing femininity from women and allowing the male performance of both gender roles, McCarthy in effect creates a closed circuit for male desire.

A merely cursory reading of Cormac McCarthy's novels reveals an unmistakable ambivalence about women, even an outright misogyny, manifested in the objectification of women as dead bodies in *Child of God* (1973), as the one-dimensional stereotypes witch, virgin, or whore in *Suttree* (1979), or as absence itself in much of *All the Pretty Horses* (1992) and *The Crossing* (1994). Particularly telling is McCarthy's turning from southern gothic novels to the Western, a genre which contemporary critics such as Tompkins and Lee Clark Mitchell recognize as a reaction against feminism and female authority (Mitchell 152; Tompkins, *West* 39–40).

All the Pretty Horses begins with John Grady Cole's betrayal by the two most important women in his life, his mother and his girlfriend, but the narrative soon avenges him. When his mother fails to register at the Menger Hotel under her married name and is escorted by a man other than his father, John Grady has no further contact with her. At the end of the novel, Lacey Rawlins asks if he has seen her, and he replies simply, "No" (298). He abjures his mother again in *Cities of the Plain* when Billy, hinting that John Grady might acquire the money to go to veterinary school from her, asks if John Grady ever writes her. Here, his response is a little more telling: "What's my mother got to do with anything?" (*COP* 217). Mary Catherine Barnett is not merely excluded, but visually contained at their final parting. John Grady sees no tears of remorse in her eyes, and when she offers her hand in farewell, he does not "know what she was doing" because he has "never shaken hands with a woman before" (*APH* 29). The narrative then encloses her within a "frame" so that she may never again exceed her proper limits:

> He stood back and touched the brim of his hat and turned and went on up the street. He didnt look back but he could see her in the windows of the Federal Building across the street standing there and she was *still* standing there when he reached the corner and stepped out of the glass forever. (29, emphasis added)

The implication is clear: John Grady steps out of the glass, moving beyond the moment, while Mary Catherine remains frozen there forever.

Even the women for whom John Grady retains affection are dispatched. Alejandra, who might be considered the second most important character in the novel if it is viewed as a traditional heterosexual love story, rides into the narrative on a horse and leaves on a train without much fanfare (John Grady works harder to reclaim his horse Redbo than to convince Alejandra to marry him). Abuela, who never really makes an appearance in the novel, is buried in "the unmarked earth" at the end of the novel; as John Grady stands tearfully at her grave, her chief value is revealed: "she had known and cared for the wild Grady boys" (APH 301).

The Crossing's Library of Congress subject heading, "Boys—New Mexico—Fiction," affirms that "boys" are the subject of this book, and this fact becomes readily apparent as the women one-by-one fade from view: Billy's grandmother Margarita and younger sister Margarita are dead before the novel begins; his mother Carolyn is killed by the end of part I; the primadonna appears only long enough to inspire in Billy a very pale passion that serves as a "disclaimer" against his implicit homosexuality or zoophilia;[2] and the girl whom Boyd and Billy save in Mexico disappears with Boyd but never even has a proper name. The only fully developed female character is not a woman at all, but a she-wolf, who dies in part I.

Before her death, the wolf faces increasingly deadly forms of confinement, from the wolftraps set early in the novel, to the muzzle, the *carretero*'s tent where a ten-centavo admission is charged (104), and the dogfight pit where she is chained to a stake. Finally, Billy himself buries the she-wolf and the unborn pups "under a cairn of scree. . . . [H]e buried them all and piled the rocks over them" (C 129).[3] Later, in another burial of sorts, Billy attends a tawdry carnival where the shill tries to entice him with the promise of "the attractions" inside, but he "had already seen bleeding through the garish paintwork old lettering from a prior life and . . . recognized the caravan of the traveling opera company" (377). The primadonna, who once complained about being killed night after night by the Punchinello who knew her secret (229), now becomes enclosed in the spectacle, or rather, is the spectacle itself, and Billy refuses to look upon her again despite the narrative's earlier (overwrought) insistence that seeing her naked beauty altered his life (220).[4]

Cities of the Plain features only four major women characters within the action proper (Betty appears in the Epilogue). Socorro, whose name means *help*, effectively raised the late Margaret Johnson McGovern and is Mac's housekeeper, but she rarely ever speaks; and, true to her name, she serves in the traditional helpmeet function. The one-eyed *criada* (maid) is Socorro's dark mirror, serving as Eduardo's housekeeper and Magdalena's surrogate mother, just as Socorro was Margaret's. Margaret Johnson McGovern is herself merely a ghost and a name. Billy tells John Grady that he decided to stay on at Mac's ranch only after Margaret died (COP 12). Although he professes admiration for the woman who was alive, he seems to prefer ghosts named Margaret (his sister and grandmother both are named versions of "Margaret"). The wedding ring that Margaret declined to be buried with is for Mac the symbol of their enduring love because, he says, "she set more store by that ring and what it meant than anything else she ever owned" (216). But the ring becomes a symbol of enclosure and the male circuit of desire when Mac gives it to John Grady, to give to Magdalena (215–16), a transaction that is prevented by Magdalena's death at the hands of John Grady's rival Eduardo, who, like the Punchinello in the primadonna's opera, kills Magdalena because he has "seen into her heart" and therefore knows her secret (COP 213).[5]

Like the she-wolf in *The Crossing*, Magdalena moves through a series of increasingly lethal forms of confinement. She moves from La Venada to the White Lake brothel, but John Grady imagines installing her in the little adobe house on the outskirts of Mac's ranch. Instead, we see her restrained during epileptic seizures in two different scenes at the White Lake; in the first, the *criada* forces a piece of broomstick between Magdalena's teeth (72), in an act reminiscent of Billy's attempts to subdue the she-wolf by muzzling her with a stick in her mouth. During the second seizure, Tiburcio forces a leather belt between her teeth and then gropes her prone body like an "incubus of uncertain proclivity" (COP 183). The final chapters of the novel show her moving from the hospital room with the concrete ceiling where she is "strapped to a steel table" (208), to Eduardo's bedroom with its "small barred window" (213), to the morgue with its smell "of damp concrete" and its overhead lights "covered with small wire baskets" (229). Ultimately, we see Magdalena framed as Mary Catherine Barnett is in John Grady's final image of her. The police captain shows Billy the coroner's photo: "The girl in the photo looked made of wax. She'd been turned so as to afford the best view of her severed throat" (242). The captain returns the photo "face down" to "an oakwood tray at the corner of his desk" (242).

The coroner's photo and its placement are apt metaphors for Magdalena's fate as a woman in the trilogy, for she is contained, reduced, and ultimately relegated to the margins. Although Magdalena receives more narrative space than any other female in the trilogy, she is, as the blind maestro says, "at best a visitor. . . . She does not belong here. Among us," among men (81). She, too, must eventually give way for the action between men and their dream of femininity without women.

Although flesh-and-blood women are absent or marginalized, the repressed feminine emerges in unexpected ways, for like the spirit of the she-wolf, "the world cannot lose it"(C 127). Perhaps the characterization of Billy Parham in *The Crossing* most clearly demonstrates the destabilization of gender roles that both complicates and transgresses the generic conventions of the Western in the Border Trilogy. An apparent reference to Billy's three forays into Mexico, the titular "crossing" is equally a reference to his "gender crossing," as he crosses the illusory yet socially-endorsed boundaries between the masculine and the feminine. While the feminine itself may be omnipresent, the "gender trouble" in the Border Trilogy is that biological males—"boys"—ultimately perform both gender roles to create a closed system of desire that effectively makes women unnecessary.

Twenty years before *The Crossing*, McCarthy depicted gender trouble with *Child of God*'s Lester Ballard, whose adoption of feminine styles is also associated with dead women, but Lester displays the feminine superficially by cross-dressing in his female victims' clothing and hair. In the scene where he dons a frightwig and dress to attack Greer, he is merely a man in drag, still toting his precious phallic rifle (COG 172–73). Without the costume changes, Billy Parham's performance of the feminine in *The Crossing* is perhaps more subtle than Lester's but no less real. As the psychoanalyst Joan Riviere first argued in her 1929 essay "Womanliness as a Masquerade," womanliness can "be assumed and worn as a mask, both to hide the possession of masculinity and to avert the reprisals expected" from parental figures (Riviere 38); further, such a mask can be assumed by a man to protect himself within masculine rivalry (40), just as Lester Ballard does when he attacks Greer. In fact, according to Riviere, "genuine womanliness" and the masquerade are "the same thing"(38); that is, despite the biological sex of the performer, femininity is always an act.

Working from the theories of Riviere, Jacques Lacan, and others, Judith Butler argues that gender is not an essence but a performance independent of biological sex, "a stylized repetition of acts" including "bodily gestures, movements, and styles of various kinds" that "constitute the illusion of an abiding gendered self" (140). Erroneously regarded as constant and essential, gender identity is in reality tenuous and contingent. As *The Crossing* progresses, the two Parham brothers each adopt the "stylized repetition of acts" associated with a particular gender. Boyd, whose name contains "boy" within it, acts out the stereotypical roles of chivalric male and oedipal son. He is the oedipal son insofar as he not only suffers the symbolic guilt for his father's death, as does Billy, but seemingly admits his complicity when he confesses the anguish of his partial identification with the killers: "They called for me. Called Boyd. Boyd. . . . Like we was friends"(173). Boyd's role as the chivalric male is really an extension of his role as oedipal son, since once the son has "killed" the father and taken his place, he must thereafter enforce taboos. Attempting to insure the girl's chastity, he chides Billy for cursing in front of her and frets when she may have seen some young boys swimming in the nude. Conversely, Billy, whose name is a diminutive and sometimes feminine version of William (his father's name), denies having trouble at home because his father "never allowed it" (166). Moreover, he acknowledges Boyd's superiority and his father's recognition of that superiority: "He was a born natural. He was smarter than me too. . . . About everthing. Daddy knew it too. He knew it and he knew I knew it and that's all there was to say about it" (420). Less smart, less spontaneous, less "natural," Billy becomes increasingly feminized and emotive, a singer of *corridos*, while Boyd becomes the hero celebrated in *corridos* (375, 381).

The catalyst for Billy's transformation from traditional masculine identity to a feminized one is the she-wolf. Robert Jarrett suggests that the wolf is the "supreme representation of the Other . . . embodying an alternate consciousness to that of the human" (118). I would contend that this otherness issues as well from the wolf's femininity, for, as Billy suggests to Mr. Sanders, women are fundamentally inscrutable and Other: "I guess I've got to say that I dont understand the first thing about em"(C 352). In the absence of human women, the she-wolf embodies the mythic feminine with her inscrutability, fecundity, and fidelity—her mate must force her to leave him (24). In stereotypically masculine manner, Billy tries to subdue her in physically transgressive ways that uncomfortably recall rape: "It aint no use to fight it," he tells her, "You aint got no damn sense" (56–57). This transgression inevitably extends to touching: "He sat stroking her. Then he reached down and felt her belly. She struggled and her eye rolled wildly. He spoke to her softly. He put the flat of his hand between her warm and naked teats. He held it there for a long time" (74).

But that which Billy would subdue, he must ultimately subsume. Having already been warned that "[w]omen are crazy" (C 37), Billy begins early on to exhibit an affinity for the feminine point of view. He himself is accused of being "crazy" and "peculiar" for wanting to return the wolf to Mexico (59, 68) but claims to be "just like everbody else" (68). The rancher who tells him, "Well you aint" (68), clearly excludes females from his "everbody" since his own wife Jane Ellen also expresses sympathy for the wolf. "That poor thing," she says, insisting on getting medical attention for the wolf's injured leg (69–70). From the rancher's perspective, the wolf, Billy, and Jane Ellen are symptomatic of an "epidemic" of "craziness" that clearly threatens stalwart men like himself (70).

With the wolf's death at the end of part I, Billy introjects this feminine ideal, the "better angel" that he associates not only with the wolf but alternately with other dead or absent women, especially his grandmother. *The Crossing* could even be considered an aborted sentimental fiction. McCarthy's maudlin depiction of the wolf's death certainly rivals anything out of Stowe or Dickens and seems to grant a kind of power to the victim. As in the sentimental novel, the death of the innocent feminine sufferer—the she-wolf—becomes her apotheosis, a sacrificial death that radically transforms its witness, Billy:[6]

He took up her stiff head out of the leaves and held it or he reached to hold what cannot be held, what already ran among the mountains at once terrible and of a great beauty, like flowers that feed on flesh. What blood and bone are made of but can themselves not make on any altar nor by any wound of war. What we may well believe has power to cut and shape and hollow out the dark form of the world surely if wind can, if rain can. But which cannot be held never be held and is no flower but is swift and a huntress and the wind itself is in terror of it and the world cannot lose it. (C 127)

However, unlike that of nineteenth-century sentimental fiction, Billy's feminization does not have a salvific effect.

Billy's feminization commences with his exposure to the "matrix"[7]

—which connotes mother/womb/menses—in short, the female generative principle that both opposes and complements the Lacanian concept of the Phallus in the context of *The Crossing*.[8] As Ellie Ragland-Sullivan explains, the Lacanian Phallus or "phallic signifier" is not identical to, although it is sometimes confused with, the penis. Instead, it is the "representational agent of separation" that imposes a "scission" in the mother-child dyad and thus initiates the infant's "true passage from nature to culture in ternary or Oedipal terms" (Ragland-Sullivan 55). The first section of the novel, where neither Parham boy has made that passage fully, is imbued with the abjection of the maternal body, as Julia Kristeva would refer to the novel's matrix motif. The wolf becomes the perfect vehicle for the abject, combining the animal and the maternal, for, according to Kristeva, "The abject confronts us . . . with those fragile states where man strays on the territories of *animal*" and "within our personal archeology, with our earliest attempts to release the hold of *maternal* entity even before ex-isting [sic] outside of her" (12–13). Searching Mr. Echols's cabin for the wolf traps, Mr. Parham finds the vial labeled "No. 7 Matrix." The masculine antipathy or fear of the generative female body surfaces in the exchange between father and son:

Good God, he whispered.
Let me smell it, Boyd said.
No, said his father. He put the vial in his pocket. . . . (17)

Boyd (not Billy) exhibits an attraction that his father protects him from, schooling him in the appropriate revulsion ("Good God") and imposing the scission that insures his transition "from nature to culture." Don Arnulfo later tells Billy that "the matrix was not so easily defined. . . . He said that in his opinion only shewolves in their season were a proper source" (45). For the human women in the trilogy, the onset of menses marks them as objects of desire but also as objects of dread and violent revulsion; as the Mexican girl's would-be rapist informs Billy, "if they were old enough to bleed they were old enough to butcher" (209), a dictum that echoes in Magdalena's death later in the trilogy.

While Lester Ballard keeps close tabs on his rifle in *Child of God*, Billy willingly trades his own father's phallic rifle for the she-wolf's corpse after first shooting her, a gesture that arguably places Billy squarely in the patriarchal *if-I-can't-have-her-no one-will* camp (123–24). The implications of the trade are teased out later when Billy admits to the sheriff that his family was left defenseless since he had the "forty-four forty carbine," his father's only gun, in Mexico (167). Billy's possession of the rifle is perhaps a form of usurpation of the father's authority, as suggested by the sheriff's reproachful "It wasnt much use to em, was it?"(167). Upon his return, his parents' bloody mattress itself possibly constitutes a sign, a sort of perverse hymeneal bed, proof not of the mother's defloration but the father's castration. When the sheriff asks the gun's current whereabouts, he insinuates something even more problematic than usurpation—a sort of abdication on Billy's part:

I see that scabbard boot. Where's the rifle at?
I traded it.
What did you trade it for?
I dont think I could say.
You mean you wont say.
No sir. I mean I aint sure I could put a name to it. (170)

Billy's inability to "put a name to" what he has traded for suggests the same ineffable, indefinable quality that Don Arnulfo has previously attributed to the matrix; in fact, Billy has traded the phallic carbine for a form of vicarious menstruation[9] that he first experiences as he rides away with the wolf's corpse and feels "the blood of the wolf against his thigh where it had soaked . . . through his breeches"(125). The bleeding between the legs invokes a primitive castration anxiety, underscoring the symbolic effect of trading his gun for the she-wolf's corpse. The moment when he "put his hand to his leg and tasted the blood which tasted no different than his own" (125) is also telling in that Mr. Parham previously has forbidden Boyd to smell the No. 7 Matrix, perhaps because, as Kristeva notes, "An unshakeable adherence to Prohibition and Law is necessary if that perverse interspace of abjection is to be hemmed in and thrust aside" (16). Here, Billy not only smells, but tastes the wolf's blood, and it could be argued that the act mimics transubstantiation: He takes in the spirit of the she-wolf—hence the feminine—along with her blood. Noting Bruno Bettelheim's theory of "cross-sex envy," James Brain argues that male simulation of menstruation is "a conscious attempt to undertake voluntarily . . . by males what occurs naturally in females" (312). As Billy bears the wolf's corpse to the hills, the narrator pointedly calls attention to the presence of the moon (C 125), which both induces lunacy (the "craziness" that Billy is accused of) and governs the twenty-eight day menstrual cycle—two sinister faces of the same female moon. A few pages later, he deliberately cuts himself and watches "the slow blood dropping on the stone"(130), an act of phlebotomy that suggests a conscious attempt to feminize himself. Billy also experiences this mock bleeding when he is once again powerless to protect a loved one and Boyd is shot; his trouserlegs are "stiff with dried blood," with the "last thin paring of the old moon" watching over him (273, 274).[10]

At the beginning of part IV of *The Crossing*, when he returns without Boyd from his second Mexican expedition, Billy once again attempts to align himself with the patriarchal order by enlisting in the armed forces. When the border guard issues the challenge, "Hell fire, boy. This country's at war" (333), Billy begins a futile quest to find his place in the action, traveling to Deming, El Paso, and finally Albuquerque trying to enlist: "I think I need to be in the army" (341), he tells the doctor at Albuquerque. The army appeals to Billy as an antidote to his orphan status, providing a sense of belonging, but it would also confirm, or perhaps (re)constitute, his masculinity. According to Margaret Higgonet, war is the ultimate "*gendering* activity," for women purportedly stay home and men head to the front (4). Gender identity is simplified during wartime by this easy division. But Billy is rejected at three different recruitment centers because he has a heart murmur, which symbolizes the weak or soft heart that his experiences have wrought within him, the "[d]oomed enterprises" that have divided his life "into the then and the now"(129). Being left on the homefront in the wake of his failure to save the she-wolf, his parents, and ultimately his brother Boyd, Billy experiences another impediment to his masculine identity. His exclusion from the community of warriors, the *comitatus*, is demonstrated by the confrontations with the G.I., who disparages Billy by saying, "Uniform dont mean nothin to him" (349), and with the drunken Mexican patriot who shows Billy his war wounds. This same lack continues to haunt Billy throughout *Cities of the Plain*, where he listens to "Troy's war stories" (COP 7)[11] and explains why he did not serve, "I was four-F. . . . I tried to enlist three different times but they wouldnt take me," to which Elton responds consolingly, "I know you did. I tried to get overseas but I spent the whole war at Camp Pendleton" (26). The Mexican police captain investigating

Magdalena's murder rebukes the insolent Billy with a narrative of his own family's distinguished military heritage:

Every male in my family for three generations has been killed in defense of this republic. Grandfathers, fathers, uncles, brothers. Eleven men in all. Any beliefs they may have had now reside in me. Any hopes. . . . I pray to these men. Their blood ran in the streets and gutters and in the arroyos and among the desert stones. They are my Mexico and I pray to them and I answer to them and to them alone. I do not answer elsewhere. (243)

Billy respectfully replies: "If that's true then I take back what I said" (243).

The heart murmur is a hidden defect that finds its outward sign in the tears that Billy sheds throughout the novel. While real men do cry, the accepted fiction is that they do not. At any rate, fictional men, particularly heroes of the Western genre, do not cry. Thus it is significant that McCarthy includes such lachrymose male characters, since tears and flagrant displays of emotion are the *sine qua non* of sentimental fiction, for "emotions of the heart bespeak a state of grace, and these are known . . . in moments of greatest importance, by tears" (Tompkins, "Sentimental" 89). Billy's eyes are "swimming" with tears during the trade of his father's rifle for the she-wolf's corpse (C 122). In the descriptions of the she-wolf's death and burial, emotion escapes the confines of the text as the narrative exacts the reader's identification with Billy's grief. When he discovers his parents' bloodstained mattress, Billy "fell to his knees in the floor and sobbed into his hands" (165). In the Sheriff's office, he conspicuously wipes his eyes, suggesting tears (168). After the ordeal of Niño's stabbing, Billy wakes from dreaming of Boyd only to weep (400). And the final page of the novel sees him crying ostensibly because he cannot find the dog he has driven off the night before (426), but the lost dog merely stands in for all of Billy's losses as the novel's culminating sorrow.

Billy's feminization is underscored when he adopts the *materna lingua* of his grandmother. Jane Tompkins notes the distrust of language within the Western, where "only actions are real" (*West* 51); in *The Crossing*, however, Billy's actions become more futile, and words—particularly the *materna lingua* of comforting stories and lullabies—become the only true thing. When the *alguacil* confiscates the she-wolf, Billy enters the enclosure and tells her "what was in his heart," including "promises that he swore to keep in the making" (105). As he rides away with the wolf's corpse, he begins to sing "songs his father once had sung in the used to be"[12] but then changes to "a soft corrido in spanish from his grandmother that told of the death of a brave soldadera who took up her fallen soldierman's gun" (125); in his grandmother's *corrido*, it is the woman, "a brave soldadera," who is heroic and powerfully armed.[13] In the scene where he must push the faltering Niño beyond his endurance, Billy once again reverts to his grandmother's tongue: "He told it stories in spanish that his grandmother had told him as a child and when he'd told all of those that he could remember he sang to it" (274).[14] At a pivotal moment in the novel when Billy reaches out and begs Boyd, "I need for you to talk to me," Boyd refuses to talk and finally rejects him for the girl (330). It is telling that when Billy tries to deny his maternal side and revert to a gruff, macho nature by shooing off the stray dog in the final chapter, he ultimately breaks down and ends up crying, himself abject, and abjected. While tears and emotional displays may suggest "salvation, communion, reconciliation" in the sentimental novel (Tompkins, "Sentimental" 89), they suggest the opposite in *The Crossing*: utter despair, loneliness, and irremediable loss.

The fluidity of gender identity and its existence primarily as performance are underscored by Billy's modeling of "masculine" behavior at the beginning of *Cities of the Plain*. If, as Riviere claims, femininity can "be assumed and worn as a mask" to "hide the possession of masculinity" (38), then masculinity can perhaps be worn to mask femininity. As Edwin Arnold notes, the Billy we meet in *Cities* is so different that he seems to be wholly "disconnected from the Billy of the previous book" (227). This new, macho Billy is not very likable. He trades crass banter with Troy about the nature of whores (*COP* 4) and draws an unflattering comparison between women and horses as he tells John Grady, "Get that one I had. She's five gaited or I never rode"(6). Ironically, he later reproaches John Grady for selling his horse to finance his future with Magdalena, a move he characterizes as "Losin your head over a piece of tail"(136). This new Billy reads *Destry* as a primer for modified masculinity (59)[15] but eventually takes his cue from Hollywood action films. While searching for John Grady, Billy roughs up Tiburcio, calling him "You little son of a bitch," hitting him "squarely in the mouth" and slamming him "back against the wall"(237). He then threatens Eduardo, saying with bravado, "You better have a shoebox full of pistols in there" (239). McCarthy deflates Billy's ironic hyper-masculinity by having Eduardo calmly pull out a cigar (the more benign phallic symbol) and ask pointedly, "Why would I need a pistol?" (239). In the Epilogue, Billy even becomes a professional actor, performing the masculine in his role as a cowboy extra in a Western filmed in El Paso in the "second year of the new millenium" (264). Indeed, Billy is an "actor" throughout both *The Crossing* and *Cities of the Plain*, alternating between masculine and feminine roles as needed.

The perfect foil for Billy Parham would seem to be John Grady Cole, who is the *ne plus ultra* of masculinity: silent, strong, superior—a leader. Emilio Pérez tells him, "The world wants to know if you have cojones" (APH 193), but we already know that he does. We learn early in *All the Pretty Horses* that the Grady men all die manly, that is, violent deaths. And so it will be for John Grady Cole, the last of the Grady men, who himself dies at the hand of another "serious man" (COP 198). Nonetheless, the same gender anxiety that besets Billy eventually creeps into McCarthy's characterization of John Grady Cole as well.

John Grady's status as the superior male is established early in *All the Pretty Horses*. Hearing John Grady's plans to go to Mexico, Lacey Rawlins asks, "If I dont go will you go anyways?" But John Grady is "already gone" (27), so Lacey follows him. Don Héctor is surprised to learn that Lacey is actually older than John Grady because John Grady is so clearly "the leader" (114). When Lacey fears for his life in prison, John Grady sternly orders him not to give up, sprinkling his pep-talk with several paternal *clichés*, "You listen to me," "You hear me?" and "I know it and I dont care" (182–83). This leadership dynamic also exists between John Grady and Blevins, whom John Grady protects with the same paternal gruffness: "Do like I told you," he tells the slow-moving Blevins when danger is imminent (77). In *Cities of the Plain*, Billy understands John Grady to be superior to him in the same ways that Boyd was. He is being only mildly facetious when he dubs John Grady the "all-american cowboy" (3). He admits that John Grady reminds him of Boyd (146), and though he seems annoyed that John Grady "cant do no wrong where Mac's concerned" (16), he eventually shares Mac's opinion as he says of John Grady: "He's as good a boy as I ever knew. He's the best"(244).

Like the "all-american cowboy" that he is, John Grady abides by the cowboy's code of silence. In *All the Pretty Horses*, a man commends John Grady's silence as "a good trait to have" (19). When Mary Catherine suggests they could remain friends, John Grady says contemptuously, "It's just talk, Mary Catherine" (28). And just as Boyd refuses to communicate with Billy, John Grady eventually shuts Lacey out, deferring, perhaps indefinitely, a discussion of the events at Saltillo: "I'll tell you. Let's just sit here. Let's not talk. Let's just sit here real quiet," John Grady tells Lacey, later repeating, "Let's just sit here real quiet" (208). The lack of verbal communication is part of his general affective reticence. Early in *All the Pretty Horses*, his father forbids him to shed tears in their conversation about Grandfather Grady (12); he does cry at least twice in *All the Pretty Horses*—once for his father, once for Abuela (286, 301)—but remains mostly dry-eyed in *Cities*, the notable exception being the scene in which he recognizes but refuses to identify Magdalena's corpse.

However, more telling than the lack of tears is perhaps the sheer volume of blood that John Grady loses in the Border Trilogy. Like Billy Parham, he experiences vicarious menstruation, but the implications of this bleeding vary drastically between *All the Pretty Horses* and *Cities of the Plain*. Gail Kern Paster notes the connection between dramatic representations of bleeding and menstruation: "The bleeding body signifies as a shameful token of uncontrol, as a failure of physical self-mastery particularly associated with woman in her monthly 'courses'" (92). Twice in *All the Pretty Horses* John Grady suffers wounds that cause his boots to fill with blood (202, 268). His boots "sloshed" and his clothes "sagged with the weight of the blood" after the knife-fight in prison (201). After being shot in the thigh, his "trousers were dark with blood and there was blood on the ground" (266), and later the captive captain notes the wound, which is "still bleeding" (272). But in this scene, the anxiety surrounding male blood loss is abated because even in displaying the feminine, John Grady manages to display the phallic at the same time. As the captain looks on in disbelief, John Grady cauterizes his thigh wound with his own pistol by "jamm[ing] the redhot barrel ash and all down into the hole in his leg" (274). His "manly" suffering mirrors Boyd's in the bullet extraction scene of *The Crossing* (311–13). Both scenes involve an unsettling, vaguely phallic probing of adolescent male flesh, but whereas the doctor probes Boyd's wounds, John Grady probes his own, serving effectively as both penetrated and penetrator.

Paster describes phlebotomy as "the cultural inversion of involuntary bleeding in any form" because it requires "professional skill and strategic application on the part of the surgeon and self-mastery on the part of the patient" (91). Although John Grady does not deliberately bleed himself, he does control the flow of his blood as the phlebotomist would and thus mitigates the feminizing effects of incontinent bleeding through "self-mastery."

In *Westerns: Making the Man in Fiction and Film*, Lee Clark Mitchell notes the centrality in the Western of "the image of the male body violated" (175), which often develops into a "convalescence narrative" involving the rehabilitation of the hero in "a process of slow recovery [that] leads to renewed strength" (177). John Grady's two woundings in *All the Pretty Horses* become just such convalescence narratives in which his seemingly imperiled manhood is in fact strengthened. However, the typical convalescence narrative features a woman who "serves as catalyst for that recovery, a midwife between two states of consciousness, who ensures through a feminine presence . . . that masculine restraint will be restored, unimpaired, to full strength" (Mitchell 178). By contrast, men alone serve as "midwives" in the convalescence in *All the Pretty Horses*, underscoring yet again the superfluity of women. At Saltillo, it is "Pérez's *man*" who "gather[s] him up in his arms" (202, emphasis added), and when John Grady cauterizes his own wound, he himself facilitates the process. The meaning of this self-sufficiency is demonstrated in the courtroom scene where "there aint no women present" and the judge asks John Grady to "show the court them bulletholes"(288). After he denies receiving "medical attention" for those "nasty lookin holes," there ensues a dialogue that underscores his masculinity and confirms the respect of all those present for this superior male:

. . . You were lucky not to of got gangrene.
Yessir. I burnt em out pretty good.
Burnt em out? . . . What did you burn em out with?
A pistolbarrel. I burnt em out with a hot pistolbarrel.
There was absolute silence in the courtroom. The judge leaned back.(289)

Breaking the awed silence, the judge orders the horses returned to "Mr Cole" and frees him, referring to him once more as "Son."

While John Grady's facility with a pistol saves him from feminization in *All the Pretty Horses*, he seemingly repeats many of the steps toward feminization in *Cities of the Plain* that Billy Parham experiences in *The Crossing*. His relationship with Magdalena (the abject female, object of male dread and desire) effectively represents a narrative return to Billy's relationship with the she-wolf. Just as the wolf catalyzes Billy's transformation from the traditional masculine identity to a feminized one, Magdalena triggers symptoms of gender trouble in John Grady. The same dangerous "craziness" (the lunacy coinciding with vicarious menstruation) found in *The Crossing* pervades *Cities of the Plain*, where Magdalena tells John Grady his actions are "loco" (102), and Billy berates John Grady in almost the same terms he himself is berated for helping the wolf in *The Crossing*:

> Have you lost your rabbit-assed mind? I'm an absolute son of a bitch, bud. I never in my goddamn life heard the equal of this. . . . Do you know what they're goin to do with you? They're goin to hook your head up to one of them machines and throw a big switch and fry your brains to where you wont be a menace to yourself no more. (COP 119)

Even Eduardo, who is arguably as implicated in lunacy as John Grady, taunts him for believing "craziness is sacred" (251).

Just as Billy trades his father's rifle for the she-wolf's corpse, John Grady eventually pawns his grandfather's gun to gain access to Magdalena. He tells the pawnbroker that he will return for the gun, but the pawnbroker nods toward a case "where half a dozen old Colt revolvers lay displayed" and tells him knowingly, "All of them belonged to somebody's grandfather" (94). The pawnbroker knows that the transaction is not reversible. John Grady has relinquished his inheritance from those wild Grady boys; he has also renounced the very thing that allowed him, in the cauterization scene, to maintain his self-mastery, his masculinity. To lay claim to Magdalena, he renounces the symbol of his phallic power, and that renunciation proves lethal in the final bloodletting scene.

Eduardo's final words in the dialogue-as-knife-fight taunt John Grady with his sexual fall: "For a whore, the pimp said. For a whore" (253). Just as Billy is infected by the feminine when he tastes the she-wolf's blood, Magdalena "contaminates" John Grady through intercourse and weakens him. Pollution theories, which abound in many cultures (even our own), posit menstruation as a sign of women's inferiority and corruption, and thus account for much of the anxiety and ritual surrounding heterosexual intercourse. The anthropologist Ian Hogbin found that among certain Melanesian tribes, men use bloodletting and scarification as "artificial menstruation," to purify themselves after exposure to female impurity during intercourse (88). The ritual re-enactment of a female biological process suggests that the male body is feminized through heterosexual intercourse. But the very bleeding itself marks the male body as feminized, if not emasculated, because as Paster notes, "The male body, opened and bleeding, can assume the shameful attributes of the incontinent female body as both cause of and justification for its evident vulnerability and defeat" (92). We see this vulnerability in John Grady's evisceration, the "gray tube of gut" protruding from his abdomen (COP 254), and in the "soft sloshing sound" his boots make (COP 253),[16] but also most strikingly in the thigh wounds inflicted so precisely by Eduardo: "the boy's thigh was laid open in a deep gash and the warm blood was running down his leg" with "the letter E in the flesh of his thigh" (COP 249, 252). The "medical transplant" Eduardo performs (250) is a symbolic emasculation, one which John Grady reciprocates in the final knife thrust. *Cities of the Plain* is not a "convalescence narrative"; this time John Grady Cole will not be restored to full strength but will instead become Billy's "burden"(262) in a *pietà*: "The dead boy in his arms hung with his head back and those partly opened eyes beheld nothing at all"(261). In John Grady's quest to prove himself "a serious man," his masculinity defeats itself, and in the epilogue of *Cities of the Plain*, he is symbolically reincarnated as Betty's daughter, the young girl so "in love with" the colt, she would "go out at night after supper in the cold and sit in the straw floor of the shed and talk to it" (290).

In her study of male homosocial desire, Eve Kosofsky Sedgwick posits "a continuum between homosocial and homosexual—a continuum whose visibility, for men, in our society, is radically disrupted" (1–2). Desire appears in many guises along the male homosocial continuum, but always as "the affective or social force, the glue, even when its manifestation is hostility or hatred or something less emotively charged, that shapes an important relationship" (2). Edwin Arnold notes that the trilogy's real love stories are "between men and men" (236) but cautions that in spite of "the sexual ambivalence" that attends their relationship, we should not confuse Billy's love with "overt physical desire" for John Grady (237–38). While it is true that genital sexuality is not a component of the relationship between the two men, there is an undeniable cathexis of desire between them; such palpable desire between a man and a woman would certainly be labeled sexual even if it were never consummated. Conditioning in an outwardly homophobic culture often prevents recognition that all male-male relationships are of a piece. In *Love and Death in the American Novel*, for example, Leslie Fiedler carefully constructs a paradigm of "innocent homosexuality" for such American classics as *Moby-Dick* and *Adventures of Huckleberry Finn* (531), a paradigm in which *innocent* clearly signifies *non-genital*. In *Cities of the Plain*, McCarthy seemingly confirms this signification in the negative, where Tiburcio, who is clearly coded as gay (Arnold 238), is likewise coded as nefarious and depraved, a "morbid voyeur" and an "incubus of uncertain proclivity"(COP 183).[17] Nonetheless, McCarthy shows Tiburcio as merely an adjunct to Eduardo, playing "alcahuete" to Eduardo's "grand alcahuete"(196) and murdering Magdalena on his behalf. It is not entirely clear whether Tiburcio is motivated by money, sadism, or fealty to his superior. In all its manifestations along the male homosocial continuum, the attraction between men is often more passionate than that between a man and a woman, as it is in the trilogy, whether that attraction be John Grady's failed paternal instincts with Blevins (whom John Grady later avenges), Billy's homoerotic desire for John Grady (a desire incorporating the paternal), or even, ultimately, John Grady's final obsession with Eduardo. Although they often take on sublimated or disguised forms in the Border Trilogy, the homosocial and the homoerotic commingle; sexual and other forms of desire overlap. It is precisely this blending that allows desire to circulate exclusively among men.

The circuit of male desire in the trilogy takes two paths. The first involves triangular desire, in which the ostensible female object is really a catalyst for a male-male relationship. The second is direct homoerotic or homosocial longing, rarely reciprocated with equal fervor by the object (perhaps as a strategy for maintaining the "innocence" of the relationship). Although the continuity of male desire may not be immediately discernible, the two forms of desire are aspects of the same phenomenon and have the same result: the removal of the female from the equation of desire.

As René Girard notes, triangular desire is desire mediated by a rival or an idol and so defined *"according to Another"* in a primitive movement that is easily confused "with the will to be Oneself" (4). "In the birth of desire,"

Girard says, "the third person is always present" (21). Competition and rivalry are therefore really forms of covert desire; that the competition is "about" or over a woman is a moot point. Perhaps with a beautiful woman, a rival is always implicit, but certainly so with a whore. Thus John Grady Cole first posits his desire for Magdalena in the terms of an imaginary competition; rebuffing Troy's offer to procure Magdalena for him, he declares: "I can get her if I want her" (COP 6), a declaration he will spend the rest of the novel trying to prove. Later, he tells the maestro, "I'd give her up if I thought I could not protect her" (197), but when the skeptical maestro asks if he really would, he replies, "I dont know" (198). In this conversation, he seeks the maestro's confirmation that he is Eduardo's equal, for when the maestro warns that Eduardo is "a cuchillero. A filero [synonyms for "knife-wielding man].... A man of a certain rigor. A serious man," John Grady insists, "I am serious myself" (198). His desire for Magdalena is clearly in reference to Eduardo, another man. She is thus trapped within the "phantom corpus" of male homosocial desire, "that bodiless structure" that "contained her life" (COP 212).

Although John Grady's *inamoratas* seem to be vastly different women—a West Texas school girl, a young Mexican debutante, and an epileptic prostitute—they become disturbingly interchangeable. The descriptions of both Alejandra and Magdalena fixate on their long black hair and their blue clothing (APH 94, 123, 141; COP 6, 229). In fact, Alejandra prophesies Magdalena in her final meeting with John Grady, telling him of a dream she had "Long ago. Before any of this": "They carried you through the streets of a city I'd never seen. It was dawn. The children were praying. Lloraba tu madre. Con más razón tu puta" (APH 252; Your mother was weeping. More to the point your whore), a scene that occurs at the end of *Cities of the Plain*. Dianne Luce suggests that Alejandra herself might be a substitute for Mary Catherine, whom John Grady lost to an older boy with a car; he can symbolically defeat this older male by winning Alejandra from the father Don Héctor ("When You Wake" 158–59). Magdalena, in turn, is described in her first narrative appearance as a "young girl of no more than seventeen and perhaps younger" who "fussed with the hem of her gaudy dress like a schoolgirl" (COP 6), a description that aligns her with the prelapsarian Mary Catherine. "She was so goddamned pretty, bud," John Grady tells Billy (259). But he never calls Magdalena by name in the final pages, an omission that makes possible a conflation of all the women in his life.

John Grady's women are interchangeable because ultimately their identities are not as important as their function within a structure. "If it is women who are being transacted, then it is the men who give and take them who are linked, the woman being a conduit of a relationship rather than a partner to it," Gayle Rubin explains in her critique of Claude Lévi-Strauss's *The Elementary Structures of Kinship* (174). In describing John Grady's first liaison with Alejandra, McCarthy uses the term "larceny," a crime that usually applies to property: "Sweeter for the larceny of time and flesh, sweeter for the betrayal" (141). What is John Grady stealing, and from whom? Luce notes the possibility of his material ambition in his courtship with Alejandra ("When You Wake" 156, 157). When Lacey Rawlins asks, "You got eyes for the spread?"(APH 138), he hints at Alejandra's potential to forge an alliance between Don Héctor and John Grady, in the manner described by Lévi-Strauss in *The Elementary Structures of Kinship*.[18] When John Grady dines with Alejandra in public, he remarks the other male diners' admiration of her (249) and is so reminded of her value. Eduardo makes more explicit this notion of women as property to be exchanged between men according to certain formalized rules when he makes his case to Billy: "everything that has come to pass has been the result of your friend's coveting of another man's property and his willful determination to convert that property to his own use" (COP 240).

"The woman is dead and the lover remains. There is no longer an object but the mediator . . . still exerts an irresistible attraction," Girard says of Dostoevsky's *The Eternal Husband* (45), but his words could just as aptly describe the confrontation between Eduardo and John Grady. According to Girard, "Only someone who prevents us from satisfying a desire which he himself has inspired in us is truly an object of hatred" (10–11). Though it results from the contention over Magdalena, the putative beloved, the knife fight between Eduardo and John Grady becomes a highly eroticized ballet. Eduardo first suggests the erotic nature of their fight: "Come, he said. We must make a beginning. It is like a first kiss" (COP 248). After this first kiss, Eduardo takes on a sexually suggestive pose: "He was suddenly very low before John Grady. Almost kneeling. Almost like a supplicant" (249), almost like a courtly suitor or like one about to perform fellatio. He intends to lay claim to John Grady as he has to Magdalena—"I name you completely to myself"(250)—and insists that John Grady's object is not Magdalena, but Eduardo himself, for as he carves his initial in John Grady's inner thigh, he tells the boy that he is performing "A medical transplant. To put the suitor's mind inside his thigh"(250). That is, having read John Grady's mind, Eduardo now inscribes what he finds there on the boy's flesh—"E" for Eduardo, not "M" for Magdalena. While John Grady receives most of the knife wounds, the two men take turns penetrating each other, for Eduardo receives the final blow, through the vulnerable submandibular triangle. The violence of the knife fight is almost a parodic (perhaps just sublimated) form of intercourse, so the aftermath parodies post-coital intimacy. Just as Alejandra wears his shirt after their last night together (APH 252), John Grady wears Eduardo's shirt, after a fashion, when he cuts away "the silk shirt from his dead enemy" and ties it around himself as a bandage (COP 254). "I just wanted him," he tells Billy three times before dying (259), admitting, however ambiguously, the desire that is integral to male rivalry.

But John Grady Cole is himself the object of intense, undisguised homoerotic desire. In the Border Trilogy, this form of desire seems to commence from an aborted (futile) rivalry, such as in Lacey's relationship with John Grady, Billy's respective relationships with Boyd and John Grady, and even Tiburcio's relationship with Eduardo. Perhaps because these desiring males have been feminized, they no longer need the feminine mediation of triangular desire. In all of these relationships, the male object originally spurns the desiring man for a woman, but in his relationship with Billy, John Grady ends up in the arms of the desiring man, albeit briefly.

This homoerotic longing is evident in the verbal and nonverbal expressions of jealousy so prevalent in the trilogy. Lacey is jealous not only of Alejandra, but of Blevins, as is evident when he advocates leaving Blevins behind. When John Grady asks how Lacey would feel if it were he, Lacey replies, "I wouldnt leave you and you wouldnt leave me. That aint no argument," implying that the bond between John Grady and himself should exclude Blevins (APH 79). His feelings of betrayal are clear when he refuses to meet John Grady's eyes after the two are arrested (153). In *The Crossing*, Billy resents the unnamed peasant girl who threatens to come between him and his brother. Billy asks sullenly, "You aint above just goin with her. Are you?" (237), and when he watches the girl embrace Boyd, he spits "dryly into the road" to express his disgust (238). In *Cities of the Plain*, we see jealousy expressed openly. The drunken Billy reveals his nascent heartache when he asks John Grady, "Have you got a girl you're seein?" (85). When John Grady tells him the affair with Magdalena "dont have nothin to do with you," Billy responds angrily, "The hell it dont" (121). He later protests, "I aint jealous you know" (156). The language of jealousy is ambiguous, for while the assumption is that Billy envies John Grady for having Magdalena, in truth he envies Magdalena for having John Grady. Oren's exchange with John Grady hints at this possibility:

Parham tells me she's pretty as a speckled pup.
He thinks I'm crazy.
Well. You might be a little crazy. He might be a little jealous. (202)

Implicit in John Grady's courtship with Magdalena is the possibility that, like Boyd, he "aint above just goin with her" and leaving Billy alone. Given Billy's vocal antipathy for the relationship with Magdalena, it is ironic that John Grady asks him to negotiate with Eduardo. He does so half-heartedly at best, a perverse Cyrano de Bergerac who is not in love with the beloved but with the lover. He concedes every point to Eduardo, even admitting that he does not believe that Magdalena loves John Grady (133), and ends by asking a rhetorical question, "He's in trouble, aint he?" (135).

The desperate longing for male-male intimacy that is forbidden in physical form (except when disguised as violence) will find its expression in songs and words, which are, of course, stereotypically part of the feminine realm. Billy's bawdy song, "John Grady Cole was a rugged old soul. . . . With a buckskin belly and a rubber asshole" (*COP* 76), is not only a comic elevation of "the boy to folk status" (Arnold 229); it is Billy's most explicit expression of homoerotic desire, its humor only thinly veiling the physical, even genital, nature of that longing. Lacey Rawlins' more demure expression occurs when he sings, "Will you miss me, will you miss me. Will you miss me when I'm gone" (*APH* 37), a musical version of his earlier question, "If I dont go will you go anyways?"(27), or more simply, how much do you love me? At the end of the novel, he discovers the answer when John Grady rebuffs his offer of comfortable domesticity, "You could stay here at the house" (299).

Along with homoerotic longing come terms of endearment, which are reserved exclusively for men in the trilogy. Just as Paul Fussell finds the word *lad* to be the foremost expression of World War I homoeroticism (282),[19] the word *bud* or *buddy* is a homoerotically charged expression for McCarthy's cowboys. When Rawlins sees John Grady after their extended separation, he hails John Grady jubilantly, "Bud is that you?" (*APH* 298). In *The Crossing*, Billy refers to his beloved brother as "[m]y bud" (420), as he does John Grady in *Cities*. As Billy frantically searches for the missing John Grady, he asks the *criada*, "Dónde está mi compañero?" (Where is my friend?) but quickly revises his question: "Dónde está mi cuate?" (*COP* 238). Billy refers to John Grady as *mi cuate*, which means both "my twin" and "my buddy" in Spanish. The connotation of kinship here does not preclude erotic attachment—only consider Rinthy and Culla in *Outer Dark* (1968) or the unnamed Mexican girl who claims to take the place of Boyd's dead twin sister in *The Crossing* (323). In calling John Grady *mi cuate*, Billy is claiming the same intimate identification that blends eroticism and kinship in the Mexican girl's relationship with Boyd. In the final pages of part IV, Billy and John Grady reconcile the differences they have had during John Grady's pursuit of Magdalena. Here, Billy uses the same paternal gruffness to express tenderness that John Grady once used in *All the Pretty Horses*, responding to John Grady's "I cant make it" with "I aint listenin to that shit. Hell, I've had worse scratches than that on my eyeball"(*COP* 258). In the final moments of John Grady's life, the two drop all pretenses and invoke "bud" twenty-one times between them (257–61); John Grady uses it almost as a punctuation mark: "I seen her, bud. . . . Like a sumbitch, bud. . . . Hurts, bud" (259–60). Billy tells John Grady, "Dont quit on me now, goddamn it" (258), articulating the anxiety he has suffered all along: losing John Grady. But it is too late, and Billy's lamentation echoes John Grady's anguished discovery of Magdalena's corpse in the morgue (229): "Billy called to him. As if he could not have gone far. Bud, he said. Bud? Aw goddamn. Bud? . . . Oh God. Bud. Oh goddamn" (261).

When Magdalena is dead and John Grady himself dying, he asks Billy to reclaim his gun: "There's a pawnshop ticket in the top of my footlocker. If you wanted to you could get my gun out and keep it" (*COP* 260). In essence, John Grady is asking Billy to reclaim the phallus and assume the masculine prerogative in his wake. Although it is unclear whether Billy ever redeems the Grady gun, he does honor John Grady's request that he take the puppy, the symbolic child of their *hierogamos*, spalded from his rocky keep by the two men after they destroy the mother (177), and Billy does become "Mr Parham" on the final page of the trilogy, where he tells Betty ambiguously, "I aint nothin" (292). As the double negatives cancel each other out, we understand that Billy (unlike Tiburcio's version of Magdalena) is *something*. With her loving words and gaze, Betty confirms his worth, serving as mother/mirror in the final pages, a role that returns us to both the original biological and psychological functions of women. For Billy, the infantile oedipal fantasy finally comes to fruition: the mother's adoring gaze and voice conferring the father's place upon the son. It is appropriate, then, that McCarthy uses the Dedication to end *Cities* and the Border Trilogy in what Arnold calls "the place of lullabies" (243).

With its destabilization of gender identity, the Border Trilogy could be regarded as McCarthy's most subversive work. Yet, while male performance of the feminine seemingly undermines the notion of "natural" male domination, it also becomes one more strategy to contain feminine power and obviate women. As feminist theorist Tania Modleski notes, men "deal with the threat of female power by incorporating it. . . . [M]ale power frequently works to efface female subjectivity by occupying the site of femininity"(7). In this sense, the gender trouble experienced by the trilogy's boys may be yet another symptom of McCarthy's narrative misogyny: the text of male desire appropriating the feminine while perpetually striving to make women themselves unnecessary. Magdalena's presence in *Cities of the Plain* offers little consolation. Betty's maternal presence on the last page suggests that at least until men have mastered parthenogenesis and thereby can become the infant's first mirror, women will have some place in the narrative. However, McCarthy undercuts even this grudging inclusion by carefully constructing a paradigm of desire as a masculine *cul-de-sac*, a paradigm that demands the systematic expulsion of women from the narrative.

Notes

1. Travis tells John Grady the same thing, in almost identical terms, shortly before John Grady's fateful encounter with Eduardo in *Cities of the Plain*: "They aint worth it, son." John Grady replies sarcastically, "I've heard that" (226).

2. In *Hollywood from Vietnam to Reagan*, Robin Wood calls those characters who exist only to prove the hero's heterosexuality "disclaimers" (229).
3. The image of the funereal "cairn of scree" evokes Wanda's premature burial under the "wall of slate" in *Suttree* (361–62).
4. McCarthy invokes an early scene in Marcel Carné's *Les Enfants du Paradis* (1944), in which the bathing Garance—the object of male desire in the film and the ultimate destroyer of all the men's lives—is the star attraction inside a tent.
5. Dianne Luce notes the implicit comparison between Magdalena and the diva in the passage where Magdalena has a vision of herself as "some young diva remanded to a madhouse" (COP 225). See "The Road and the Matrix" (217 n18).
6. For further discussion of the traits of sentimental fiction, see Jane Tompkins, "Sentimental Power" (85–87).
7. Throughout the novel, McCarthy also uses the term *matrix* as a synonym for the Creation. The narrator refers to "the rich matrix of creatures" (127). In the tale of the old man of Caborca, the ex-priest refers to creation as a "matrix" (149). In "The Road and the Matrix," Dianne Luce discusses the matrix as a metaphor for narrative.
8. See Lacan's "The Signification of the Phallus," in *Ecrits: A Selection*, trans. Alan Sheridan (New York: Norton, 1977): 281–91. Another version of the essay appears as "The Meaning of the Phallus" in *Feminine Sexuality: Jaques Lacan and the Ecole Freudienne*, ed. Juliette Mitchell and Jacqueline Rose, trans. Jacqueline Rose (New York: Pantheon, 1985): 74–85.
9. "Vicarious menstruation" is a term coined by K. A. Menninger. See James L. Brain, "Male Menstruation in History and Anthropology."
10. Shortly after burying the wolf, Billy "whittled a bow from a holly limb, made arrows from cane" (C 129), taking up the bow and effectively joining the cult of Diana. Diana is the goddess of the hunt, conducted with the bow in Roman times, but she is also the goddess of the moon, which in turn dictates the twenty-eight-day menstrual cycle. McCarthy again invokes Diana when Billy reenacts, in less violent form, the Actaeon myth by watching the primadonna bathing (C 220). The moon is also prominent in John Grady's first interlude with Alejandra, who is compared to the "moon that burned cold" (APH 141).
11. Both Troy and John Grady's father use a "Third Infantry Zippo lighter"(APH 7; COP 6).
12. Lacey Rawlins, whose relationship with John Grady in some ways parallels Billy's relationship with Boyd, is also a singer (APH 37).
13. The *corrido* evokes the she-wolf, who inherits her mate's struggle with the trappers after his final stand in Mexico (C 24), but it also evokes Dueña Alfonsa, who tells John Grady that either she or Alejandra "could have been a soldadera" in "a different life" (APH 230).
14. Although he represents Spanish dialogue elsewhere in the novel, McCarthy never transcribes these stories or songs directly, suggesting perhaps their ultimate Otherness to the discourse of the novel. The same otherness is suggested in *Cities of the Plain*, where Oren remarks of John Grady, "there's things about a horse he can only say in spanish"(114). Like Billy, John Grady associates Spanish with the grandmother, as he stands at Abuela's grave, "call[ing] her his abuela" and saying "goodbye to her in spanish" (APH 301). According to José Limón, John Grady's fluency in Spanish and McCarthy's refusal to translate or italicize the Spanish blur John Grady's "bio-racial-cultural categorization" and mark him as a member of both the Anglo and Mexican-American families (202). Limón also stresses the centrality of Mexican women to John Grady's development in *All the Pretty Horses* (206). This argument could be extended

to claim Spanish as the language of the feminine and domestic intimacy throughout the trilogy. Magdalena, for example, speaks no English.

15. Edwin Arnold identifies *Destry* as "most likely *Destry Rides Again* by Max Brand, which tells of a peaceful cowboy who attempts to enforce justice without the use of a gun"(232). Destry is thus a fitting model for the gunless Billy, who has traded the family rifle for the she-wolf's corpse, and who will confront Tiburcio and Eduardo unarmed.

16. John Grady's blood-filled boots in *All the Pretty Horses* and *Cities of the Plain* have their narrative counterpart in Magdalena's bleeding feet. After the long walk home from the hospital, she leaves "bloody footprints in the carpet as if a penitent had passed"(COP 212) and during her final trek to the café on the Calle de Noche Triste, her feet bleed "in her shoes and she could feel the wet blood and the coldness of it" (222).

17. This connection between homosexuality and evil does not exist in McCarthy's characterization of Trippin' Through the Dew in *Suttree*. This discrepancy suggests that it is not Tiburcio's homosexuality *per se* that marks him as evil.

18. Jarrett notes a different axis of power, in which Alfonsa and Alejandra control John Grady's fate through the transaction that denies him access to Alejandra but insures his release from prison (110).

19. According to Fussell, "In Great War diction there are three degrees of erotic heat attaching to three words: *men* is largely neutral; *boys* is a little warmer; *lads* is very warm" (282). To revise Fussell, in the trilogy we have *man*, *boy*, and *bud*.

Works Cited

Arnold, Edwin T. "The Last of the Trilogy: First Thoughts on *Cities of the Plain*." Arnold and Luce 221–47.

Arnold, Edwin T., and Dianne C. Luce, eds. *Perspectives on Cormac McCarthy*. Rev. ed. Jackson: UP of Mississippi, 1999.

Brain, James L. "Male Menstruation in History and Anthropology." *Journal of Psychohistory* 15.3 (1988): 311–23.

Butler, Judith. *Gender Trouble: Feminism and the Subversion of Identity*. New York: Routledge, 1990.

Fiedler, Leslie A. *Love and Death in the American Novel*. New York: Criterion, 1960.

Fussell, Paul. *The Great War and Modern Memory*. New York: Oxford UP, 1975.

Girard, René. *Deceit, Desire, and the Novel: Self and Other in Literary Structure*. Trans. Yvonne Freccero. Baltimore: Johns Hopkins P, 1976.

Hall, Wade, and Rick Wallach. *Sacred Violence: A Reader's Companion to Cormac McCarthy*. El Paso: Texas Western P, 1995.

Higonnet, Margaret Randolph, et al. "Introduction." *Behind the Lines: Gender and the Two World Wars*. Ed. Margaret Higonnet et al. New Haven: Yale UP, 1987. 1–17.

Hogbin, Ian. *The Island of Menstruating Men: Religion in Wogeo, New Guinea*. Scranton: Chandler, 1970.

Jarrett, Robert L. *Cormac McCarthy*. New York: Twayne, 1997.

Kristeva, Julia. *Powers of Horror: An Essay on Abjection.* Trans. Leon S. Roudiez. New York: Columbia UP, 1982.

Limón, José E. *American Encounters: Greater Mexico, the United States, and the Erotics of Culture.* Boston: Beacon, 1998.

Luce, Dianne C. "The Road and the Matrix: The World as Tale in *The Crossing.*" Arnold and Luce 195–219.

———. " 'When You Wake': John Grady Cole's Heroism in *All the Pretty Horses.*" Hall and Wallach 155–67.

McCarthy, Cormac. *All the Pretty Horses.* New York: Vintage, 1993.

———. *Child of God.* New York: Vintage, 1993.

———. *Cities of the Plain.* New York: Vintage, 1999.

———. *The Crossing.* New York: Vintage, 1995.

———. *Suttree.* New York: Vintage, 1986.

Mitchell, Lee Clark. *Westerns: Making the Man in Fiction and Film.* Chicago: U of Chicago P, 1996.

Modleski, Tania. *Feminism Without Women: Culture and Criticism in a "Postfeminist" Age.* New York: Routledge, 1991.

Paster, Gail Kern. *The Body Embarrassed: Drama and the Disciplines of Shame in Early Modern England.* Ithaca: Cornell UP, 1993.

Ragland-Sullivan, Ellie. *Jacques Lacan and the Philosophy of Psychoanalysis.* Urbana: U of Illinois P, 1986.

Riviere, Joan. "Womanliness as a Masquerade." *International Journal of Psychoanalysis* 10 (1929). Rpt. in *Formations of Fantasy.* Ed. Victor Burgin, James Donald, and Cora Kaplan. London: Methuen, 1986. 35–44.

Rubin, Gayle. "The Traffic in Women: Notes on the 'Political Economy' of Sex." *Toward an Anthropology of Women.* Ed. Rayna R. Reiter. New York: Monthly Review P, 1975. 157–210.

Sedgwick, Eve Kosofsky. *Between Men: English Literature and Male Homosocial Desire.* New York: Columbia UP, 1985.

Tompkins, Jane. "Sentimental Power: *Uncle Tom's Cabin* and the Politics of Literary History." *The New Feminist Criticism: Essays on Women, Literature, and Theory.* Ed. Elaine Showalter. New York: Pantheon, 1985. 81–104.

———. *West of Everything: The Inner Life of Westerns.* New York: Oxford UP, 1992.

Wood, Robin. *Hollywood from Vietnam to Reagan.* New York: Columbia UP, 1986.

Crossing from the Wasteland into the Exotic in McCarthy's Border Trilogy

J. Douglas Canfield

Cormac McCarthy's Border Trilogy ends where it began: with the screenplay called "Cities of the Plain," written in the 1980s and revised as the trilogy's final volume.[1] In its genesis, then, as well as in its final form, the trilogy is set in a wasteland in the American Southwest, where modern technology and weaponry have corrupted the pastoral frontier that is already slipping through the hands of John Grady Cole after the death of his grandfather in *All the Pretty Horses*. In a sense, the encroachment of the U.S. Army on Mac McGovern's cattle ranch, among others, in the early 1950s portends not just a physical wasteland caused by the nuclear testing, first glimpsed by Billy Parham at the end of *The Crossing*, but a spiritual wasteland as well, marked already in the 1930s by Martin Heidegger:

From a metaphysical point of view, Russia and America are the same; the same dreary technological frenzy, the same unrestricted organization of the average man. At a time when the farthermost corner of the globe has been conquered by technology and opened to economic exploitation; when any incident whatever, regardless of where or when it occurs, can be communicated to the rest of the world at any desired speed; when the assassination of a king in France and a symphony concert in Tokyo can be "experienced" simultaneously; when time has ceased to be anything other than velocity, instantaneousness, and simultaneity, and time as history has vanished from the lives of all peoples; when a boxer is regarded as a nation's great man; when mass meetings attended by millions are looked on as a triumph—then, yes then, through all this turmoil a question still haunts us like a specter: What for?—Whither?—And what then?

The spiritual decline of the earth is so far advanced that the nations are in danger of losing the last bit of spiritual energy that makes it possible to see the decline . . . , for the darkening of the world, the flight of the gods, the destruction of the earth, the transformation of men into a mass, the hatred and suspicion of everything free and creative, have assumed such proportions throughout the earth that such childish categories as pessimism and optimism have long since become absurd. (31)

My citation of Heidegger is not random. Some recent interpretations of McCarthy's Border Trilogy read the whole as a quest with barely a mention of its vatic passages—or even a denial of their significance. Here is Barcley Owens, first on *The Crossing*, then on *All the Pretty Horses*:

Along the way the two boys [Billy and Boyd] are warned by older, wiser counsel in the form of McCarthy's anchorites, who materialize along the trail to offer gloomy, oblique advice concerning the mystery of life, how a man's will is not the stuff of reality but rather a striving of "doomed enterprises [that] divide lives forever into the then and the now" ([C]129). But the advice is never taken, as the boys venture on, seeking their impossible dreams and rebelling against authority.

Like so many of McCarthy's characters, Alfonsa ponders the relationships between free will, chance, and fate. . . . And like so many of McCarthy's older characters, she is unable to untangle enough of the puppet strings of life to trace in them any definite meaning. Although Alfonsa was once a young idealist herself, as an old woman she becomes entrenched in the intractable society she once detested. Throughout the Border Trilogy, young heroes always reject such older voices of wisdom, stubbornly defying chance and fate and the authority of society in favor of their own indomitable will. (90–91)

For Owens, then, these "older voices of wisdom" are significant only in that they are rejected by the protagonists of the trilogy. And here is Daniel Cooper Alarcón, arguing that the novels of the trilogy are themselves "doomed enterprises," that they never transcend the flattest stereotypical quest into and exoticization of Mexico:

In conclusion, McCarthy's Mexican novels [I note that he has discussed only one out of four] fit neatly within the Infernal Paradise tradition, doing little to challenge its assumptions and conventions. Like his storyteller, the fallen priest, he has done a wonderful job of appearing to tell a different Mexican story, when in fact, he has retold a very familiar one. (64–65)

For Cooper Alarcón, then, the storytellers and their stories—and he examines only the priest's out of so many—are by implication all merely the purveyors of stereotypes and therefore of no other, more philosophical significance.

Other interpretations, most notably by Edwin T. Arnold and Dianne C. Luce, take the trilogy's vatic passages—especially those of *The Crossing*—much more seriously. In a forthcoming essay, Arnold glosses *The Crossing* with the Christian mystic Jacob Boehme, whom McCarthy cites in one of the epigraphs to *Blood Meridian*. Arnold reads out the implications of the sacred revealed by such glossing:

For an author who details so often and so explicitly the violence and despair and randomness of life, the possibilities of grace, love, and charity in the world might seem a bit remote, and yet these qualities appear again and again in his work. "You think God looks out for people?" Lacey Rawlins asks John Grady Cole in *All the Pretty Horses*, and when John Grady answers affirmatively, Rawlins agrees: "Way the world is . . . [y]ou dont know what's goin to happen. I'd say He's just about got to. I dont believe we'd make it a day otherwise" (*APH* 92). In one sense this is a simplistic answer, made before both boys experience the awful consequences of their journey, but in another, it seems to be a core belief in McCarthy's work, and nowhere moreso than in *The Crossing*.

Implicitly answering deconstructionist interpretations of the failure of the novel to capture Presence in its "tracings," Luce weaves the vatic passages into a tapestry that reveals story as witness to truth:

This matrix of witnessing, in which individuals' tales encompass and are embedded in one another's, and in which we are our lives not only as we live them from day to day but also as we are tabernacled in the hearts and memories of others who participate in creating the meaning of our lives, validates story as life itself even where particular stories may be seen as lies or fiction. . . . At its truest, narrative is equivalent to spiritual insight into the world itself: a vision that is not related to eyesight, but that penetrates to the black mystery at the core of things. ("The Road and the Matrix" 198, 210)[2]

I should like to support Arnold's and Luce's readings of the trilogy by reference to existentialism (hence the Heidegger). But I should also like to problematize them by revisiting Cooper Alarcón's objection to the stereotyping of Mexico, by way of José Limón and Robert Canfield. Canfield has well analyzed the nostalgic deployment of Mexico as the site for the restaging, the theatralizing, of western anxiety, but Limón has suggested, perhaps, a way out of the box through McCarthy's portrayal of the Mexican-American community. I myself want to conclude with an analysis of a reflexivity I find in the trilogy which comments on the central narrator's nostalgia for the spiritual. Is that reflection strong enough to counter the imperial masking of Mexico?

Existentialism, following Heidegger, posits a *Dasein*, a *being-there* in the world into which humans are thrown, a world which stands outside of human consciousness. In perhaps a Laurentian move, McCarthy glimpses that world most memorably in the trilogy in the blood-consciousness of horses and wolves. Human consciousness, at its best, attempts to understand that world by constructions of its Being—constructions which can never coincide with the Kantian *Ding-an-sich*, the Thing Itself, the *Grund* which is presumed to underlie the phenomenal world. Compare the existential version with that of Boehme, as explicated by Arnold: "Boehme held that in the terrestrial state, man isolated himself from the rest of creation, caught up in his (illusive) individual consciousness and will, a state of essential exile, separated from the whole; whereas in the celestial state he would return to his place in the matrix, resign his individual personality, his 'selfish will,' to the greater 'nothingness' of spiritual existence" ("Sacred"). For Boehme, for the existentialists, human consciousness remains "illusive," never fully capturing the Thing Itself—a phrase that runs through the trilogy like a mantra indeed.

In the epilogue to *Cities of the Plain*—and to the entire trilogy—McCarthy's last vatic soothsayer, apparently a Mexican (who may represent Death, though he denies it, or who may represent Christ Himself, vouchsafing to McCarthy's chief witness an extreme unction), seems to have the last word on the possibilities of stories to capture meaning, Presence, once and for all: "The thing that is sought is altogether other. However it may be construed within men's dreams or by their acts it will never make a fit" (*COP* 287). Thus, in the concluding Dedication, McCarthy tells us, *"The* story's told / Turn the page" (293). His story, just one among myriad, is now finished. It is time to begin a new (anew).

Existentialism can be either secular, atheistic, materialist; or theological, spiritual. That is, it can portray this world as absurd, meaningless; or it can portray the world as a dark mystery, whose signs and ciphers may point to the noumenal ground of Being assumed by Kant. Jean-Paul Sartre and Albert Camus may be the most famous proponents of the former existentialism; Karl Jaspers and Gabriel Marcel—and the later Heidegger himself—may be the best known proponents of the latter. Heidegger privileges the language of poets as approximating the language of the gods. He writes in *An Introduction to Metaphysics*, "[W]ords and language are not wrappings in which things are packed for the commerce of those who write and speak. It is in words and language that things first come into being and are" (11). Such is the paradox of language in existentialism. Words can discover that which is concealed, hidden—not directly but cryptically. In answer to Nietzsche and the nihilists, Heidegger asserts, "[U]ltimately what matters is not that the word 'being' remains a mere sound and its meaning a vapor, but that we have fallen away from what this word says and for the moment cannot find our way back" (33).[3] When McCarthy insists repeatedly in the trilogy that man's history is one and that it is his only history, a history he cannot fully know, I am reminded of Heidegger's project for the philosopher and the poet: "to restore man's historical being-there [*Dasein*]—and that always includes our own future being-there in the totality of the history allotted to us—to the domain of being, which it was originally incumbent on man to open up for himself" (34). The theological existentialist believes that full understanding of the meaning of that history exists only in the mind of God. Nevertheless, such an existentialist assumes the fundamental ground of what Jaspers calls "The Comprehensive," of which we can "gain only an intimation": "It is not manifested to us, but everything else is manifested in it" (31). For the theological existentialist, as Søren Kierkegaard proclaimed at the dawn of existentialism, one must make a leap of faith in the face of apparent absurdity—an injunction that is especially salient today, given the implied absurdity in deconstruction's eternal deferral of meaning.[4]

I know of no direct, biographical evidence that McCarthy read the existentialists. But they were certainly in the air in the 1950s and 60s when he was enrolled at the University of Tennessee and beginning his writing career. I cite these particular texts by Heidegger and Jaspers and Kierkegaard because they were popular paperbacks in the mid to late 50s and were ubiquitous among intellectuals, of which McCarthy surely was one during his formative years. As he has obviously remained.

Both kinds of existentialism, secular and theological, have been attributed to McCarthy. Linda Townley Woodson reads McCarthy's language in the trilogy from a Nietzschean perspective, where all truths are lies, constructed to comfort us in the face of death, nothing more. George Guillemin—following Dana Phillips—and David Holloway interpret the trilogy as materialist, providing no transcendence (except, very interestingly, through ecocriticism, in which both Guillemin and Holloway discover a *material* transcendence in McCarthy's concrete descriptions). Arnold and Luce, on the other hand, read the trilogy as spiritual, providing intimations of traditional transcendence. I myself have read McCarthy's *Blood Meridian* as a negative theodicy. In that great novel, as in much of McCarthy's work and for the Christian existentialist generally, it is as if, after Auschwitz, one must seek God in the ashes of human violence; one must seek Him in the bloodstains on one's hands, in the hearts of which one has eaten, in the flotsam and jetsam of humanity's rivers of destruction; one must wrestle with His angel in the very jakes of abjection. Like the blind man of *The Crossing* (who is in turn like Shakespeare's Gloucester and who must learn to eschew despair and await the final ripeness), the Christian existentialist must find his way feelingly. If there is a Holy Trinity, then it is the dark one McCarthy envisions in *Outer Dark*. If there is a redemptive sacrifice, then it must be discovered in that novel's bloody child. Even the psychotic Lester Ballard must be seen somehow, paradoxically, as a child of God. Suttree has immersed himself in the detritus of civilization, and only in his feverish hallucinations does he dream of possibilities. As the hermit asserts in *Blood Meridian*, "It's a mystery" (19), despite the judge's denials.

The hermit of *The Crossing*, the heretic of the church in Huisiachepic, has come to believe "terrible things" of God (148). Like Job, he demands an answer, a reckoning from God, Whom he beards in His own house. Ironically, as the priest interprets, even the heretic's theodicean challenge is itself necessary as witness: "[H]ad he not rather been appointed to take up his brief by the very Being against whom it was directed?" (154). The heretic eventually sees "that he was indeed elect and that the God of the universe was yet more terrible than men reckoned. He could not be eluded nor yet set aside nor circumscribed about and it was true that He did indeed contain all else within Him even to the reasoning of the heretic else He were no God at all" (156).

In the dream within the dream of the epilogue to *Cities of the Plain*, McCarthy presents us with the last parable, a story of sacrificial substitution. As in René Girard's *Violence and the Sacred*, a scapegoat is found, perhaps to point to the ultimate end of our endless reciprocal violence, an Omega to the story that is also its Alpha. The storyteller administers to Billy his final lesson, complete with the ultimate question for humans, according to McCarthy:

> Every man's death is a standing in for every other. And since death comes to all there is no way to abate the fear of it except to love that man who stands for us. We are not waiting for his history to be written. He passed here long ago. That man who is all men and who stands in the dock for us until our own time come and we must stand for him. Do you love him, that man? Will you honor the path he has taken? Will you listen to his tale? (288–89).

Typical of McCarthy's western protagonists, Billy does not have the consciousness of the existentialist philosopher or poet. But has he who has suffered and seen so much, and who now uncharacteristically questions his interlocutor and pragmatically challenges him, been, in effect, the perfect—if skeptical—witness after all? A doubting Thomas? Heidegger writes: "To know how to question means to know how to wait, even a whole lifetime" (172). The woman who tends Billy at the very end, another of McCarthy's peasant women, seems an avatar of Goethe's *Ewig-Weibliche*, the Eternal Feminine, a ministering *Mater Dolorosa*, who indeed knows who he is and why she—and her Divine Son—put up with him.

As an atheist, I hold no particular brief for this reading of McCarthy. But as a critic, I have tried to do him justice. Now let me problematize: As if it were an anticipatory direct challenge to my reading (though his study does not include McCarthy), Robert Canfield has written of the American male "who searches across the wasteland of a misrepresented Mexico for his mantra, his masculinity, or his meaning": "[T]he tragedies of the West continue to be resolved or dissolved via a fetishizing misconception and misrepresentation of the 'primitive,' the 'primal,' and the 'revolutionary' nature of an essentialized Other" (178–79). Indeed, for Canfield and Cooper Alarcón, such writings re-stage colonization. Has McCarthy anticipated such objections through his own reflexivity? Let me propose a case.

First, as many others have noted, the questers fail in their primary objectives. Their hubris—from John Grady's defying the cultural superego in sleeping with the daughter of the Father, to Billy's undertaking the three impossible tasks of returning the wolf to the mountains, reclaiming his father's stolen horses, and reburying his brother in a situation that would reconstitute kin—marks their stories in *All the Pretty Horses* and *The Crossing* as tragedies of loss and alienation. "Eres huérfano," calls the old *indio* to Billy ominously (C 134). And he is right. Billy is literally already an orphan, but like so many of McCarthy's protagonists, he is a metaphoric orphan, a drifter who as he ages becomes not so much an agent as an observer of tragedy. Then *Cities of the Plain* replays John Grady's and Billy's tragedies as farce, wherein the capturing and taming of wild horses or the trapping of a wolf degenerates into the capturing and violently decapitating of wild dogs.[5] The aristocratic Alejandra has degenerated into the epileptic whore-with-a-golden-heart, Magdalena (whatever else her name may signify). Crossing into the exotic has become a trip to a Juárez whorehouse. Great schemes have dwindled into a hut, a dog, a woman, and a day's wages. Tragedy has dwindled into country music.

Second, the vatic soothsayings of *The Crossing*, which serve to locate in a primitive and primal Mexico the mysterious, the mystical, are flanked in the other two novels by more modern, urbane, cynical wisdom. In *All the Pretty Horses* Doña Alfonsa's initial sympathy with John Grady transforms itself into inveterate enmity. Why? What emerges from her narrative of the Mexican Revolution that explains her motivation? I propose that it is finally, for all her freethinking, her inability to transcend class and to become a real revolutionary. She represents the tenacious *hacendado* class that still retains power despite the Revolution. Moreover, Alfonsa's narrative reveals that John Grady cannot have Alejandra because he, like a Jamesian New World protagonist in the Old World, does not, cannot understand class. Finally, Alfonsa is at heart a Nietzschean: "I've no sympathy with people to whom things happen. It may be that their luck is bad, but is that to count in their favor?" (APH 240).[6] That John Grady could falter for an instant marks him as ignoble and hence unworthy of the straight-backed Alejandra, of the class she herself does not wish to leave. In *Cities of the Plain* Eduardo mocks John Grady and his fellow *gringos* for seeking in Mexico what they have lost at home: "They drift down out of your leprous paradise seeking a thing now extinct among them. A thing for which perhaps they no longer even have a name" (COP 249). What they find is a land of illusion:

> In his dying perhaps the suitor will see that it was his hunger for mysteries that has undone him. Whores. Superstition. Finally death. For that is what has brought you here. That is what you were seeking.

After another pass with his knife, Eduardo continues:

> That is what has brought you here and what will always bring you here. Your kind cannot bear that the world be ordinary. That it contain nothing save what stands before one. But the Mexican world is a world of adornment only and underneath it is very plain indeed. While your world . . . your world totters upon an unspoken labyrinth of questions. And we will devour you, my friend. You and all your pale empire. (253)

Cooper Alarcón argues that there are not enough contemporary, realistic details in the trilogy to redeem it from being a nostalgic stereotype of Mexico. But these comments by Eduardo satirize that nostalgia as a quest for the spirituality, the sense of mystery, that the United States has lost. And it is not spirituality that will "devour" its "pale empire." It is Mexico's reality.

The reality of Mexico shines through not just in the tawdriness of Juárez but, as John Wegner has clearly demonstrated, in the constant references to the Revolution of 1910–1917—a revolution that failed, particularly in its attempt at land reform. Moreover, the very spirituality of Mexico seems compromised in Mr. Johnson's description of the everyday absurdity of the Revolution:

> He talked for a long time. He named the towns and villages. The mud pueblos. The executions against the mud walls sprayed with new blood over the dried black of the old and the fine powdered clay sifting down from the bulletholes in the wall after the men had fallen and the slow drift of riflesmoke and the corpses stacked in the streets or piled into the woodenwheeled carretas trundling over the cobbles or over the dirt roads to the nameless graves. There were thousands who went to war in the only suit they owned. Suits in which they'd been married and in which they would be buried. Standing in the streets in their coats and ties and hats behind the up-

turned carts and bales and firing their rifles like irate accountants. And the small artillery pieces on wheels that scooted backwards in the street at every round and had to be retrieved and the endless riding of horses to their deaths bearing flags or banners or the tentlike tapestries painted with portraits of the Virgin carried on poles into battle as if the mother of God herself were authoress of all that calamity and mayhem and madness. (COP 64–65)

McCarthy's Hemingwayesque terse specificity finally yields here to *Ewig-Weibliche* as Bellona or Kali.

Do these and similar intrusions of everyday reality and Alfonsa's and Eduardo's cynicism and bravado undercut McCarthy's portrayal of a longing for mystery *per se*? No. But they reveal an awareness of the problem of situating the sense of mystery in the exotic. Yet José Limón thinks that *All the Pretty Horses* finally avoids stereotypes, and he applauds the novel's quiet celebration of a sympathy between John Grady and the Mexican-American community. He applauds also the crossing implied in the novel's code switching between Mexican Spanish and English. We can extrapolate from Limón's more limited survey of the trilogy's first volume: throughout the Border Trilogy, McCarthy's respect for Mexican culture and especially its spirituality, especially among its peasants, its *serranos*, its *indios*, its gypsies, is enormous and even infectious. We understand why Billy in *Cities of the Plain* cannot pass the truckload of Mexicans because he remembers a similar truckload who saved his brother's life in *The Crossing*. Travis too explains, in *Cities of the Plain*, why he admires the Mexican people, who despite the Revolution's failing them have maintained a hospitality in the midst of abject poverty:

Those people would take you in and put you up and feed you and feed your horse and cry when you left. . . . They didnt have nothin. . . . But you could stop at some little estancia in the absolute dead center of nowhere and they'd take you in like you was kin. You could see that the revolution hadnt done them no good. A lot of em had lost boys out of the family. Fathers or sons or both. Nearly all of em, I expect. They didnt have no reason to be hospitable to anybody. Least of all a gringo kid. That plateful of beans they set in front of you was hard come by. But I was never turned away. Not a time. (90)

Travis's description embraces *la gente* encountered by the other *gringo* kids of the trilogy, as well.

In short, McCarthy's representation of Mexicans is indeed positive, even romantic, but his reflexivity seems to me to reveal that he is aware of the problem of the exotic, that he has critiqued it. Stephen Tatum argues, "[S]uch critiques . . . center on the permeability of the boundaries and of the borders so desired and so ferociously defended by imperialists and colonizers of any political persuasion" (314). This "permeability" allows crossings that foster a cultural exchange among peoples and not just markets.

Perhaps despite this reflexivity, McCarthy's vision is still too romantic, too primitive. Perhaps, as Guillemin argues, his pastoralism is melancholic and nostalgic and refers to nothing but its own desire. Perhaps, as Eduardo suggests, McCarthy has given us only a mask. Masks by their very nature misrepresent. And what right has McCarthy, *pace* Tatum, to appropriate Mexico for his own purposes in yet another act of *gringo* imperialism? Is he not guilty, like young Isaac McCaslin in Faulkner's Go Down, Moses, of misrepresenting and valorizing the racial Other: "They are better than we are" (281)?

Perhaps. But perhaps living on the border invites crossings that do not result in steel walls, in murdered *gringos*, in desiccated *campesinos*. Indeed, travelers to Mexico in this last century have constantly remarked, alongside smoldering revolutionary fervor, an amazing hospitality and grace and joy among the penniless poor. It's a paradox. Whatever John Grady and Billy Parham absorb from their failed crossings, McCarthy obviously intends for the reader to absorb respect and perhaps even wisdom. Wisdom is a key word for understanding the function of the vatic utterances of The Crossing. It is as if, between his two more realistic novels of the trilogy, we are vouchsafed in the middle volume glimpses of Wisdom-literature, where Sophia, who plays at the feet of the Lord, manifests herself through a glass darkly. For the secular existentialist, such tropes are the rhetoric of desire for a Transcendental Signifier whose Signified, to employ the language of deconstruction, circles back to that desire itself. For the theological existentialist, such tropes are the signs that prompt a leap of faith.

I myself cannot condemn McCarthy, *pace* Robert Canfield and Cooper Alarcón. I am willing to accept the trilogy's locating of the spiritual in the people of Mexico, who, as anyone who has ever interacted with them knows, are a genuinely spiritual people. As Charles Bailey has noted, quoting Don Arnulfo's attendant nurse, for *la gente mexicana* "La fe es todo" (C

49; faith is everything; Bailey 65). I honor the mask McCarthy places over them, knowing it to be a mask. For as Gaspar, the *arriero* who explains the opera buried in the middle of Mexico, affirms, "El secreto . . . es que en este mundo la mascara es la que es verdadera [The secret is that in this world the mask is that which is truth]" (C 229). Even an existential atheist can find truths if not The Truth amid the acknowledged misrepresentations of the Border Trilogy. For McCarthy, as for Faulkner, they are the old truths of the heart—a construct, of course, a mask, (mis)representing a consummation devoutly to be wished.

Notes

1. See Arnold, "The Last of the Trilogy."
2. See also Bailey, who recognizes the fideism inherent in McCarthy and for whom McCarthy "deconstructs deconstruction" (65).
3. Luce captures the paradox of language in McCarthy as she juxtaposes passages from McCarthy's unpublished play, "Whales and Men," on the failure of language with those from *The Crossing* that celebrate story even while despairing of its ability to capture the Thing Itself:

> *The Crossing* suggests that rather than any physical sense, the human capability for narrative—not for language, which is another kind of artifact, but for formulating the tale that carries our past, gives meaning to our present, and right intention to our future—is our primary means of accessing and perhaps communicating the thing itself: the world which is a tale. For McCarthy, "the thing itself" carries connotations of truth, ultimate essence, the sacred heart of things that inspires reverence, and he implies that humans access the thing itself only by transcending the obstacles posed by artifact, language, and physical sense in moments of spiritual insight that constitute a direct and immediate apperception of the "world as given" ("The Road and the Matrix" 208–09).

4. For Kierkegaard, see especially the entire argument of *Fear and Trembling*.
5. For a reading of this degeneration in the light of José Ortega y Gasset's classic essay on hunting, see Luce, "Vanishing World" 184. And see Arnold, "The Last of the Trilogy" for discussion of the "diminished" world of *Cities of the Plain* (esp. 222, 235, 238).
6. Woodson too sees Alfonsa as embodying a Nietzschean attitude toward history and truth (49, 53), but she does not discuss this example of the strong's disdain of the weak, as in the Nietzsche of *The Genealogy of Morals*.

Works Cited

Arnold, Edwin T. "The Last of the Trilogy: First Thoughts on *Cities of the Plain*." Arnold and Luce, *Perspectives* 221–47.

———. "McCarthy and the Sacred: A Reading of *The Crossing*." *Cormac McCarthy*. Ed. James Lilley. U of New Mexico P, 2002.

Arnold, Edwin T., and Dianne C. Luce, eds. *A Cormac McCarthy Companion: The Border Trilogy*. Jackson: UP of Mississippi, 2001.

———. *Perspectives on Cormac McCarthy*. Rev. ed. Jackson: UP of Mississippi, 1999.

Bailey, Charles. " 'Doomed Enterprises' and Faith: The Structure of Cormac McCarthy's *The Crossing*." *Southwestern American Literature* 20.1 (1994): 57–67.

Canfield, J. Douglas. "The Border of Becoming: Theodicy in *Blood Meridian*." *Mavericks on the Border: The Early Southwest in Historical Fiction and Film*. Lexington: UP of Kentucky, 2001. 37–48.

Canfield, Robert. " 'Such Continuous Tragedies': The Theatralization of Mexico in the Master-Narrative." *Discourse: Theoretical Studies in Media and Culture* 18. 1 & 2 (1995–96).

Cooper Alarcón, Daniel. " 'Doomed Enterprises': McCarthy's Mexican Representations." *Southwestern American Literature* 25.1 (1999): 58–66.

Faulkner, William. *Go Down, Moses*. New York: Vintage, 1990.

Girard, René. *Violence and the Sacred*. Trans. Patrick Gregory. Baltimore: Johns Hopkins UP, 1977.

Guillemin, George. " 'As of some site where life had not succeeded': Sorrow, Allegory, and Pastoralism in Cormac McCarthy's Border Trilogy." Arnold and Luce, *Companion* 92–130.

Heidegger, Martin. *An Introduction to Metaphysics*. Trans. Ralph Manheim. New York: Anchor-Doubleday, 1961.

Holloway, David. " 'A false book is no book at all': The Ideology of Representation in *Blood Meridian* and the Border Trilogy." *Myth, Legend, Dust: Critical Responses to Cormac McCarthy*. Ed. Rick Wallach. Manchester and New York: Manchester UP, 2000. 185–200.

———. "Modernism, Nature, and Utopia: Another Look at 'Optical Democracy' in Cormac McCarthy's Western Quartet." *Southern Quarterly* 38.3 (2000): 186–205.

Jaspers, Karl. *Way to Wisdom: An Introduction to Philosophy*. Trans. Ralph Manheim. New Haven: Yale UP, 1954.

Kierkegaard, Søren. *Fear and Trembling and The Sickness unto Death*. Trans. Walter Lowrie. Garden City, NY: Anchor-Doubleday, 1954.

Limón, José E. *American Encounters: Greater Mexico, the United States, and the Erotics of Culture*. Boston: Beacon P, 1998.

Luce, Dianne C. "The Road and the Matrix: The World as Tale in *The Crossing*." Arnold and Luce, *Perspectives* 195–219.

———. "The Vanishing World of Cormac McCarthy's Border Trilogy." Arnold and Luce, *Companion* 161–97.

McCarthy, Cormac. *All the Pretty Horses*. New York: Vintage, 1993.

———. *Cities of the Plain*. New York: Vintage, 1999.

———. *The Crossing*. New York: Vintage, 1995.

———. *Blood Meridian or The Evening Redness in the West*. New York: Vintage, 1992.

Owens, Barcley. *Cormac McCarthy's Western Novels*. Tucson: U of Arizona P, 2000.

Phillips, Dana. "History and the Ugly Facts of Cormac McCarthy's *Blood Meridian*." *American Literature* 68.2 (1996): 433–60.

Tatum, Stephen. "Topographies of Transition in Western American Literature." *Western American Literature* 32.4 (1998): 310–52.

Wegner, John. " 'Wars and rumors of wars' in Cormac McCarthy's Border Trilogy." Arnold and Luce, *Companion* 73–91.

Woodson, Linda Townley. " 'The Lighted Display Case' ": A Nietzschean Reading of Cormac McCarthy's Border Fiction." *Southern Quarterly* 38.4 (2000): 48–60.

NOTES ON CONTRIBUTORS

Edwin T. Arnold is professor of English at Appalachian State University in Boone, NC. He is co-editor with Dianne C. Luce of *Perspectives on Cormac McCarthy* (1993; rev. ed. 1999) and has written widely on McCarthy and other Southern writers.

J. Douglas Canfield is Regents' Professor of English and Comparative Cultural and Literary Studies at the University of Arizona. He specializes in both English Restoration literature and American literature of the Southwest. His latest book is *Mavericks on the Border: The Early Southwest in Historical Fiction and Film* (2000).

Christine Chollier wrote the first PhD thesis on Cormac McCarthy in France. She teaches American literature at the University of Reims, France, and has published articles on Fitzgerald, Dos Passos, and Brett Easton Ellis. She continues to work on McCarthy.

George Guillemin, who wrote his thesis on Cormac McCarthy, is a member of the Graduate Seminar at the John F. Kennedy-Institute for North American Studies at the Free University in Berlin, Germany.

Dianne C. Luce chairs the English Department at Midlands Technical College in Columbia, SC. She has written on William Faulkner, Cormac McCarthy, William Gilmore Simms, and other Southern authors. She is co-editor with Edwin T. Arnold of *Perspectives on Cormac McCarthy* (1993; rev. ed. 1999).

Jacqueline E. Scoones received her PhD in English in September 2000 from the University of California, Irvine, where she is currently a Lecturer in the School of Humanities. Her dissertation, "Dwelling Poetically: Environmental Ethics in Contemporary Fiction," includes a chapter on Cormac McCarthy's Border Trilogy.

Phillip A. Snyder is an associate professor of English at Brigham Young University, specializing in 20th century British and American literature, Western Studies, and autobiography. His recent publications include "Zora Neale Hurston's *Dust Tracks*: Autobiography and Artist Novel" in *Critical Essays on Zora Neale Hurston* (1998) and "Artist-by-Artist Deconstruction: Mediated Testimony in Bellow's 'Zetland: By a Character Witness'" in *Small Planets: Saul Bellow and the Art of Short Fiction* (1999).

Nell Sullivan received a PhD in American Literature from Rice University and is currently assistant professor of English at the University of Houston-Downtown. Her previous publications include essays on Eavan Boland, William Faulkner, Nella Larsen, and Cormac McCarthy.

John Wegner is an assistant professor of English at Angelo State University in San Angelo, TX, and the Editor of *The Cormac McCarthy Journal Online*. He teaches an Interdisciplinary Southwest Studies course, as well as courses in the American Novel, World Literature, and Freshman Composition. He has published articles on McCarthy, Hawthorne, and Ellen Glasgow.

INDEX

Aaron, 40
Abbey, Edward, *The Monkey Wrench Gang*, 196n 31
Abuela (APH), 96, 109, 231, 242
Agamben, Giorgio, *Homo Sacer*, 152n 3, 158n 26
Alamogordo, N.Mex., 139, 154n 10, 190
Albuquerque, N.Mex., 238
Alejandra Rocha (APH), 6, 10, 11, 15, 16, 18, 24, 29, 33n 12, 50, 51–52, 54, 55, 93, 96, 97, 100, 101, 112, 114, 121, 209, 217, 230–31, 247, 248, 249, 263, 264
Alfred A. Knopf Publishing Company, viii
Alighieri, Dante, 121
"All the Pretty Little Horses" (lullaby), 51
Allen, Rex (and horse "Ko-Ko"), 210
Amarillo, Tex., 84
Anderson, H. Allen, 182
Anderson, Sherwood, "Death in the Woods," 60
Animas Foundation, 189
Animas Mountains, 173, 174, 176, 189
Animas National Wildlife Refuge, 189
Animas, N.Mex., 179
Animas Plains, 173–74
Apache Indians, 216
"Apocalypse" (in Christian literature), 58
Aquinas, Saint Thomas, 181

Armageddon, 64
Arnold, Edwin T., x, 145, 153n 5, 154n 9, 157n 23, 240, 245, 252, 254n 15, 258, 259, 261
Arnold, Edwin T., and Dianne C. Luce, *Perspectives on Cormac McCarthy*, vii, ix
Arthur "Ather" Ownby (OK), 41–42, 108
atomic bomb, 81, 83–84, 85
Atomic Bomb Test (White Sands, N.Mex.), 62–64, 78, 88n 6, 114, 132, 136, 139, 142, 154n 10, 158n 27, 163, 190
Auschwitz (Poland), 261
Autry, Gene (and horse "Champion"), 210

Bailey, Charles, 266–67, 267n 2
Bakhtin, Mikhail, 3, 4–5, 9, 15, 28, 31–32, 33n 2, 33n 3; "Discourse in the Novel," 4
bartender (in Winslow, Ariz.) (C), 83
Barthes, Roland, 22
Bataan Death March, 84, 139, 147
Baumann, John, 199–200
Bell, Madison Smartt: *All Souls' Rising*, viii; *Master of the Crossroads*, viii
Bell, Vereen, *The Achievement of Cormac McCarthy*, ix
Ben Telfair (St), 55–56, 63, 64, 68n 8, 70n 22

Benjamin, Walter, 99, 102, 105, 106, 108, 128 n 7
Beston, Henry, 188, 196 n 30; *The Outermost House*, 188
Bettelheim, Bruno, 237
Betty (COP), 67, 87, 144, 145, 156 n 20, 158 n 27, 225, 231, 252
Bible, 39–40, 47, 49, 58, 63, 131, 151
Billy the Kid (William H. Bonny or Henry McCarty), 86, 188
Bird (horse) (C), 214
Blake, William: "The [First] Book of Urizen," 47; "The Marriage of Heaven and Hell," 48; "A Memorable Fancy," 48–49
Blanca (wolf), 182, 185
Blevins's horse (APH), 121–22, 213
blind maestro (COP), 107
blind revolutionary (C), 74, 100, 107, 166–68, 191 n 7
Boehme, Jacob, 46, 258, 259
Bolsón de Cuatro Ciénagas, 70 n 18
Booth, Wayne, 3–4
Borges, Jorge Luis, 41
Boyd Parham (C), 12, 13, 15, 16, 17, 20, 27, 31, 34 n 19, 54, 55, 57–58, 60–61, 66, 67, 74, 80, 82, 93, 100, 125, 142, 145, 150, 155 n 16, 165, 177, 178, 190, 200, 208, 209, 231, 234, 236, 237, 238, 239, 240, 241, 242, 249, 250, 251, 257
Brain, James, 237
Brand, Max, *Destry [Rides Again]*, 240, 254 n 15
Brannaman, Buck, 211
Brown, David E., 176, 177, 179; *The Wolf in the Southwest*, 173, 193 n 17
Burbank, James, 173, 174, 179, 180, 186; *Vanishing Lobo*, 168, 193 n 17
Burroughs, William, *Naked Lunch*, 42
Butler, Judith, 233–34

Caborca, Mexico, 62
Cameron, Craig, 211
Camus, Albert, 260
Canfield, Douglas, x
Canfield, Robert, 259, 262–63, 266

Captain White (BM), 77
Cárdenas, Lázaro, 79, 193 n 16
Carné, Marcel, *Les Enfants du Paradis*, 253 n 4
Carolyn Parham (Billy's mother)(C), 20, 231
Carranza, Venustiano, 76
carretero (C), 9
Carson National Forest (N.Mex.), 169
Casas Grandes, Mexico, 156 n 17
Casey, Edward, *The Fate of Place*, 135
Cassidy, Hopalong (and horse "Topper"), 210
Castaneda, Carlos, 41
Castro, Bill, 177
Chihuahua, Mexico, 192 n 11
Chollier, Christine, x
Cloverdale, N.Mex., 174, 179, 180, 221
Coahuila, State of Mexico, 50, 70 n 18
Coates, Peter, 190 n 2, 191 n 3, 192 n 10
Cobley, Evelyn, 32
Cochise County, Ariz., 173
Cohn, Dorrit, 13, 14, 18
coldforger (BM), 47–48
_____ Cole (John Grady Cole's father) (APH), 15, 74, 84, 93, 100, 119–20, 212
Columbus, N.Mex., 80
Comanche Indians, 50, 51, 100, 125, 136, 142, 145, 163, 166, 205
Comonfort, Melchor Ocamp Ignacio, 76
Cooper Alarcón, Daniel, 257–58, 259, 263, 264, 266
Cormac McCarthy Society, ix
Cornelius Suttree (S), 39, 42–44, 261
corrido (traditional song), 80, 104, 234, 240
criada (mother of Tiburcio) (COP), 8, 232
Culla Holme (OD), 39, 42, 43, 45, 251
Currumpaw Ranch (Clayton, N.Mex.), 182

Daniel, 40
Danow, David K., 5
Dary, David, *Cowboy Culture*, 198–99
Daugherty, Leo, 152 n 4
De Baca County, N.Mex., 188
De Man, Paul, 95, 106
"Dedication" (COP), 127–28, 132–35, 154 n 9, 163, 259–60
Deming, Tex., 101, 238

Derrida, Jacques, 48, 202–03
Díaz, Porfirio, 75, 76
Dobie, J. Frank, 212
Don Arnulfo (C), 27, 59–60, 62, 166, 175, 179–81, 186, 218, 236, 237
Don Héctor Rocha y Villareal (APH), 10–11, 24, 29, 51, 52, 53, 78, 79, 96, 105, 209, 241, 247, 248
Donne, John, 121
Donoghue, Denis, 38–39, 45
Dorrance, Bill, 211
Dorrance, Tom, 211
Dos Passos, John, *U.S.A.*, viii-ix
Dostoevsky, Feodor, *The Eternal Husband*, 248
Dreamer (Epilogue) (COP), 23, 30–31, 40, 54, 66–67, 77, 107, 136, 143, 148–49, 158n 28, 163–64, 188, 262
drunken Mexican patriot (C), 74, 82, 238
Dueña Alfonsa Rocha (APH), 10, 11, 15–16, 24, 25, 26, 29, 34n 20, 52–53, 65, 77, 78, 97, 99, 100, 101–02, 105, 107, 113, 121, 217, 257, 263–64, 265

Echols, W. C., 168, 173, 174, 175–76, 177
Eduardo (COP), 8, 11–12, 27, 30, 32, 65, 76, 87, 149, 150, 153n 7, 192n 12, 217, 218–19, 224, 232, 240–41, 244, 245, 246, 247, 248–49, 250, 264, 265, 266
Egyptian revolution, 81
El Paso, Tex., 75, 80, 84, 154n 10, 238, 241
Eldorado, Tex., 84
Elihu, 40
Elrod (BM), 75
Elton (COP), 238
Emilio Pérez (APH), 15, 241
"Epilogue" (COP), 5–6, 30–31, 40, 54, 66–67, 69n 12, 77–78, 136, 143, 146–49, 153n 5, 163, 188, 241, 259, 262
Erdrich, Louise: *The Bingo Palace*, viii; *Love Medicine*, viii; *Tracks*, viii
Evans, Dale (and horse "Buttermilk"), 210
Everyman Library, x

Faulkner, William, 267; *Go Down, Moses*, 60, 68n 8, 69n 17, 266; "Snopes Trilogy," ix

Fiedler, Leslie, 229; *Love and Death in the American Novel*, 246
Fisketjon, Gary, viii
Fitzgerald, F. Scott, *The Great Gatsby*, 116
Fitz-Randolph, Louis, 182
Flader, Susan, 170
Fort Bliss, Tex., 86
Fort Sumner, N.Mex., 188
Foucault, Michel, *The History of Sexuality*, 152n 3
Fountain, Colonel Albert Jennings, 89n 17
Francisco Madero (APH), 11, 15–16, 74, 78, 79
Freud, Sigmund, 40
Fussell, Paul, 251, 254n 19

García Márquez, Gabriel, 41
Gare, Arran, "MacIntyre, Narratives, and Environmental Ethics," 155n 14
Gaspar (C), 267
Gatlinburg, Tenn., 43
Gene Edmonds (COP), 84, 162
Genesis, 131, 151
Girard, René, 246–47, 248; *Violence and the Sacred*, 262
gitano (gypsy) (C), 23, 31, 100, 102–03, 107
Glanton, John Joel, 76, 77, 81
God, 39–40, 58, 59, 62, 68n 8, 123, 151, 180, 186, 261–62
Goethe, Johann Wolfgang von, 262
――――― Grady (grandfather of John Grady Cole) (APH), 84, 85, 96, 142–43, 144, 146, 163, 242
Grandmother (of Billy Parham) (C), 240
Grandmother (of unnamed girl) (C), 13
Grant County, N.Mex., 87, 193n 14
Grant, Ulysses S., 87
Gray Ranch (N.Mex.), 189–90
Greene, Brian, *The Elegant Universe*, 70n 21
Guillemin, George, x, 261, 266
Gustavo Madero (APH) 11, 15–16
Guy Schuler ("WAM"), 159n 30, 186–88, 191n 5, 195n 29

hacendado (younger) (C), 26
Hadley, Drum, 189–90

Hall, Wade, and Rick Wallach, *Sacred Violence*, ix
Hawthorne, Nathaniel, *The Scarlet Letter*, 42
Hearst, William Randolph, 76, 139
Héctor (COP), 166
Hedges, Mackey, *Last Buckaroo*, 204, 223
Heidegger, Martin, x, 256–57, 259, 260, 261, 262; *Anaximander Fragment*, 134; *An Introduction to Metaphysics*, 260
Hemingway, Ernest, *The Sun Also Rises*, 191n3
heretic (at Huisiachepic) (C), 71n24, 100, 261–62
hermit (BM), 261
Hidalgo County, N.Mex., 87, 156n17, 173, 174, 175, 188, 190
Hidalgo, Guadalupe, 87
Hidalgo y Costilla, Miguel, 76
Higgonet, Margaret, 238
Hiroshima, Japan, 83–84
Hochbaum, H. Albert, 170
Hogbin, Ian, 245
Holloway, David, 261
Holmes, Robert L., *On War and Morality*, 81–82
Huerta, Victoriano, 76, 79
Huisiachepic, Mexico, 22, 261
Hunt, Alex, 85, 158n26
Hunt, Ray, 211
huntsman (S), 44
Husserl, Edmund, 135

Indian (murderer of Billy's parents) (C), 155n16, 190, 221
Indian sage (C), 207, 263
Iturbide, Agustín de, 76

Jacob, 39
James, William, *The Varieties of Religious Experience*, 69n12
Jane Ellen (wife of rancher) (C), 235
Jarrett, Robert L., 115–16, 140, 146, 153n5, 229, 234, 254n18; *Cormac McCarthy*, ix
Jaspers, Karl, 260, 261
Jeffers, Robinson, 195n28
Jeremiah, 49, 140–41

Jesus Christ, 47, 49, 259; Second Coming of, 63; Sermon on the Mount, 63
Jimmy Blevins (companion to John Grady and Rawlins)(APH), 9–10, 15, 17, 24, 34n19, 35n25, 54, 96, 165, 206, 221, 224, 241, 246, 249
Jimmy Blevins (preacher) (APH), 10
Joaquín (COP), 158n29, 184, 185
Job, 40, 261
John Wesley Rattner (OK), 41, 42, 43
John Western ("WAM"), 159n30, 187, 195n29
Joseph, 39, 40
Joseph (father of Jesus), 40
Joyce, James, *Ulysses*, 42
Juárez, Benito, 75, 76
Juárez, Mexico, 28, 34n14, 74, 88n5, 149, 154n10, 263, 264
judge ("Charles") (APH), 23, 165, 243
Judge Holden (BM), 32, 45–49, 65, 75, 81, 109, 217
Jung, Carl, 40

Kant, Immanuel, x, 259, 260
Kelly McAmon ("WAM"), 71n24, 159n30, 186–87, 195n29
Keno (horse) (C), 12, 31, 214
Kevil, Mike, 226n4
kid, the (BM), 39, 45–47, 74, 75, 76
Kierkegaard, Søren, 260, 261
Kiowa Indians, 145
Knoxville, Tenn., 43, 44
Korean War, 74, 81
Kreml, Nancy, 94
Kristeva, Julia, 95, 97, 99, 100–01, 236, 237
Kundera, Milan, *The Art of the Novel*, 73, 81

La Babícora (Hearst Ranch), 76, 79, 80, 139
La Púrisima (ranch) (APH), 6, 51, 70n18, 111
La Venada (brothel) (COP), 232
Lacan, Jacques, 100, 122, 233, 236
Lacey Rawlins (APH), 6, 8, 9–10, 15, 18–19, 21, 24, 26, 29, 34n19, 50–51, 52, 53, 54, 69n13, 74, 84, 96, 111, 112, 113, 115,

121, 123, 165, 206, 208, 213, 221, 224, 229, 230, 241, 242, 248, 249, 250, 251, 258
L'Amour, Louis: *Conagher*, 204; *Hanging Woman Creek*, 204; *Hondo*, 216, 220; *Shalako*, 216
Langtry, Tex., 165
Las Margaritas (wolf), 176–77, 193n 20
Lawrence, D. H., 259
Lee, Oliver, 86, 89n 17
Leopold, Aldo, 168–73, 174, 175, 180, 182, 183, 187, 192n 11, 192n 12, 192n 13, 194n 23; "The Land Ethic," 151n 1; *Sand County Almanac*, 168, 169; "Southwestern Game Fields," 169; "Thinking Like a Mountain," 169–72
Lester Ballard (COG), 42, 46, 59, 108, 233, 236, 261
Levinas, Emmanuel, 205, 219–20
Lévi-Strauss, Claude, *The Elementary Structures of Kinship*, 248
Ligon, J. Stokely "Stoke," 169, 174, 176; "Southwestern Game Fields," 169
Limón, José, 253n 14, 259, 265
Lincoln County, N.Mex., 86
Lincoln County Wars, 86
Lobo (wolf), 182–83, 185
Lone Ranger (and horse "Silver"), 210
Lopez, Barry, 184–85, 187, 192n 10, 193n 19, 194n 21, 194n 26, 194n 27, 195n 27, 195n 29–30; *Of Wolves and Men*, 168
Los Alamos, N.Mex., 154n 10
Louverture, Toussaint, viii
Lowry, Malcolm, *Under the Volcano*, 35n 26
Luce, Dianne C., x, 20, 41, 82, 155n 14, 157n 25, 205–06, 207, 247, 248, 253n 5, 258, 261, 267n 3
Luis (APH), 79, 120–21
Luisa (APH), 145
Lyons, John, 211

Mac McGovern (COP), 78, 86, 93, 100, 112, 114, 208, 209–10, 231, 232, 241, 256
MacIntyre, Alisdair, *After Virtue*, 140
Madero, Francisco I., 76, 78, 82
Magdalena (COP), 8, 11, 18, 27, 28, 30, 33n

12, 55, 65–66, 76, 93, 100, 125, 157n 21, 166, 209, 210, 218–19, 229, 232–33, 236, 240, 242, 244, 247, 248, 249, 250, 251, 252, 263
Malpai Borderlands Group, 188–90
Mammon, 47
Manhattan Project, 139, 143, 154n 10
map drawer (C), 31
Marcel, Gabriel, 260
Margaret McGovern (COP), 142, 155n 12, 210, 231, 232
Margarita Evelyn Parham (Billy's dead sister) (C), 54–55, 188, 231, 251
Marx, Leo, 110, 111–17, 118; *The Machine in the Garden*, 114
Mary Catherine Barnett (APH), 156n 21, 229, 230, 232, 242, 247
Mary (mother of Jesus), 40
Matthiessen, Peter: *Bone by Bone*, viii; *Killing Mister Watson*, viii; *Lost Man's River*, viii
Maximilian, 75
McBride, Roy, 176–77, 193n 20
McCarthy, Cormac
Works: *All the Pretty Horses* (novel), vii, viii, 6–7, 9–11, 14, 15–16, 17–19, 21, 22–23, 24–25, 26, 29, 49–57, 58, 59, 65, 67, 69n 13, 71n 27, 74–75, 77–78, 79, 82, 84, 86, 92, 93, 94, 95, 96, 97–98, 99, 100, 101–02, 103, 104, 105, 107, 109–11, 112, 113, 114, 116, 118, 119–25, 127, 129n 14, 136, 142–46, 163, 164, 165, 166, 200, 205–06, 207, 212–13, 214, 217, 221, 222, 224, 228–29, 230–31, 241, 242–43, 247, 249, 250, 251, 256, 258, 262–63, 265; *Blood Meridian or the Evening Redness in the West* (novel), vii, 3, 6, 32, 38, 39, 44–49, 68n 6, 74, 75, 76, 77, 81, 108–09, 147, 163, 217, 258, 261; *Child of God*, 3, 39, 42, 46, 59, 70n 21, 108, 230, 233, 236; *Cities of the Plain* (novel), vii, viii, ix, 5–6, 8, 11–12, 15, 18, 22, 23, 26, 27–28, 29–31, 32, 40, 54–55, 58, 61, 64–67, 69n 12, 71n 24, 73–74, 76, 77, 78, 83, 84, 85–87, 92, 93, 94, 95, 96, 98, 99, 100, 107, 108, 112, 113, 114, 115, 116, 125–26, 127–28, 131, 132–35, 136,

141–42, 143, 144, 145, 146, 147–51, 161–63, 164–65, 166, 170, 179, 184, 185, 188, 198, 200–01, 206, 208–10, 212, 213, 214, 218–19, 221–22, 224–25, 228, 229, 230, 231–33, 238–39, 240–41, 242, 244–45, 246, 247–49, 250, 251–52, 257, 259–60, 262, 263, 264–65; "Cities of the Plain" (screenplay), vii–viii, 157n 23, 256; *The Crossing* (novel), vii, viii, ix, 7–8, 9, 12–14, 15, 16–17, 19–22, 23, 25–27, 29, 31–32, 39, 52, 54, 56, 57–64, 67, 71n 24, 73–74, 77, 79–80, 82–83, 85, 87, 92, 93, 94, 95, 96, 98, 99, 100, 101, 102–03, 104, 106–07, 112, 113, 114, 116, 125, 127, 136, 137–39, 141, 162, 163–64, 165, 166–68, 173–75, 176, 177–78, 179–81, 183, 186–87, 188, 190, 200, 206–08, 215, 217–18, 221, 224, 230, 231, 232, 233–40, 242, 244, 249–50, 251, 256, 257, 258, 261–62, 263, 265, 266–67, 267n 3; *The Orchard Keeper* (novel), 3, 38, 39, 41–42, 108, 127, 162; *Outer Dark* (novel), 3, 39, 42, 43, 44, 45, 57, 71n 28, 94, 251, 261; *The Stonemason* (play), vii, 55–56, 63, 64, 68n 8, 68n 12, 70n 22, 71n 24; *Suttree* (novel), 3, 42–44, 53, 230, 253n 3, 254n 17; "Wake for Susan" (story), 41; "Whales and Men" (screenplay), 37, 48, 70n 19, 71n 24, 159n 30, 162, 168, 186–88, 191n 5, 195n 29
McDonald, Bill, 189, 190
McLaury, Buster, 211
McMurtry, Larry: *Lonesome Dove*, 204, 216, 220, 223; *Streets of Laredo*, 216, 220–21
Meine, Curt, *Aldo Leopold*, 169
Melville, Herman, *The Confidence-Man*, 68n 12; "The Encantadas," 26, 35n 29
Merleau-Ponty, Maurice, 135
Mexican girl (Boyd's companion) (C), 13, 209, 234, 236, 249, 251
Mexican Revolution, 13, 15–16, 29, 54, 74, 75–77, 78–81, 86, 142, 263–65, 266
Mexican/American War (1846–48), 74
Mexico, 74, 117, 150, 174, 180, 199; history of, 10–11, 15–16, 29, 74–77, 138; hospitality of, 222, 265; language of, 23–26, 27–28, 253n 14, 265; romantic view of, 93, 111–13, 126, 149–50, 257–58, 262–67
Miller, Robert M., 211
Miriam, 40
Mitchell, Lee Clark, 230; *Westerns*, 243
Mix, Tom (and horse "Tony"), 210
Modleski, Tania, 252
Morelos, Mexico, 12
Morris, Michele, 225n 3
Morrison, Gail M., 97, 109, 118, 205, 206, 207
Morrison, Toni: *Beloved* (novel), viii; *Jazz* (novel), viii; *Paradise* (novel), viii
Moses, 40
Mother (of John Grady Cole) (APH) (COP), 14, 15, 96, 110, 143, 158n 27, 229, 230
Mr. Echols (C), 174, 175–76, 177–81, 217–18, 236
Mr. Johnson (COP), 65, 66, 78, 81, 86, 100, 107, 108, 125, 141, 142, 154n 12, 164, 264–65
Mr. Sanders (C), 83, 175, 179, 218, 234

Namiquipa, Mexico, 13
Native Americans, 126, 156n 17, 192n 10
Nature Conservancy, 70n 18, 189
Nebuchadnezzar, 39
Newhouse wolf traps, 177, 193n 18
Nietzsche, Friedrich, 260, 261, 263–64
Niño (horse) (C), 20, 22, 214, 239

Obregón, Alvaro, 76
OK Bar Ranch (N.Mex.), 174, 175, 176
old rancher (C), 19–20
Orange and White (student newspaper), 41
Oren (COP), 71n 16, 214, 250
Ortega y Gasset, José, 171–73, 177, 178, 179, 180, 181, 184, 193n 13; *On Hunting*, 171–72
Owens, Barcley, 257; *Cormac McCarthy's Western Novels*, ix
Ozona, Tex., 165

"Papaw" Telfair (St), 56, 64, 70n 22
Parelli, Pat, 211
Partido Revolucion Institucional (PRI), 77

Pascal, Roy, *The Dual Voice*, 14
Paster, Gail Kern, 242–43
Paul, 40
pawnbroker (COP), 244
Peloncillo Mountains, 173
Pérez, Francisco, xi
Pershing, John Joseph, 80
Peter Gregory ("WAM"), 48–49, 159n 30, 187–88
Philippines, 139, 147
Phillips, Dana, 6, 261
Phoenix, The (literary supplement of *Orange and White*), 41
Plato, 181
Pluto (God of Underworld), 47
Poland, Tim, 117–18, 121
police captain (of Juárez) (COP), 232, 238–39
police captain (Raúl, of Encantada) (APH), 17, 79, 242
Portales, N.Mex., 188
Predator and Rodent Control Program (PARC), 169, 174, 177, 186
priest (at Huisiachepic) (C), 22, 56, 63, 71n 24, 107, 207
primadonna (diva) (C), 20, 231, 253n 5, 253n 10

Quijada (C), 77, 80, 139

Raat, Dirk, 80
Ragan, David Paul, 41
Ragland-Sullivan, Ellie, 236
rancher (C), 235
Redbo (horse) (APH), 213, 214
Reis, Dennis, 211
Riffaterre, Michael, 4
Rinthy Holme (OD), 39, 71n 28, 251
Rivers, Jacob, 193n 13
Riviere, Joan, 240; "Womanliness as a Masquerade," 233
Roberts, Monte, 211
Rogers, Roy (and horse "Trigger"), 210
Roth, Phillip, viii
Rubin, Gayle, 248

Saltillo, Mexico, 53, 242, 243
San Angelo, Tex., 84, 146
San Antonio, Tex., 110, 111, 166
San Luis Mountains, 173
San Luis Pass, N.Mex., 189, 190
Santa Anna, Antonio Lopez de, 76
Sartre, Jean-Paul, 260
Schaefer, Jack, *Monte Walsh*, 200, 204, 220
Schaeffer, Pierre, 32
Scoones, Jacqueline, x, 165
Scribner's (magazine), 182
Sedgwick, Eve Kosofsky, 245
Seton, Ernest Thompson, 182–83, 187, 194n 23, 194n 24, 194n 25; "Lobo, King of the Currumpaw," 182–83; *Wild Animals I Have Known*, 182, 185
Shakespeare, William: *Hamlet, Prince of Denmark*, 49–50; *King Lear*, 261
sheriff (of Lordsburg, N.Mex.) (C), 237
she-wolf (C), 7–8, 9, 12, 16, 17, 19, 25, 26–27, 57, 59, 61–62, 113, 137–38, 141, 143, 161, 164, 166, 168, 173–74, 175, 178, 179, 180–81, 183, 186–87, 208, 217–18, 231, 232, 234–38, 239–40, 244
shoeshine boy (COP), 27
Siringo, Charlie, *A Texas Cowboy*, 200, 220
Slatta, Richard W., *Cowboys of the Americas*, 199
Slotkin, Richard, *Gunfighter Nation*, 201–02
Smith, Henry Nash, *Virgin Land*, 201
Snyder, Phillip, x
Socorro (COP), 93, 100, 231–32
Socorro Rivera (C), 17
Sodom and Gomorrah (Biblical cities), 154n 10, 196n 31
soldier (in bar in Winslow, Ariz.) (C), 83, 238
Solomon, 39
Sonora, Mexico, 138
Sophia, 266
Southern Quarterly, ix
Southwestern American Literature, ix
Spanish language, McCarthy's use of, 23–28, 253n 14, 265
Spenser, William, *The Fairie Queen*, 47

Sullivan, Nell, x
sutler (BM), 44

Tarahumara Indians (C), 106
Tatum, Stephen, 266
Temple, Shirley, 84–85
Tennessee, University of, 261
Thomas, Dylan, "Fern Hill," 70n 21
Thoreau, Henry David, 119, 171; *Walden*, 188
three-legged dog (C), 62, 63
Tiburcio (COP), 8, 27–28, 65, 66, 228, 229, 232, 240, 246, 249, 252
Tobin (BM), 46
Tompkins, Jane, 216–17, 223, 229, 230, 239, 240
Tonto (and horse "Scout"), 210
Travis (COP), 74, 79, 82, 184, 222, 252n 1, 265
Treaty of Guadalupe Hidalgo, 75, 88n 4, 88n 5
Trinity, N.Mex. (White Sands Atomic Test Site), 62
Trippin' Through the Dew (S), 254n 17
Troy (COP), 74, 84, 161, 162, 185, 221, 238, 240, 247
Turner, Frederick, "The Invented Landscape," 154n 11
Turner, Frederick Jackson, 182, 201

Updike, John, viii
U.S. Forestry Service, 168, 189

Vera Cruz, Mexico, 80
Villa, Pancho, 74, 76, 79, 80

Wager, Douglas, 16
Wallace, Garry, "Meeting McCarthy," 38
Wallach, Rick, ix, 22; *Myth, Legend, Dust*, ix
Watson, Edgar J., viii
Wegner, John, x, 264
Wes ("Wake for Susan"), 41
Western Horseman (magazine), 211
White Lake (brothel) (COP), 8, 34n 14, 76, 232
White Sands Missile Range, 62, 78, 86, 88n 6, 154n 10, 190
Will Parham (Billy's father) (C), 19, 20, 149, 175, 176, 178, 181, 224, 234, 236, 237
Winslow, Ariz., 83
Wolfenbarger (COP), 26
Woodson, Linda Townley, 261
World War I, 73, 78, 81, 83
World War II, 73, 74, 78, 81, 82–85, 87, 139, 142, 147

Zacatecas, Mexico, 29
Zapata, Emiliano, 76, 79

www.ingramcontent.com/pod-product-compliance
Lightning Source LLC
Chambersburg PA
CBHW030337240426
43661CB00052B/1657